D0559488

The Collapse
of the
Anglo-French Alliance

The Collapse

of the

Anglo-French Alliance

1727–1731

JEREMY BLACK

ALAN SUTTON · Gloucester
ST. MARTIN'S PRESS · New York

First published in Great Britain in 1987 by
Alan Sutton Publishing Limited
30 Brunswick Road
Gloucester GL1 1JJ

British Library Cataloguing in Publication Data

Black, Jeremy
    The collapse of the Anglo-French Alliance.
1. Great Britain—Foreign relations—France
2. France—Foreign relations—Great Britain
3. Great Britain—Foreign relations—18th century
4. France—Foreign relations—1715–1793
I. Title
327.41044   DA47.1

ISBN 0-86299-300-8

First published in the United States of America in 1987 by
St. Martin's Press, Inc.
175 Fifth Avenue
New York, NY 10010

Library of Congress Cataloging in Publication Number
    87-40237

ISBN 0-312-01211-X

Typesetting and origination by
Alan Sutton Publishing Limited.
Printed in Great Britain

To Those Whose Hospitality Made This Possible,
particularly John Blair and Paul Zealander

Contents

Abbreviations

1. Abbreviations relating to manuscript sources

Add.	Additional Manuscripts
AE.	Paris, Quai d'Orsay, Archives du Ministère des Affaires Étrangères
AG.	Paris, Vincennes, Archives de la Guerre
Althorp	Althorp deposit, Poyntz papers
AN. AM.	Paris, Archives Nationales, Archives de la Marine
Ang.	Angleterre
ASG.	Genoa, Archivio di Stato di Genova
ASM.	Modena, Archivio di Stato di Modena
AST.	Turin, Archivio di Stato di Torino
ASV.	Venice, Archivio di Stato di Venezia
Aut.	Autriche
B7	Pays Étrangères series
BL.	London, British Library, Department of Manuscripts
Bodl.	Oxford, Bodleian Library, Department of Western Manuscripts
Br.	Brunswick – Hanovre
Bradfer Lawrence	Norwich, County Record Office, Bradfer-Lawrence Collection, Townshend State Papers and Letters
C(H).	Cambridge, University Library, Cholmondeley (Houghton) papers
Chewton	Chewton Mendip, Chewton House, Waldegrave papers
CP.	Correspondance Politique
CRO.	County Record Office
Darmstadt	Darmstadt, Staatsarchiv
Dresden	Dresden, Hauptstaatsarchiv, Geheimes Kabinett, Gesandtschaften
Eg.	Egerton Manuscripts
EK.	Englische Korrespondenz
Fonseca	Nachlass Fonseca

GK.   Grosse Korrespondenz
Hanover   Hanover, Hauptstaatsarchiv
Hull   Hull, University Library, Hotham papers
Ing.   Inghilterra
LM.   Lettere Ministri
Marburg   Marburg, Staatsarchiv, Bestand 4: Politische
                     Akten nach Philipp d. Gr.
MD.   Mémoires et Documents
Munich   Munich, Hauptstaatsarchiv, Bayr. Gesandtschaft
Münster   Münster, Staatsarchiv, Deposit Nordkirchen,
                     papers of the Plettenberg family
Nancy   Nancy, Archives de Meurthe-et-Moselle, Fonds
                     de Vienne, serie 3F
Osnabrück   Osnabrück, Staatsarchiv, Repertorium 100, Ab-
                     schnitt 1
PRO.   London, Public Record Office, State Papers
RA.   Windsor Castle, Royal Archives, Stuart Papers
Rawl   Rawlinson Letters
SRO.   Edinburgh, Scottish Record Office
sup.   supplément
HHStA.   Vienna, Haus-, Hof- und Staatsarchiv, Staaten-
                     abteilung
Vienna, Kinsky   Vienna, Palais Kinsky, Correspondence of Count
                     Philip Kinsky
Wolfenbüttel   Wolfenbüttel, Staatsarchiv

2. *Abbreviations relating to published material*

Armstrong   E. Armstrong, *Elisabeth Farnese the Termagant of
                     Spain* (1892)
Baudrillart   A. Baudrillart, *Philippe V et la cour de France*
                     (5 vols, Paris, 1890–1901)
Boyer   A. Boyer, *Political State of Great Britain* (60 vols,
                     1711–1740)
Browning   R. Browning, *The Duke of Newcastle* (New
                     Haven, 1975)
Cady   P. S. Cady, *Horatio Walpole and the making of the
                     Treaty of Seville, 1728–1730* (unpublished Ph.D.
                     thesis, Columbus, Ohio, 1976)
Carlisle   Historical Manuscripts Commission, *Manuscripts
                     of the Earl of Carlisle* (1897)
Cobbett   W. Cobbett, *Parliamentary History of England
                     from . . . 1066 to . . . 1803* (36 vols, 1798)
Dureng   J. Dureng, *Mission de Théodore Chevignard de
                     Chavigny en Allemagne Septembre 1726–Octobre
                     1731* (Paris, 1912)

Egmont	Historical Manuscripts Commission, *Manuscripts of the Earl of Egmont, Diary of the Earl of Egmont* (Viscount Perceval) (3 vols, 1920–23)
EHR	*English Historical Review*
Gibbs	G. C. Gibbs, *Parliament and Foreign Policy, 1715–1731* (unpublished MA. thesis, Liverpool, 1953)
Goslinga	A. Goslinga, *Slingelandt's Efforts towards European Peace* (The Hague, 1915)
Hatton	R. Hatton, *George I* (1978)
HCJ	*The Journal of the House of Commons*
Hervey	John, Lord Hervey, *Some Materials towards Memoirs of the Reign of King George II* (ed.) R. R. Sedgwick (3 vols, 1931)
HLJ	*The Journals of the House of Lords*
HMC.	Historical Manuscripts Commission
Höfler	C. Höfler, *Der Congress von Soissons, Nach den Instructionen des Kaiserlichen Cabinetes und den Berichten des Botschafters Stefan Grafen Kinsky* Fontes Rerum Austriacarum, vols XXXII, XXXVIII (Vienna, 1871, 1876)
Hughes	M. Hughes, *The Imperial Supreme Judicial Authority under the Emperor Charles VI and the crises in Mecklenburg and East Frisia* (unpublished Ph.D. thesis, London, 1969)
Ilchester	Earl of Ilchester (ed.), *Lord Hervey and his Friends* (1950)
King	Peter, Lord King, 'Notes on Domestic and Foreign Affairs during the last years of the reign of George I and the early part of the reign of George II', in appendix to P. King, *Life of John Locke* (2 vols, 1830) vol. 2
Knatchbull	A. N. Newman (ed.), *The Parliamentary Diary of Sir Edward Knatchbull 1722–1730* (1963)
Marini	R. A. Marini, *La Politica Sabauda alla Corte Inglese dopo il trattato d'Hannover 1725–1730 nella Relazione dell' ambasciatore piemontese a Londra* (Chambéry, 1918)
Michael	W. Michael, *Englische Geschichte im achtzehnten Jahrhundert* (5 vols, Berlin/Basel and Berlin/Leipzig, 1896–1955)
Plumb	J. H. Plumb, *Sir Robert Walpole, The King's Minister* (1960)
Quazza	G. Quazza, *Il Problema Italiano e l'Equilibrio Europeo 1720–1738* (Turin, 1965)
Recueil	*Recueil des Instructions données aux Ambassadeurs et Ministres de France depuis les Traités de Westphalia jusqu'à la Révolution Française* (Paris, 1884–)

Sedgwick | *The House of Commons 1715–1754* edited by R. R. Sedgwick (2 vols, 1970)

Williams | B. Williams, *Carteret and Newcastle* (Cambridge, 1943)

Wilson | A. M. Wilson, *French Foreign Policy during the Administration of Cardinal Fleury, 1726–1743* (Cambridge, Mass., 1936)

Notes on Dates

In this work the New Year is always taken as starting on 1 January. The convention by which the English New Year began on 25 March has been ignored. In the early eighteenth century Britain conformed to the Julian calendar. Dates recorded in this calendar are referred to as old style. Most of the continent conformed to the Gregorian calendar and recorded its dates in new style. In this work dates mentioned in the text are consistently given in new style (ns) which was eleven days ahead of old style (os). In the footnotes the dates given are those found on the documents cited except that the year is assumed to have started on 1 January. In the footnotes, unless otherwise stated, all dates are in new style.

Preface

This study has two linked aims. The first is to demonstrate that in order to appreciate eighteenth-century British foreign policy it is necessary to consider not only diplomatic relations, but also domestic politics. The second is to fill a significant gap in the published work on British foreign policy, that of the years 1727 to 1731. The magisterial work of J. F. Chance and the stimulating study of Ragnhild Hatton come to an end in 1727; Vaucher's important survey of Anglo-French relations commences in 1731.[1] There is an only partially filled gap between these works. In attempting to fill it I have sought to demonstrate the relationship between diplomatic and domestic pressures, and to indicate that beneath the smooth progression described by certain diplomatic historians there was confusion and indecision, an active debate over diplomatic objectives and a foreign policy that cannot be understood simply as a diplomatic response. A study of foreign policy in this period throws much light on the political system, and, in particular, on the role of the King.[2]

My initial publication on British foreign policy in the age of Walpole, a book with that title, was published in August 1985 in Edinburgh. It presented a conceptual approach to foreign policy and sought to cover the whole of the subject in the 1720s and 1730s. In this work I have adopted a different approach, the chronological method, and taken a more restricted topic, policy from the summer of 1727 until the summer of 1731. This was the period I covered in my thesis and I have retained my interest in it. I have sought to examine in greater detail the development of British diplomacy in a crucial period, the collapse of the Anglo-French alliance of 1716–31. This was of vital importance in British foreign policy, as it inaugurated a period of 85 years of near-constant hostility between the two powers that was to be of major significance for British political, economic and colonial history. This study also benefits from fresh archival work undertaken after I completed the writing of my first book in April 1984. Since then I have made three research trips to Paris and have visited Munich and Vienna. Most significant has been the deposit in 1985 of the Poyntz papers, to which I was denied access when writing my thesis and my first book, in the British Library. These are of the greatest value and have been used by no earlier diplomatic historian scholar. Stephen Poyntz was one of the British Plenipotentiaries at the Congress of Soissons and his correspondence with senior political figures, such as Townshend and Horatio Walpole, with officials, such as Delafaye, Weston and Tilson; with diplomats, such as Waldegrave, Keene and Holzendorf; and with parliamentarians, such as Selwyn, is of the greatest importance both for

British foreign policy and for ministerial politics in this period. Also of value was the acquisition by the library in the summer of 1986 of two volumes of the papers of Horatio Walpole.

In the course of many years' research on this topic I have been fortunate enough to receive help from a large number of individuals and institutions. Without it I would have been unable to produce this work. I am very grateful for it. I have been privileged to use several private collections of manuscripts in the course of my research. It is an honour to be able to head my list of acknowledgements with the name of Her Majesty Queen Elizabeth II by whose gracious permission I was allowed to use the Stuart papers. Prince Kinsky, the Duke of Richmond, the Earl of Egremont, the Earl of Harrowby, the Earl Waldegrave, Lady Agnew, Lady Lucas, and John Weston-Underwood permitted me to consult their manuscripts. The generosity of several institutions has been most helpful. I would particularly like to mention the British Academy, the British Council, the Staff Travel and Research Fund of Durham University, the Deutscher Akademischer Austauschdienst, the Zaharoff Foundation, Merton College Oxford and the Gladys Krieble Delmas Foundation. I am most grateful to the friends who provided invaluable hospitality and the scholars who generously gave their time and advice, reading drafts, lending material and discussing issues. I would particularly like to mention David Aldridge, Leopold Auer, Peter Barber, Peter Bassett, Richard Berman, John Blair, Tony Brown, Hilmar Brückner, Marco Carassi, Roy Clayton, Jonathan Dent, Michel Fleury, Graham Gibbs, Robert Gildea, James and Janet de Groat, Anthony Gross, Dan and Stella Hollis, Peter Hore, Harold James, James Lawrie, Jeremy Mayhew, Gerhard Menk, Armin Reese, Peter Spear, Charles Stephens, Mark Stocker, Peter Tibber, Philip Winston and Paul Zealander. Four scholars in particular, Eveline Cruickshanks, Paul Langford, Derek McKay and Reg Ward, have provided vital encouragement. I would like to thank Bill Speck and Harry Dickinson, the examiners of my thesis, for some very helpful advice. I would like to thank Wendy Duery for her exemplary typing of a distinctly unexemplary manuscript. The assistance of my parents has been most helpful over the last few years. They generously provided funds which aided my research in British archives. Sarah has often been bemused by my interest in the stygian depths of history. It is largely thanks to her encouragement that I finished this work, and I hope that she is not too disappointed with the result.

Notes

1. J. F. Chance, *The Alliance of Hanover*, (1923); R. M. Hatton, *George I*, (1978); P. Vaucher, *Robert Walpole et la Politique de Fleury, 1731–42* (Paris, 1924)
2. J. Black, 'George II Reconsidered. A Consideration of George's Influence In The Conduct Of Foreign Policy In the First Years Of His Reign', *Mitteilungen des Österreichischen Staatsarchivs*, 35 (1982), pp. 35–56; J. Black, *British Foreign Policy in the Age of Walpole* (Edinburgh, 1985), pp. 27–48; J. Black, 'British Foreign Policy in the Eighteenth Century: A Survey', *Journal of British Studies* 26 (1987) pp.39–41.

CHAPTER ONE

The European and British Setting

The general peace treaties of the 1710s which ended the various wars then afflicting Europe left many questions unsettled. Territorial and dynastic disputes affected large areas of Europe. Throughout the 1710s and 1720s diplomatic tension produced military mobilisations and the threat of war. Professor Hatton has viewed the period as one 'when progress was made in limiting wars and achieving a longish period of peace by conscious rational efforts . . . [and] . . . the idea of the Society of Europe in which peace was regarded as the natural state was being transferred from the blue-prints to reality on a practical level'. However, whilst Hatton has seen a generally rational, hopeful 'climate of opinion' which reached its apogee in a series of Congresses that served to 'deflate' problems and make them more amenable to solutions, the politicians of the period felt defeated by the interminable nature of the Congress system and its inability to settle issues. The French first minister Cardinal Fleury felt that Congresses were unhelpful, and his view was shared widely.[1] If the Congress system produced pessimism, the other major diplomatic innovation of the period which has been praised by historians, the system of collective security involving reciprocal guarantees[2], failed. The Congress of Cambrai, begun in 1724, was a failure, and by 1725 Europe was at the brink of war, split by two conflicting alliances, those of Hanover and Vienna.

The basic causes of European tension were twofold. First, it proved difficult to adapt to the rather sudden shifts in the power of particular European states. Four changes posed major problems. In the Baltic, the rise of Russian and the collapse of Swedish power had been both sudden and frightening.[3] Russia under Peter the Great had proved able to deploy troops inside Europe, in Mecklenburg and Jutland. The defeat of Charles XII of Sweden at Poltava in 1709, the conquest of the Swedish Baltic provinces, and the internal conflicts affecting Sweden in the 1720s, all helped to destroy the possibility of Sweden continuing to serve as an effective anti-Russian barrier. Frederick William I of Prussia was too scared of Russian power to seek the role, and Augustus II, King of Poland and Elector of Saxony, too weak to do so. The attempt by Britain and France to force Russia to restore her Baltic conquests to Sweden had proved a failure.

The rise of Russian power would have been less threatening if Russia, once she had beaten Sweden, had devoted her attentions to the conquest of territories from Turkey and Persia, as indeed seemed to be the case in 1723. However, for dynastic reasons, Peter I became deeply involved in German politics. In 1716 Peter's niece Catherine married Charles Leopold, Duke of Mecklenburg-Schwerin, and in 1725 Peter's daughter Anna married Charles Frederick, Duke of Holstein-Gottorp. Both these German princes had interests which were espoused by Peter, interests that clashed with those of Hanover. The ducal lands of Holstein-Gottorp in Schleswig had been seized by Frederick IV of Denmark, and Britain, as well as France, had guaranteed Danish possession of them. Hanover had been authorised by the Emperor to intervene in Mecklenburg, where the conflict between the Duke and his nobility had deteriorated into a state of civil war. Russian support for the Duke challenged the Hanoverian position.[4] Hopes were expressed in 1725, when Peter was succeeded by his widow Catherine I, that Russia would collapse into anarchy. The theme of a possible Russian return to barbarism was a common one in the diplomatic correspondence of the period and in the British press.[5] Such hopes proved to be unfounded, and, though the British government received reports of a decline in Rusian naval strength, Catherine showed herself able to control Russia, and willing to aid her German relatives. She espoused the cause of the Duke of Holstein-Gottorp with vigour, and ordered major military mobilisations in 1725–27 which threatened the other Baltic powers. Unpleasant rumours about Russian intentions began to circulate. In November 1725 the Duke of Newcastle, the Secretary of State for the Southern Department, informed Horatio Walpole, the British Ambassador in Paris, that war with Russia was probable. The Russian accession in 1726 to the Vienna Alliance, the alliance formed in 1725 by Austria and Spain, linked Baltic rivalries more firmly into the general pattern of European conflict. Russia appeared as an unpredictable, unstable power, able and willing to risk war, and averse to seeing its position limited by any Congress.[6]

At the opposite end of Europe, aggression by another state which had suddenly increased in power gave rise to tension. Under Charles II, who had ruled Spain from 1665 until 1700, Spain had been regarded as a cipher, and this view was reinforced by the War of the Spanish Succession, when Spain was fought over by other powers, and deprived of the bulk of her European empire: Sicily, the island of Sardinia, the Milanese, Naples, and the Southern Netherlands. Louis XIV's second grandson, Philip, Duke of Anjou, had become King of Spain as Philip V, defeating the rival claims of the Austrian Archduke Charles, who became the Emperor Charles VI in 1711. Philip was a markedly eccentric character, prone to acute melancholia and bouts of hysteria, and strongly influenced by his second wife Elisabeth Farnese, whom he married in 1714. Under Philip there was a marked increase in Spanish power, a development that owed much to the nadir reached during the 1700s, from which it could only improve, and something to the administrative reforms and Bourbon governmental methods which were introduced partially under Philip. A particular concern for other powers was the increase in Spanish naval power and a growing Spanish interest in schemes for commercial and oceanic trade. The growth in Spanish power, coupled with a desire to reverse recent territorial losses, most threatened the Austrians, who had acquired the bulk of Spain's Italian possessions. In 1717 the Spaniards conquered the island of Sardinia, and in 1718 invaded Sicily, beginning a war which lasted until 1720. The Austrians fought badly and their military system was shown to be singularly unable to defend their Italian possessions. It was a combination of British naval power, which smashed the Spanish fleet off Cape Passaro in 1718 and isolated the Spanish army in Sicily, and a French invasion of Spain in 1719, that forced Philip V to abandon, for a while, his Italian schemes.[7]

By the Peace of Utrecht in 1713, Britain had gained various concessions from the Spaniards. Gibraltar and Minorca, captured in 1704 and 1708 respectively, and ceded to Britain in 1713, were believed to strengthen Britain's control over her Mediterranean trade and to improve her naval position. In the same year Britain acquired the *asiento*, the contract to supply the Spanish colonies with slaves. A clause in it permitted limited trade in British manufactures with New Spain, in an annual permission ship. The growth in Spanish naval power and commercial pretensions, a growth particularly associated with Patiño, Intendant of the Marine from 1717, challenged British rights as well as the more general British aspiration to gain a large share in the trade to America and the South Seas.[8]

Although the British would not have accepted the premise, the rise of British power was another cause of European instability. Under the later Stuarts Britain, wracked by internal conflict and willing to become the pensioner of France, could be dismissed as an effective force in European affairs. William III's success in smashing his opponents within the British Isles ended this state of affairs. It was not that William dragged Britain into European politics, as is customarily assumed. In the 1650s and 1670s various British governments had sought to play a prominent role in Europe. Rather, it was the brutal, crushing successes of William in Scotland and, in particular, Ireland, and the consolidation of authority around the parliamentary monarchy, which permitted Britain to act in an effective manner as an opponent of France. There was a massive increase in the size of the British navy and army. The French fleet was defeated at La Hogue in 1692, and British control of the Channel was not to be seriously challenged again until 1744. From 1694–5, when the fleet wintered in the Mediterranean for the first time, using Cadiz as its base, British naval power became a major instrument of policy and influence in the politics of southern Europe. Elisabeth Farnese complained in 1727 of the British who had burnt 'their fleet and pretended to lord it over everybody'.[9] British fleets were dispatched to the Baltic, and under George I intervened in Baltic affairs with great frequency. British armies were regularly deployed on the Continent. The accession of George I in 1714 led to increasing British involvement in Baltic and German affairs. Hatton has painted a rather charitable picture of George, but contemporaries, both in Britain and Europe, had little doubt that British strength was being used to support Hanoverian pretensions. Hanover's formal acquisition in 1719 of the former Swedish Duchies of Bremen and Verden was widely attributed to British aid. For the Spaniards, concerned to defend their commercial position in the Indies and anxious to wipe out the humiliating concessions of Utrecht, the growth of British power was a major threat, a view shared by Austrian ministers concerned to resist Hanoverian pretensions, Dutch ministers worried about the threat to Dutch commerce, and French ministers, uneasily aware of their need for a British alliance, but unhappy at growing British assertiveness. Though some British ministers appreciated these feelings (George I, Stanhope and Townshend being willing, for instance, to return Gibraltar as the price for better Anglo-Spanish relations), most of the British political public failed to appreciate the degree to which Britain was regarded in Europe as a selfish, arrogant and aggressive power, and a source of tension. They were therefore surprised in the late 1720s when their Dutch and French allies proved willing to consider the abandonment of British pretensions as a reasonable price to pay for European peace, and when they were increasingly isolated in European diplomacy.[10]

The fourth major power whose rise in strength was an important cause of instability was Austria. Between 1683 and 1720 Austria had witnessed a spectacular growth in territorial power, a growth only surpassed by Russia. In Italy she had gained Naples, Sicily, Mantua and the Milanese; in the Balkans, Hungary, Transylvania, Little Wallachia, much of Serbia and the Banat of Temesvar; and further west she had acquired the Southern Netherlands. Accompanying this expansion was a growth in military strength and reputation, and a determination to enforce Austrian power and Imperial authority in every area possible. The Wittelsbach diplomat Jacob van Gansinot wrote in 1725 that the current Emperor, Charles VI, was the most powerful since the foundation of the Holy Roman Empire. In Italy, where she had become the strongest power, Austrian rule was marked by financial exactions and became bitterly unpopular. Diplomats of all powers believed that Italy was ready to rebel against Austrian rule, a belief which was shared by the European press. Within the Empire, Charles VI appeared as an insensitive ruler, determined to use the legal instruments of Imperial authority, such as the Aulic Council, to enhance Austrian power. Charles was widely accused of seeking to establish a despotism inside the Empire. The situation was exacerbated by the increase in religious hostilities within the Empire. The Emperor used Imperial authority to interfere in confessional disputes in a manner which appeared to Protestant powers, such as Hanover and Prussia, to be flagrantly unfair. To the Austrians, these Protestant powers were selfish and disloyal members of the Empire. The Austrian maritime trading companies, at Trieste and Ostend, worried Britain and the United Provinces.[11]

Aside from major changes in the power of particular European states, the second basic cause of European tension was dynastic insecurity. Several major states had insecure dynasties, or successions which were unclear or could be challenged. The only children of Charles VI to survive for any length of time were three daughters, the youngest of whom died in 1730 aged four. Charles VI hoped to secure the undivided succession of his various territories for his own children rather than for Maria Josepha and Maria Amalia, the daughters of his elder brother, the Emperor Joseph I. This, as much as the stipulations of the indivisibility of the inheritance and the reversion to female in the absence of male descendants, was the most troublesome aspect of Charles' promulgation of the Pragmatic Sanction, an attempt to settle his succession on his eldest daughter. Maria Josepha and Maria Amalia, born in 1699 and 1701, were considerably older than Charles' two eldest daughters, Maria Theresa and Maria Anna, born in 1717 and 1718. To reinforce the exclusion of the Josephine archduchesses, Charles ensured that their marriages were accompanied by solemn renunciations of all claims to the succession. In 1719 the marriage of Maria Josepha and the heir to the Electorate of Saxony, Frederick Augustus, the future Augustus III, was preceded by a renunciation sworn to by bride, groom and groom's father. In 1722 the marriage of Maria Amalia to the heir to Bavaria, Charles Albert, was preceded by a similar renunciation. Neither the Saxons nor the Bavarians paid much attention to these renunciations. Both believed that neither the acts of parents nor renunciations could abnegate inalienable rights, and both were convinced that dynastic and inheritance rights were not transferable. In 1725, to fortify the position of the Bavarians, who had only won the younger of the Josephine archduchesses, Charles Albert's father Max Emanuel forged a copy of the Emperor Ferdinand I's will, purportedly awarding the Wittelsbachs the Austrian hereditary lands upon the extinction of the dynasty's male line. Charles VI's continued failure to produce a male heir and his efforts to secure European support for the Pragmatic Sanction helped to make the Austrian Succession more critical. Under Charles VI Austrian policy became increasingly dominated by the issue, whilst powers opposed to Austria resorted to the device of encouraging pretensions upon the Austrian Succession, Saxon and Bavarian in the Empire, Sardinian and Spanish in Italy. Within the Empire, Bavaria fostered the development of a close alliance, a *Hausunion*, between the closely related Wittelsbach Electors of Bavaria, Trier, Cologne and the Palatinate, and made it clear, in response to Anglo-French efforts in 1725–26 to secure their alliance against Austria, that a committment to help the Bavarian succession was expected.[12]

Until the birth of a Dauphin in September 1729 the succession to the young Louis XV of France was also very uncertain. As part of the Utrecht settlement Louis' uncle Philip V of Spain had renounced his claims to the French throne, leaving as the next in line Philip V's second cousin, Louis XIV's nephew, Philip II, Duke of Orléans, and, after his death in 1723, his son Louis. Philip V doubted the validity of the Utrecht renunciation and maintained his claim to the French throne. He showed particular interest whenever Louis XV was very ill, especially during the time of his smallpox attack in late 1728. A formidable 'Spanish' party existed in France, and the Orléans family felt threatened. Partly to safeguard his position Orléans, as Regent for the young Louis XV, signed the Triple Alliance in January 1717 with Britain and the United Provinces. The alliance stated that all those articles of the Peace of Utrecht which concerned the three powers, including those relating to the successions to the crowns of Britain and France, should retain full force. Orléans therefore closely associated the British alliance with the exclusion of all claims by the Spanish Bourbons. After Orléans' death the Duke of Bourbon, chief minister from 1723 to 1726, maintained a hostile stance to Philip V. Philip continued to aspire to the French throne, particularly after his shortlived abdication of the Spanish crown in 1724 convinced him that he had no real right to the Spanish throne. It was widely believed that secret Austro-Spanish agreements in 1725 included an understanding that Austria was to support Spain in any French succession dispute. Until Louis XV sired his eldest son much speculation persisted about the French succession, and 'it was not until the late 1750s that the succession to the throne was firmly assured in Louis XV's line'.[13]

As a result of the Triple Alliance of 1717 France was committed to supporting the Hanoverian succession in Britain. The challenge of Jacobitism posed a major problem for successive British governments. It was suggested at the time that the threat of Jacobitism was deliberately exaggerated to discredit opposition within Britain, and it has been suggested recently that the group most impugned, the Tories, were largely free from Jacobitism. Such a view would have found little support from George I and George II, both of whom believed that although individual Tories were loyal and could be trusted, the party as a whole was factious and disloyal. Equally serious was the manner in which foreign powers, hostile to Britain and to her Hanoverian rulers, could be encouraged to support Jacobitism, and were themselves encouraged in their stance by a belief in the strength of Jacobitism. Jacobite chances were seen to depend on help from European powers. The Jacobites were delighted by the Austro-Spanish alliance of 1725, and sought to enlist the support of both powers for an invasion of Britain. The Jacobite factor was of greater importance by the late 1720s in British foreign policy, where it could influence the views of other states, than it was in British internal affairs.[14]

The insecurity of the Russian succession was closely linked in the eyes of the rest of Europe to the general belief in an imminent collapse of Russian power. The position of Peter's widow Catherine was believed to be threatened by his grandson Peter, who succeeded Catherine – killed, according to one rumour, by means of poison administered in a bottle of her favourite beer from Burton-upon-Trent in 1727. Whether Peter II was to have a Russian or a foreign bride became a major issue of debate linked to the long-standing tension between foreign and 'Old Russ' influences within Russia. In 1730 Peter II died suddenly of smallpox leaving no child. He was succeeded by Peter I's niece, Anne, the childless widowed Duchess of Courland, but her position was challenged by an attempt to restrict her power in favour of the higher aristocracy. Peter I's daughters by his marriage to Catherine I – Anne, the wife of the Duke of Holstein-Gottorp and Elizabeth, who eventually became Czarina in 1741 – also possessed strong claims to the throne. A Holstein coup in Russia, such as was rumoured in 1727, or Russian support for the Holstein interest, were major threats to Baltic stability, as Charles Frederick of Holstein-Gottorp claimed not only Schleswig but also the throne of Sweden, as the son of Charles XII of Sweden's elder sister, Hedvig Sofie. Britain and France supported Frederick I, the elder son of Landgrave Karl of

Hesse-Cassel, who had become King of Sweden in 1720 upon the abdication of his wife Ulrika Eleonore, the younger sister of Charles XII. There was a powerful Holstein interst in Sweden, and Russia attempted to coerce the Swedes to accept Charles Frederick, either as King or as the heir to the childless Frederick I. Russian policy was greatly affected by the succession of so many monarchs within a short interval. Catherine I did not pursue her husband's policy of Caspian expansion and devoted much attention to Baltic affairs. Peter II, who showed much favour to Old Russ families such as the Dolgorukiis, reaffirmed Catherine I's alliance with Austria and promised to send Russian troops into Europe in support of the Vienna alliance, but during his reign Russian military action declined, the Baltic fleet was allowed to rot and a reversion of Russia to barbarism was widely anticipated. Anne in 1730 reaffirmed the Austrian alliance and adopted a much more active stance in European politics.[15]

Aside from influencing the disputed succession in Sweden, Russian power was also of great importance in Poland, another country whose unsettled succession was a major cause of instability in eastern Europe. There were two kings of Poland alive. Stanislaus Leszczynski, after 1725 the father-in-law of Louis XV, had been set up by Charles XII of Sweden as King of Poland in rivalry to Augustus II Elector of Saxony. The defeat of Charles XII at Poltava in 1709 had led to Stanislaus being driven into exile. Stanislaus maintained his claim to the Polish throne, and the existence of a strong anti-Saxon movement within Poland, able to express itself freely thanks to the somewhat anarchic nature of the Polish system of government, encouraged European opponents of Augustus to consider supporting Stanislaus. Poland was an elective monarchy and Augustus' attempts to have his son accepted as his successor failed. Saxon aspirations clashed with Prussian determination to prevent Saxony from becoming a major power. Frederick William I was very interested both in the Polish succession and in the succession to the Polish vassal-Duchy of Courland, where the dynasty was dying out. The growing ill health of Augustus II and his unrelenting addiction to the bottle, and the chase of both deer and women, led to frequent reports of his death: that he was to survive until 1733 came as a great surprise.

Aside from these major territories there were several other states whose succession was uncertain and contested. Several European dynasties were failing to reproduce themselves. The Cirksena family, the Dukes of East Friesland, was one of these and their extinction in 1744 had been long anticipated. In 1691 a mutual succession agreement between Hanover and East Frisia was confirmed, providing for the eventual succession of the Welfs to East Friesland if the Cirksenas died out. Three years later the Emperor Leopold I granted Frederick III of Brandenburg-Prussia a right of succession. Danish and Dutch interest in the area compounded the tension, and a civil war broke out in the 1720s between the ruler George Albert and the powerful Estates. The East Friesland issue embittered Hanoverian-Prussian relations, and the exercise of Imperial authority in the dispute fortified fears about Austrian intentions.[16]

Further south the Wittelsbach family was in dynastic difficulty largely due to its policy of donating too many younger sons to the rule of such ecclesiastical principalities as Liège, Cologne, Münster, Paderborn, Hildesheim and a clutch of south German bishoprics. The Elector Palatine Karl Philipp, who was due to die childless in 1742, ruled, besides his Electorate to which the Wittelsbach house of Palatine-Sultzbach had a clear right to succeed, the Rhenish Duchies of Jülich and Berg. These were a part of the old succession of the house of Cleves which had been provisionally divided in 1614 between the two principal claimants, the Elector of Brandenburg and the Count Palatine of Neuberg, a division confirmed, after much conflict, in the partition of 1666. The rights of the house of Palatine-Sultzbach to succeed in the Jülich-Berg inheritance were open to dispute, and Frederick William I of Prussia made it clear that he intended to pursue his claims with vigour, and if necessary with violence. Though Frederick William claimed to be ready to accept a compromise, the Wittelsbachs displayed no such readiness.[17]

In Italy the Medici Grand Dukes of Tuscany and the Farnese Dukes of Parma were dying out. The succession to both Duchies was claimed by the eldest son of Philip V and Elisabeth Farnese, Don Carlos. Though John Gaston the last Medici Grand Duke was not to die until 1737, and the last of the Farnese died in 1731, the succession issue had been much discussed in the 1720s. Imperial authority (and Austrian power) was involved, as both Tuscany and Parma were within the Empire, and the Austrians did not wish to see their strong position within Italy challenged by Carlos. Elisabeth Farnese sought to have Carlos' succession confirmed by the introduction of Spanish garrisons into the principal strongpoints in the Duchies, and by permission being granted for Carlos to reside in them. The Dukes, disinclined to see their authority infringed, and supported by the Austrians, opposed any such scheme.[18]

The role of these dynastic concerns is difficult to evaluate. However, in general it could be suggested that the dynastic element should be stressed at the expense of any analysis centring on, for example, commercial factors. Foreign policy was the most essential prerogative of majesty, and the attitudes of individual rulers are central to any analysis of international relations in this period. Any attempt at model building fails before the stubborn facts of personal whim.[19]

The Austro-Spanish treaties of 30 April and 1 May 1725 came as a considerable surprise to the rest of Europe. The two parties had been considered irreconcilable because of their differences over Italy. Early in 1725 a Dutch adventurer, Ripperdá, arrived in Vienna. He had been sent secretly by Elisabeth Farnese to offer a Spanish guarantee of the Pragmatic Sanction and concessions for Charles VI's favourite commerical scheme, the Ostend Company, in return for guarantees for Don Carlos' succession to Parma and Tuscany, and marriages between Philip V's eldest sons, Carlos and Philip, and two of the Emperor's daughters. The eventual treaties avoided committing Charles on the fate of his daughters, but provided for Carlos' rights in Italy, the mutual recognition and guarantees of each ruler's possessions and successions, trading concessions to the

Ostend Company, and Austrian support for the return of Gibraltar and Minorca from England. The treaties created a lot of unease in Britain and France. Bourbon's ministry was concerned about the prospect of Austrian support for Philip V's claim on the French throne and the British were worried by rumoured secret articles in support of the Pretender, fears which were unfounded insofar as the actual Austro-Spanish agreements were concerned. Both powers feared that the threat to the balance of power represented by the new treaties could force them into making concessions in the myriad of disputes in which they were involved. On 3 September 1725 Britain, France and Prussia signed the Treaty of Hanover guaranteeing each other's territories and rights inside and outside Europe. This provoked a new Austro-Spanish treaty two months later. Spain promised Austria subsidies, and in return Charles VI agreed that two of his daughters should marry the sons of Philip and Elisabeth.[20]

The next eighteen months saw a period of acute diplomatic tension, described aptly by McKay as a 'cold war', and by the leading opposition weekly, the *Craftsman*, as 'a sort of earthly purgatory, or a middle state between Peace and War.' Each of the alliances sought to acquire new allies. The Hanover alliance gained Sweden, Denmark and the United Provinces; the Vienna alliance, Russia, and largely thanks to Prussian fears of Russia and the prospect of Austrian support over Jülich-Berg, Prussia. Most of the German powers, whichever alliance they formally joined, followed an ambivalent policy. This was true of Saxony, Bavaria and Hesse-Cassel, whilst Sardinia attempted to conduct an auction for her support. The period saw massive military mobilisations. Britain dispatched three large fleets, one to the Baltic to persuade Sweden and Denmark that an accession to the Hanover alliance would not leave them vulnerable to Russia, one to the West Indies to blockade the Spanish treasure fleet and thereby prevent Spain from being able to provide Austria with subsidies, and one to Spanish waters to menace invasion and prevent a blockade of Gibraltar. The Spaniards fired the first shots when they besieged Gibraltar in February 1727. George I, anxious about Hanoverian vulnerability to Prussian and Austrian attack, persuaded France to move large forces towards the Rhine. War plans were drawn up and Townshend considered naval action against Sicily and an invasion of the Austrian Netherlands. Throughout the period of tension negotiations had continued between some of the powers of the two alliances. Cardinal Fleury, Louis XV's former tutor, became chief minister of France in 1726 and he was determined to avoid war. He attempted to restrain the more aggressive British ministry, and this led to some British doubts about the degree of his commitment to the Anglo-French alliance. Fleury realised that Austria was less interested in conflict than Spain. An ultimatum was sent to Austria threatening war if she would not agree to 'quelques articles préliminaires, qui puissent faire envisager une prompte conciliation'. Charles VI, averse to war, in a difficult fiscal position due to disappointments over Spanish subsidies, and hopeful that he would be able to gain advantages at the Congress table, agreed.[21]

On 31 May 1727 the Preliminaries of Paris, the terms for a pacification of Europe, were signed by the representatives of Britain, France, the United

Provinces and Austria.[22] Spain did not have an envoy in Paris and it was agreed that the Spanish envoy in Vienna, Bournonville, should be asked to sign there on behalf of Spain. Two weeks later, on 14 June, George I embarked at Greenwich for a visit to his Electorate and eight days after that, on the 22nd, he died at Osnabrück. On the 23rd the news of his death reached The Hague, on the 26th Paris and on the 28th Vienna. On Wednesday 25 June towards 3 pm the news reached Whitehall by means of a courier sent by Viscount Townshend, the Secretary of State for the Northern Department, who had been following George I to Hanover. The First Minister, Walpole, gave orders to double the guard throughout London and then left for Richmond to inform George Prince of Wales that his father had died. That evening George came to London and the following morning was proclaimed King.

It might seem that George I left on his last trip to Europe and George II came to the throne against the background of impending peace. After the Preliminaries had been signed the ministerial press was full of praise for a government that had brought peace to Europe. Hope was held out that British trade would revive. The day before George died *Stanley's News Letter* reported

> The merchants and traders of the City of London are overjoy'd at the prospect there is, that both our domestick and foreign trade, which has for a considerable time met with obstructions from the undeserved ill usage this nation had met with, will by the great wisdom and conduct of our wise administration flourish again; some of these good effects begin already to appear among our woollen and silk manufacturers here.[23]

Prosperity at home would be accompanied by peace abroad. It was confidently predicted that the Jacobites would see their chances of foreign support disappear, and indeed, many of the Jacobites were very pessimistic about the consequences of the Preliminaries. Owen O'Rourke, the Jacobite agent in Vienna, reported, 'all doors seem to be shut up by the preliminarys agreed upon'.[24]

However, alongside these tidings of peace, sounds of war and notes of discord were still heard. Some diplomats doubted whether Austria or Spain were sincere in their desire for peace. Fears were expressed that the Preliminaries would lead to France abandoning Britain and joining Spain and Austria.[25] It was well known that there had been much Anglo-French tension over the conduct of negotiations. These doubts and fears were to grow in intensity after the accession of George II, and it was to be speedily realised that the Preliminaries of Paris had not improved the British diplomatic situation to any appreciable extent.

The British Ministry

When George II acceded, the principal British ministers were Sir Robert Walpole, who ran the Treasury and led the ministerial group in the House of Commons, Lord Townshend, the Secretary of State for the Northern

Department, and the Duke of Newcastle, his colleague in the Southern Department. Walpole was First Commissioner of the Treasury and Chancellor of the Exchequer. They were referred to in an anonymous French memoir as 'le triumvirat'.[26] Opinions varied and still vary as to the abilities of each and their relations with each other. The last five years of George I's reign, the period after the deaths of Stanhope and Sunderland, have received very little scholarly attention. The ministerial rivalries of this period, and in particular the falls of Carteret and Cadogan, have received far less attention than the feuds of the first five years of the reign, and the latest biographer of George I, Hatton, is disappointingly brief in her survey of these years. She sees the last years of George's reign as years of political quiescence: 'The consensus among ministers achieved by the Townshend–Walpole coup of 1724 . . . the absence of factional strife made for relative ease of cabinet business'.[27] It was certainly the case that Walpole and Townshend acted to remove those of different views and put in their place people they could trust. Former adherents of Sunderland were removed, such as the Duke of Roxburgh, Secretary of State for Scotland, sacked in 1725; Lord Carteret, Secretary of State for the Southern Department, 1721–4, sent to Ireland as Lord Lieutenant in 1724 (a form of exile in the view of many); and the Earl of Macclesfield, impeached successfully as Lord Chancellor in 1725 in a move which some blamed on Walpole. Diplomats closely associated with Carteret, such as Sir Luke Schaub and the Earl of Marchmont, were denied posts. However, as George Baillie, one of the Lords of the Treasury, had pointed out in 1723, 'Walpole doubtless has secret enemies', and the conduct of several ministers in 1727 when George Dodington, a Lord of the Treasury, and the Duke of Dorset, the Lord Steward, deserted Walpole for his challenger Spencer Compton, confirms this view. Within the Council there was a superficial air of unity concealing envy and tension. Many hoped that the accession of George II would lead to the removal of Walpole.[28]

Walpole's relations with Townshend, his brother-in-law until 1726, and Newcastle were reasonably good. Tension has been detected between the two brothers-in-law, particularly in 1725 when Walpole was displeased by the financial consequences of Townshend's expensive attempt to recruit allies for the Hanover alliance by means of subsidies.[29] These tensions have probably been exaggerated by historians conscious of the future rivalry between the two ministers. Townshend was quite aware of the political difficulties of persuading Parliament to grant peacetime subsidies to foreign powers. He showed this in 1726 over discussions about offering Bavaria such subsidies, and the Hessian envoy Diemar found him very firm in negotiations over subsidies and concerned about parliamentary attitudes. To pretend that Townshend, an experienced debater in the House of Lords, was unconcerned by parliamentary and popular opinion, is inaccurate. The French Chargé d'Affaires, Chammorel, pressing Townshend in March 1726 against a projected tax upon French cloth imports, reported that the minister was very concerned about the possibility of the Opposition exploiting the issue.[30]

The respective roles of the three principal ministers are difficult to distinguish, because of the paucity of private correspondence surviving between them. Newcastle seems to have followed the lead of his colleagues. He was not noted for his abilities, and was profuse in his protestations of loyalty towards Walpole and Townshend. He also stressed his willingness to follow the advice of the senior Secretary, Townshend. After George I died Newcastle wrote to Townshend, 'you may be assured, that no one thing shall be done or step taken by us, till we have the pleasure of seeing you here'.[31] However, Newcastle was a stubborn man determined to protect his position and desirous of seeming to influence policy. Despite his apparent pliancy, he was increasingly adopting views of his own.[32] In 1725 he sought to block the dispatch of Lord Waldegrave to Paris on an embassy to congratulate Louis XV on his marriage. The details are obscure, but it appears that Newcastle resented an appointment in his own department of someone he did not approve of. Newcastle failed to block the appointment.[33] Possibly the increased speculation about Newcastle being replaced as Secretary, speculation particularly noticeable in the winter of 1726–1727, reflected real tension within the ministry, but if it did, there are few other signs of such tension. Newcastle accepted both a position as ministerial second fiddle in the House of Lords, and the independent attitude and position of Sir Robert Walpole's brother, Horatio, who held Paris, the most important embassy in Newcastle's department. Newcastle describing his position in the 1720s noted that he 'then, never thought, nor could be thought by anybody, but to act a subordinate part in the House of Lords'.[34]

The relations between Townshend and Walpole are unclear. Differences of opinion existed about a range of matters, and historians have been able to draw attention to clashes between the two ministers. However, it would be absurd to suppose that differences should not have existed. Any attempt to define respective spheres of interest, with Townshend dealing with foreign affairs, and Walpole with the House of Commons and fiscal matters, needs to cope with the interdependence of these spheres. Foreign policy entailed fiscal obligations which had to be supported by Parliament. During Townshend's absences in Hanover, Walpole was involved in the conduct of foreign policy. Plumb has suggested that tension between the two men steadily increased, that Walpole acquired sufficient self-confidence to challenge Townshend's control of foreign policy, that Townshend resented Walpole's growing strength in Norfolk politics symbolised by the building of his grandiose seat at Houghton, and that the death in 1726 of Walpole's sister, who had been Townshend's wife, helped to weaken the links between the two men.[35] Against this must be set the continued successful partnership of the two men and the relative absence of contemporary suggestions of division between them. Contemporary commentators were always very keen to see signs of conflict, and they are, within limits, a guide to the perception of tension in this period. George I's ministry, when he set out for Hanover in the summer of 1727, was a successful administration. The three principal ministers were united and the jealousy of them that existed within the ministry was held in check by governmental success and royal favour. The maverick Tory Lord Bolingbroke was foolish to believe that George was going to dismiss Walpole.[36] Nevertheless Walpole, aware of opposition within the ministry, was conscious of the need to maintain royal support.

Walpole's relations with George, Prince of Wales, were not particularly good, though they were not as bad as the Prince's relations with Newcastle. During the mid-1720s the Prince had played little part in politics and had led a rather retired life. The spectacular disputes with his father of the late 1710s had been replaced by a mutual coldness. There is little sign of any difference of opinion between father and son over policy, but there was tension over the Prince's position. George I refused to have his son as Regent in England, during his absences in Hanover, and he vetoed his request to have a military post in any European conflict which might involve Britain.[37] The ministry sought to smooth matters. Townshend was instrumental in securing the Garter for the Earl of Scarborough, the Master of the Horse to the Prince of Wales and one of his principal favourites. The Prince was kept informed of government policy through the Lord Privy Seal, the Duke of Devonshire, who had close connections with the Princess, Caroline of Ansbach.[38] Foreign diplomats had little hope that the accession of George II would alter British policy, which suggests a belief that the Prince was as committed to the French alliance as his father.

Though his views on policy might be a mystery, the Prince was known to possess a distinct group of friends and confidants, some of whom were distinctly at odds with his father's ministers. This group has never received major scholarly attention, and its importance and potential strength have been underrated. Its leading member was the Honourable Spencer Compton, son of the third Earl of Northampton and MP for Sussex. Throughout George I's reign he was Speaker of the House of Commons and Treasurer to the Prince of Wales. In 1722 the ministry, seeking to please the Prince, bestowed on Compton the extremely lucrative office of Paymaster General. In her diary Lady Mary Cowper presented Compton as an active politician seeking to create a party that would include some of the Tories, but views of Compton's effectiveness and abilities varied. Browning has referred to 'the peculiarly gutless manner that characterised so much of his public life', and this view is widely, if less vividly, held. Compton's abilities and influence are difficult to assess, but in 1727 he was held to be a plausible candidate for chief minister.[39] Prince George's circle had a distinctly aristocratic tone. Aside from Compton, prominent members included Frederick Nassau, first Earl of Grantham, Richard Lumley, second Earl of Scarborough, William Capel, third Earl of Essex and Philip Stanhope, fourth Earl of Chesterfield. Apart from Compton, few members of this group possessed any governmental experience and none, apart from Scarborough, had distinguished himself in Parliament. Aside from Compton the group was relatively young, younger than George II, who acceded in his forty-sixth year. Scarborough had been born in 1688, Chesterfield in 1694. The abilities of these men were unknown, their political interest untested. None was a great borough patron. The other confidant of the Prince who was believed to enjoy great influence was his mistress Henrietta Howard, Countess of Suffolk. She had links with the parliamentary opposition and was in touch with the critics of Walpole. After George II came to the throne she enjoyed little power, but this had not been predicted, and George's earlier favour for her had been seen as a sign that Walpole would not survive the change of monarch.[40] Given the significant political changes which had followed the accession of recent monarchs it was understandable that the fall of the Walpole ministry was anticipated. What is surprising is that more sweeping alterations were not expected by many.

Notes

1. R. Hatton, *War and Peace 1680–1720* (1969), pp. 26, 22; Fleury to Austrian diplomat Pentenriedter, 3 Mar., reply, 22 Mar. 1727, A. Drodtloff, *Johann Christoph Pentenriedter* (unpublished Ph.D., Vienna, 1964), pp. 227, 238; Fleury to the Emperor, 12 Mar., Pentenriedter to Austrian Chargé d'affaires in Paris, Fonseca, 4 Aug., 6, 20 Sept. 1727, HHStA. Frankreich Varia 11, Fonseca 21; Viscount Townshend, Secretary of State for the Northern Department, to William Finch, Envoy Extraordinary at The Hague, 6 Feb. (os) 1728, PRO. 84/299; *Craftsman*, leading opposition newspaper, 2 Dec. (os) 1727.

2. Hatton, *George I*, p. 216; J. H. Shennan, *Philippe Duke of Orléans* (1979), p. 61.

3. J. Chance, *George I and the Great Northern War* (1909); W. Mediger, *Moskaus Weg nach Europa* (Brunswick, 1952); Mediger, *Mecklenburg, Russland und England – Hannover* (Hildesheim, 1967); R. Hatton, *Charles XII of Sweden* (1968); D. Aldridge, *Sir John Norris and the British Naval Expeditions to the Baltic Sea, 1715–1727* (unpublished Ph.D., London, 1971); H. Bagger, *Ruslands Alliancepolitik efter freden i Nystad* (Copenhagen, 1974), English summary; Black, 'Anglo-Russian Diplomatic Relations in the Eighteenth Century', *Study Group on Eighteenth-Century Russia Newsletter 12* (1984).

4. Hughes, pp. 77–84, 108–280; St. Saphorin, British agent in Vienna, 'Relation sur les affaires du Mecklenbourg', [1727], PRO. 80/61.

5. Black, 'Russia and the British Press, 1720–1740', *British Journal for Eighteenth-Century Studies*, 5 (1982), 'Russia and the British Press in the early eighteenth century', *Study Group on Eighteenth-Century Russia Newsletter* 11 (1983).

6. Newcastle to Horatio Walpole, 15 Nov. (os) 1725, BL. Add. 32744; Horatio Walpole, 'Considerations', – Aug. 1727, PRO. 84/294 f.138.

7. Armstrong; Quazza, pp. 19–24; G. J. Walker, *Spanish Politics and Imperial Trade* (1979), pp. 93–113, 159–73; D. McKay, *Prince Eugene of Savoy* (1977), pp. 172–3; Black, 'Parliament and the Political and Diplomatic Crisis of 1717–18', *Parliamentary History* 3 (1984).

8. L. Vignols, 'L'asiento français, 1701–13, et anglais, 1713–50, et le commerce france-espagnol vers 1700 a 1730', *Revue d'histoire économique et sociale* 17 (1929).

9. Journal of James Lord Waldegrave, British Ambassador to Austria, 10 Nov. 1727, Chewton; S. F. Gradish, 'The establishment of British seapower in the Mediterranean, 1689–1713', *Canadian Journal of History*, 10 (1975); Black, 'The development of Anglo-Sardinian Relations in the first half of the eighteenth century', *Studi Piemontesi*, 12 (1983); Black, 'The British Navy and British Foreign Policy in the Eighteenth Century', in Black and K. Schweizer (eds.), *Essays in European History in honour of Ragnhild Hatton* (Lennoxville, 1985).

10. Townshend to William Finch, 29 Sept. (os) 1727, Horatio Walpole to Charles Delafaye, Under Secretary in the Southern Department, 7 Sept. 1728, PRO. 84/294, 78/188; Waldegrave journal, 16 Oct. 1727, Chewton; Benjamin Keene, Minister in Spain, to Horatio Walpole and Stephen Poyntz, envoys in Paris, 20 Oct. 1729, BL. Add. 32763; Villars, pp. 19–20; Goslinga, pp. 160–1, 259–60, 283–4.

11. Gansinot to the Cologne minister Count Plettenberg, 22 Dec. 1725, Münster, NB. 259; A. Arneth, *Prinz Eugen von Savoyen* (Vienna, 1858); M. Braubach, *Versailles und Wien von Ludwig XIV bis Kaunitz* (Bonn, 1952); Braubach, *Prinz Eugen von Savoyen* (Vienna, 1963–5); McKay, *Eugene*; Quazza, pp. 25–43; H. Naumann, *Österreich, England und das Reich 1719–32* (Berlin, 1936); K. Borgmann, *Der Deutsche Religionstreit der jahren 1719–20* (Berlin, 1937); H. Schmidt, *Kurfürst Karl Philipp von der Pfalz als Reichfürst* (Mannheim, 1963), pp. 114–49; M. Huisman, *La Belgique Commerciale sous l'Empereur Charles VI. La Compagnie d'Ostende* (Brussels, 1902); Dunthorne, pp. 57–74.

12. A. Philipp, *August der Starke und die Pragmatische Sanktion* (Leipzig, 1908); L. Hüttl, *Max Emanuel* (Munich, 1976); C. Ingrao, 'The Pragmatic Sanction and the Theresian Succession: A Reevaluation', *Topic* 34 (1980).

13. A. Baudrillart, 'Les prétensions de Philippe V à la couronne de France', *Séances et travaux de l'Academie des Sciences Morales et Politiques*, 127 (1887); Armstrong, p. 214; Thomas Robinson, Minister in Vienna, to Horatio Walpole, 28 May 1734, PRO. 80/107; J. M. J. Rogister, 'A Minister's Fall and its Implications: The case of Chauvelin, 1737–46', D. J. Mossop, G. E. Rodmell and D. B. Wilson (eds.), *Studies in the French Eighteenth Century* (Durham, 1978), p. 213; Black, 'The Anglo-French Alliance 1716–31', *Francia* 13 (1986).

14. G. H. Jones, *The Mainstream of Jacobitism* (Cambridge, Mass., 1954); P. Fritz, *The English Ministers and Jacobitism* (Toronto, 1975); L. Colley, *In Defiance of Oligarchy: the Tory Party 1714–60* (Cambridge, 1982); Black (ed.), *Britain in the Age of Walpole* (1984), pp. 2–6, 159–60.

15. D.J. Taylor, *Russian Foreign Policy 1725–39* (unpublished Ph.D., Norwich, 1983).

16. Hughes, pp. 84–95, 99–100, 281–362; memorandum, AE. MD. Hollande 60 f.65–124; B. Kappelhoff, *Absolutisches Regiment oder Ständerherrschaft ?Landesherr und Landstände in Ostfriesland im ersten Drittel des 18 Jahrhunderts* (Hildesheim, 1982).

17. A. Rosenlehner, *Kurfürst Karl Philipp von der Pfalz und die jülichsche Frage, 1725–1729* (Munich, 1906).

18. G. H. Jones, 'Inghilterra, Granducato di Toscana e Quadruplice Alleanza', *Archivio Storico Italiano* (1980); Quazza, pp. 61–7; R. Moscati, 'La Politica Estera Degli Stati Italiani dalla Caduta di Alberoni al Terzo Trattato di Vienna', *Rassegna Storica Del Risorgimento* (1948).

19. Black, 'The theory of the balance of power in the first half of the eighteenth century: a note on sources', *Review of International Studies* 9 (1983), pp. 56–7.

20. G. Syveton, *Une cour et un aventurier au XVIII siècle: le Baron de Ripperdá* (Paris, 1896), review by E. Armstrong, *EHR* 12 (1897), pp. 796–800; Syveton, 'Un traité secret de mariage et d'alliance', *Revue Historique* 54 (1894); Horatio Walpole to Newcastle, 26 June 1726, BL. Add. 32746; extract of dispatch from Keene, 15 June 1726, C(H) Mss., papers 26/23; Townshend to General Diemar, Hesse-Cassel envoy in London, 4 Jan. (os) 1727, PRO. 100/15; Hervey, p.58; Fritz, *Jacobitism*, p.134.

21. McKay, *Eugene*, p. 208; *Craftsman* 4 May (os) 1728; Wilson, pp. 151–67; R. Lodge, review of Chance, 'Alliance of Hanover', *EHR* 39 (1924), pp. 293–7.

22. Chance, *Alliance of Hanover* pp. 731–5; A. Pribram, *Österreichische Staatsverträge: England bis 1748* (Innsbruck, 1907), pp. 457–64.

23. *Wye's Letter* 27 May (os), 6, 10 June (os) 1727.

24. O'Rourke to James III, the Pretender, 14 June, HHStA. England Varia 8; Sir Henry Goring, Jacobite agent in Paris, to James, 8 June, Charles Caesar, Jacobite MP to James, 29 June 1727, RA. 107/34, 141; G. V. Bennett, *The Tory Crisis in Church and State 1688–1730* (Oxford, 1975), p. 293.

25. Horatio Walpole to Delafaye, 13 June, Townshend to Newcastle, 19 June, George Tilson, Under Secretary at the Northern Department, to Delafaye, 19 June, Richard Sutton, Envoy in Cassel, to Townshend, 23 June, Francis Vandermeer, Dutch Ambassador in Spain, to Horatio Walpole, 22 Sept. 1727, PRO. 78/308, 43/9, 81/122, 94/98; Townshend to Admiral Norris, 24 June (os), Horatio Walpole to Newcastle, 30 July 1727, BL. Add. 28156, 32751; Fleury to Charles VI, 7 June 1727, HHStA. Frankreich Varia 11; Fleury to Richelieu, 4 June 1727, A. de Boislisle (ed.), *Mémoires authentiques du Maréchal de Richelieu* (Paris, 1918), p. 26.

26. Memoir, 31 Dec. 1728, AE. CP. Ang. 346.

27. Hatton, p. 276.
28. Sedgwick, I, 35, 95, 501; HMC. Onslow, p. 465; E. Fitzmaurice, *Life of William Earl of Shelburne* (1875), I, 44.
29. Coxe, I, 49–50.
30. Townshend to St. Saphorin, 14 Jan. (os) 1726, Townshend to Earl of Chesterfield, Ambassador at The Hague, 29 Apr. (os) 1729, PRO. 80/57, 84/304; Townshend to Horatio Walpole, 22 Aug. (os) 1728, BL. Add. 32757; Chammorel to Morville, French foreign minister, 11 Mar. 1726, AE. CP. Ang. 354.
31. Newcastle to Townshend, 15 June (os) 1727, BL. Add. 32687; Browning, p. 48.
32. Plumb, p. 195; Browning, pp. 49–50; Williams, pp. 60–66.
33. 'Notes relating to my coming here', undated, Chewton.
34. Newcastle to Lord Chancellor Hardwicke, 14 Oct. (os) 1739, BL. Add. 35046; newsletter to George I's brother, Ernst August, Prince Bishop of Osnabrück, 7 Jan. 1727, Osnabrück, 299.
35. J. B. Owen, *The Eighteenth Century 1714–1815* (1974), pp. 28–29; Walpole to Newcastle, 19 Sept. (os) 1725, PRO. 35/38; Plumb, pp. 132–3, 151, 171; Hervey, pp. 80–5; Black, 'An "ignoramus" in European affairs?' *British Journal for Eighteenth-Century Studies* 6 (1983).
36. Sir Henry Goring to James III, 24 Mar. 1727, RA. 105/49; Bolingbroke to Sir William Wyndham, 20 Feb. (os) 1736, Coxe, II, 340; Hervey, pp. 13–16; Coxe, I, 264–5; A. Foord, *His Majesty's Opposition 1714–1830* (Oxford, 1964), p. 115; H.T. Dickinson, *Bolingbroke* (1970), p. 219.
37. Newcastle to Townshend, 28 June (os) 1723, BL. Add. 32686; Thomas Southcoat to James III, 6 July 1722, RA. 60/125; Duke to Duchess of Portland, 15 Oct. (os) 1723, BL. Eg. 1711; Broglie, French Ambassador in London, to Morville, 30 Nov. 1724, 2 June 1727, Chammorel to Morville, 11 June 1725, AE. CP. Ang. 349, 359, 351; D'Aix, Sardinian Envoy in London, to Victor Amadeus II of Sardinia, 26 June 1727, AST. LM. Ing. 35; Coxe, I, 193, 271; Foord, *Opposition*, p. 107, n.6, p. 116.
38. Coxe, I, 193–4, 283; Plumb, p. 163; Le Coq, Saxon Envoy in London, to Marquis de Fleury, Saxon Minister, 3 May 1726, Dresden, 2674.
39. S. Cowper (ed.), *Diary of Mary Countess Cowper, 1714–20* (2nd ed., 1865), p. 144; Browning, p. 51; Coxe, I, 284–5; Sedgwick, I, 568–9; P. D. G. Thomas, *The House of Commons in the Eighteenth Century* (Oxford, 1971), pp. 291–4.
40. Hervey, 39–44; Coxe, I, 276–81; L. Melville, *Lady Suffolk and her Circle* (1824).

CHAPTER TWO

The Accession of George II

George II came to the throne determined to be his own master. He had no intention of being a roi fainéant, and made it clear from the beginning of his reign that he wished to control all the activities of government. Such a wish was not new and, particularly since Louis XIV's bombastic remarks of 1661, every monarch at his accession to power spoke of his intention to rule himself. George energetically threw himself into the business of government, and contemporaries noted this. The Sardinian envoy, the Marquis D'Aix, and his Saxon counterpart Le Coq, noted that George wanted to be informed of everything and that he worked hard; points frequently made in the diplomatic correspondence of this period.[1] Indeed he worked so hard that fears were expressed about his health.[2] Hill Mussenden informed his brother Carteret Leathes, soon to be elected an MP for Sudbury, that George was determined to sit in person on the Admiralty, Treasury and War Office Boards. When George came to the throne he spoke of his intention to supervise the Treasury in person, and of his determination to cut pay, particularly for officials who held more than one post. It was believed that he would cut the number of pensions paid from the civil list, and Le Coq argued that these changes were due not to George's avarice, but to a coherent fiscal and political strategy, an attempt to reduce the need for governmental borrowing and the dependence upon parliamentary grants. There is no independent evidence for this suggestion, but it is symptomatic of the belief that George was seriously attempting to intervene in the processes of government.

George's initial determination to rule himself survived the summer of 1727. He continued to work hard. Throughout the autumn and winter of 1727 he showed that he was determined to maintain his authority. Carteret's new instructions as Lord Lieutenant of Ireland, drawn up in October, limited his power over the Irish army and increased that of the King. Two months later the manuscript newsletter sent regularly from London to George's uncle, Ernst-August, the Prince-Bishop of Osnabrück, reported that George was intervening in the pay of his household and guard officers, and devoting a lot of attention to administration.[3]

Countering these signs of royal activity were others suggesting that George was, as one biographer has claimed, a 'King in toils'. The Jacobite Earl of Strafford informed James III that

The same violent and corrupt measures taken by the father will be pursued by the son, who is passionate, proud and peevish, and though he talks of ruling himself, he will just be governed as his father was.[4]

The continued power of Walpole, the few ministerial changes and the decision not to change government policies led many to adopt Strafford's conclusion. By the autumn of 1727 Walpole's continued power was regarded as unremarkable, and this has led historians to ignore just how surprising such a continuation was.

Eight days before the death of George I, the London weekly newspaper *Applebee's Original Weekly Journal* printed a letter from 'Terre-Filius', warning 'all designing statesmen, and unwary politicians' that

> as their power only depends upon the breath of their sovereigns, an angry blast of that flings them at once from the summit of their glory, and height of their ambition; or at most, their authority generally determines with the life of their Prince, it being very rarely found that the most expert statesman can continue a favourite to two Princes successively.[5]

Many endorsed this view, and the accession of George II led to widespread expectations of Walpole's fall. Most of the major Tory peers and MPs flocked to court, hoping that George would drastically reconstitute the ministry. On 26 June the Earls of Strafford and Lichfield and Lords Gower and Scarsdale came to court and kissed George's hand. Strafford and the Duke of Somerset accompanied George to the Chapel Royal on 6 July. These visits were public and were well reported, both in Britain and in Europe. *Stanley's Letter*, a manuscript newsletter used by many provincial newspapers, such as the *Ipswich Journal*, as a source of London and European news, reported on 5 July that 'there is the greatest court that has been known, most of the Popish and Tory Lords so called, have been to wait on their Majesties and were very graciously used'. The newsletter sent to George's uncle Ernst-August observed that many notables who had not been to court for years, such as Somerset, Strafford, Scarsdale, the Duchess of Marlborough and the Earl of Arran, had paid their respects to George and been received very graciously. Tories such as Lord Bathurst hoped that George would turn to them. Charles Caesar, soon to be elected MP for Hertfordshire, informed James III that 'several of the Tories . . . had formed to themselves ridiculous notions of favour from the Prince', but he suggested that some of the Tories who went to court had mixed motives, 'hoping to so lull the government asleep that they would disband some of their forces and seeking to defeat the plans of those Tories who would serve George'. George did make a few moves in the direction of the Tories. He was most gracious to those who came to court, sufficiently so that there was speculation that some, such as Sir Thomas Hanmer (Tory MP for Suffolk), would be raised to the peerage, and he took steps to increase the number of Tory Justices of the Peace.[6] However, the Tories were swiftly disabused of their hopes of George. On 5 August the newletter sent to Osnabrück noted that most Tories were no longer going to court because they realised George would not include them in the ministry. Charles Caesar wrote on 12 August that the Tories were increasingly conscious of the vanity of their hopes.[7] It is most doubtful whether George ever intended to do anything more than make a few concessions to the

Tories, and to favour individuals whom he liked, as his father had done. As Prince of Wales in the 1720s, George had had little to do with the Tories and the aristocratic clique he mixed with was overwhelmingly Whig. Compton, earlier in his career, had had close links with the Tories, as Walpole had done, and there were later to be suggestions that he was willing to make such an alliance, but there are no signs that he considered one in the summer of 1727. When George gave the Lord Chancellor Lord King his instructions about altering the composition of the Bench, he told him to 'still keep a majority of those who were known to be most firmly in his interest', though he ordered him to keep that part of his instructions secret, a move which suggests George was really seeking to curry popularity. There are no signs in this period that George seriously thought of turning to the Tories, and this appears to have been a decision stemming from George's personal distrust of Toryism and his concern about the Jacobite sympathies of many Tories, rather than the result of Walpole's persuasion.[8]

On the day that George was proclaimed king, 26 June, Newcastle wrote to Townshend of 'the concern and distraction we are all in here . . . we can make no judgement of affairs here, in all probability the speaker will be the chief man'. Arthur Onslow, the MP for Guildford, who was in London at the time, noted

> that everybody expected, that Mr. Compton the Speaker would be the Minister, and Sir Robert Walpole thought so too, for a few days . . . the new king's first inclination and resolution, which were certainly for Mr. Compton . . . who had long been his treasurer, and very near to him in all his counsels. It went so far as to be almost a formal appointment, the king, for two or three days directing everybody to go to him upon business . . . but by the Queen's management, all this was soon over-ruled.[9]

Onslow's interpretation was shared by many others. It was generally believed that George was heavily influenced by his wife. In March 1726, in a memoir drawn up by the French foreign ministry for their envoy in Britain Count Broglie, Caroline was stated to possess a lot of influence over George. In November 1727 Walpole, telling Lord King 'of the great credit he had with the king', attributed it to 'the means of the Queen, who was the most able woman to govern in the world'.

The contrast between the Queen's bright, sparkling, witty nature and George's more dour, boorish demeanour greatly influenced contemporaries such as Lord Hervey. Coxe regarded George as a puppet manipulated by his wife, 'Caroline . . . almost entirely governed the king . . . contrived that her opinion should appear as if it had been his own'. By such guileful methods Caroline earned a reputation as a shrewd intriguer, and it was because of this reputation that contemporaries and historians, such as Coxe and Vaucher, have largely attributed Walpole's continuance in office to the Queen.

Without overthrowing this analysis, it is possible to suggest that Caroline's influence has been exaggerated and that there were other reasons for Walpole's continuance in power. In her diary Lady Mary Cowper, a Lady-in-Waiting to Caroline as Princess of Wales, suggested that Caroline and others overestimated her influence, a view later expressed by Sarah Duchess of Marlborough.[11] The picture of George as a headstrong, blinkered boor, manipulated by his wife and by Walpole, is one which has enjoyed much support, but it is largely based on the malicious views of a few contemporaries such as Hervey. Many of the statements used by historians to support this interpretation of the events of 1727 are open to question. Hervey and Onslow both wrote their accounts several years later. Hervey did not begin his memoirs until 1733 or 1734, whilst Onslow's account is based upon papers and correspondence that no longer exist but were transcribed by his son in 1769. These papers were certainly drawn up after Walpole's death in 1745 and their accuracy is open to question.

The notes made by Lord King are a more useful source as they were made at the time of the events recorded or only shortly afterwards. King's account of the failure of Compton does not mention the Queen, but suggests that George was persuaded, by personal experience, to continue Walpole in power,

> . . . by his constant application to the King by himself in the mornings, when the Speaker, by reason of the sitting of the House of Commons, was absent, he so worked upon the King, that he not only established himself in favour with him, but prevented the cashiering of many others, who otherwise would have been put out.

There were several obvious reasons why it would have been foolish to remove Walpole at once. The accession of a new monarch meant that Parliament had to be summoned, the Civil List settled and elections held for a new Parliament. Walpole was needed for these purposes. Parliament sat from 8 to 28 July, and during this time Walpole made himself extremely useful to George, securing an enlarged Civil List of £800,000 per annum. As Prince of Wales, George had accumulated substantial debts; Le Coq suggested that they exceeded a million pounds. Furthermore the king had a reputation for avarice and meanness. Whatever the importance to George of the enlarged Civil List, it is certain that Walpole's command of the House of Commons and the ease with which he secured parliamentary consent for the new fiscal arrangements were very impressive, though it is doubtful whether politicians seeking to win royal favour would have found it helpful to oppose the Civil List in Parliament.[12]

Possibly as significant was Walpole's success in the elections. Le Coq suggested that Walpole was given an opportunity to display his skill to the king, and that George had decided to delay any governmental changes until after the elections, in order to be in a state to gratify those who had helped with the elections and those whose help would be needed in the subsequent Parliament. If this was so, Walpole certainly passed the test with flying colours. After the election petitions were heard, the new House of Commons consisted of 415 ministerial supporters, 15 opposition Whigs, and 128 Tories, a government majority of 272, the largest since George I's accession. The comparable figures after the 1722 election were 389 Whigs and 169 Tories, a majority of 220.[13]

In his lengthy and thoughtful dispatch of 22 July Le Coq had reported that other reasons were being advanced as to why it was against the king's interest to change the government. First, Walpole's influence with Parliament and with the great chartered corporations – the Bank of England, East India Company and South Sea Company – was held to be very important for the credit-worthiness and stability of the government. Second, to change the government was held to be inadvisable for British foreign policy. The current policy was the product of the Walpole/Townshend ministry, so it was held to be dangerous to replace them by men who were poorly informed about British foreign policy and the European situation. Furthermore, it was felt that such a change would alarm Britain's allies at a tricky diplomatic juncture.

The importance of these last factors in the mind of George II is difficult to evaluate. However interested he might be in the Civil List or in the general election, George was probably at least as concerned about the European situation, and during the first few years of his reign he was to display far more interest in European than in domestic affairs. Britain's allies certainly expressed some concern about the possibility of a change in the British government. Fleury pressed George II to maintain the Walpoles in power. Concern was expressed in The Hague. It is possible that the French view was of great importance to George, as British foreign policy depended on a continued alliance with France. Opposition supporters blamed Fleury for Walpole's continuance in office.[14]

Whatever the reasons, Walpole's continuance in power was clear within a fortnight of George's accession. The achievement was however subject to two questions: first, whether Walpole would be forced to accept many changes in the ministry, and second whether George would follow the advice of his ministers. Both these problems were to be of great significance during the first six months of the reign and each was to raise many questions about the stability of the Walpolean system. Though it rapidly became clear that the Tories had little to hope for from George, other politicians, both those associated with George as Prince of Wales, and those Whigs who had fallen out with Walpole, had high hopes from the new monarch. The dismissal of Viscount Malpas, Walpole's son-in-law and the Master of the Robes to George I, the day after the accession, led many to assume there would be major changes. On 1 July Newcastle had to confess to Waldegrave, 'we can yet make no certain judgment what turn things will take here'. Hill Mussenden noted rumours 'that Sir Robt. will be continued in the Treasury, but not with the same authority, and that Ld. Carteret and Mr. Pulteney will certainly be brought into play in the room of some of Sir. Robt.'s friends'. It was suggested that Carteret would replace Newcastle. The Saxon agent Zamboni reported rumours that the ministry was to be replaced by Pulteney, Chesterfield, Compton, and other friends of George whilst Prince of Wales. D'Aix suggested that those who had the ear of George were Scarborough and Compton, and that

Chesterfield would join the ministry. Suggestions were made that George's aristocratic friends would be raised in the peerage and that several would receive dukedoms. The press published these suggestions far and wide. On 28 June *Stanley's News Letter*, for example, reported 'We hear that Sir Spencer Compton, the Earl of Grantham and Lord Carteret will have some high posts conferred on them'.[15]

The rumours proved to be wildly exaggerated. Though such sound supporters of Walpole as Malpas and Sir William Yonge, one of the Lords of the Treasury, lost their places, they soon gained others. Malpas became a Lord of the Admiralty and Yonge gained the same position in 1728. Whilst dismissed supporters of Walpole thus gained compensation, the same was not true for Walpole's opponents. The accession of George and the subsequent changes in the ministry provided an opportunity to remove some of the opposition Whigs and it is difficult to believe that Walpole was not behind these removals. The Earl of Berkeley, First Lord of the Admiralty since 1717, was dismissed and his post given to Viscount Torrington, after the Earl of Orford had declined it on the grounds of age. The Chetwynd brothers were dismissed as 'Sir Robert Walpole's declared ill-wishers', William Chetwynd, a friend of Bolingbroke and Lady Suffolk, losing his Lordship of the Admiralty, and Walter Chetwynd his Rangership of St. James's Park.[16]

George's aristocratic friends won a few positions. Essex gained the Rangership of St. James's, one of the more important posts of its type as it gave access to the monarch. Grantham was raised to the Privy Council and made Lord Chamberlain to the Queen. Scarborough was made Master of the Horse. Sir Charles Hotham, a friend of George II's and MP for Beverley, was made a Groom of the Bedchamber. With all these men it is unclear how much personal ambition they possessed. Most seemed to have been content with honourable, fashionable and profitable posts in the Household and to have shown little interest in gaining the more arduous posts of power. Essex, a flashy womaniser, was to be Ambassador to Sardinia from 1732 until 1736, but during his embassy his principal concerns were seduction and securing leaves of absence so that he could visit the carnivals of Italy. Hotham's ambition was restricted largely to the army where he sought a regiment, a goal not attained until 1732. Scarborough is a difficult man to evaluate. He was highly intelligent and profoundly melancholic, a courtier who ended his life in suicide. He was never noted for his ambition.

Two members of George's aristocratic group were politically ambitious. Compton's maladroit conduct in June 1727 did not mean that he was the 'amiable noncnity' depicted by Basil Williams. It is probable that Compton was disinclined to accept responsibility for the financial management of the crown. John Scrope, the Secretary of the Treasury, suggested it was this in particular that led him to decline the Treasury. Compton was outmanoeuvred by Walpole, and lacked his ability, but it is difficult to accept Hervey's characterisation of him as a weak and vicious man. He has been used as a foil to Walpole's ability, but Walpole was clearly concerned about Compton and regarded his continuance in the Commons as a threat.[17]

Chesterfield sought office as Secretary of State. He had no diplomatic or governmental experience, but in this he was little worse prepared than Newcastle, who was only a year his senior and had never been abroad. Chesterfield's lively spirit attracted the notice of several foreign diplomats and he was seen as possessing considerable potential. Instead of being appointed Secretary he was named for the Hague Embassy, as successor to William Finch. Some saw this as a form of diplomatic exile, and Chesterfield himself was less than keen to go and did not arrive at The Hague until May 1728. However, it was generally understood that the posting was a form of training, and that if Horatio Walpole was appointed as a Plenipotentiary at the forthcoming Peace Congress, Chesterfield would succeed him at Paris, the most important of the British embassies. It was believed George hoped to appoint Chesterfield Secretary of State after this training. Chesterfield had never troubled to cultivate Walpole, and he had a reputation for being his enemy. Horatio Walpole was deeply disturbed by Chesterfield's apparent rise. On 9 August he informed his brother that should Chesterfield come to Paris, 'he will stand in the eye of the world, as the person designed by his majesty to be hereafter Secretary of State', and three months later he returned to the same point.[18] Chesterfield's ambition and the favour in which George held him was to be a major problem for the Walpoles for several years.

George's aristocratic friends were not therefore promoted to high office. Chesterfield received his embassy, and Compton was ennobled as Lord Wilmington in January 1728, but neither had gained what he sought. Their continued ambition, combined with their ease of access to George, was a major threat to Walpole. Others were similarly disappointed. Carteret was sent back to Ireland with diminished powers; the opposition Whigs under Pulteney were not heeded; while on 8 July Hervey, having dined the previous night with Walpole, was able to inform Stephen Fox that 'the political world rolls on just as it did'. A month later Newcastle informed Lord Blandford that George 'has been pleased to make but very few and those immaterial alterations amongst the late king's servants'. Having mentioned Berkeley's dismissal, he stated that 'the other changes are not worth troubling you with'.[19]

If Walpole had secured not only his own position but also that of his colleagues and political allies, he was nevertheless still faced with the problem of defining a relationship with his new master. Mussenden, five days after the Proclamation, stated that 'all that can be gathered for the present is that whatever side be uppermost, they will not have the same authority, that the last ministry had, since the king seems resolved to enter into all manner of affairs himself'. Lord King was soon to be made aware of this fact. Early in July George told him he expected to nominate to all benefices and prebendaries which the Chancellor usually nominated to, and when Lord King defended his prerogative George retorted that Lord Cowper, a former Chancellor, had told George such nominations were a royal right.

George's wishes were not always translated into action. He did not persevere in his dispute with Lord King about the nominations, and allowed Grafton's views about the appointment of Suffolk JPs to conquer his own wish to appoint Tories. In 1732 Viscount Perceval recorded a visit from his cousin Mary Dering, Dresser Extraordinary to the Princesses:

> 'She gave an instance how princes are imposed upon by their Ministers. She said that when the King came to the Crown, his resolution was to continue in his service as chaplains all those who had been so while he was Prince, and to fill up the number belonging to him as King with as many of his father's chaplains as could be admitted, but one of his chaplains he particularly named to be continued on account of some extraordinary services he had done him when Prince. But when the then Lord Chamberlain . . . brought him the lists to sign, he did it without further examination than observing the chaplain's name was there, yet afterwards it proved that the man was removed, and neither all his old chaplains, nor many of his father's continued, but a good many new persons placed.[20]

There was simply not enough time for George to supervise all that he wished to control and for him to see that his orders were carried out. Some of the bold claims he made soon after his accession about what he would do as monarch can be attributed to inexperience and nervous excitement. In some spheres, such as the church and the law, George's interventions were episodic, though he could be extremely determined in the defence of his prerogatives. The ministry were to find it difficult to persuade George to prefer ecclesiastics he disliked.

In two spheres, the army and foreign affairs, George displayed particular interest from his accession. There was no doubt of his great interest in and affection for the army. He enjoyed attending military reviews and drilling troops, both his own, whether British or Hanoverian, and those of his allies, such as the Hessians whom he usually reviewed on each trip to Hanover. George was keen to discuss military matters, and he enjoyed the company of military men such as Hotham, Richard Sutton and William Stanhope. He also showed favour to foreign envoys who had a military background, such as D'Aix and Broglie. George kept a close eye on military developments in other countries and followed European campaigns with great interest. He was determined to control military patronage within Britain and he refused to accept ministerial suggestions in this sphere. He had the Guards' regimental reports and returns sent to him personally every week, and when he reviewed his troops he did so with great attention to detail.

George associated the army with his 'gloire', and believed that the military reviews he conducted were the most obvious and impressive display of his power and importance. Possibly the fondest memory from his youth was of his campaigning in the Spanish Netherlands against the French in the War of the Spanish Succession. He had displayed great personal bravery when, in 1708 at the battle of Oudenarde, he had charged the French at the head of the Hanoverian dragoons, and had his horse shot under him. George bored people with his reminiscences of this period for many years. In this he was not alone. His brother-in-law, Frederick William I of Prussia, had fought in Prince Eugene's army against the

French at Malplaquet in 1709, and held annual celebrations on the anniversary of the battle. For these German princes, the campaigns of the 1700s represented a time of youthful freedom and excitement which they later sought to rediscover.

For the British ministers, George's close personal interest in the army was only an occasional nuisance, although they would have preferred to enjoy some of the military patronage George wielded, and they were embarrassed by opposition attacks upon George's militaristic tendencies. Due to George's military interests, the government had less room for concession and parliamentary manoeuvring over such issues as the size of the British army and the policy of paying subsidies to secure the use of Hessian troops. It was the effect of George's martial temperament upon his conduct of foreign policy which most concerned the government.

When George came to the throne he did not alter the direction of British foreign policy and as a result historians have concluded that the change of monarch made no difference to British foreign policy. In fact, George's accession made a substantial, twofold difference. First, however much he may have followed similar policies, he did so in a distinctly aggressive fashion, as the French diplomat Chavigny, who had previously served in London, had predicted;[21] and second, from George's accession until the spring of 1730 there was considerable uncertainty as to which ministers enjoyed George's confidence in the field of foreign policy. This produced a general situation of tension and ministerial strife.

Pugilistic diplomatic methods were not unknown in early eighteenth-century British foreign policy. Due to Britain's insular position and small army they did not resemble the martial bravado of Prussian methods, but tended to take a naval form. The best known instance was Commodore Martin's arrival at the head of a squadron in the Bay of Naples in 1742 and his peremptory demand that Naples should agree to remain neutral in the War of the Austrian Succession or face destruction. The politics of bombardment were not unknown in the Walpolean period. John Hedges, British Envoy Extraordinary at Turin, suggested naval action against Genoa, whilst Lord Tyrawly, Envoy Extraordinary at Lisbon, was a strong believer in the efficacy of violence. In February 1729 he urged treating the Portuguese roughly and in July 1729 he suggested that they should be brought to reason 'by the roughest means', adding that as Portugal lacked allies nobody would intervene if George 'had a mind to lay this country to ashes'. These views were controlled during peacetime, and Newcastle kept Tyrawly in order.[22]

The House of Lords' Address of 7 February 1728 referred to George as 'formed by Nature for the greatest military Achievements' and contemporaries were in no doubt of George's eagerness for conflict. The French general and politician, Marshal Villars, a member of the Conseil d'État where the dispatches of French diplomats were read out, noted in his diary that George was believed to desire war ardently and to wish to lead his army into battle. Le Coq noted the fear that George would push British foreign policy with more vigour, but he argued that George's warlike penchant would be restrained by his allies' opposition to war, by just considerations of state, and by the fact that the views of a Prince of Wales were naturally different from those of a King of Britain. Whatever might be the generic case for heirs succeeding to a kingdom, George II did not lose his desire to serve at the head of an army. In the late 1720s and then again during the War of the Polish Succession of 1733–1735, ministers were made uneasily conscious of George's wish, though the king was not to achieve his objective until the Dettingen Campaign in 1743. This was a major reason for ministers seeking to dissuade George from visiting Hanover, for they felt, quite correctly, that in Hanover George's propensity for violent solutions would be harder to tame, and the Anglo-Prussian war scare of 1729 confirmed their fears. George's willingness to entertain the idea of war was probably closely linked to his personal wish to fight.[23]

More significant than George's pugilistic diplomatic methods was his decision to seek advice from whom he wished. Historians have been misled by the manner in which Walpole routed Compton into assuming that after a few days' uncertainty Walpole's position was scarcely affected by the accession of George. This was not the case. George allowed Walpole to run Parliament and the Treasury, but he retained a tight control over foreign policy and proved willing to listen to politicians who disagreed with Walpole. From his accession George had made it clear he wished to control foreign policy. He read the dispatches of British envoys with great attention.[24] George began to show an independence that alarmed his ministers. His changes in the diplomatic corps were not of great significance, but they indicated a willingness to reject ministerial advice. The major diplomats of the last years of George I's reign continued in office with few changes in posting. William Stanhope, who was to be much favoured by George II and to be one of the British Plenipotentiaries at Soissons, had been very well received by George I on his return from Spain. Waldegrave, who had been ordered to go to Vienna as soon as good relations were restored, had been a favourite of George I. He was regarded favourably by George II; on 13 July 1727 Townshend informed Waldegrave 'that H.M. expresses a very particular regard for your Lordship'. Suggestions had already been made as to who would be the British Plenipotentiaries at the forthcoming Congress. Although the *Daily Journal* late in May had mentioned reports that Carteret and Stanhope would be selected, most suggestions included the names of those whom George II was eventually to appoint: Stanhope, Stephen Poyntz and Horatio Walpole.[25]

Despite these signs of continuity there were indications of George's determination to appoint whomever he wished. Chesterfield was sent to The Hague. William Finch, a protégé of Carteret's who had been brought in as MP for Cockermouth by his brother-in-law the Tory Duke of Somerset, was informed that he would be replaced at The Hague, but he was assured of the Madrid embassy, a post which he never took up but for which he was paid after he returned from The Hague. His brother Edward, another protégé of Carteret's, was sent to Sweden in 1728, after the Sardinian envoy had indicated that his Protestant zeal would make him an unacceptable envoy at Turin. Whilst Edward Finch's posting was undecided, British interests in Stockholm were represented by the new Hanoverian envoy appointed by George II, Baron von Diescau. Diescau was to embarrass the British government considerably by failing to cooperate with Finch. George decided to appoint the Hanoverian diplomat Friedrich von Fabrice as Hanoverian envoy in Dresden and considered giving him responsibility for British interests there. This was a particularly insensitive step for two reasons. First, Saxony in 1727 was a very significant diplomatic posting, because Augustus II was trying to negotiate a neutrality for the Empire, a step which would provide for the security of Hanover; and because Augustus was willing to act as a go-between in the restoration of Anglo-Prussian and Anglo-Austrian relations. Second, Fabrice was an old enemy to Townshend with very different views on European matters. Townshend had failed in 1726 to get Fabrice sacked as one of George's chamberlains and, thanks to their excellent system of postal interception and decyphering, the British ministry had discovered that Fabrice was in touch with hostile foreign envoys, in particular the Austrian Resident Palm and the Modenese agent Riva. He had used information supplied by them to seek to dissuade George I from anti-Austrian steps and to persuade him to sever his links with France. Fabrice had been secretly in touch with Berlin. George II's attempt to send Fabrice to Dresden failed due to Fabrice's excessive personal demands, but it is clear from Le Coq's dispatches that it had been a source of tension.[26] Combined with the appointments of Chesterfield and Diescau it must have led Townshend to wonder whether he would have any influence in his department.

Irritating as these moves of George's must have been, it was his attempt to consult whom he wished that created most trouble. Although George II paid little heed to Sir Luke Schaub, a diplomatic protégé of Carteret's who had been disgraced in 1724 and had hoped that the new reign would witness a revival of his fortunes, he showed sufficient confidence in St. Saphorin to upset Townshend and Walpole. Lieutenant-General François Louis de Pesmes, Seigneur de St. Saphorin, a Swiss Protestant, had represented British interests at Vienna from 1718 until he was expelled in April 1727. He had been widely blamed for the deterioration in Anglo-Austrian relations in 1725. Townshend criticised St. Saphorin in the instructions he sent to his successor Waldegrave, whom he instructed to inform the French Ambassador, the Duke of Richelieu, 'that you chuse rather to imitate his example of politeness and good breeding, than to follow the steps of Mor. de St. Saphorin, who has been censured as having acted too rough and forbidding a part'.[27]

Having left Vienna St. Saphorin set off for a Swiss spa to take the cure, and went via Schaffhausen to Lausanne. He was then ordered to wait on George I at Hanover, but this was prevented by George's death. Hoping that he would find favour with the new king he travelled to London, though Townshend had instructed him to remain in Switzerland. Count Dehn, sent on a special mission to London by the Court of Wolfenbüttel, claimed St. Saphorin had no impact, but there are indications that Dehn was wrong. D'Aix reported that George saw St. Saphorin often, and it is clear from Le Coq's dispatches that George used St. Saphorin as a confidential intermediary with foreign envoys. The French were concerned about St. Saphorin's influence. St. Saphorin was the acknowledged expert on Austrian affairs, and Townshend sent Waldegrave St. Saphorin's 'Relation secrette sur la Cour de Vienne', noting that it included 'a great deal of truth'.[28]

Seeking St. Saphorin's advice would not have mattered so much, had there not been by the autumn increasingly obvious tension between George and his ministers. D'Aix reported ministerial anger at George's supervision of them and his willingness to listen to others. Le Coq pinpointed another area of tension when he suggested that George's attempts at financial reform were weakening the position of his ministers by denying them an undisputed control of governmental patronage.[29] These tensions were made more serious by the apparently deepening problems with which British foreign policy was faced, and by the growing possibility that this policy might change direction and Britain acquire different allies. The identification of the Walpole brothers and Townshend with the French alliance meant that such changes would have important repercussions in domestic politics.

Notes

1. D'Aix to Victor Amadeus II, 11 Aug. 1727, AST. LM. Ing. 35; Le Coq to Augustus, 22 July 1727, Dresden, 2676, 18a; Broglie to Chauvelin, 4 Aug. 1727, AE. CP. Ang. 361; newsletter, 11 July 1727, Osnabrück 299; King, p. 47.
2. Le Coq to Augustus, 22 July, 26 Aug. 1727, Dresden, 2676, 18a.
3. Mussenden to Leathes, 20 June (os) 1727, Ipswich, East Suffolk CRO., Leathes papers, HA 403/1/10; Le Coq to Augustus, 12 Aug., 23 Sept. 1727, Dresden 2676, 18a; D'Aix to Victor Amadeus II, 15 Dec. 1727, AST. LM. Ing. 35; newsletter, 30 Sept., 7 Nov., 16 Dec. 1727, Osnabrück, 291, 295; L'Hermitage to States General, 7 Nov. 1727, BL. Add. 17677 KKK 9; Tenth article of Carteret's instructions, 23 Oct. (os) 1727, PRO. 63/389; Knatchbull, p. 73.
4. J. D. Griffith Davies, *A King in Toils* (1938); Lord Mahon, *History of England* (5th ed., 1858) II, xxxii.
5. *Applebee's* 3 June (os) 1727; O. Burrish, *Batavia Illustrata* iv.
6. Viscount Perceval to his brother Philip, 14 June (os) 1727, BL. Add. 47032; Caesar to James III, 29 June (os), Charles Earl of Orrery to James, 30 June (os), Graham to O'Rourke, 1 Aug. 1727, RA. 107/141, 150, 109/3; Duchess of Somerset to Earl of Nottingham, 18 July (os) 1727, Leicestershire CRO., Finch Mss. DG/7/4952; Charles, Lord Bruce to the Earl of Wilmington, 29 Dec. (os) 1729, Wiltshire CRO., Savernake Mss. 1300, 1238; King, pp. 49–50.
7. Newsletter, 5 Aug. 1727, Osnabrück, 291; James Hamilton to James III, 14 July (os), Caesar to James, 1 Aug. (os), Strafford to James, 1 Aug. (os) 1727, RA. 108/73, 109/6, 2; Bathurst to Mrs. Howard, 24 Oct. (os) 1727, BL. Add. 22626.
8. King, pp. 49–50.
9. Newcastle to Townshend, 15 June (os) 1727, BL. Add. 32687; HMC. *Onslow*, pp. 516–17; Villars, p. 77.
10. Instructions for Broglie, 9 Mar. 1726, AE. CP. Ang. 354; D'Aix to Victor Amadeus II, 30 June 1727, AST. LM. Ing. 35; King, p. 50; Le Coq to Augustus, 12 Dec. 1727, Dresden 2676, 18a; Hervey, 39, 44–5, 47–8, 69; Coxe, I, 282, 285–6, 288; Vaucher, *Walpole*, p. 35.
11. *Diary of Mary Countess Cowper*, pp. 163–4; Marlborough to Captain Fish, 31 July (os) 1727, BL. Add. 61444.

12. King, p. 46; Newcastle to Townshend, 15 June (os) 1727, BL. Add. 32687; Le Coq to Augustus, 22 July 1727, Dresden, 2676, 18a.
13. Le Coq to Augustus, 22 July 1727, Dresden, 2676, 18a; Sedgwick, I, 34, 37.
14. Fleury to George II, 2, 11 July, Robinson, Secretary of Embassy in Paris, to St. Saphorin, 14 July 1727, PRO. 100/7, 80/61; James Hamilton to James III, 14 July (os), Atterbury to James, 20 Aug. 1727, RA. 108/73, 109/87; *Craftsman* 18 July (os) 1730; Broglie to Morville, 30 Nov. 1724, AE. CP. Ang. 349.
15. Newcastle to Waldegrave, 20 June (os) 1727, Chewton; Mussenden to Leathes, 22, 17 June (os) 1727, Ipswich, HA 403/1/10; Zamboni to De Brosse, Saxon envoy at The Hague, 11 July 1727, Bodl. Rawl. 120; D'Aix to Victor Amadeus II, 26 June, 4 Aug. 1727, AST. LM. Ing. 35.
16. Lady Chetwynd to Lady Suffolk, 29 July (os) 1727, BL. Add. 22627.
17. B. Williams, *The Whig Supremacy* (Oxford, 1962) p. 202; Coxe, I, 286, II, 519–20; Hervey, 46; Egmont, II, 156–7; Le Coq to Augustus II, 22 July 1727, Dresden, 2676, 18a.
18. BL. Add. 63749; Le Coq to Augustus, 29 July 1727, Dresden, 2676, 18a; Hervey, 71, 73; newsletter, 1 Aug. 1727, Osnabrück 291.
19. Ilchester, p. 21; Newcastle to Blandford, 24 July (os) 1727, BL. Add. 32993.
20. Mussenden to Leathes, 20 June (os) 1727, Ipswich, HA 403/1/10; King, pp. 47–8; Egmont, I, 228.
21. Chavigny to Chauvelin, 8 July 1727, AE. CP. Allemagne 373.
22. Hedges to Delafaye, 8 Feb. 1727, Tyrawly to Newcastle, 14 Sept. 1728, 5, 25 Feb., 2, 26 June, 17 July, Tyrawly to Delafaye, 7 Aug., Newcastle to Tyrawly, 17 June (os) 1729, PRO. 89/35–6; *Stanley's Newsletter* 22 July (os) 1727.
23. *House of Lords Journals* XXIII, 167; Villars, p. 96; Le Coq to Augustus, 22 July 1727, Dresden, 2676, 18a.
24. Le Coq to Augustus, 19, 26 Aug. 1727, Dresden, 2676, 18a.
25. Townshend to Waldegrave, 2 July (os) 1727, PRO. 80/62; L'Hermitage, Dutch agent in London, to the States General, 6 June 1727, BL. Add. 17677 KKK. 9.
26. Le Coq to Augustus II, 15, 19 Aug., 31 Oct. 1727, Dresden, 2676 18a; Coxe II, 500–1; Du Bourgay to Tilson, 6 Dec. 1725, PRO. 90/19; R. Grieser (ed.) *Die Memoiren des Kammerherrn Friedrich Ernst von Fabrice* (Hildesheim, 1956).
27. Townshend to Waldegrave, 26 Oct. (os) 1727, PRO. 80/62.
28. Townshend to St. Saphorin, 23 June (os) 1727, PRO. 80/61; Dehn to Ferdinand Albrecht, 20 Sept., 10 Oct. 1727, Wolfenbüttel, 1 Alt 22, Nr 534; D'Aix to Victor Amadeus II, 6 Oct. 1727, AST. LM. Ing. 35; Horatio Walpole to Tilson, 3, 21 Oct. 1727, BL. Add. 48928; Woodward, British Secretary at Vienna, who left with St. Saphorin, to Tilson, 29 July, Townshend to Waldegrave, 26 Oct. (os) 1727, PRO. 80/61, Chewton.
29. D'Aix to Victor Amadeus II, 29 Sept. 1727, AST. LM. Ing. 35; Le Coq to Augustus, 23 Sept. 1727, Dresden, 2676, 18a.

CHAPTER THREE

From the Accession of George II to the Convention of the Pardo
(Summer 1727 – Spring 1728)

Hard upon the news of George II's accession Britain's envoys and allies received profuse assurances that the new King would remain firm to old alliances.[1] Foreign envoys in Britain assured their rulers that this would be the case.[2] Britain's French and Dutch allies received firm promises that Britain would not depart from the Alliance of Hanover,[3] whilst the Hessian envoy General Diemar was assured that George II was as conscious of the importance of Hessian troops for the defence of Hanover as his father had been.[4]   Despite these assurances, many doubted that Britain would be able to help her allies. In particular, it was widely assumed in Catholic Europe that the accession of a new monarch would be accompanied by major disturbances and, possibly, by a successful Jacobite uprising. Belief in such a development varied. The French government had few doubts about the stability of the Hanoverian succession and their representatives in London swiftly reassured them of the popularity of the new government. Chammorel assured Chauvelin that George was popular. The Austrians were well informed of the weak state of British Jacobitism. Prince Eugene told the Jacobite envoy in Vienna, O'Rourke, 'that whatever change might be expected hereafter, he was confident, the son would succeed quietly the father in the beginning'.[5] Two prominent groups anticipated disorders in Britain, the Spaniards and the Jacobites. The news of the death of George I led James III to leave his court at Bologna and set off for the Channel coast hoping that by the time he arrived an uprising would enable him to return to Britain. James was aware that France was unlikely to assist his scheme, but he hoped Austria would send him money and troops. The Jacobite Secretary of State, Sir John Graham, instructed O'Rourke on 4 July to press the Austrians for assistance. Austrian assistance was crucial as, in the Austrian Netherlands, Austria controlled the only ports near Britain which were not held by a British ally. Over the previous years the Jacobites had urged the Austrians to sponsor an invasion of Britain from Ostend, which they believed to be militarily practical, proximity to the target providing the opportunity for surprise that would offset the strength of the British navy, and they now hoped to execute the scheme.[6]

Alarmist rumours circulated that the Pretender would receive major support from the Catholic powers, but these rumours were totally inaccurate. France refused to heed Jacobite requests, while on 10 July Eugene reminded O'Rourke of the principle he had frequently enunciated during the previous two years, namely that the Jacobites would receive no open support or military assistance until war was declared between Britain and Austria, and that until such a time the Austrians believed that all previous agreements between Austria and Britain subsisted. Eugene therefore refused to promise support, telling O'Rourke he thought James's journey precipitate and foolish, a view held by most commentators.[7] Eugene and Sinzendorf refused to answer James's letter requesting support and on the 15th reaffirmed their refusal to help, Sinzendorf declaring that there would be no help unless there was war, and that Austria was bound by the Preliminaries. These points were echoed by Prince Eugene, who added the ominous advice that he did not believe James would be safe in the Austrian Netherlands. Sinzendorf told the Dutch envoy that 'though in case of a rupture the Emperor would have thought all fair play, yet they had no *positive* engagement with the Pretender, much less would they have any now the Preliminarys were signed.' The Pretender's half-nephew, the Duke of Liria, in Vienna on his way to take up his post as Spanish envoy in St. Petersburg, informed him that Austrian support would not be forthcoming unless James could show himself 'at the head of a good party', and that the Austrian government would not let itself be persuaded that Britain would declare for James.[8]

Despite reports to the contrary the Pretender did not reach the Austrian Netherlands but ended his journey in the Duchy of Lorraine, whence, as a result of French pressure on Duke Leopold, he moved to the Papal enclave of Avignon.[9] Austria had proved to be a great disappointment for the Jacobites, which pleased the British. The British press praised the Austrians for their stance. *Farley's Bristol Newspaper* informed its readers in September that Charles VI had written in his own hand to George to assure him that he knew nothing of Jacobite plans, and other newspapers reported that the Austrians had pressed Leopold to expel James.[10]

The British were less satisfied with the attitude of the Spaniards. The Jacobite diaspora had spread over most of Europe but there was a major concentration of Jacobites in Spain, where considerable favour had been shown to them.[11] Several Jacobites were prominent at Court, and they encouraged the Spanish government to believe that the change of British monarch would lead to disturbances and make Britain weaker.[12] Spain was dissatisfied with the Preliminaries of Paris, and her belief that the Alliance of Hanover would be weakened by the accession of George II stimulated her to press for her own interpretation of the Preliminaries.[13] Philip V maintained the blockade of Gibraltar, refused to return the South Sea Company permission-ship, the *Prince Frederick*, and disputed the British right to trade in the West Indies. In addition the privateering activities of Spanish ships upon British merchantmen, which had caused so much disquiet during the previous two years, continued. The Spaniards demanded that the British possession of Gibraltar and Minorca should be discussed at the forthcoming Congress. They also claimed damages for the disruption caused to Spanish trade by the British maritime blockade, and suggested that, pending discussion of British commercial pretensions at the Congress, the *Prince Frederick* should be held by a third power, such as the French or the Dutch.[14]

These Spanish demands were skilfully presented in an attempt to sow dissension amongst the Hanover Allies. It was known that neither the

French nor the Dutch were keen to fight either for British maritime pretensions or for the British possession of Gibraltar and Minorca. Both powers were jealous of the privileges the British had acquired at Utrecht and both had suggested the return of Gibraltar in order to placate Spanish feelings. There were rumours that the French had a secret agreement with Spain for the return of Gibraltar.[15] Sinzendorf suggested that France and Austria should jointly mediate Anglo-Spanish differences at the forthcoming Congress.[16] Chauvelin felt it necessary to order French envoys to deny reports that the Franco-Spanish reconciliation would lead to France abandoning the interests of her allies.[17] The British refused to accept the Spanish position and demanded that the Preliminaries should be executed without alteration. As the Spaniards refused to withdraw their troops from before Gibraltar, the British declined to yield to Spanish demands that they should withdraw their squadrons from Spanish waters.[18] Admiral Wager complained bitterly about the taking of British merchantmen after the Preliminaries, and threatened that he would detach ships to follow any Spanish warships sent to American waters.[19] The British response to Spanish intransigence was slow, delayed by the government's concern with elections, which fully occupied Walpole and Newcastle, and by the illness of Townshend. British relations with Spain had been handled since the departure of William Stanhope in March by Francis Vandermeer the Dutch ambassador. George II confirmed this arrangement, but it was far from satisfactory, as Vandemeer's alarmism and self-importance made him an unreliable envoy.[20] There seemed to be only three means to end the Anglo-Spanish dispute: naval action,[21] French diplomatic pressure and Austrian diplomatic pressure. Austrian aid could not be relied upon, as Austria was believed to be encouraging Spain in its obduracy in order to delay European peace.[22] The Austrians denied these accusations, though they lent diplomatic support to most of the Spanish demands.[23] Waldegrave informed Tilson on 12 September that 'the professions made by the Imperial ministers of their masters sincere desire of peace are hard to be reconciled with the encouragement it's evident they give Spain to cavil and stand out'.[24]

The British refused to exchange with Spain the ratifications of the Preliminaries of Paris. Due to the absence of diplomatic links between Britain and Spain it had been intended that Waldegrave should exchange the ratifications when he took up his post at Vienna but, as Waldegrave told the Austrian envoy in Paris, Baron Fonseca, on 20 August

> . . . till the Spaniards had agreed to the two points relating to Gibraltar and the *Prince Frederick* my going there could be of no use, for that it was not reasonable to suppose we could exchange ratifications with Spain whilst they dispute the construction and meaning of two of the articles, that our exchanging would be acquiescing to their interpretation which England would never submit to.[25]

Fleury had followed up the Preliminaries by making a major attempt to develop good relations with Spain, which he believed to be the best way to limit Austrian influence there.[26] Despite British fears and Jacobite hopes to the contrary,[27] he did not aim to abandon the Hanover alliance, but rather to broaden it to include Spain. Fleury offered to try to settle Anglo-Spanish differences and those still persisting between Britain and Austria. Despite their fears of the real purpose of the Franco-Spanish negotiations, the British government yielded to French pressure not to resort to naval action.[28] On 6 October Newcastle informed Horatio Walpole that

> His Majesty is willing as the Cardinal desires to suspend any further declaration, either to the Court of Vienna or Madrid, till the success of Count Rottembourg's negotiation and the letter wrote to the Duke de Richelieu is known.[29]

Rottembourg, the French envoy at Berlin,[30] was sent to Spain. He reached the Spanish court at St. Ildefonso on 12 October. Although his ostensible instructions, shown to Horatio Walpole, committed him to support the British position,[31] he carried secret instructions which suggested that he should attempt to produce a compromise settlement, more in line with Spanish demands.[32] The ambivalence of his mission was suspected from the outset. Waldegrave noted in his journal on 21 September his suspicion that such secret instructions existed, though four days later he wrote to Townshend of his certainty that 'those that send him are much in earnest to have this matter terminated to our satisfaction'.[33] However, the British government was surprised in December when news arrived that Rottembourg had accepted a protocol which entirely surrendered the British position over the *Prince Frederick*.

By entrusting the settlement of Anglo-Spanish differences to Rottembourg, the British had surrendered the diplomatic initiative to the French.[34] This was a policy advocated by Horatio Walpole, who prided himself on his close links with Fleury and believed the replacement that summer of the anglophile foreign minister Morville by the relatively unknown Chauvelin did not threaten his position or the Anglo-French alliance.[35] Waldegrave assured Townshend that the appointment of Chauvelin would secure the continuance of the alliance. He presented Chauvelin as a 'disciple' of Fleury's,[36] a view doubted by many others.[37] The policy was a continuation of the reliance upon French diplomacy earlier in the year when the Preliminaries had been settled as a result of Fleury's initiative in arranging Franco-Austrian negotiations.

The Walpole ministry's close identification with the French alliance[38] had produced considerable criticism.[39] Sir Edward Knatchbull recorded that the Commons' debates on the Treaty of Hanover in February 1726 and on the Address in January 1727 were marked by opposition claims that France was an unreliable ally whose aggrandisement was dangerous.[40] The French were aware of British jealousy and fear; Morville believed it was essential to persuade the British that the Anglo-French alliance operated for the benefit of both powers.[41] Such a belief was held by the Walpole ministry. The war plans drawn up early in 1727, when war was envisaged against Spain and Austria, had placed great reliance on the French army, particularly for the defence of Hanover. The success of the Preliminaries led to an increase of ministerial confidence in the alliance. In a draft dispatch for John Hedges, British Envoy Extraordinary at Turin, Newcastle noted

> . . . the preserving and cementing the union betwixt England and France, which has proved so useful and advantageous to both kingdoms, is what His Majesty looks upon as a principle not to be departed from . . . this prosperous turn of affairs, which, next to the wisdom of His Majesty's Councils, and the cheerful concurrence of his Parliament, must, in justice, be ascribed greatly to the constancy, firmness and upright behaviour of France.

The next section of the draft was deleted, but it serves to illustrate the attitude in 1727 of Newcastle, a minister not later noted for his French sympathies:

> where the present administration appears to act upon different maxims from those which may have been pursued in a former reign.[42]

Ministerial newspapers and newsletters stressed the solidity of the Anglo-French alliance, and France's firm adherence to her engagements.[43] This view was to be increasingly challenged in the autumn of 1727 and, as the Anglo-French alliance failed to settle Anglo-Spanish difficulties, the foreign policy associated with the Walpole ministry came under increasing – and for the Walpoles, worrying – strain.[44] This strain was compounded by two other developments. Severe ill-health incapacitated and threatened to remove Townshend, leading to speculation as to who would be his successor. This was made yet more serious by increasing signs that the varied attempts made since the summer to improve Britain's relations with various German powers, attempts George was closely identified with, would bear fruit and produce either a rapprochement with Austria or a system of German alliances which would have but a tenuous connection with Britain's French alliance.

Townshend had been dogged with ill-health before the autumn of 1727. In September 1727 Waldegrave noted that he had often and unsuccessfully pressed Townshend to look after his health.[45] However, none of Townshend's illnesses was as serious as that which nearly killed him in 1727.[46] Various diagnoses were offered at the time, ranging from gout, rheumatism and dropsy to more exotic illnesses, but the diagnoses only reveal the clumsy state of medical science in this period, as did the treatments, which included the provision of horse medicines by Walpole. Soon after Townshend returned to London on 30 June the first signs of illness were visible.[47] On 9 August Waldegrave wrote to Townshend's under-secretary, George Tilson:

> I am sorry to find mylord has been laid up with the gout, but hope it will be no longer than what may contribute to his health and settle those humours I used to fear were floating about him.[48]

Such optimistic notes were soon stilled when it became apparent that the illness was far more serious than had been believed. Medical cures were tried without success. Townshend was confined to his chamber and fears were expressed about his life. At one stage the doctors gave him up. 1727 had already witnessed several unexpected deaths, including those of George I, Catherine I, Viscount Harcourt and Lord Lechmere. It is impossible to state what Townshend was suffering from but it is conceivable that he had suffered a stroke. This seems to be the diagnosis that best fits the few recorded symptoms.

After being particularly severe in September the illness seems to have abated in October. During this period Townshend was able to discharge some of the functions of his office. He discussed with Diemar the Freudenberg affair, a dispute between Hesse-Cassel and Hanover. On 20 October, at his home, he was able to question Dehn about the size of the Wolfenbüttel army and to offer a subsidy treaty.[49] He wrote himself the most sensitive section of Waldegrave's instructions, that dealing with George I's will.[50] On 14 November he met the judges in the Exchequer Chamber at Westminster, where the sheriffs were being chosen. On 18 November, though 'in a very bad way with his rheumatism', he was able to dine with Charles Delafaye.[51] Thereafter his health seems to have declined again. On the 24th, the *Daily Journal* reported that on the 22nd Townshend 'was judged to be at the last extremity'.[52] In December Townshend seems to have recovered a little,[53] although he continued weak and reports persisted that he was very ill. In mid-December he was still confined to his chamber, though able to walk. He did not recover until the spring, missing the opening of Parliament. He took the oaths in the Lords on May 1728, having been reported ill in late April.[54]

Townshend's illness produced a governmental crisis which has been ignored by historians. His illness put a lot of pressure upon his colleague as Secretary, Newcastle, who took over the correspondence with the British envoys in the northern department. Doubts were expressed about Newcastle's ability to cope.[55] Townshend's illness was given by Le Coq as the reason for the serious delay in diplomatic negotiations.[56] Townshend excused himself to Du Bourgay, the British envoy at Berlin, for failing to write.[57] The British diplomatic system appeared to be drifting into a state of chaos. Diemar reported that Townshend's illness deranged the business of the ministry. Townshend had instructed St. Saphorin to write a report on his mission to Vienna, but St. Saphorin was able to develop personal relations with George II because of Townshend's illness. George ordered St. Saphorin to bring the report directly to him. Horatio Walpole complained that Newcastle was not keeping him informed, and he anxiously questioned his brother about Townshend's health.[58]

In November Le Coq sugguested that Townshend's death would cause a major problem, 'parce qu'il est seul au fait des affaires'.[59] Fleury pressed Horatio Walpole on the matter, 'with the greatest concern', doubting Horatio's assurances that Townshend would recover.[60] Speculation began as to who would replace Townshend, and suggestions were made that Newcastle would be replaced. Broglie informed his government that as soon as the diplomatic situation settled down Newcastle would go.[61]

Townshend's illness and the effective vacancy in the northern department (for Newcastle displayed little interest in the affairs of Townshend's department and did not maintain an extensive private correspondence with the diplomats in it), meant that George's views on the conduct of Anglo-German relations were given free rein. Since his accession, George had been defining his own views on foreign policy, and in the winter of 1727–1728 he piloted a policy of his own with considerable independence. George's policy differed from that of his ministers in two important respects, one relating to the prime area of concern and the second to the best means for executing policy. Unlike his ministers, George displayed very little interest in Anglo-Spanish relations and his concern for the issues at stake was at best fitful. He believed that the key to the diplomatic situation was Austria. Though Townshend certainly agreed with his analysis, he, in common with the other ministers, gave great attention to parliamentary views on the diplomatic situation. These tended to concentrate on the commercial disputes at stake between Britain and Spain and on Gibraltar, and to ignore the niceties of German politics.

George was particularly concerned with the rights of Protestant German princes, such as himself, faced with what he saw as a despotic Catholic Austrian threat.[62] Hanoverian grievances against the manner in which the Emperor exercised Imperial jurisdictional rights in the Mecklenburg and East Friesland disputes fortified his determination to force Charles VI to be a good Emperor. Allied to these particular Hanoverian interests was George's belief that Austria was to blame for European instability and that it was secretly encouraging Spain to resist British demands.[63] It was felt that Austria hoped, by delaying peace, to weaken the Hanover allies and gain opportunities to split the alliance, charges Austria denied.[64] Vandermeer suggested that Rottembourg would encounter major difficulties in persuading Spain to be reasonable unless Austria changed her policy.[65] This was a view shared by the British ministry. Townshend had informed William Finch in September that 'all the difficultys we meet with come from the Imperial court'.[66] Two months later Newcastle wrote to Finch:

> tho' the Emperor does not openly himself act contrary to the Preliminaries, yet the king sees plainly enough by the whole tenour of the conduct of Vienna and by many instances of the behaviour of Count Konigsegg at Madrid during this negociation, that at the bottom the design of the Impl. Ministry is, to encourage Spain in their dispute about the execution of the Preliminarys, and to endeavour to embroil the Allys of Hanover.

Newcastle made the same point to Horatio Walpole,[67] who had been informed in August by Vandermeer that Austria was directing Spanish policy.[68] Given this view it was not surprising that some attempt should be make to define British relations with Austria. Early in 1727 they had plummeted to a distinct low when the British expelled the Austrian Resident Palm for making public a Memorial he presented to George I which accused George of falsely impugning Austrian conduct in his speech to Parliament. This had led the Austrians to retaliate by expelling St. Saphorin, and the British to step up plans for a military conflict with Austria. In order to forestall an Austrian attack upon Hanover and Hesse-Cassel, an invasion of the Habsburg hereditary lands was considered. Relations were still frosty when George I left for Europe. The British were averse to reopening diplomatic relations with Austria. Waldegrave's instructions, drawn up at the end of May, noted

> We had many scruples and objections to the sending any minister thither till we have had some satisfactory explanation upon the ill treatment we have received from that Court in several respects.[69]

The British had however yielded to French pressure[70] and decided to send Lord Waldegrave, a diplomat noted for his charm, affability and easy manner, to Vienna. Newcastle wrote that Waldegrave had been selected because he was 'known to be perfectly agreable to the Court of France'.[71] Waldegrave went as far as Paris, where he had been ordered to discuss matters with Fleury, but the unfavourable diplomatic scene produced by the death of George I persuaded him to go no further, and on 22 June he informed Townshend:

> What weighed most with me and determined me to stay here was the caution yr. Lordship had given me, not to proceed unless I had the strongest assurances of being well received, and in this I thought the king's honour too much concerned to run any hazard.

Waldegrave's decision was in accordance with his orders, but it was regretted by those who wished to see improved relations, such as Slingelandt, the Dutch Pensionary, and the Wolfenbüttel diplomat Count Dehn. The Austrian Chargé d'affaires in Paris, Fonseca, told Waldegrave that his 'being at Vienna might and would certainly have facilitated matters'. Waldegrave was ordered to remain in Paris pending diplomatic developments.[72] In addition, the French negotiations with Austria which had produced the Preliminaries had been viewed with suspicion by the British. Suggestions that the French would betray the British position were openly voiced, and they were shared by some members of the government.[73] Du Bourgay reported from Berlin that the Austrian envoy Seckendorf had told Frederick William I that a secret Austro-French agreement had been negotiated.[74] The French Ambassador at Vienna, Richelieu, was particularly distrusted.[75]

However, there was considerable ambivalence in British attitudes towards Austria.[76] This ambivalence was best summed up in letters dispatched to Waldegrave on 18 August. In the instructions sent to the envoy he was ordered to co-operate with the Austrians. The hope was expressed that 'you will find an equal inclination at Vienna to suppress all reflections on past measures and to look forward only upon the best means for reestablishing a strict friendship for the future'. On the same day

Townshend informed him that George was 'very sensible of the ill treatment which has been received from the court of Vienna'.[77] Suspicion was therefore coupled with a hope that it would somehow be possible to restore amicable relations, a possibility which appeared more likely when the Austrians clearly disavowed the Jacobites. Some understanding with Austria was needed if Britain was not to be totally outmanoeuvred at the forthcoming Congress, for, otherwise, France could act the role of arbiter of Europe, and Britain would be isolated if France should decide to support Spanish or Austrian pretensions. Sinzendorf took the credit for better Franco-Spanish relations, attributing them to Austrian pressure on Spain. The advantage of some sort of agreement with Austria was clear, and indeed it was openly advocated by the opposition Whigs, but the French orientation of the Walpole ministry prevented any independent approach to Austria. It was in concert with France that Horatio Walpole proposed in September 1727 to send Waldegrave to Vienna informally 'to see if the Emperor can be persuaded not to encourage Spain in so unreasonable demands as those now made'.[78] The ministry did not wish to jeopardise French support by appearing to follow an independent German policy. Horatio Walpole assured Morville in July that Britain would only listen to Prussian proposals in concert with France.[79]

In October 1727 O'Rourke wrote of the Austrians:

> their politicks are all passive, that is to say that like pretty women, they will make noe advances, but receave those that are made to them if to their liking, and take hold of such overtures, and occurrences, as offer of themselves.[80]

The Austrians, disinclined to upset their allies and quizzical about the stability of the Walpole ministry, had made no overtures to George II, but waited for Waldegrave's arrival in Vienna, hoping that he would bring proposals for them to consider. Sinzendorf instructed Fonseca to seek the advice of the exiled Jacobite Atterbury on British affairs, and to press France not to yield to British demands. Despite Waldegrave's appointment the Austrians did not name an envoy for Britain.[81] The Prussians had been more adventurous. Frederick William I greeted the news of George I's death with the tears then conventional upon the news of a father-in-law's death, and with assurances to Du Bourgay that a high ranking envoy would be sent to Britain to offer condolences.[82] Baron Wallenrodt was sent to London to sound the British about the possibility of a new treaty.[83] Noises were made in Berlin and in the British press about the projected marriages between George's eldest son Frederick, now Prince of Wales, and Frederick William's eldest daughter Wilhelmina, and between the Prussian Crown Prince Frederick and the British Princess Royal, Anne.[84] In his audience in July Wallenrodt gave George 'very strong assurances from the king his master of his friendship and affection, and of his earnest desire to live in a perfect good understanding with his Majesty'.

George's response to the Prussians was curt. Wallenrodt was told 'that as to any engagements or joint measures, he could enter into none, unless they were concerted with France likewise'.[85] Du Bourgay was sharply reprimanded for exceeding orders in his discussions with the Prussians, and for 'meddling'. George denied that he had any plans for the marriage of his children, and stated that such marriages must wait until the European situation was more stable.[86] George was criticised for his negative response to the Prussian approaches. The Reverend Henry Etough, rector of Therfield in Hertfordshire, kept extensive records of his conversations with Robert Walpole, Horatio Walpole, and John Scrope. He noted in his papers that Frederick William I had been tactlessly irritated by George's refusal to publish his father's will.[87] George II did so because he wished to suppress the provisions it included for the eventual separation of Hanover from Britain. George I had stipulated that if his grandson Frederick should have more than one son, the first-born should inherit the royal crown and the second the electoral cap. If Frederick had only one son, that son should become King of Great Britain, while the Electorate would pass into the Wolfenbüttel branch of the house of Brunswick. Frederick William I believed George II had deprived Frederick's wife Sophia Dorothea of her father, George I's legacy to her, by suppressing the will.[88]

Etough noted that 'the friends and foes of the present establishment were nearly unanimous in their opinion, that had this opportunity been improved to procure the amity of the King of Prussia, and had not been perverted to increase his enmity, all payments to Hesse Cassel might have been absolutely saved'. Etough was referring to the subsidy treaty with Hesse-Cassel which had been negotiated in 1726 in order to commit Hessian troops to the defence of Hanover. St. Saphorin pressed for an Anglo-Prussian alliance in order to limit Austrian power in the Empire.[89] Townshend excused the British response by claiming that Britain was being faithful to her allies. He informed Du Bourgay of 'the rule H M has laid down to go hand in hand with the most Christian king in all things that concern the publick affairs of Europe'.[90] The French had already expressed concern over Anglo-Prussian discussions, particularly that British support for Prussia would upset the Wittelsbachs, concerned over the Jülich-Berg inheritance. Townshend complained about French distrust.[91]

In fact the British response was not simply due to compliance with French wishes, however much the British might attempt to persuade the French that this was the case.[92] The British did not want to become embroiled in conflicts as an ally of Prussia. The Prussians had made it clear that they expected assistance over Jülich-Berg from their allies, and in addition the Courland succession dispute, in which Prussia had a major interest, had erupted into violence. Furthermore, it was felt that Frederick William could not be trusted,[93] and as Etough pointed out, his 'inconsistent and deceitful practices, with regard to the treaties of Vienna and Hanover . . . discouraged all political dependence'.[94] Newcastle informed Horatio Walpole in October that George believed Frederick William should be made 'to feel the effects of his late behaviour'.[95]

In his rejection of Prussian approaches and his antagonism towards the Austrians George could be seen as a faithful ally, but he displayed considerable independence in his attempts to develop a league of German princes.[96] A note of vigour was injected into Britain's German policy. Wallenrodt reported that George had told him he was determined 'to maintain the constitution of the Empire, but if the Emperor trod upon his toe, H.M. would let him know, whom he had to do with'.[97] The Hanoverian ministry urged George to make the Congress the stage for an airing of Hanoverian grievances against imperial policy, in particular the alleged despotic moves of the Imperial court contrary to the Imperial constitution, and religious grievances. In August Horatio Walpole received a letter from Delafaye: 'Your Excellency will perhaps think us too full of the scheme for taking care at the Congress of the Libertys of the Germanic Body, as being pretty strong meat for the Cardinal's digestion: But Mylord Townshend ordered me to tell you that it arises from the King himself, who sees with regret the Emperor gaining such an absolute influence throughout Germany as may make him an overmatch for us and France too'.[98] The Hanoverian envoy at the Imperial Diet in Regensburg received direct orders from London to consult with the French envoy, Chavigny, in stirring up the German princes against the Emperor.[99] George drafted Horatio Walpole instructions demanding that France should provide a declaration that she would respect the rights of Protestants in the Empire.[100] Townshend informed Horatio Walpole that 'a stop must be put to the absolute power which the Emperor is daily acquiring in Germany'.[101]

During the period of near-conflict which had preceded the Preliminaries of Paris the French had been eager to beat the same drum, and had sought to develop an alliance with the Wittelsbach princes, but after the Preliminaries the French advocated a moderate approach to Austria. As a result the lead in finding new supporters for the Alliance of Hanover was taken by George II. D' Aix noted that George was trying to acquire a party in the Empire and to persuade the Princes to demand independent representation at the forthcoming Congress and not to permit the Emperor to represent them.[102] This was of great importance for George because he feared that in any Congress restricted to the signatories of the Preliminaries of Paris, Britain would be isolated, and France and Austria would decide German matters themselves and display no concern for the grievances of the Protestant princes. Were the latter included, George would be able to play a more prominent role at the Congress. For this reason he pressed for the widest representation possible, denied that the Emperor had the right to represent the princes[103] and urged that the Scandinavian powers should be admitted to the Congress.[104] France gave only grudging support to this policy.

A major motive for George's actions was concern over the security of Hanover. The Electorate was an exposed territory, lacking sound fortifications. Visitors to Hanover commented frequently upon its defencelessness. In 1729 Townshend wrote that George had 'a great extent of country to defend which is open and unguarded by any strong place'. A British visitor noted of the town of Hanover that 'the fortifications are not considerable'. Chauvelin argued that the conquest of the Electorate could be settled by one battle, because there were no fortifications which required a siege, whilst Boissieux, the French envoy to the Elector of Cologne, stated that the Electorate of Hanover would take less than three weeks to conquer.[105]

The agreements between Austria, Prussia and Russia signed in 1726 had badly shaken George I. George II was very concerned at signs of military movements by these powers, and at their attempts to bring Mecklenburg, Brunswick-Wolfenbüttel and Saxony-Poland into their system. In early October 1727, Le Coq reported a revival of earlier British fears that Augustus II was permitting the Austrians to construct magazines in Saxony, that an Austro-Saxon agreement existed for the assembly of Austrian troops to attack Hanover and Hesse-Cassel, and that August Wilhelm of Brunswick-Wolfenbüttel was negotiating the entry of Austrian troops into the fortress of Brunswick. Austrian military preparations in the Rhineland were noted widely by diplomats, and were also reported in the British press.[106] In October Augustus II's leading minister Count Flemming visited Berlin, ostensibly to discuss toll disputes between Saxony and Prussia. This explanation of his mission was believed by few, and though Du Bourgay was unable to find out the true motive, Villars noted the belief that it was to discuss plans for an invasion of Hanover and commented on the improvement of relations between Austria and Prussia. Le Coq informed Flemming that he had had to reassure the British about the purpose of his mission.[107]

Among the foreign envoys who arrived in Britain to attend the coronation were the Württemberg envoy Count Gravanitz and the Wolfenbüttel envoy Count Dehn. George opened discussions with both men about the possibility of an alliance with Britain. Gravanitz's dispatches do not survive, and it is difficult to discover information about his mission. Le Coq reported that the British were anxious to win the alliance of Württemberg, and both he and D'Aix believed that Württemberg was interested in such an arrangement, though, as Le Coq pointed out, she required subsidies. The British urged France to satisfy the Württemberg claim to Montbéliard. This policy had been advocated by St. Saphorin the previous spring.[108]

To contemporaries Dehn's mission was charged with significance. Dehn himself does not seem to have been a terribly impressive diplomat, though his parties appear to have been quite lavish.[109] Pöllnitz, the Prussian courtier who printed his travel notes in the 1730s, referred to Dehn in very disparaging terms as a frivolous politician who delighted in splendour, enjoyed balls and liked making treaties.[110] Pöllnitz is not a reliable source. In some respects he was a German equivalent of Lord Hervey. However, his view was corroborated by Sutton who served as the British Envoy Extraordinary in Brunswick-Wolfenbüttel in 1729. Sutton, who managed to combine debauchery and ability, thought little of Dehn who only managed the former.[111] Largillière's portrait of Dehn, now hanging in the Herzog Anton-Ulrich museum in Brunswick, is a portrait of a shallow and flashy courtier.

Delayed by contrary winds Dehn arrived in London in early October. There he negotiated the Treaty of Westminister with Townshend. The agreement included a mutual guarantee of dominions, mutual assistance in case of attack, a British subsidy, an arrangement under which the fortress of Brunswick was to be kept for the common safety of the house of Lüneburg, and the delivery of the copy of George I's will held by Brunswick-Wolfenbüttel. The will was not mentioned in the treaty, but George's ratification was conditional upon its delivery. The British ministers who signed the treaty were Walpole, Townshend, Newcastle, Devonshire and Lord Trevor, the Lord Privy Seal. Fleury had suggested to Horatio Walpole in August that efforts should be made to keep the will secret.[112] This was seen by the British as a considerable triumph. Newcastle informed Horatio Walpole that it would make Brunswick-Wolfenbüttel 'a Barrier against any attempts of the Emperor, who has cerainly flattered himself with the hopes of making Brunswick a place of arms'.[113] Fleury told Horatio that he was delighted by the treaty, and the government proclaimed it as a triumph of foreign policy, though they were less keen on advertising the amount of money promised to Brunswick-Wolfenbüttel.[114]

More attention was devoted to the suggestions that Dehn sought to achieve an Anglo-Austrian rapprochement. Reports to this effect circulated widely. In the previous year Brunswick-Wolfenbüttel had signed an alliance with Austria. The Duke, August Wilhelm, was the uncle of Charles VI's wife. It was suggested that, in addition to an Anglo-Austrian reconciliation, Dehn would arrange a marriage between George II's eldest daughter, Anne, and Ferdinand Albrecht of Brunswick-Bevern's eldest son Charles. Dehn was very optimistic about the possibility of a reconciliation. Dehn's brother, the Wolfenbüttel envoy at Vienna, wrote that Austria sought better relations with Britain and information from Dehn, to whom they were willing to give a special commission to negotiate should circumstances prove propitious. The Wolfenbüttel minister Schleinitz believed that George II, in order to break a projected alliance between Austria, France and Spain, would negotiate an alliance with Charles VI. There are hints that the Dutch sought to encourage an Anglo-Austrian reconciliation.[115] Zamboni informed the Landgrave of Hesse-Darmstadt that August Wilhelm had decided to attempt such a rapprochement and that he had ordered Dehn to secure it. According to Zamboni the Austrians disliked the idea and persuaded August Wilhelm to desist.[116] From St. Petersburg the French agent Magnan reported that the Danish envoy there, Westphalen, was displeased at reports of an Anglo-Austrian reconciliation, and that the Wolfenbüttel minister Cramm was attempting to secure an Anglo-Russian reconciliation on orders from the Hanoverian Regency.[117] Cramm was suspected of being a British envoy and in order to cover his costs the government of Brunswick-Wolfenbüttel sought money from Britain, claiming that he represented British interests. In early 1729 a Wolfenbüttel envoy in St. Petersburg made soundings on the possibility of better Anglo-Russian relations. On 11 November 1727 Waldegrave recorded in his journal:

Mr. Wal. told me that the Card. had taken notice . . . . that the D of N had acquainted the French ambassador at London with a proposal made the king by the Wolfenbüttel minister about a private pacification with the Emp. but had been rejected by the king, Mr. Wal. was surprised that the D of N had taken no notice of it in any of his letters to him.[118]

The *Post Boy* linked a potential improvement in Anglo-Austrian relations to the state of the Anglo-French alliance: 'to guard against all events, some talk of renewing the Grand Alliance, in case France and Spain do not give speedy satisfaction to the crown of Great Britain'.[119]

The British certainly assured the French that they had rejected an approach from Dehn, but it is difficult to disentangle the course of events. Only a portion of Dehn's correspondence survives and it is not particularly helpful. It does however reveal that internal Wolfenbüttel politics may have played a major role in developments. The politics of the Duchy were notoriously intricate and unstable.[120] August Wilhelm had no children and there was a strong reversionary interest in the duchy centred on his brother's son-in-law Ferdinand Albrecht, the Duke of Brunswick-Bevern, who was eventually to succeed to Wolfenbüttel in 1735. Ferdinand Albrecht was a staunch supporter of Austria and a regular correspondent of Prince Eugene's. He had a private correspondence with Dehn. In October 1727 the principal Wolfenbüttel minister Münchhausen fell. This upset Dehn who feared that he would follow Münchhausen, a point Ferdinand Albrecht also made. This helped to make Dehn very cautious, and lent weight to Ferdinand Albrecht's advice that he should return to Wolfenbüttel and do nothing to upset the Austrians.[121]

Dehn was notoriously keen to exaggerate the favour with which his approaches were received. It is probable that had George received his approach with greater favour he would have made more of the matter. Equally, it is possible that George used the Dehn mission in order to frighten the French into lending him more diplomatic support. In their correspondence with Horatio Walpole the ministry downplayed Dehn's importance, possibly in response to Horatio's warning in June 1727 that any suggestion of an Anglo-Austrian reconciliation would lead to tension between Britain and France.[122] Townshend informed Horatio in August that Dehn's mission was essentially complimentary and linked to the will.[123] Tilson assured Horatio that Townshend had George's orders to reject any approach from Dehn.[124] However it is possible that such letters were sent to Horatio in order to be shown to the French, or that an attempt was made to mislead him. St. Saphorin had suggested in August in the draft of a letter to the Portuguese envoy in Vienna, Count Tarouca, who had close links with the Austrian ministry, that George wished for good relations with Austria and was prepared to listen to Austrian proposals, provided that nothing prejudical to his dignity, his allies or the security of Europe was proposed. This draft was probably intended to serve as the basis of an approach to Austria.[125] In October O'Rourke reported from Vienna that an Anglo-Austrian alliance was possible, and that he had been told by a minister that George II had told 'a friend of the Empr.s' [Dehn?] that he wanted good relations and was willing to support the Pragmatic Sanction. O'Rourke commented that he believed Austria wanted a British alliance and would attempt to obtain one.[126] Whatever the truth of the matter it is certain that the episode increased uncertainty over George's intentions and over British policy in general. In December 1727 Newcastle informed Horatio Walpole that, faced with the apparent failure of Rottembourg's negotiation, George believed the powers of the Alliance of Hanover should ask Charles VI whether he was willing to execute the Preliminaries of Paris and, if so, should settle with him on those terms.[127]

The Dehn mission was no secret, but British approaches to the Saxons that winter were, and have remained so. They have received no scholarly attention and the only evidence about the approaches is to be found in the Saxon archives. The uncorroborated nature of the evidence calls its veracity into question, but it should be noted that Le Coq's dispatches reveal an intelligent and perceptive mind at work, and that the British never complained about the accuracy of Le Coq's dispatches as they were to complain about those of other envoys, such as the Prussian Reichenbach. On 12 December 1727 Le Coq sent a messenger to Augustus II with a lengthy dispatch. This dispatch, subsequently endorsed 'lettre de Mr Le Coq contenant quelques overtures faites par Mr. de St. Saphorin', contained the details of several conferences between Le Coq and St. Saphorin. The conferences were undated, except for the last on 10 December. St. Saphorin, on the 10th, dwelt on the threat to the German princes represented by the alliance of Spain and Austria and argued that both powers intended that Don Carlos should marry Maria Theresa and succeed to the Austrian inheritance. In October Tilson had observed that it seemed as if Austria and Spain intended to persevere with the marriages.[128] St. Saphorin stated that to face this threat, a league in the Empire was necessary to defend its rights and liberties. He stated that he was sure Bavaria would join, a view that probably owing something to his mission there in 1725,[129] and suggested that Prussia would, despite the instability of its recent policy. St. Saphorin added that France would have to be excluded from any agreement between Britain and the German powers because France was distrusted in the Empire,[130] a point he did not enlarge upon, and which contrasted with Chavigny's enthusiasm for a similar scheme.[131]

Le Coq was at pains to affirm that St. Saphorin's approach was not a personal one. He reiterated that he was sure St. Saphorin was speaking in the name of the king.[132] St. Saphorin informed Le Coq that Saxony had been approached first because the British hoped Saxon approval would have a good effect upon other powers.[133] He might have added that there was no Wittelsbach representative in London and that Wallenrodt's death in October had reduced Prussian representation to a low level. Le Coq was further convinced St. Saphorin was acting on royal instructions by the fact that on 9 December Le Coq had had an audience of over an hour with the Queen, who had stated that George needed allies in the Empire and that an Anglo-Saxon alliance without France was necessary.[134]

This approach to Saxony, rather than the response to Dehn's mission, confirmed that George was willing to adopt schemes of his own, and to ignore his ministers. Le Coq reported that Newcastle knew nothing of the matter and that George wanted St. Saphorin to handle the negotiation unbeknownst to his ministers or the French.[135]

George was not only challenging the French orientation of British foreign policy in the Empire. His anger at the French failure to settle Anglo-Spanish differences to the satisfaction of the British led him to demand that action should be taken against the Spaniards, a policy France opposed.[136] During the autumn of 1727 criticism of France had been growing in London.[137] Broglie had assured George that France was still true to the British alliance.[138] Horatio Walpole informed all and sundry that this was the case.[139] Horatio was, nevertheless, anxiously aware that this was doubted and he feared that his brother was no longer happy with the French alliance. On 23 September he wrote to him to reassure him on the point. However Horatio himself was increasingly doubtful about the French. On 21 September he went for a walk with Waldegrave who recorded that he 'seemed under a good deal of uneasiness at his own situation' and that Horatio had told Fleury that if he deceived him Horatio would probably be sent to the Tower. The next day 'Mr. Wal. told the Cardinal that everybody said that nothing but his answering for his Em. made people believe him in earnest'. On the 25th Horatio showed Waldegrave letters he had received the previous day from his brother and from Newcastle. Newcastle's praised the conduct of France towards Spain, but 'his brother's seemed a good deal suspecting the worst in every point, and that Fr. Sp. and the Emp. might have some underhand dealings to humble us'.[140]

Sir Robert Walpole's fears were shared by others.[141] In the summer the ministry had derided fears, voiced by such varied sources as John Bagshaw, the British Consul in Genoa, and d'Ittersum, the Overyssel nobleman who was one of Townshend's principal informants on Dutch affairs, of an alliance between Austria, Spain and France, the hope of the Jacobites.[142] The failure of these powers to unite in support of the Pretender seemed to lend credence to the ministerial viewpoint, and the government had dismissed reports, encouraged by the Spaniards, that Spain had been responsible for the replacement of Morville by Chauvelin. However, Rottembourg's failure to settle Anglo-Spanish affairs to British satisfaction led to a revival of doubt about the French.[143] George was very angry at the unsettled state of affairs and he vented his spleen on Broglie, who reported being told by George that the delays angered him.[144]

The ministry were placed in a very difficult position by Rottembourg's agreement, which ignored the British position on the *Prince Frederick*, a position made worse by the fact that the British Minister Plenipotentiary, Benjamin Keene, had signed the agreement, though 'without the least colour of order or instruction'.[145] Waldegrave wrote of the Spaniards, 'they must think that we should have very little reason to depend on allies, that would give way to such chimerical notions'. Newcastle described the agreement as 'perfect madness'.[146] Had Britain refused to accept the agreement she would have risked angering the French by forcing them to choose between supporting or breaking it. The latter course of action would have entailed the French sacrificing their new-found good relations with Spain.[147] The former course could have led to the diplomatic isolation of Britain. If the ministry had accepted the agreement they would have faced tremendous domestic criticism and they would have found it very difficult to persuade Parliament that the French alliance was serving any purpose.[148] The proximity of the parliamentary session and the campaign in the opposition press attacking the French alliance made the decision more difficult.

Compounding the problem for the ministry was the fact that they were having to consider a successor to Townshend. The sudden deaths of ministers earlier in the decade, Craggs and Earl Stanhope in 1721, Sunderland the following year, underlined the need to make contingency plans. On 8 December Waldegrave noted in his journal that Sir Robert Walpole

> seems under a good deal of difficulty on account of my Lord Townshend's illness, which he says will be such as should he ever recover will not give him leave to do any business this winter, the Cabals are great about a successor or a substitute in case there should be a prospect of his recovery.[149]

There was no shortage of available candidates, and the names mentioned included Carteret, Chesterfield, Dodington, Stanhope and Sir Paul Methuen. Horatio Walpole does not appear to have been seriously considered as he was to be in 1729–1730 and again in 1733. Possibly this reflects the fact that Horatio was too closely identified with the French alliance, or that Sir Robert Walpole was politically on the defensive. Horatio hinted in a letter to Newcastle that he was being harmed by his association with the French alliance.[150] He had earlier written to the Duke 'I cannot sufficiently lament the want of Lord Townshend at so great a juncture of affairs both at home and abroad by the behaviour of Spain and the approaching sessions of Parliament'.[151] There is very little evidence about the struggle to succeed Townshend. One newspaper report claimed that 'our coffee-house politicians have been laying out a secretary of state in case of Lord Townshend's death'.[152] General George Wade, the Commander-in-Chief in Scotland, was in London in November 1727. In a letter he sent to Duncan Forbes he claimed that he knew 'nothing of what passes in the Grand Monde', because he was confined to his chamber with the ague. This may be doubted, since he was then in touch with Newcastle, and visited by Stanhope, among others. He noted speculation that Methuen, Carteret, Stanhope or Horatio Walpole might succeed Townshend, but concluded that 'Methuen may have it if he pleases'.[153] Zamboni agreed, though he wrote to the Landgrave of Hesse-Darmstadt that Townshend's successor was likely to be Stanhope if Methuen refused it, as looked possible.[154]

Broglie reported that Methuen would succeed Townshend.[155] Opinions of Methuen's ability differed. Hervey's unfavourable judgement is usually cited whenever he is discussed,[156] but Broglie thought highly of him, and Methuen's experience of office was very impressive.[157] He had represented British interests at Lisbon, Turin and Madrid, served as a Lord of both the

Admiralty and the Treasury, and been Secretary of State for the Southern Department. In the 1720s he held household appointments, first as Comptroller and then as Treasurer, and acted as a leading ministerial spokesman in the Commons.[158] He would have made a good choice as secretary but he lacked political connections and would have brought the ministry little added weight in the Commons. The Earl of Ailesbury wrote to his brother from Brussels concerning Townshend: 'he had all the foreign affairs under his care and there are very few capable to succeed him'. He thought that Stanhope, thanks to his distinguished diplomatic record, would be chosen.[159] Speculation about a successor did not cease until Townshend's recovery in the spring.

Methuen and Stanhope could probably have been relied on to support the Walpoles, though Methuen's resignation in 1729 was ostensibly on the grounds that he disapproved of general government policy.[160] Carteret, Chesterfield and Dodington would have been less fortunate choices for the ministry. Dodington had diplomatic experience, having proved an able envoy to Spain, and had considerable governmental experience. However, he was a friend of the Countess of Suffolk, and had urged Compton to supplant Walpole, turn to the Tories for support and make Dodington Secretary of State.[161] Chesterfield was continually postponing his departure for the United Provinces hoping to receive a domestic post.

Horatio Walpole was extremely concerned by the uncertainty as to Townshend's successor. He wrote to his brother in November:

> Should anything happen, the replacing of him will be of vast consequence to the management of affairs at home, as well as to the credit and influence of the Government among the foreign powers . . .[162]

A month later Le Coq informed Augustus II that the problem was not simply to find competent individuals, but to ensure that they would cooperate with the ministry.[163] This truism was of particular importance for Walpole, because George showed signs of being ready to break from the Walpolean policy of cooperation with France. As the parliamentary session approached, with no settlement in the Anglo-Spanish disputes, domestic pressure increased for naval action against Spain.[164] George expressed openly his irritation at the diplomatic impasse. It could be suggested that one of the reasons for his irritation was that Anglo-Spanish differences prevented a concentration upon German issues and the need to protect Hanover from a possible Austrian and/or Prussian attack.

The British fleet had remained in Spanish waters after the Preliminaries were signed. Reports that the Spaniards intended to mount an invasion of the British Isles in support of the Jacobite cause had led to a strengthening of the fleet in Spanish waters.[165] Admiral Norris was recalled from the Baltic and his ships were used to strengthen Sir Charles Wager's squadron off Cadiz. On 16 August Townshend ordered Wager to destroy the Spanish fleet if it should sail towards Britain. Similarly aggressive orders

Wager was instructed to seize the Spanish treasure ships which were due to return from the Indies. Newcastle feared that the arrival of these ships would make the Spaniards 'more insolent'.[167] Rottembourg's initial failure to secure Spanish recognition of the British position led to domestic pressure for a war with Spain and the issue was discussed at length in the press.[168] The Spanish Indies were believed to be poorly defended and ripe for attack. The French ministry feared that the British would attack the Indies, and the Earl of Stair, formerly British envoy in Paris, mentioned the possibility to the Austrian agent Visconti.[169] Foreign diplomats reported that the British government was ready to fight Spain. Townshend informed Du Bourgay that 'we shall never submit to any terms, but what shall be entirely for the honour and interest of the nation'. Jacquemin, the Lorraine envoy at Vienna, noted 'on soupçonne toujours que l'Angleterre veut absolument la guerre'. The diplomat, Fiorelli, reported the possibility of a British naval bombardment of Spanish ports.[170]

War was considered. Townshend wrote to William Finch on 23 December 'the King is most nearly touched with the turn this affair has taken, and will risque the coming to the utmost extremitys rather than submit to those scandalous conditions Spain would impose upon him; . . . if the Spanish Court persist in their unreasonable proceedings, his Majesty must, and will, sooner enter into a war with that crown than suffer his own Honour and Royal Dignity, and the interests of his people to be treated in so ignominious a manner'.[171] On the following day Horatio Walpole was warned of the possibility of war.[172] D'Aix reported that George II wanted war with Spain. British merchants were instructed to withdraw their ships from Spanish ports.[173] Marquis Scaramuccia Visconti, an Austrian diplomat in London, without character, was in correspondence with Sinzendorf and sent an interesting letter on the subject. Judging by his letters he was a very well-informed source. He was aware that one of the major reasons for the large subsidy paid to Brunswick-Wolfenbüttel was the need to gain its copy of George I's will. The British government thought him sufficiently important to order the interception of his mail. He was in close touch with many of the foreign diplomats in London and with several members of the British government, being received by Townshend on 1 February.[174] On 13 January 1728 he informed Sinzendorf that Sir Robert Walpole had been rebuked by the Duke of Argyll at a council meeting for suggesting that Gibraltar be returned, and that either Argyll or George II had pressed for an immediate declaration of war on Spain. According to his account George and most of his favourites were for war, Walpole and Queen Caroline against.[175] Count Berkentin, the well-informed Danish envoy in Vienna, who according to Ferdinand Albrecht was secretly responsible for representing George II's interests there,[176] reported that the Austrians had been informed from London that most of the ministers, and particularly Argyll, had pressed for war in order to please George.[177] There is little evidence to support this account in the British sources. Lord King recorded a ministerial meeting on 13 January to discuss Rottembourg's new instructions, but there is no mention in his account either of Gibraltar or of Argyll's presence. In his account of the Cabinet held at Lord

Townshend's on 31 January he noted Argyll's presence and a discussion whether the British possession of Gibraltar should be examined at the Congress, but he gave no details of the views of individual ministers.[178] He recorded the presence of thirteen ministers, some of whom – Scarborough, Wilmington and Dorset – were not noted for their support of Walpole. Argyll, who had replaced Cadogan as the Master General of the Ordnance, had close links with George II due to their shared political views. It was believed that Argyll had first persuaded George to indulge in extra-marital affairs.[179] Visconti's account may have been correct, but even if he was in error, it was true that Walpole's policy was in difficulties. Parliament had to be prorogued until the international situation became clearer, and it was widely believed that Walpole's success in Parliament would depend upon this situation. Duncan Forbes, then in London, informed his brother 'whether we shall in the ensuing Parliament have any heats will probably depend upon the state of foreign affairs'.[180]

The British ministry urged the French to support their case with Spain, arguing that if they failed to do so the ministry might fall and the Anglo-French alliance be destroyed. George warned Broglie that unless the situation improved 'it would raise such dissatisfaction in the Parliament and nation, as would be of the utmost ill consequence to His Majesty as well as to his allies'. Horatio Walpole complained of sleepless nights, Waldegrave was warned that 'unless France speaks firm and plain and gets out of C. Rottemburg's scrape' the alliance was in great danger.[181] Urgency was lent to this pressure by the proximity of the session.[182] Horatio Walpole pressed Fleury to force the Pope to expel the Pretender from Avignon, to produce a declaration that France would stand by Britain, and to order Rottembourg to present Spain with an ultimatum. Fleury was told that this was 'the only means to stop the mouths of the malintentionés en Angle'.[183] Fleury was persuaded to send fresh instructions to Rottembourg on 19 December 1727 ordering him to insist on the implementation of the Preliminaries without any conditions.[184] The British attempted to persuade the French and the Dutch that in case Spain refused to comply, their envoys should immediately leave Spain, a move which would have been regarded as a prelude to war.[185] Britain's allies refused to accept this proposal, and Horatio Walpole was very concerned about the support he could expect from them. William Finch was told by Slingelandt that the United Provinces were opposed to war and feared France would not support them.[186] The Pretender was expelled from Avignon thanks to French pressure.[187] Waldegrave noted in his journal on 9 December 'tho' the Card. did not directly say that France must declare war, yet he satisfied Mr. Wal. that he was sincere in his design of acting vigorously'. However, Horatio feared that when it came to the crunch Britain would be isolated and the French alliance discredited.

Fortunately for the British, French hostility towards Spain was increased by the high *indulto* or duty imposed in 1727 on the cargo of Spanish *flotilla*, in which French merchants had a major interest. Waldegrave argued that it was this which persuaded Fleury to discard his policy of moderation. Villars and the Spanish envoys in Paris attributed Fleury's decision to pressure from Horatio Walpole, a view held also by the latter.[188] On 13 January 1728 Elisabeth Farnese accepted a project largely in accordance with the British interpretation of the Preliminaries. She was discouraged by lack of Austrian support and by continued French backing for the British, but she was chiefly affected by the chronic ill-health of her husband, whose death appeared imminent.[189] The Dutch and the French approved the new project, details of which reached London on the evening of 30 January. The Cabinet considered the project next day and approved it, having concluded that it did not allow Spain to raise her pretensions to Gibraltar at the Congress. With a minor addition, designed to ensure that the engagements between Britain and Spain were made reciprocal, the project returned to Paris and The Hague where the British amendment was accepted.

After delays, largely caused by Britain's unintentional failure to provide Keene with the correct credentials, and some anxiety as to whether the agreement would in fact be settled, the project, later known as the Convention of the Pardo, was signed in Spain on 6 March. Spain promised to raise immediately the blockade of Gibraltar, deliver up the *Prince Frederick* and its cargo to the South Sea Company, and restore the *indulto* to its usual rate. Britain agreed to withdraw its fleet from Spanish and Spanish-American waters and accepted that the Congress could discuss 'all the respective pretensions on each side', including 'the contraband trade and other causes of complaint which the Spaniards might have in relation to the ship *Prince Frederick*'. Both powers promised to abide by the decisions of the Congress. The news that Spain had largely accepted the British position was received in London with delight. The government press hailed it as a triumph for British diplomacy, trade, the willingness to prefer negotiations to force, and the French alliance.[190]

Notes

1. Newcastle to Waldegrave, 20 June (os) 1727, Chewton; Townshend to Sutton, 20 June (os), Sutton to Townshend, 10, 17 July, St. Saphorin to Tarouca and to Törring, undated drafts, PRO. 81/122, 80/61; Le Coq to Augustus, 22 July 1727, Dresden, 2676, 18a.
2. D'Aix to Victor Amadeus II, 30 June 1727, AST. LM. Ing. 35.
3. Newcastle to Townshend, 15 June (os) 1727, BL. Add. 32687 f.21–3 (misfiled in 1726 papers); Newcastle to Horatio Walpole, 16 June (os), Horatio to Townshend, 22 June 1727, BL. Add. 32750, 48982; Newcastle to William Finch, 16 June (os) (misfiled in 1726 papers), Fleury to George II, 2, 11 July 1727, PRO. 84/290 f.21–3, 102/7; Fonseca to Sinzendorf, 7 July 1727, HHStA, Fonseca 11.
4. Diemar to Landgrave Karl, 4, 18 July 1727, Marburg, England, 178, 195.
5. O'Rourke to Graham, 11 July 1727, HHStA, England, Varia 8; Chammorel to Chauvelin, 14, 21, 28 July 1727, AE. CP. Ang. 359; D'Aix to Victor Amadeus II, 26 June, 28 July 1727, AST. LM. Ing. 35; Fleury to George II, 2 July 1727, PRO. 102/7.
6. Graham to Hay, 1 Feb ., Caesar to James III, 9 Feb. 1727, RA. 102/102, 103/52.
7. Graham to Hay, 5, 26 Apr. 1727, RA. 105/118, 106/64; O'Rourke to Graham, 17, 24, 31 May, 11, 15 July, 27 Sept., O'Rourke to James III, 7 June 1727, HHStA, England, Varia 8; James to George Lockhart, 14 June, 22 July 1727, *Lockhart Papers*, II, 345, 356; Jacquemin to Duke Leopold, 14 Aug. 1727, Nancy 139.
8. O'Rourke to Graham, 15 July 1727, HHStA, England, Varia 8; Solaro di Breglio,

Sardinian envoy in Vienna, to Victor Amadeus II, 23 July 1727, AST. LM. Aut. 58; Horatio Walpole to Newcastle, 5, 13 Aug. 1727, BL. Add. 32751; Sinzendorf to Fonseca, 14 July, 3 Aug. 1727, HHStA, Fonseca 11; Poyntz, envoy in Stockholm, to Tilson, 30 Aug. 1727, PRO. 95/47; Liria to James III, 15 July 1727, RA. 108/79.

9. Graham to O'Brien, 9 Aug., James III to Atterbury, 9 Aug., Graham to Atterbury, 12 Sept. 1727, RA. 109/53, 55, 110/38; Waldegrave Journal, 19 Aug. 1727, Chewton; Jacquemin to Leopold, 28 July 1727, Nancy 139.

10. *Farley's Bristol Newspaper* 12 Aug. (os), 9, 16 Sept. (os), *Stanley's Newsletter* 5 Aug. (os), *Evening Post* 12 Aug. (os), *Kentish Post* 16 Aug. (os) 1727.

11. Stalpaert, French consul in Spain, to Maurepas, French naval minister, 5 July 1727, AN. AM.B7 290; Keene to Horatio Walpole, 6 Oct., Horatio to Keene, 6, 20 Oct. 1727, BL. Add. 32752; Waldegrave Journal, 10 Nov. 1727, Chewton.

12. De Buy to Flemming, 14 July 1727, Dresden 3105; Waldegrave Journal, 29 Oct. 1727, Chewton; Robert Daniel, British agent in Brussels, to Tilson, 31 Dec. 1727, PRO. 77/74; Armstrong, p. 216.

13. De Buy to Flemming, 8 July 1727, Dresden 3105.

14. Townshend to William Finch, 11, 18 July (os), Vandermeer to Horatio Walpole, 29 July, memorial of South Sea Company, 4 July (os), Thomas Burnett, Consul in Lisbon to Newcastle, 23 Sept. 1727, PRO. 84/294, 94/98, 36/2, 89/34; Marquis de la Paz to Vandermeer, 4 July, reply 5 July 1727, C(H) papers 23/4–5. Königsegg to Rialp, 7 July, 29 Aug. 1727, HHStA, GK.49; De Buy to Flemming, 28 July, 30 Aug. 1727, Dresden 3105; Villars, pp. 92, 98, 102–3; Wilson, p. 173; Goslinga, pp. 139, 184; Baudrillart, III, 346, 360–1; S. Conn, *Gibraltar in British Eighteenth Century Diplomacy* (New Haven, 1942) pp. 90–1.

15. Graham to Hay, 1 July 1727, RA. 108/1.

16. Sinzendorf to Fonseca, 26 June 1727, HHStA, Fonseca 11.

17. Chauvelin to Chavigny, 29 Sept. 1727, AE. CP. Allemagne 373.

18. De Buy to Flemming, 4 Aug. 1727, Dresden 3105.

19. Stalpaert to Maurepas, 28 July 1727, AN. AM. B7 290.

20. Gansinot to Plettenberg, 5 Sept. 1724, Münster, NB. 259[1].

21. Newcastle to Horatio Walpole, 5 Sept. (os) 1727, BL. Add. 32751.

22. Delafaye to Horatio Walpole,5 Sept. (os), Vandermeer to Horatio, 13, 27 Oct., Newcastle to William Finch, 21 Nov. (os) 1727, PRO. 78/187, 94/98, 84/294.

23. Sinzendorf to Fonseca, 3, 10, 20 Aug., 20 Sept., 12 Oct., 17 Dec., Fonseca to Sinzendorf, 9, 13 Nov., Fleury to Fonseca, 27 Nov., Eugene to Fonseca, 12 Oct. 12 Nov., Pentenriedter to Fonseca, 17 Dec. 1727, HHStA, Fonseca 11, 21, 3.

24. Waldegrave to Tilson, 12 Sept. 1727, PRO. 80/62.

25. Waldegrave Journal, 21 Aug. 1727, Chewton; Fonseca to Sinzendorf, 28 Sept. 1727, HHStA, Fonseca 11. Fleury and Fonseca were angered by the way in which the dispute over the *Prince Frederick* prevented the settlement of other European problems, Fleury to Charles VI, 18 Sept., Fonseca to Sinzendorf, 23 Sept. 1727, HHStA., Frankreich, Varia 11, Fonseca 11.

26. The Austrians were suspicious of these French approaches, Sinzendorf to Fonseca, 10 Aug. 1727, HHStA., Fonseca 11.

27. Newcastle to Horatio Walpole, 25 July (os) 1727, BL. Add. 32751; Graham to O'Rourke, 29 Sept. 1727, RA. 110/127.

28. Newcastle to Horatio Walpole, 10 Sept. (os) 1727, BL. Add. 32751.

29. Newcastle to Horatio Walpole, 25 Sept. (os) 1727, BL. Add. 32752.

30. He was regarded as a supporter of the Anglo-French alliance, Waldegrave to Townshend, 25 Sept. 1727, PRO. 80/62.

31. Tilson to Waldegrave, 27 Nov. (os) 1727, Chewton; Newcastle to William Finch, 28 Nov. (os) 1727, PRO. 84/294.

32. Baudrillart, III, 349, 355–63; Wilson, pp. 175–6.

33. Waldegrave Journal, 21 Sept. 1727, Chewton; Waldegrave to Townshend, 25 Sept. 1727, PRO. 80/62.

34. Townshend to Horatio Walpole, 8 Aug. (os) 1727, BL. Add. 32751; Delafaye to Horatio, 10, 15 Sept. (os) 1727, PRO. 78/187; Le Coq to Augustus, 23 Sept. 1727, Dresden, 2676, 18a.

35. Horatio Walpole to Newcastle, 9, 19 Aug., 23 Sept., Horatio to Townshend, 26 Aug.,

Townshend to Horatio, 21 Aug. (os) 1727, BL. Add. 32751; Horatio to Robert Walpole, 23 Sept., 24 Oct. 4 Nov. 1727, C(H) corresp. 1481, 1485, BL. Add. 63749.
36. Waldegrave to Townshend, 27 Aug. 1727, Chewton.
37. Sinzendorf to Fonseca, 23 Aug. 1727, HHStA., Fonseca 11; Atterbury to James III, 20 Aug. 1727, RA. 109/87; Vandermeer to Horatio Walpole, 9 Sept. 1727, PRO. 94/98; E. Cruickshanks, *The Factions at the Court of Louis XV* (unpublished Ph.D., London, 1956), p. 8.
38. Atterbury to James III, 19 Jan. 1728, RA. 113/97.
39. Newsletter, 24 June 1727, Osnabrück 291; Broglie to Chauvelin, 6 Nov. 1727, AE. CP. Ang. 360.
40. Knatchbull, pp. 52, 59; Le Coq to Augustus, 5 Feb. 1726, Dresden 2674.
41. Morville to Chammorel, 12 June 1727, AE. CP. Ang. sup. 8.
42. Newcastle to Hedges, 27 May (os) 1727, PRO. 92/32; Newcastle to Horatio Walpole, 28 May (os), Horatio to Townshend, 22 June 1727, BL. Add. 32750, 48982.
43. *Flying Post* 19 Sept. (os), *Whitehall Evening Post* 12 Oct. (os), *Wye's Letter* 6 May (os), 19 Oct. (os), 16 Nov. (os) 1727.
44. Chammorel to Chauvelin, 22 Sept. (os), 13 Oct. (os) 1727, AE. CP. Ang. 360; *Craftsman* 30 Sept. (os) 1727.
45. Waldegrave to Townshend, 25 Sept. 1727, PRO. 80/62.
46. I would like to thank Dr. A.M. Cooke FRCP. and Dr. S.E. Black for their advice.
47. Poyntz to Tilson, 9 Aug. 1727 (referring to Tilson to Poyntz, 14, 18, 21 July (os)), PRO. 95/47.
48. Waldegrave to Tilson, 9 Aug., Richard Edgcumbe to –, 27 Aug. (os), Duncan Forbes to Delafaye, 15 Sept. (os), Du Bourgay to Tilson, 20 Sept. 1727, PRO. 80/62, 36/3, 54/18, 90/22; Newcastle to his wife, 23 Aug. (os) 1727, BL. Add. 33073; Delafaye to Waldegrave, 24 Aug. (os) 1727, Chewton; newsletter, 5 Sept. 1727, Osnabrück 291.
49. Dehn to Ferdinand Albrecht, 24 Oct. 1727, Wolfenbüttel, 1 Alt 22, Nr. 534.
50. Townshend to Waldegrave, 26 Oct. (os) 1727, PRO. 80/62.
51. *Daily Journal* 6 Nov. (os) 1727; Delafaye to Duncan Forbes, 7 Nov. (os) 1727, H.R. Duff (ed.), *Culloden Papers* (1815) p. 102.
52. *Daily Journal* 13 Nov. (os), *Stanley's Newsletter* 11 Nov. (os), *Craftsman* 18 Nov. (os), *Wye's letter* 21 Nov. (os) 1727; newsletter, 28 Nov. 1727, Osnabrück 291; General Wade to Forbes, 23 Nov. (os) 1727, Duff (ed.), *Culloden Papers*, p. 356.
53. *Daily Journal* 4 Dec. (os) 1727; L'Hermitage to the States General, 16 Dec. 1727, BL. Add. 17677 KKK 9.
54. Townshend to Horatio Walpole, 13 Dec. (os) 1727, BL. Add. 48982; *Ipswich Journal* 9, 16 Dec. (os), *Craftsman* 9 Dec. (os) 1727; *Wye's Letter* 4 May (os) 1728.
55. D'Aix to Victor Amadeus II, 8 Dec. 1727, AST. LM. Ing. 35.
56. Le Coq to Augustus, 23 Sept., 13 Oct., 28 Nov., 9, 19 Dec. 1727, Dresden, 2676; Philip Yorke, Attorney General, to Delafaye, 21 Sept. (os) 1727, PRO. 54/18; King, pp. 50–1.
57. Townshend to Du Bourgay, 27 Oct. (os) 1727, PRO. 90/22.
58. St. Saphorin to Townshend, 4 Sept. (os) 1727, PRO. 80/61; Diemar to Landgrave Karl, 5 Dec. 1727, Marburg, England 195; Waldegrave Journal, 11 Nov. 1727, Chewton; Horatio to Robert Walpole, 11 Nov. 1727, BL. Add. 63749
59. Le Coq to Augustus, 25 Nov. 1727, Dresden, 2676, 18a.
60. Horatio to Robert Walpole, 11 Nov. 1727, BL. Add. 63749.
61. Broglie to Chauvelin, 6 Nov. 1727, AE. CP. Ang. 360.
62. M. Hughes, *The Imperial Supreme Judical Authority under the Emperor Charles VI and the crises in Mecklenburg and East Frisia* (unpublished Ph.D., London, 1969).
63. Newcastle to Horatio Walpole, 5 Sept. (os), 23, 30 Nov. (os) 1727, BL. Add. 32751–2; Delafaye to Horatio, 5 Sept. (os), St. Saphorin to Tarouca, Portuguese envoy in Vienna, [-Aug.] 1727, PRO. 78/187, 80/61.
64. Gansinot to Plettenberg, 3 Oct. 1727, Münster NB. 259; Sinzendorf to Fonseca, 20 Aug. 1727, HHStA., Fonseca 11.
65. Vandermeer to Horatio Walpole, 13 Oct. 1727, PRO. 94/98.
66. Townshend to Finch, 5 Sept. (os) 1727, PRO. 84/294.
67. Newcastle to Finch, 21 Nov. (os), PRO. 84/294; Newcastle to Horatio Walpole, 23, 30 Nov. (os) 1727, BL. Add. 32753.

68. Vandermeer to Horatio, 25 Aug., Waldegrave to Tilson, 12 Sept. 1727, PRO. 94/98, 80/62.
69. Instructions, 26 May (os) 1727, PRO. 80/62.
70. Instructions; Townshend to Horatio Walpole, 27 May (os) 1727, BL. Add. 48982; Townshend to Chesterfield, 6 Sept. (os) 1728, PRO. 84/301.
71. Newcastle to Horatio Walpole, 27 May (os) 1727, BL. Add. 32750.
72. Waldegrave to Townshend, 22 June, draft memorandum to Waldegrave, 29 May (os) 1727, PRO. 80/62, 78/187; Dehn to Ferdinand Albrecht, 23 Sept. 1727, Wolfenbüttel, 1 Alt 22 Nr. 543; Waldegrave Journal, 24 Sept. 1727, Chewton; Newcastle to Horatio Walpole, 30 Nov. (os) 1727, BL. Add. 32753.
73. Delafaye to Horatio Walpole, 8 Aug.(os) 1727, PRO. 78/187.
74. Du Bourgay to Townshend, 9 Sept. 1727, PRO. 90/22.
75. Woodward to Tilson, 9 Apr., 2 May, St. Saphorin to Townshend, 16, 22 Apr., 29 May, Delafaye to Horatio Walpole, 8 Aug. (os) 1727, PRO. 80/61, 78/187; Waldegrave Journal, 8 Nov. 1727, Chewton; Newcastle to Horatio Walpole, 30 Nov. (os) 1727, BL. Add. 32753.
76. The possibility of a reconciliation was discussed, *Post Boy* 30 Sept. (os) 1727.
77. Instructions for Waldegrave, 7 Aug. (os), Townshend to Waldegrave, 7 Aug. (os) 1727, PRO. 80/62.
78. Waldegrave Journal, 21 Sept. 1727, Chewton.
79. Horatio to Newcastle, 30 July 1727, BL. Add. 32751.
80. O'Rourke to Graham, 1 Oct. 1727, HHStA., England, Varia 8.
81. Sinzendorf to Fonseca, 14 July, 3 Aug. 1727, HHStA., Fonseca 11; St. Saphorin to Tarouca, [Aug. 1727], PRO. 80/61.
82. Du Bourgay to Townshend, 28 June, 12 July 1727, PRO. 90/22.
83. Sühm, Saxon envoy in Berlin, thought the Prussians serious, Sühm to Augustus, 21 July 1727, Dresden, 3378, IV.
84. *Wye's Letter* 24 Aug. (os), 7 Nov. (os) 1727; D'Aix to Victor Amadeus II, 3 Nov. 1727, AST. LM. Ing. 35.
85. Townshend to Du Bourgay, 14 July (os) 1727, PRO. 90/22; Sühm to Augustus, 22 Aug., Le Coq to Augustus, 23 Sept. 1727, Dresden, 3378, IV, 2676, 18a.
86. Townshend to Du Bourgay, 19 Sept. (os) 1727, PRO. 90/22.
87. Etogh's notes, BL. Add. 9200 f.49.
88. R. Drogereit, 'Das Testament König Georgs I' *Niedersächsisches Jahrbuch für Landesgeschichte* (1937), pp. 84–199, 'The Testament of King George I' *Research and Progress* 5 (1939), pp. 83–6; Le Coq to Augustus, 15 Aug. 1727, Dresden, 2676, 18.
89. BL. Add. 9200, f.49; St. Saphorin, 'Relation sur les affaires du Mecklenbourg', PRO. 80/61.
90. Townshend to Du Bourgay, 14 July (os) 1727, PRO. 90/22.
91. Horatio Walpole to Newcastle, 19 Aug., Townshend to Horatio, 21 Aug. (os) 1727, BL. Add. 32751, 48982; Horatio to Robert Walpole, 24 Oct. 1727, C(H) corresp. 1485.
92. Townshend to Horatio Walpole, 14 Aug. (os) 1727, BL. Add. 32751.
93. Du Bourgay to Townshend, 12 July 1727, PRO. 90/22; Solaro di Breglio, Sardinian envoy in Vienna, to Victor Amadeus II, 1 Oct. 1727, AST. LM. Aut. 58; Newcastle to Horatio Walpole, 16 Oct. (os) 1727, BL. Add. 32751.
94. Horatio Walpole to Newcastle, 30 July 1727, BL. Add. 32751; Chavigny to Chauvelin, 12 Aug. 1727, AE. CP. Allemagne 373; BL. Add. 9200 f.49–50.
95. Newcastle to Horatio Walpole, 16 Oct. (os) 1727, BL. Add. 32752.
96. Townshend to Horatio Walpole, 21 Aug. (os), Delafaye to Horatio, 29 Aug. (os), [Delafaye or Newcastle] to Horatio, 25 Dec. (os) 1727, PRO. 78/187.
97. Du Bourgay to Townshend, 9 Aug. 1727, PRO. 90/22; Le Coq to Augustus, 25 July 1727, Dresden, 2676, 18a.
98. Hanoverian council to George II, 5 Aug. 1727, Hanover, Cal. Brief. 11, EI 274 M; Delafaye to Horatio Walpole, 8 Aug. (os) 1727, PRO. 78/187; Townshend to Waldegrave, 7 Aug. (os) 1727, PRO. 80/62.
99. Hughes, p.366.
100. Draft Instructions for Horatio Walpole, – 1727, PRO. 78/187 f.1–7.
101. Townshend to Horatio Walpole, 8, 21 Aug. (os), Newcastle to Horatio Walpole, 9 Nov. (os) 1727, BL. Add. 32751–1; Townshend to the Dutch nobleman d'Ittersum, 18

Aug. (os) 1727, PRO. 84/296.
102. D'Aix to Victor Amadeus II, 3 Nov. 1727, AST. LM. Ing. 35.
103. Le Coq to Augustus II, 17 Oct., 16 Dec. 1727, Dresden, 2676, 18a.
104. Townshend to Horatio Walpole, 17 Aug. (os) 1727, BL. Add. 32751.
105. Townshend to Chesterfield, 2 Sept. 1729, PRO. 84/305; Anon. travel account, Bodl. Rawl. letters, 72 f.2; Chauvelin to Chavigny, 21 Aug., Boissieux to Chauvelin, 13 Sept. 1729, AE. CP. Br. 47, Cologne 70.
106. Le Coq to Augustus II, 3, 7 Oct. 1727, Dresden 2676, 18a; Waldegrave Journal, 8, 10 Nov. 1727, Chewton; *Whitehall Evening Post* 30 Sept. (os), *Craftsman* 27 Sept. (os) 1727.
107. Du Bourgay to Townshend, 28 Oct., 4 Nov. 1727, PRO. 90/22; Le Coq to Flemming, 18 Nov., 2 Dec. 1727, Dresden, 2676 18a; Villars, pp. 100, 106.
108. Le Coq to Augustus II, 24 Oct., 7 Nov. 1727, Dresden, 2676, 18a; St. Saphorin to Townshend, 22 Apr. 1727, PRO. 80/61; Dureng, p. 62.
109. Ferdinand Albrecht to his mother-in-law, Christine Louise von Öttingen, wife of Ludwig Rudolf of Brunswick-Wolfenbüttel, 3 Apr. 1728, Wolfenbüttel, 1 Alt 22 Nr. 529; *London Evening Post*, 22 Feb. (os) 1728.
110. Pöllnitz, *Lettres et Mémoires* (5th ed., Frankfurt, 1738) I, 86–7.
111. Sutton to Townshend, 8 Mar., Sutton to Tilson, 11 Mar., 17 May 1729, PRO 81/123.
112. Treaty of Westminster, 25 Nov. (os) 1727, BL. Add. 32753, Wolfenbüttel, 1 Alt. 22, Nr. 534; Dehn to Townshend, 6 Dec. 1727, BL. Add. 32753; Townshend to Dehn, 25 Nov. (os), Newcastle to Dehn, 25 Nov. (os), draft of a declaration to Dehn, – Nov. (os) 1727, PRO. 100/15; Fleury to Horatio Walpole, 2 Aug. 1727, BL. Add. 48982; King, pp. 50–4; Naumann, *Österreich, England und das Reich* pp. 135–6.
113. Newcastle to Horatio Walpole, 2 Nov. (os) 1727, BL. Add. 32752.
114. Horatio Walpole to Newcastle, 20 Nov. 1727, BL. Add. 32752.
115. Anon to anon., undated, HHStA., England, Varia 10 f.39. This document has been dated as 1750? but clearly relates to the winter of 1727–8; Schleinitz to Dehn, 3 Oct. 1727, BL. Add. 48982; Le Coq to Augustus II, 9 Dec. 1727, Dresden, 2676, 18a; Baron Dehn to Count Dehn, 20 Aug. 1727, PRO. 84/294; Count Dehn to Ferdinand Albrecht, 2 Sept. 1727, Wolfenbüttel, 1 Alt 22, Nr. 534.
116. Zamboni to Landgrave of Hesse-Darmstadt, 16 Dec. 1727, Bodl. Rawl. 119.
117. Magnan to Chauvelin, 15 Nov. 1727, *Sbornik Imperatorskago Russkago Istoricheskago Obshchestva* (148 vols, St. Petersburg, 1867–1916) 75, 126.
118. Dehn to August Wilhelm, 13 July 1728, Wolfenbüttel, 2 Alt. 3632; Liria, pp. 28–9; Rondeau to Townshend, 28 Feb. (os) 1729, *Sbornik* 66, 37; Waldegrave Journal, 11 Nov. 1727 Chewton.
119. *Post Boy* 30 Sept. (os) 1727.
120. Private Instructions for Sutton as Envoy Extraordinary to the Duke of Wolfenbüttel, 21 Jan. (os) 1729, PRO. 81/123.
121. Dehn to Townshend, 14 Feb., Townshend to Diescau, 31 May (os) 1728, PRO. 100/15, 95/50; Ferdinand Albrecht to Dehn, 12 Sept., 27 Nov., Dehn to Ferdinand Albrecht, 31 Oct., 18 Nov., Ferdinand Albrecht to Christine Louise von Öttingen, 4 Nov. 1727, Wolfenbüttel, 1 Alt 22, Nr. 534, 529.
122. Horatio Walpole to Townshend, 17 June 1727, BL. Add. 48982.
123. Townshend to Horatio Walpole, 21 Aug. (os) 1727, BL. Add. 48982.
124. Tilson to Horatio Walpole, 12 Oct. (os) 1727, BL. Add. 48982.
125. St. Saphorin to Tarouca, – Aug. 1727, PRO. 80/61.
126. O'Rourke to Graham, 22 Oct. 1727, HHStA., England, Varia 8.
127. Newcastle to Horatio Walpole, 14 Dec. (os) 1727, BL. Add. 32753; Townshend to William Finch, 2 Jan. (os) 1728, PRO. 84/299.
128. Tilson to Horatio Walpole, 12 Oct. 1727, BL. Add. 48982.
129. J. Black, 'Britain and the Wittelsbachs in the Early Eighteenth Century', *Mitteilungen des Österreichischen Staatsarchivs* 40 (1987).
130. 'Lettre de Mr. Le Coq contenant quelques ouvertures faites par Mr. de St. Saphorin', 12 Dec., Le Coq to Flemming, 7 Oct., Flemming to Le Coq, 25 Oct., Le Coq to Augustus II, 28 Nov. 1727, Dresden, 2676, 18a.
131. Chavigny to Morville, 8 July 1727, AE. CP. Allemagne 373.

132. 'Lettre de Mr. Le Coq . . .' f.412.
133. Le Coq to Flemming, 12 Dec. 1727, Dresden, 2676, 18a.
134. 'Lettre de Mr. Le Coq . . .' f.412–3.
135. 'Lettre de Mr. Le Coq . . .' f.414–5.
136. Villars, pp. 96–7; Townshend to William Finch, 19 Sept. (os), [Newcastle or Delafaye] to Horatio Walpole, – Sept. (os) 1727, PRO. 84/294, 78/187 f.53; Horatio Walpole to Tilson, 3 Oct. 1727, BL. Add. 48982.
137. Newsletter to Prince-Bishop, 4 Nov. 1727, Osnabrück 291; Chammorel to Chauvelin, 15 Dec. 1727, AE. CP. Ang. 360; *Craftsman* 4, 11 Nov. (os) 1727.
138. Newsletter to Prince-Bishop, 4 Nov. 1727, Osnabrück 291; Villars p. 100; Visconti to Sinzendorf, 29 Sept. 1727, HHStA., EK. 65.
139. Horatio Walpole to Newcastle, 10, 18 Dec. 1727, BL. Add. 32753.
140. Horatio to Robert Walpole, 23 Sept. 1727, C(H) corresp. 1481; Waldegrave Journal, 22, 24, 25 Sept. 1727, Chewton.
141. Visconti to Sinzendorf, 19 Sept. 1727, HHStA., EK. 65.
142. Townshend to d'Ittersum, 18 Aug. (os) 1727, PRO. 84/296; Townshend to Horatio Walpole, 17, 21 Aug. (os) 1727, BL. Add. 32751, PRO. 78/187; Horatio Walpole to Tilson, 6 Sept., Schleinitz to Dehn, 3 Oct. 1727, BL. Add. 48982.
143. Waldegrave Journal, 2 Nov. 1727; *Daily Journal* 12 Dec. (os), *Craftsman* 23 Dec. (os) 1727.
144. Broglie to Chauvelin, 22 Dec. 1727, 1 Jan. 1728, AE. CP. Ang. 360, 362; Newcastle to Horatio Walpole, 14, 21 Dec. (os) 1727, BL. Add. 32753, 9138.
145. Newcastle to Horatio Walpole, 8 Dec. (os), Newcastle to Keene, 8 Dec. (os), Horatio Walpole to Keene, 15 Dec. 1727, BL. Add. 32753.
146. Waldegrave to Tilson, 4 Dec. 1727, Chewton; Newcastle to William Finch, 8 Dec. (os) 1727, PRO. 84/294.
147. Chavigny to Belle-Isle, French general, 6, 27 Jan. 1728, AG. A1 2643; Horatio Walpole to Newcastle, 18 Dec. 1727, BL. Add. 32753; Waldegrave to Newcastle, 21 Feb. 1728, Chewton.
148. [Townshend] to Horatio Walpole, 13 Dec. (os) 1727, BL. Add. 48982; Le Coq to Augustus II, 23 Dec. 1727, Dresden 2676, 18a.
149. Waldegrave Journal, 8 Dec. 1727, Chewton.
150. Horatio Walpole to Newcastle, 27 Dec. 1727, BL. Add. 32753.
151. Horatio Walpole to Newcastle, 10 Dec. 1727, BL. Add. 32753.
152. *Farley's Bristol Newspaper* 2 Dec. (os) 1727.
153. Wade to Forbes, 23 Nov. (os) 1727, Duff, *Culloden Papers* p. 356.
154. Zamboni to Landgrave, 16 Dec. 1727, Bodl. Rawl 119.
155. Broglie to Chauvelin, 8 Dec. 1727, AE. CP. Ang. 360.
156. Hervey, 101–2.
157. Broglie to Chauvelin, 8 Dec. 1727, AE. CP. Ang. 360.
158. Zamboni to Manteuffel, 31 May 1727, Bodl. Rawl. 120; Knatchbull, pp. 56, 72, 93; Sedgwick, II, 254.
159. Ailesbury to brother, 10 Dec. 1727, Trowbridge, Wiltshire CRO. Savernake Mss. 1300 x 691.
160. Hervey, 101–2; Zamboni to Manteuffel, 31 May 1729, Bodl. Rawl. 120. Sedgwick is inaccurate in stating that he resigned in 1730, II, 254.
161. Sedgwick, I, 501.
162. Horatio to Robert Walpole, 11 Nov. 1727, CUL. C(H) corresp. 1489.
163. Le Coq to Augustus II, 19 Dec. 1727, Dresden, 2676, 18a.
164. Sinzendorf to Fonseca, 22 Nov. 1727, HHStA., Fonseca 11; Chammorel to Chauvelin, 15 Dec. 1727, AE. CP. Ang. 360; Le Coq to Augustus II, 26, 30 Dec. 1727, Dresden, 2676, 18a; *Post Boy* 16 Sept. (os), *Craftsman* 23 Sept. (os), *Ipswich Journal* 7 Oct. (os) 1727; Newsletter to the Prince-Bishop, 4 Nov. 1727, Osnabrück 291.
165. Anon. draft to the Earl of Portmore, Governor of Gibraltar, 5 Aug. (os), Brigadier Dormer, Envoy Extraordinary in Lisbon, to Vandermeer, Dutch Ambassador in Spain, 7 Oct., Wager to Vandermeer, 21 Oct., Holloway, consul in Malaga, to Newcastle, 23 Sept., 11, 18 Nov. 1727, PRO. 36/2, 94/98, 215; L'Hermitage to States General, 31 Oct. 1727, BL. Add. 17677 KKK 9; Baudrillart, III, 347, 350; Goslinga, p. 167.

56   THE COLLAPSE OF THE ANGLO-FRENCH ALLIANCE

166. Townshend to Wager, 5 Oct. (os), Newcastle to Wager, 12, 18 July (os), 12 Sept. (os) 1727, PRO. 42/78.
167. Newcastle to Wager, 18 Nov. (os), 25 Dec. (os), Newcastle to Finch, 28 Nov. (os) 1727, PRO. 42/78, 84/94; Newcastle to Horatio Walpole, 25 Nov. (os) 1727, BL. Add. 32753.
168. Wye's Letter 28, 30 Sept. (os), 3, 5, 12, 14, 24, 26 Oct. (os), 11 Nov. (os), Stanley's Letter 26 Oct. (os), Craftsman 9 Dec. (os) 1727.
169. Horatio to Robert Walpole, 11 Nov. 1727, CUL. C(H) corresp. 1489; Fleury to Charles VI, 18 Sept. 1727, HHStA., Frankreich, Varia 11; Visconti to Sinzendorf, 20 Jan. 1728, HHStA., EK. 65.
170. Townshend to Du Bourgay, 17 Jan. 1728, PRO. 90/24; Jacquemin to Duke Leopold of Lorraine, 14 Feb. 1728, Nancy 139; Fiorelli to Doge of Venice, 23 Jan. 1728, ASV. LM. Ing. 97; Villars, pp. 80, 106.
171. Townshend to Finch, 12 Dec. (os) 1727, PRO 84/294.
172. Townshend to Horatio Walpole, 13 Dec. (os) 1727, BL. Add. 48982.
173. D'Aix to Victor Amadeus II, 5 Jan. 1728, AST. LM. Ing. 35, Marini, p. 95; Newcastle to Wager, 25 Dec. (os) 1727, PRO. 42/78.
174. Townshend to the Postmasters General, 18 July (os) 1727, PRO. 36/2; Zamboni to Manteuffel, 6 July 1728, Bodl. Rawl. 120.
175. Visconti to Sinzendorf, 13 Jan. 1728, HHStA., EK. 65.
176. Ferdinand Albrecht to his mother-in-law, 3 Apr. 1728, Wolfenbüttel, 1 Alt 22, Nr. 529.
177. Berkentin to -, 17 Mar. 1728, PRO. 80/326.
178. King, pp. 54–5.
179. Dickinson, Walpole, pp. 52–3; Wodrow, Analecta III, 459.
180. Duncan to John Forbes, 6 Jan. (os) 1728, D. Warrand (ed.) More Culloden Papers III (Inverness, 1927) pp. 27–8.
181. Newcastle to Horatio Walpole, 8, 14, 21 Dec. (os), Horatio Walpole to Newcastle, 17, 29 Dec., Townshend to Horatio Walpole, 13 Dec. (os) 1727, BL. Add. 32753, 9138, 48982; Tilson to Waldegrave, 14 Dec. (os) 1727, Chewton.
182. Newcastle to Horatio Walpole, 5 Dec. (os), Horatio Walpole to Finch, 22 Dec., Horatio Walpole to Newcastle, 27 Dec., Townshend to Horatio Walpole, 13 Dec. (os) 1727, BL. Add. 32753, 48982; Draft of a declaration to Broglie, unused, 20 Dec. 1727, PRO. 100/5; D'Aix to Victor Amadeus II, 5 Jan. 1728, AST. LM. Ing. 35.
183. Waldegrave Journal, 2 Dec. 1727, 15 Jan. 1728, Chewton.
184. Horatio Walpole of 8 Jan. 1728, enclosing Chauvelin to Rottembourg, CUL. C(H) papers 23/10–11; King, pp. 54–5; Villars, pp. 111–112; Goslinga, pp. 192–3, 196; Wilson p. 189; St. Cruz and Barrenechea, Spanish envoys in Paris, to De la Paz, Spanish foreign minister, 20 May 1730, BL. Add. 32767.
185. Newcastle to Horatio Walpole, 18 Dec. (os), – Dec. (os) 1727, BL. Add. 32753, PRO. 78/187; Horatio Walpole to Finch, 22 Dec., Horatio Walpole to Newcastle, 24 Dec. 1727, BL. Add. 32753.
186. Newcastle to Horatio Walpole, 21 Dec. (os), Horatio Walpole to Newcastle, 24 Dec. 1727, 2 Jan. 1728, BL. Add. 9138, 32753; Waldegrave Journal, 25 Dec. 1727, 4, 5 Jan. 1728, Chewton; Townshend to Finch, 2 Jan. (os) 1728, Berkentin to –, 17 Mar. 1728, PRO. 84/299, 80/326; Fonseca to Sinzendorf, 25 Jan. 1728, HHStA., Fonseca 12.
187. Horatio Walpole to Newcastle, 27 Dec. 1727, BL. Add. 32753.
188. Horatio Walpole to Newcastle, 17, 24 Dec. 1727, BL. Add. 32753; Waldegrave Journal, 6 Jan. 1728, Chewton; Villars, pp. 111–112; Horatio Walpole, 'Apology', BL. Add. 9132 f.90–3.
189. De Buy to Flemming, 16, 26 Jan., 9, 15 Feb. 1728, Dresden, 3105; Königsegg to Pentenriedter, 4 Mar. 1728, HHStA., Frankreich, Varia 12; Villars, p. 120; Armstrong, p. 221.
190. There is a text and an English translation in PRO. 103/110; Townshend to William Finch, 21 Jan. (os), Finch to Townshend, 10 Feb. 1728, PRO. 84/299; Königsegg to Pentenriedter, 7 Mar. 1728, HHStA., Frankreich, Varia 12; Goslinga, pp. 24–7; Baudrillart, III, 385–99; Original Mercury, York Journal: or Weekly Courant 30 Jan. (os), Ipswich Mercury 10 Feb. (os), Whitehall Evening Post 9 Mar. (os), Daily Journal 28 Mar. (os), Wye's Letter 23 Apr. (os) 1728.

CHAPTER FOUR

Early 1728
The Session of 1728: Abortive Approaches to Austria

The parliamentary session of 1728 was preceded by a major pamphlet and press war.[1] The attack upon the government was concentrated on its foreign policy and on the failure of the Anglo-French alliance to secure British interests. The news of Spain agreeing to most of the British demands destroyed the opposition case. George II was able to tell Parliament on 7 February that he had received from France and the United Provinces 'the greatest proofs of their sincerity, and a renewal of the strongest assurances imaginable, that they would effectually make good all their engagements', and that 'a general pacification' was at hand.[2] The Lords' Address was a lengthy defence of ministerial foreign policy. It argued for 'the absolute necessity of supporting your allies' and stated that 'the late disagreeable situation of affairs' could not have been prevented by 'human prudence', an answer to opposition arguments that the government had been responsible for the diplomatic imbroglio Britain had been trapped in. George II's martial instincts were acknowledged and the Walpolean view that negotiation was preferable to war stated in the Address, which referred to the 'noble self-denial of all the success and glory that might attend your Majesty's arms in the prosecution of a just and necessary war, when put in balance with the ease, quiet, and prosperity of your subjects. It is a disposition of mind truly great in your Majesty . . . to choose rather to procure peace for your subjects, than to lead them to victories'.[3]

The debates on the Address were a triumph for the government. Townshend wrote that the Lords' Address 'is conceived in stronger and more zealous terms than any that has been ever made to His Majesty's predecessors'.[4] Ministerial success was attributed to the new diplomatic situation. Newcastle informed Waldegrave that 'the good news you have sent us, has made the opening of our Parliament very successful'.[5] The rest of the session went very well for the Ministry. Much time was spent on petitions arising from the recent elections. These served to increase governmental strength in the Commons.[6] The Lords were very quiet, discussing topics such as the right to salmon fishing in the Spey, and in the Commons the government enjoyed large majorities. Many Tory MPs were absent. In the debate over the subsidies for the Hessians the majority was 280 to 86, and in the army estimates debate, 290 to 86.[7] Townshend wrote to British envoys that 'the grand affairs of session have been dispatched in less time than ever was known in any parliament, and with a greater majority than was ever remembered in any reign'. Writing to Baron Diescau about the opposition failure to divide the Commons on several points, Townshend claimed 'The opposers of these resolutions dared not come to a division, they were so disheartened at their former ill success with respect to the Hessians, that they gave up the whole, and indeed it appeared by the unanimity of the House, that if they had ventured to make a formal division there would have been near 300 to between 30 and 40.'[8]

Ministerial foreign policy was fully debated. Horatio Walpole spoke at length in defence of the French alliance. According to the newsletter sent to Ernst-August, he convinced most MPs that it was a sound policy. The opposition 'let themselves into the whole state of public affairs from north to south', but their attacks had little success. The debates simply served to convince foreign diplomats that the government was in control. The French were impressed by the ministerial successes, as were the Austrians, Dutch and Spaniards. D'Aix noted that 'le Parlement est de deux, et souvent de trois contre un', and Visconti informed Sinzendorf that the degree of harmony between government and Parliament was unprecedented.[9]

The government argued that, despite the forthcoming Congress, it was necessary to remain prepared for war. The royal speech referred to the need to continue British military preparations and the Lords' Address spoke of the possibility of having to fight. Both in Britain and in Europe opinions were divided as to whether the forthcoming Congress at Soissons would bring peace. In January Delafaye had observed 'the Grand Affair is concluded so far as to have a Congress held, the issue of which is another story'. The royal speech proroguing Parliament predicted a successful Congress and Sinzendorf declared that it would only last five weeks,[10] but other more pessimistic notes were sounded. Fears were expressed that Spain[11] or Austria might delay the Congress and refuse to be conciliatory. The opposition claimed that Britain would be duped[12] and indeed the government was concerned about the diplomatic situation. Horatio Walpole attempted to persuade Fleury that the Hanover allies should settle their claims among themselves and agree to stand by them at the Congress. He also argued that their envoys at the Congress should be given common instructions:

> I thought it might not be amiss, if some plan was drawn up in writing by way of instructions to our respective Plenipotentiaries, founded upon the Preliminary articles, to be a sort of general rule and guidance to them.

Fleury agreed that the union produced by the Treaty of Hanover should continue and that the Preliminaries of Paris should serve as the basis for the actions of the Hanover allies, but he refused to accept the idea of common written instructions, arguing that it would be impossible to keep them secret.[13] Behind this dispute lay British fears that Fleury would settle with the Austrians.[14]

By temporarily shelving the differences between the major powers the Convention of the Pardo had a kaleidoscopic effect. It freed the powers from some of their most pressing engagements and created opportunities for major realignments. This created a difficult situation for the British

ministry at a time when they were still unsure about their relations with
George II.

Ministerial strife appears to have persisted during the winter of 1727–8,
fuelled by speculation that Walpole would fall as a result of his foreign
policy. The ministers opposed to Walpole seem to have felt that Britain
should break with France and turn to Austria, though there is very little
definite information about their views. In February Visconti informed
Sinzendorf that he had been told by a very well informed source, whom he
did not name, of a court cabal determined to ruin Walpole 'dans l'esprit du
Roy'. According to this account the Walpoles had fabricated evidence that
Compton, Berkeley and Pulteney were in correspondence with the
Austrians and had urged them to refuse British demands. One of the three
was supposed to have informed George of the Walpolean fabrications, and
he, livid, had determined to dismiss Walpole at the end of the session.
O'Rourke sent James III a variation of the story:

> . . . without being entirely sure, there is this good while a private correspond-
> ence betwixt some ministers here and the new vying faction in Engd. wch.
> actually aims at the ministry, I have had some imperfect glimpses of Pultney and
> Compton's being mentioned and I doc not doubt but this court backs with all
> their industry any such change.[15]

There are no signs of any letters from Wilmington, Berkeley or Pulteney in
the Viennese archives and the suggestions mentioned by Visconti and
O'Rourke are probably inaccurate. They may reflect the known links
between the opposition Whigs, led by Pulteney, and the Austrian envoy
Palm in 1726–7, and the suspicion that these links had continued after
Palm's departure. In April 1727 St. Saphorin reported the Austrians' hope
that if they could encompass the fall of Walpole the new ministry would
support them. Charles Caesar was not alone in reporting links between
Pulteney and the Austrians.[16] In the early 1720s policy over Austria was a
significant cause of division within the ministry, with Carteret and
Cadogan leading an anti-Walpole group. It is unclear how far the courtiers
opposed to Walpole in the late 1720s supported Austria, or sought to use
foreign policy in order to discredit him. It is possible that there was still
much tension in the ministry, particularly between Wilmington and
Walpole. George's independent habits were a major difficulty, particularly
to Townshend. According to D'Aix, Townshend, who had been used
hitherto to getting his way, found it difficult to accustom himself to sharing
authority, following the policies of others and seeing George act by
himself. There is no evidence to support D'Aix's claim that Townshend
told George he would retire at the end of the Congress,[17] but there are
other suggestions of tension over George's attitudes. The newsletter sent to
Ernst-August reported Walpole to be concerned that if George went on his
projected trip to Hanover in the summer he would listen to his rivals.[18]
George and his ministers clashed over the instructions for the British
Plenipotentiaries at Soissons. George was determined that no marriage
should take place between Don Carlos and any daughter of Charles VI. He

was convinced that such an event would be a major threat to the balance of power, and a challenge to the position of the major German princes, arguments advanced the previous summer by Horatio Walpole.[19] The British ministry felt it was unlikely to take place anyway, and that it was impolitic to raise the matter at the Congress as Austria would resent the discussion of such a sensitive dynastic matter. Furthermore they, the Dutch ministry and Fleury hoped that by seeming to acquiesce in the marriage they would win Spanish support and embarrass the Austrians, forcing them to publicly oppose the marriage, and thus endanger Spanish support; or, approve of it, and anger those German powers, such as Saxony, Prussia and Bavaria, who had already made clear their opposition to the match. The British ministry had been willing to insinuate to Elisabeth Farnese that the marriage of Carlos and an Archduchess would be supported 'under proper regulations for preserving the Balance of Europe'.[20] According to D'Aix, Townshend had persuaded George that no other power would support Britain in attempting to block the marriage, but George had been informed by St. Saphorin that Townshend was lying. Sardinia, fearful of the establishment of Don Carlos in Italy, was opposed to the marriage, and D'Aix was unsympathetic to Townshend. He hinted that George had given Stanhope secret instructions, and reported that on the eve of the Plenipotentiaries' departure George had altered their instructions, without consulting his ministers, because he was determined neither to connive nor to appear to connive in the marriage scheme. D'Aix wrote that George had made the same change in Chesterfield's instructions, and that he had given his particular confidence to one of the Plenipotentiaries, Stanhope, and not to his colleagues, Horatio Walpole and Poyntz.[21]

Saxon sources suggest that Stanhope received secret instructions when he left London and, according to Le Coq, Stanhope informed him that Townshend knew nothing of the matter.[22] Owing to the few drafts that have been preserved in the British State Papers Foreign Series it is usually impossible to check statements, such as D'Aix's, that instructions have been altered, and in the volumes of drafts preserved there are no drafts of these instructions. However, there is among the Townshend papers a letter from George to Townshend which confirms that George was in favour of blocking the prospect of an Austro-Spanish marriage:

> You will have seen by Lord Chesterfield's letter, that the pensionary reasons in the same way, as I allwais did, both in relation to the provisional treaty, as of the fear he is in of the princes of the empire submitting to the match, in case we should not shew all sort of vigour in opposing it. I think, mylord, you should tell him more strongly, that it is my opinion, and as you conclude this letter, desire his sentiment how to bring those princes into our measures, and how to make everybody concern'd in this affair act with the spirit they ought to do.[23]

George's tone is unmistakable. The impasse in the European diplomatic situation had to be ended. Furthermore, the letter confirms his concern about the attitude of the German princes. Anxiety over the German situation had increased early in 1728 with reports of an improvement in relations between Saxony and Prussia. The British informed Le Coq that they were pleased with this development, but in fact they were extremely concerned. Frederick William's visit to Dresden was followed with great attention.[24] Concern increased when suggestions that the Prusso-Saxon reconciliation had been viewed with disfavour by the Austrians were replaced by a growing conviction that Austria was behind the reconciliation.[25] Suggestions were made that a marriage between Maria Theresa and the Crown Prince of Saxony was being negotiated or that the Austrians were supporting a Saxon scheme to make the crown of Poland hereditary, and that Prussian compliance was to be obtained by the cession of Elbing and the bishopric of Varmia. The French Consul at Hamburg, Geffroy, noted that it was generally held that Augustus II was to abdicate and be succeeded in Poland by his son, whilst Prussia was to receive Polish Prussia. The Dresden archives are not very helpful about the state of Prusso-Saxon relations in this period, as the key arrangements were made in discussions between the two monarchs. Du Bourgay noted that most of the Prussian ministers were not consulted about the talks at Dresden.[26]

The British government was assured that the agreement signed between Prussia and Saxony was only defensive.[27] However, they feared that though its intentions might be directed towards Poland and the settlement of conflicting Saxon and Prussian claims over Jülich-Berg, it would nevertheless have a wider impact. In January the British had rejected Prussian suggestions of a reconciliation, Townshend informing Du Bourgay that 'the proceedings of your Court are such, that there can be no certain and solid judgement made of them, and consequently H.M. can have no positive orders to send you upon the various and fluctuating state of matters where you are'.[28] This view was not an unreasonable one born simply of George II's malice. It was a widely held view that Frederick William was capricious and unreliable. However much this view may have been correct the British response, combined with the Prusso-Saxon reconciliation, made the German situation more serious. Concerned about possible Austrian troop movements[29] and fearful of an attack upon Hanover, George resorted to an attempt to develop his German alliance system, and to French aid. Major efforts were made to secure the support of Württemberg.[30] Pressure brought to bear upon France succeeded in persuading the French to threaten Prussia. Chambrier, the Prussian envoy in Paris, informed Frederick William that Fleury had told him that if Prussia used violence against the Hanoverians in Mecklenburg France would suppport them 'to the utmost'.[31] Dehn had pressed George to enter into the treaty of amity and union concluded in July 1727 between Württemberg and Brunswick-Wolfenbüttel. George supported the idea and believed it could serve as the basis for an association of 'a considerable number of princes in the Empire to defend and support the rights and immunitys of the whole Germanick Body against any usurpations or encroachments on the part of His Imperial Majesty'. It could also serve to protect Hanover. Horatio Walpole was instructed to suggest to Fleury that it would be best if George entered the treaty as Elector of Hanover, rather than as King, as this would reduce the danger of the Austrians discrediting it as an alliance with foreign powers. George suggested a convention should be signed with Louis XV, in which the French would ask George to accede as Elector to the treaty and would undertake to provide help if trouble arose on account of the new treaty, 'as if it had been in pursuance of the Treaty concluded at Hanover.'[32]

George's personal diplomatic strategy was therefore well defined by the spring of 1728. Newcastle noted in February, 'His Majesty thinks that great attention should be had to the affairs of the North'. It centred on German problems and advocated a German solution, a league of German princes supported, in the last resort, by French military aid. George also wished to defend the position of the Protestants in the Empire, the policy of France for over a century. Failing prior satisfaction he wanted Hanoverian interests in Bremen, Verden and Hadeln discussed at the Congress. Le Coq had reported in December 1727 that Britain felt the prospect of a French war would dissuade Austria from any attack upon Hanover. The same hope lay behind George's policy in 1728 and, for George, it was the essential purpose of the Anglo-French alliance. By maintaining this alliance George was secure whatever became of his diplomatic initiatives in Germany, and this alliance in turn made these initiatives more hopeful.[33]

The instructions George sent to his Plenipotentiaries at Soissons, where he was represented at the Congress table only as King, not as Elector, were in accord with this strategy. By opposing the idea of a marriage between an archduchess and Carlos, and by demanding that the issue be raised in order to be publicly rejected, George hoped to establish his credentials as the great power both most willing and best placed to represent the interests of the German princes.[34] He would then be able to negotiate from strength both in German disputes and with the great powers. In particular, his freedom in diplomatic manoeuvre would be increased as France would not be able to treat him as a junior power, and as he would be able to force Austria into accepting his pretensions and reaching an agreement with him.

There were hints of the latter in the first half of 1728. O'Rourke's suggestion that the Austrians were keen on better relations with Britain was substantiated to some extent by approaches made in March to Horatio Walpole by the Imperial representative at Paris, Pentenriedter. Pentenriedter told Walpole that the Emperor wanted good relations, that Austrian conduct had been misrepresented by St. Saphorin and that it was Spain which prevented the conclusion of a firm peace. Walpole was unimpressed. He told Pentenriedter that the Austrians were responsible for Spanish policy and informed Fleury that Pentenriedter, despite his general assurances, was still intransigent when it came to detailed discussions. Walpole reported to Newcastle that Pentenriedter's approaches were not restricted to the British. The Austrian diplomat had sought to win over the Dutch and the French.[35] Walpole clearly hoped that by telling Fleury about the approaches, he would encourage him to remain firm to British interests, and would discredit the Austrian approaches to France. Waldegrave was convinced Pentenriedter was attempting to split the Anglo-French alliance, and the British suspected that this was the purpose of his mission.[36]

The fragile nature of eighteenth-century alliances encouraged diplomats to speculate on changes in the international system. The Austro-Spanish alliance of 1725 indicated that the most surprising alliances were possible. After the news of the settlement of Anglo-Spanish differences rumours of an Anglo-Austrian reconciliation increased. Ferdinand Albrecht of Brunswick-Bevern, then in Vienna, found it necessary to refute these rumours. It was suggested that Horatio Walpole would be sent to Vienna to manage a reconciliation and that the Austrians would support George II over his demand to receive the formal investiture of Bremen and Verden.[37] Waldegrave was ordered to set out for Vienna, and it was widely believed that he had been instructed to arrange an Anglo-Austrian reconciliation. He arrived in Vienna at the beginning of May and made a conspicuous impact as a popular social figure. O'Rourke wrote slightingly, 'Waldegrave is looked upon here as a mild polite man, of noe great reach, and therefore for their purpose'. Others were more complimentary, and O'Rourke's opinion improved subsequently. Count Tarouca informed Townshend that Waldegrave's good qualities had won him universal esteem, and his skill at cards soon commended him to Prince Eugene, a noted card-player.[38] The Austrians told Waldegrave they were in favour of an improvement in relations. Eugene informed him of 'his sincere desire to see a perfect reconciliation with England', and the leader of the Spanish interest at the Court of Vienna, the Marquis Ramon de Rialp, Secretary of Charles VI's Spanish Council, blamed bad relations on St. Saphorin and said that he would be delighted to see good ones restored. The Emperor bowed to Waldegrave as he was about to mount his horse 'a mark of great distinction I am told.'[39] The French were concerned about reports that Austria was seeking to improve relations with Britain, and the Saxon agent in London, Zamboni, reported that the British ministers were determined to improve them and delighted by Waldegrave's reception. He added that Townshend had communicated these views to an unofficial Austrian agent and that the British ministry were beginning to view French power with suspicion.[40] Zamboni was almost certainly referring to Visconti as the unofficial Austrian agent and it was probably from him that he derived his information. Zamboni's report might appear to be an exaggeration of whatever interest the British government was showing in an Anglo-Austrian reconciliation, but it is partially substantiated by material in the Saxon archives. In the spring of 1728 Le Coq left London and travelled to Dresden to inform Augustus II personally of diplomatic approaches he had received from George II. There is no account of his audiences with Augustus and the evidence for this episode is the instructions drawn up by Augustus for the representatives he sent to the Congress of Soissons, Le Coq and Count Hoym, the Saxon envoy in Paris. The instructions, drawn up at the end of June, referred to British requests made via Le Coq for Saxon help in settling Anglo-Austrian differences. The British had expressed a willingness to guarantee the Pragmatic Sanction and an interest in reviving the old Anglo-Austrian diplomatic alignment. They asked the Saxons to approach only Sinzendorf, who had been appointed First Austrian Plenipotentiary at Soissons, and to act in concert with Stanhope, 'à qui seul S.M. Brit. en a confié le secret.' In addition, according to the instructions, the British had suggested an Anglo-Saxon alliance.[41]

Judging by Le Coq's subsequent reports from France it is clear that St. Saphorin had been responsible for handling the London discussions about the possibility of a Saxon mediation of Anglo-Austrian differences. Le Coq reported it was St. Saphorin's idea that only Sinzendorf should be approached, and that Stanhope had told him he had received instructions from George II to cooperate with the Saxons on this approach and that Townshend knew nothing of these secret instructions. D'Aix, who was close to St. Saphorin, reported that Stanhope entirely shared his principles.[42]

It is difficult to obtain evidence to support this account. The present whereabouts of Stanhope's papers are a mystery: the current Earl of Harrington has no knowledge of them. Whereas the Anglo-Austrian talks conducted through Waldegrave attracted a lot of contemporary attention and gave rise to much rumour, there are no signs that the projected Saxon mediation attracted any attention. This can possibly be accounted for by the precautions taken to ensure the secrecy of the project. According to the instructions for Le Coq and Hoym George II had insisted that nothing be committed to paper and that the approach to Sinzendorf should be oral. No memorials summarising the British proposals were to be given to Sinzendorf. These were sensible precautions given the notorious breaches of security which occured in this period. They were also intended to prevent the Austrians exploiting the approach in order to sow dissension among the Hanover Allies. It is also possible George feared that if the approach failed the Austrians might reveal it to the British opposition, and thus embarrass the government in Parliament. Pulteney had attempted to gain documentary evidence from foreign diplomats of George I's promise, given to Spain in 1721, to try to obtain parliamentary agreement for the return of Gibraltar.

The lack of complementary documentary evidence is not therefore proof of anything more than a sensible disinclination to entrust important information to paper. It does not disprove the Saxon material. It is unlikely that Augustus II would have drawn up formal instructions to his envoys to attempt a mediation unless he believed his efforts were desired. Were it not for Stanhope's confirmation to Le Coq that he had received secret instructions from George, it could be thought that St. Saphorin had sole responsibility for the project. It therefore seems likely that the Saxon material is accurate and that George did make approaches to the Saxons for their help in arranging an Anglo-Austrian reconciliation.

Granted that this was the case, it is necessary to reconcile George's action with the fears of Prusso-Saxon reconciliation voiced earlier in the year. Unfortunately, it is impossible to date St. Saphorin's discussions with Le Coq about an approach to Sinzendorf. They may have taken place in December 1727 at the same time as the two men discussed the need for a league of German princes, but if so, it is likely that the confidential courier who took the report of these talks to Dresden would also have taken a report on the other matter. Le Coq was still in London at the end of April 1728 and it is unlikely he would have remained so long in London had the confidential approach been made to him in December 1727. St. Saphorin probably approached him after it became clear that a Congress would be held, and this was not obvious until the news of Spain's capitulation to Anglo-French pressure arrived in London in January. It is, however, conceivable that the approach was made earlier and that George envisaged an approach to Sinzendorf through the Saxon envoy in Vienna.

Despite hostility towards Augustus II as a Catholic ruler suspected of seeking the re-catholicisation of Saxony, and bad relations after the Thorn affair, a religious dispute of 1724, neither the Hanoverian monarchs nor the British ministry viewed Saxony with particular disfavour. Saxon territorial aspirations and dynastic hopes did not conflict with either Hanoverian or British interests. The Saxon claim to Jülich-Berg did not present any particular difficulties, whilst Augustus II's schemes to make Poland a hereditary monarchy aroused little concern in London. The Saxon interest in the Habsburg inheritance did not feature prominently in the diplomacy of the period, although both the British and the French were aware that the death of Charles VI would have a disruptive effect on the international situation.

It was therefore the prospect of increased support for Prussian schemes, rather than any fears about Saxon intentions, which led to concern about the Prusso-Saxon agreement. Why George, despite this concern, still entrusted Saxony with the handling of the approach to Sinzendorf is unclear. Various suggestions could be advanced. Possibly he hoped to use Augustus to restrain the Prussians, or hoped that the growing strength of his alliance system in the Empire would persuade Saxony, Prussia and Austria, together or individually, to take him more seriously. Possibly George sought to discard the French, and the abortive attempt of 1728 was a precursor of the successful Anglo-Austrian negotiations of 1731. The Saxons had suggested neutrality agreements in the Empire in 1726–7 and had seen themselves then as occupying an intermediary position between the alliances of Hanover and Vienna.

Whatever George intended, nothing came of the Saxon approach. Le Coq arrived at Soissons on 14 July 1728. A fortnight later he informed Augustus that Stanhope had told him that, though his secret instructions were unaltered, he wanted to write to both George and Caroline to seek confirmation of them. Le Coq proposed that he should follow St. Saphorin's suggestion and approach Sinzendorf with the project of an Anglo-Austrian understanding as if it originated with the Saxons. Stanhope decided that it was best if he sought new instructions before any moves were made.[43] On 11 August Le Coq reported that Stanhope, having received no new instructions for three months, was worried that George had changed his mind. Moreover St. Saphorin had promised Stanhope that on his return to his native Switzerland he would go via Paris, and his failure to do so worried both Stanhope and Le Coq. Stanhope feared the British ministry had discovered the scheme and that he would fall into disfavour. The more phlegmatic Le Coq suggested that the Saxon intervention simply depended on how much George needed it as a diplomatic expedient.[44]

Why the Saxon intervention was allowed to peter out is unclear. Possibly the answer lay in the fears Stanhope voiced to Le Coq, that an alliance between Saxony, Prussia, Russia and Austria would harm George's interests, and include a Saxon guarantee of the Jülich-Berg inheritance to Prussia.[45] Possibly George was affected by the decree on the Mecklenburg affair issued by the Aulic Council on 11 May. This angered George because it threatened the Hanoverian position in the Duchy and because it emanated from the Aulic Council in Vienna and not from the Imperial Diet.[46] The British ministry argued that this decree confirmed their view of the Austrians as a despotic threat in the Empire. Townshend informed Chesterfield that

> if the Emperor should establish such a despotism over Germany, as he plainly aims at by his way of disposing of the Dutchy of Mecklenburg, all his neighbours will soon feel the effects of such an overgrown power, and be convinc'd, tho' too late, how boundless Imperial ambition is, when back'd with the weight and force of an arbitrary sway in the Empire.[47]

Townshend's letter was written in order to persuade the Dutch that, though they were not guarantors of the Treaties of Westphalia, they should nevertheless intervene in the Mecklenburg dispute. Townshend complained about Austrian behaviour, particularly over Mecklenburg, and argued that it indicated 'that all our condescensions are looked upon both at Vienna and Madrid as proofs of our weakness; so that unless we can prevail with our allies to act a more vigorous part, the best we can hope from the Congress, will be to have our Allies settle there all that relates to their particular interests, and to transfer the consideration of ours from Soissons to Madrid'.[48] It is clear that George was greatly concerned by the matter. On 11 August Townshend sent Horatio Walpole an anxious letter:

> His Majesty's thoughts upon the points of Mecklenburg and Sleswig, on which he is very earnest and would not suffer the least delay to be made . . . I never saw the king more displeased in my life than he was upon reading what was said in this project and your dispatches upon those two articles . . . For God's sake, Dear Horace, do your best, both your reputation and mine are at stake.[49]

The Mecklenburg resolution, combined with the lack of real response Waldegrave encountered in Vienna, destroyed the basis for an Anglo-Austrian reconciliation. Horatio Walpole warned Townshend it was foolish 'to think that by turning towards the Emperor we shall find release.' Waldegrave complained 'there is a set of people here that pretend to love the English nation . . . without having the least regard for his Majesty.'[50] The British felt that Austria was trying to stir up trouble between Hanover and Prussia in Mecklenburg. George was angry at the

Austrian decision to include Prussia among the administering powers of Mecklenburg. They also blamed the Austrians for Spanish intransigence. Despite Waldegrave's sweeping social success he found that the Austrian ministers in Vienna, and in particular the influential Prince Eugene, were far from accommodating. Thus neither of the approaches intended to improve Anglo-Austrian relations had succeeded. The 'official' approach through Waldegrave had met as little success as the 'unofficial' one through Stanhope and the Saxons.

It was not surprising that the Austrians were unresponsive to Waldegrave and insensitive over Mecklenburg. In the Empire their ties with Saxony, Prussia and Russia made them oblivious to Hanoverian views.[51] At the Congress the possibility of Austria detaching France from her allies appeared to be strong. Sinzendorf was convinced he would be able to manage Fleury and thus acquire the glory of having given peace to Europe. This optimism caused the Austrians to pay less attention to British views.[52] Without French help Britain would be forced to compromise, and this opinion, widely held, led to little attention being paid to British interests at the beginning of the Congress. Horatio Walpole had feared that this would happen and had therefore pressed unsuccessfully for a set of common written instructions for the Plenipotentiaries of the Alliance of Hanover powers. His fears were to be proved correct.[53]

Notes

1. Hervey to Stephen Fox, 9 Jan. (os) 1728, Ilchester, p. 27. *The Leeds Mercury* 30 Jan. (os) 1728 referred to a 'Paper War'.
2. Newcastle to Waldegrave, 29 Jan. (os) 1728, BL. Add. 32754; Hervey, I, 75; Carlisle, p. 53.
3. *House of Lords Journals* 23, 167–8; *House of Commons Journals* 21, 30.
4. Townshend to William Finch, 30 Jan. (os) 1728, PRO. 84/299; Delafaye to Waldegrave, 29 Jan. (os) 1728, Chewton; Visconti to Sinzendorf, 10 Feb. 1728, HHStA.,EK. 65.
5. Newcastle to Waldegrave, 29 Jan. (os) 1728, Chewton; Intelligence from France, 23 Mar. 1728, C(H) papers 26/34.
6. Knatchbull, pp. 746; Hervey, I, 75–6.
7. Tilson to Waldegrave, 15 Feb. (os), Delafaye to Waldegrave, 15 Feb. (os) 1728, Chewton; Chammorel to Chauvelin, 23 Feb., 12 Apr. 1728, AE. CP. Ang. 362.
8. Townshend to Wych, 20 Feb. (os), Townshend to William Finch, 20 Feb. (os), Townshend to Diescau, 20 Feb. (os) 1728, PRO. 82/45, 84/299, 95/50.
9. Newsletter, 2 Mar. 1728, Osnabrück, 295; William Finch to Tilson, 2 Mar., Finch to Townshend, 29 Mar., Waldegrave to Townshend, PRO. 84/299, 80/61; Keene to Newcastle, 22 Mar. 1728, BL. Add. 32754; Broglie to Chauvelin, 26 Feb., 15 Mar., Chauvelin to Chammorel, 4 Mar. 1728, AE. CP. Ang. 362, sup.8; D'Aix to Victor Amadeus II, 15 Mar. 1727, AST. LM. Ing. 35; Visconti to Sinzendorf, 5 Mar. 1728, HHStA., EK. 65.
10. Delafaye to Waldegrave, 23 Jan. (os), Robinson to Waldegrave, 14 June 1728, Chewton; Waldegrave to Delafaye, 13 Feb. 1728, PRO. 78/188.
11. Fonseca to Eugene, 14 June 1728, HHStA., GK. 85a.
12. Visconti to Sinzendorf, 13 Apr. 1728, HHStA., EK. 65; Chammorel to Chauvelin, 19 Apr. 1728, AE. CP. Ang. 362.
13. Horatio Walpole to Newcastle, 23 Mar., 5, 9 Apr., 12 May 1728, BL. Add. 32754–5; King, p. 54.

14. Horatio Walpole to Newcastle, 6 Jan. 1728, BL. Add. 32753; [Delafaye or Newcastle] to Horatio Walpole, – Dec. (os) 1727, PRO. 78/187.
15. Visconti to Sinzendorf, 3, 10 Feb. 1728, O'Rourke to James III, 24 Jan. 1728, HHStA., EK. 65, England Varia 8.
16. St. Saphorin to Townshend, 22 Apr. 1727, PRO. 80/61; Caesar to James III, 29 June (os) 1727, RA. 107/141; Waldegrave Journal, 28 Sept. 1727, Chewton.
17. D'Aix to Victor Amadeus II, 21 Apr. 1728, AST. LM. Ing. 35.
18. Newsletter, 12 Mar. 1728, Osnabrück, 295; Le Coq to De Brosse, Saxon envoy at The Hague, 23 Mar. 1728, Dresden 663; Fiorelli to Venetian government, 16 Apr. 1728, ASV. LM. Ing. 97.
19. Horatio Walpole, Considerations, PRO. 84/294 f.131–3.
20. Townshend to Horatio Walpole, 14 Aug. (os) 1727, Newcastle to Horatio, 26 Mar. (os), Horatio to Newcastle, 24 Apr. 1728, BL. Add. 32751, 32755; Townshend to Horatio, 23 June (os) 1728, Bradfer Lawrence; William Finch to Townshend, 13 Apr., Chesterfield to Townshend, 25 June, 6, 16 July 1728, PRO. 84/299–301; [Newcastle] to Horatio Walpole, – Apr. (os) 1728, PRO. 78/189 f.130.
21. D'Aix to Victor Amadeus II, 9 May 1728, AST. LM. Ing. 35; Marini, pp. 105–6.
22. Instructions for Count Hoym, Saxon representative at Soissons, 30 June, Le Coq to Augustus, 11 Aug. 1728, Dresden 2733.
23. George to Townshend, undated reply to Townshend to George, 2 July (os) 1728, Coxe, II, 521.
24. Le Coq to DeBrosse, 20, 27 Jan., 30 Mar. 1728, Dresden, 663; Newcastle to Waldegrave, 27 Feb. (os) 1728, BL. Add. 320754; D'Aix to Victor Amadeus II, 29 Mar., 14 June 1728, AST. LM. Ing. 35; Villars, p. 128; H. J. Pretsch, *Graf Manteuffel's Beitrag zur österreichischen Geheimdiplomatie von 1728 bis 1736* (Bonn, 1970), p. 33.
25. Du Bourgay to Townshend, 9 Mar. 1728, PRO. 90/23.
26. Du Bourgay to Townshend,7, 28 Feb., 2, 6 Mar., Berkentin to –, 7 Apr., Chesterfield to Townshend, 20 June 1728, PRO. 90/23, 100/5, 84/301; Waldegrave to Du Bourgay, 26 June 1728, Chewton; Geffroy to Maurepas, 16 Mar.1728, AN. AM. B7 294; *Craftsman* 17 Feb. (os), *Original Mercury* 12 Mar. (os) 1728.
27. Du Bourgay to Townshend, 24 Jan. 1728, PRO. 90/23.
28. Townshend to Du Bourgay, 30 Jan. (os) 1728, PRO. 90/23.
29. Townshend to Diemar, 14 Mar. 1728, Marburg, England 195.
30. [Delafaye or Newcastle] to Horatio Walpole, 3 Oct., 2 Nov. 1727, PRO. 78/187; Newcastle to Horatio Walpole, 25 Dec. (os) 1727, BL. Add. 32753.
31. Du Bourgay to Townshend, 15 Jan. 1728, PRO. 90/23.
32. Private Instructions for Horatio Walpole, 10 Mar. (os), Newcastle to Horatio, 13 June (os) 1728, BL. Add. 48982, 32765.
33. Newcastle to Waldegrave, 27 Feb. (os), Newcastle to Horatio Walpole, 16 Apr. (os), 13 June (os) 1728, George to Townshend, no date, BL. Add. 32754–6, 38507 f.232; Townshend to Chesterfield, 14 May (os), Townshend to Diescau 31 May (os), Townshend to Diemar, 5 July (os) 1728, PRO. 84/300, 95/50, 100/15; Newcastle to Horatio Walpole, – Mar. (os) 1728, PRO. 78/189 f.93.
34. Newcastle to Plenipotentiaries, 14 June (os) 1728, BL. Add. 32756.
35. O'Rourke to James III, 24 Jan., 28 Feb. 1728, HHStA., England, Varia 8; Horatio Walpole to Newcastle, 20, 23 Mar. 1728, BL. Add. 32754.
36. Waldegrave to Townshend, 11 Jan. 1728, Chewton; Newcastle to Horatio Walpole, – Dec. (os) 1727, PRO. 78/187 f.179; Chambrier, Prussian envoy in Paris, to Frederick William, 12 Mar. 1728, AE. CP. Prusse 88.
37. Ferdinand Albrecht to Ludwig Rudolf of Brunswick-Wolfenbüttel, 6, 10 Mar. 1728, Wolfenbüttel, 1 Alt. 22, Nr. 529; Solaro di Breglio to Victor Amadeus II, 25 Feb. 1728, AST. LM. Aut. 58; Newsletter, 30 Mar. 1728, Osnabrück, 295; Chambrier to Frederick William, 5 Apr. 1728, AE. CP. Prusse 88.
38. Newcastle to Waldegrave, 7 Mar. 1728, Chewton; O'Rourke to James III, 8 May, 17 June 1728, HHStA., England, Varia 8; Tarouca to Townshend, 14 May 1728, PRO. 80/326; Wackerbarth, Saxon envoy in Vienna, to Manteuffel, 19 May 1728, Dresden 3331.
39. Waldegrave to Townshend, 7 May 1728, PRO. 80/62; Waldegrave Journal, 17 May

1728; Solaro di Breglio to Victor Amadeus II, 12 July 1728, AST. LM. Aut. 58.

40. Chauvelin to Chammorel, 8 July 1728, AE. CP. Ang. sup.8; Zamboni to Manteuffel, 21 May 1728, Bodl. Rawl. 120.

41. Instructions for Le Coq and Hoym, 24, 30 June 1728, Dresden 2733.

42. Le Coq to Augustus, 28 July, 11 Aug. 1728, Dresden 2733; Marini, p.109; D'Aix to Victor Amadeus II, 21 Apr. 1728, AST. LM. Ing. 35.

43. Le Coq to Augustus, 28 July 1728, Dresden 2733.

44. Le Coq to Augustus, 28 July, 11 Aug., 18 Sept. 1728, Dresden 2733.

45. Le Coq to Augustus, 28 July 1728, Dresden 2733; Horatio Walpole and Stanhope to Newcastle, 20 July 1728, BL. Add. 32757; *Wye's Letter* 14 May (os) 1728.

46. Copy of decree, PRO. 100/15; Chesterfield to Townshend, 8 June 1728, PRO. 84/300; Marini, p.110; Goslinga, p.242; Dureng, pp.67–72; Hughes, pp.380–1; Naumann, *Österreich, England und das Reich*, p.140.

47. Townshend to Chesterfield, 31 May (os) 1728, PRO. 84/300.

48. Townshend to Horatio Walpole, 16 May (os), 15 July (os) 1728, Bradfer Lawrence; Tilson to Waldegrave, 23 July (os) 1728, Chewton; Townshend to Diemar, 5 July (os) 1728, PRO. 100/15; Newcastle to Plenipotentiaries, 26 July (os) 1728, BL. Add. 32757.

49. Townshend to Horatio Walpole, 31 July (os) 1728, Bradfer Lawrence; Townshend to Horatio, 15 Sept. (os) 1728, BL. Add. 32758. The 'project' referred to was the proposal for the Provisional Treaty. Austrian support for the claims of the Duke of Holstein-Gottorp led to George's concern over Sleswig.

50. Waldegrave to Townshend, undated, Chewton; Horatio to Townshend, 1 July, Townshend to Horatio Walpole, 16 May (os), 3 June (os) 1728, Bradfer Lawrence.

51. [Newcastle] to Horatio Walpole, 21 May (os) 1728, PRO. 78/189.

52. Berkentin to –, 17 Mar. 1728, Newcastle to Plenipotentiaries, 13 June (os) 1728, PRO. 80/326, 78/189.

53. Newcastle to Plenipotentiaries, 27 June (os) 1728, PRO. 78/189.

CHAPTER FIVE

The Congress of Soissons

'No one can be more eager than myself to get out of this negotiation by
the shortest way possible, provided it be good and safe'.
Townshend to Horatio Walpole July 4 1728.[1]

The talks which began at Soissons in mid-June 1728 soon revealed the
incompatible interests of the participating powers, and posed a major
question as to the value of the Congress system. The views of Spain and
Britain were irreconcilable.[2] Spain demanded the restitution of Gibraltar
and an end to illegal British commercial activities in the Indies.[3] Britain
demanded that Spain should renounce all claims to Gibraltar and Port
Mahon and recompense British merchants for the effects of Spanish
depredations. Such a difference had been predicted, and it had been
anticipated in the British press.[4] The British ministry had been aware that
Spain would make such demands,[5] and they had been informed that,
despite the approaching Congress, Spain was preparing for war.[6] There
was a difference of opinion within the British ministry as to how to respond
to the Spanish demands. Officially the British government trusted in the
continued unity of the Alliance of Hanover. Townshend had informed
Chesterfield in May, 'it must be expected that Court [Spain] will be always
giving jealousys, and neither think nor act right, till they see by the strict
union between England, France, and Holland, that their artifices are of no
use, and that they must submit to such a peace as the Allys shall jointly
judge necessary for the quiet of Europe.'[7]

The British hoped that France would repeat her performance of the
previous winter, and support Britain in her demands upon Spain.[8] They
hoped a bait could be offered to Spain by France and Britain in the form of
support for Spanish pretensions in Italy and possible compliance in
Spanish marital schemes. This cosy view was shaken by anxieties over
Fleury's response to Sinzendorf's approaches.[9] Fleury pressed the Dutch
ministry to find a compromise over Gibraltar and the commercial differences,[10] the French and the Dutch ministries made clear their dissatisfaction
with the British possession of the *asiento*[11], and rumours of agreements
which would compromise the British position circulated, including reports
that the fortifications of Gibraltar would be razed, or that Gibraltar and
Minorca would be exchanged for an equivalent in the Spanish Indies.[12]
Should France and Austria reach an agreement they might seek to assuage
Spanish resentment by supporting her claims against Britain.[13] Both
Fleury and Slingelandt believed that Britain ought to return Gibraltar,[14] a
view which found support within the British ministry. Alongside the

attitude that Britain's allies were obliged to support fully her claims against Spain was the view that Britain should seek to win over Spain by the return of Gibraltar. Poyntz, one of the British Plenipotentiaries, suggested that if Britain succeeded in retaining Gibraltar at the Congress, the Spaniards would hope to persuade Britain to return it by continuing to oppress British commerce. He believed, in common with most commentators, that however much the Queen of Spain might be determined to succeed in Italy and to gain an archduchess for one of her sons, the King and 'the true Spaniards' were much more interested in Gibraltar. Poyntz therefore suggested that provided some face-saving equivalent could be found, Gibraltar should be restored.[15]

Such a project was to be suggested on several occasions in the late 1720s but discussion of it was quashed in 1728 on the grounds that it would be fatal in domestic political terms. The retention of Gibraltar had been a reiterated theme in the addresses presented to George II on his accession,[16] and in 1728 the opposition press, probably scenting governmental vulnerability, stressed the importance of 'that invaluable fortress.'[17] Townshend, who himself believed that it should be restored, rejected Slingelandt's and Poyntz's suggestions of a restoration, arguing that they would 'put the whole nation in a flame.'[18] Correct as this assumption was, it restricted Britain's freedom of diplomatic manoeuvre. Unable to settle with Spain directly, the British were obliged to rely on France or Austria being willing to bully her into compliance. Developments in the Congress made this increasingly unlikely.

In an effort to divide France from Spain, Sinzendorf secretly sounded Fleury on the possibility of an Austro-Spanish marriage and on Spain's Italian pretensions. Sinzendorf hoped to trap France into agreeing to the marriage, thereby angering the German princes and undermining the Anglo-French attempts to develop a party on the Empire, or refusing and thereby alienating Elisabeth Farnese. Fleury declared his approval of the marriage without consulting the British, but refused to commit himself to paper. Furious with Fleury, Poyntz wrote to Townshend, 'I had nothing before my eyes for 2 or 3 days together, but the Emperor, France and Spain united for the present; Princes of the House of Bourbon fixed on the 3 most powerful thrones of Europe for ages to come.'[19] George was 'strongly . . . inclined to have the marriage brought before the Congress,' but Fleury, fearing that it would draw the Congress out, refused and George gave way.[20] Stanhope argued that the best way to please Spain and persuade her to drop her pretensions to Gibraltar was to agree to the marriage, a view also advanced by Sinzendorf, but Stanhope accepted that it would be difficult to make such an arrangement.[21]

When these matters were being discussed, a new issue came increasingly to dominate the deliberations at the Congress and to excite public interest. This was the proposal, variously attributed to Sinzendorf and to Fleury, for a Provisional Treaty.[22] As first drafted by Sinzendorf, this treaty proposed that the Ostend Company should be abolished, peace be established on the basis of the Preliminaries, and all the other outstanding differences referred to special commissioners appointed by the parties concerned. It was described in 1743 by the opposition writer James Ralph as 'little more than the Preliminaries new modelled, and digested into the form of a treaty, without any specific explanation of those points which most immediately affected the interests of Great Britain.'[23] Fleury, although he would have preferred a definitive treaty, agreed to the new proposal. He told the British Plenipotentiaries that a delay would give Philip V time to abdicate or die, and Spain would then become more reasonable. Fleury believed the Provisional Treaty was necessary because of the obstinacy of Britain and Spain over Gibraltar and commercial issues.[24] The British response was far less favourable. On 7 July the Cabinet met, and its minutes noted 'The King certainly wishes to conclude things, but is doubtful how that can be done by a Provisional Treaty'.[25] George was opposed to a Provisional Treaty, because he believed it would give France an opportunity to act as the arbiter of Europe whilst Britain was trapped in a diplomatic impasse, her pretensions endlessly debated by commissioners.[26] He believed Fleury to be unduly pliant and urged the French to be firmer in the defence of their allies.[27] George told Broglie he expected France to support his pretensions, and that he was ready for war.[28] The Dutch approved the British attempt 'to excite the Cardinal to act with more spirit and vigour'.[29]

However, George's views were not shared by all his ministers. Stanhope and Horatio Walpole supported the idea of a Provisional Treaty.[30] On 26 July Townshend informed Horatio Walpole:

> the king was so much set at first against hearing of the marriage and the Provisional Treaty . . . all that could be done was to withhold H.M. from putting an absolute refusal upon them . . . this matter has been softened little by little.[31]

There are signs that Townshend and George were not working well together. Tilson informed Horatio Walpole in August that George was still altering diplomatic instructions and maintaining his opposition to the Provisional Treaty.[32] In July D'Aix reported that Townshend and St. Saphorin were still bitter enemies, that the Queen was in close touch with St. Saphorin and that Townshend was very worried by D'Aix's contacts with the King.[33] St. Saphorin told D'Aix that George was willing to embrace the first opportunity to drive the Emperor out of Italy.[34] An anonymous writer informed Horatio Walpole that his conduct was being bitterly criticised by St. Saphorin.[35]

It is possible that in order to retain Sardinian interest in an alliance with Britain and to prevent her from settling with Austria, George and St. Saphorin exaggerated their willingness to oppose Austria. Their comments to D'Aix do not correspond to the approaches made earlier in the year to Le Coq. However, Austria's provocative actions in the Empire could well account for the discrepancy. D'Aix's dispatches suggest that George was pushing his schemes for a German league with renewed vigour. On 20 July he reported that George 'a fort goûté le projet de se faire un partie en Allemagne'.[36] George pressed for the accession of Hesse-Cassel to the

Württemberg-Wolfenbüttel treaty, and the accessions of Denmark and Sweden in their capacities as Princes of the Empire, and of Würzburg, were discussed.[37] Worried about the apparent concert of Prussia, Austria, Russia and Saxony,[38] and about the possibility of Denmark joining this group,[39] George pressed for Imperial matters to be discussed at the Congress and for the German princes to be permitted to send representatives. In April 1728 Newcastle had written 'it may be very convenient that the Princes of the Empire should know, that upon a proper occasion,' they might be able to depend on Britain and France.[40] The issue of German representation was closely related to the assistance Hanover could expect, and the British accused Fleury of failing to support her interests.[41] George feared the Provisional Treaty would allow Fleury to abandon his support of the German princes and of Hanoverian interests.[42] George's concern was apparent to many. According to Zamboni he blocked a ministerial proposal to reduce the size of the army,[43] and D'Aix reported in August that George was very worried and had declared he would prefer war to the continuation of the current state of diplomatic delay.[44]

Given George's attitude it is necessary to explain why Sinzendorf's proposal was accepted. Early in August 1728 discussions between the Plenipotentiaries of the Hanover allies produced an expanded version of Sinzendorf's document, and in mid-August a draft Provisional Treaty was formally communicated to all the powers at the Congress. The British attitude changed to a grudging acceptance of the need for a Provisional Treaty.[45] On 13 August Townshend informed Chesterfield that George wanted 'a general and definitive pacification' but had been forced to change his mind by Fleury.[46] The change followed close upon the departure of St. Saphorin. He had sought leave to retire on health grounds, claiming that the London air was very bad for him, and he embarked at Dover on 16 July. St. Saphorin was given a very generous pension, but he failed to gain the Vienna embassy and was sent back to Switzerland, without being permitted to stop off at Soissons.[47] His departure might be seen as a victory for Townshend,[48] but D'Aix had written of the latter in May that he seemed to have decided to conform to the wishes of George II and Queen Caroline, who were determined to have their way.[49]

Townshend, whose health still gave cause for concern,[50] seems to have been somewhat milder and more co-operative with George in 1728 than in the previous year. With neither Secretary of State at the Congress, Britain was not represented at the level of France and Austria. In May Delafaye had informed Horatio Walpole that George approved of Townshend's corresponding with him without Newcastle's knowledge.[51] Townshend complained of 'the dificulties that arise often with the D. of Newcastle upon forming the draughts of orders'.[52] Newcastle in his turn had a confidential corresponence with Stanhope,[53] who blamed Sir Robert Walpole for his failure to get a peerage and for his brother's blocked promotion.[54] Horatio Walpole suspected, correctly, that there was a confidential correspondence between Poyntz and Townshend.[55] Despite Poyntz's claim that the British Plenipotentiaries were united,[56] the opposite appears to have been the case. It is difficult to disentangle the secret ties of the period. The few scraps of surviving evidence might suggest that the St. Saphorin-Stanhope link, responsible for executing George's German policy earlier in the year, had been broken by St. Saphorin's departure and by the absence of a confidential correspondence between Stanhope and George. Stanhope made it clear to Le Coq that he feared he had lost royal favour. Though Newcastle assured Stanhope that he still enjoyed 'the entire confidence' of the king, Stanhope was greatly disappointed by his failure to get a peerage.[57]

The evidence suggests George had transferred his confidence, at least in part, from St. Saphorin and Stanhope to Townshend.[58] Within his own department Townshend's authority increased. He developed a good working relationship with Chesterfield at The Hague. He was on very good terms with Edward Finch, sent to Stockholm in 1728, Richard Sutton the envoy to Hesse-Cassel, and Waldegrave. Postings which might have created difficulties, such as St. Saphorin to Vienna and Fabrice to Dresden, were not made. Townshend's confidential correspondence with Horatio Walpole and Poyntz gave him more influence over the Soissons negotiations than that possessed by Newcastle. George's anger with Austria over the Mecklenburg question, by shelving his interest in an Anglo-Austrian reconciliation brought his views more into line with those of Townshend, though D'Aix's evidence would suggest that the process was mutual. George agreed to support the Provisional Treaty, and thereby save the Anglo-French alliance from serious trouble, whilst Townshend cooperated with George's German schemes. It was the need to retain the French alliance which was probably the most persuasive reason from George's point of view. Prussian pressure to move troops into Mecklenburg[59] and heightened concern over the Jülich-Berg issue made the German situation more serious. The illness of the Elector Palatine made conflict over Jülich-Berg appear imminent.[60] Renewed difficulties in East Friesland over the conduct of the Imperial commissioners sent into the Duchy by the Aulic Council increased tension with Austria.[61]

Given this situation it was not surprising that the British clung to the French alliance and sought to persuade Fleury and the Dutch to adopt a more forceful approach to German problems. The price of French support was British compliance with the draft Provisional Treaty. This draft confirmed the major international agreements from the Treaty of Utrecht to the Convention of the Pardo and agreed that special commissioners were to be appointed to deal with such outstanding problems as Spanish depredations and British contraband trade in Spanish America.[62]

The widely held view that Austria was able to dictate Spanish policy[63] was disproved by Spain's response to the project, described by Tilson as 'a medley of Spanish phrases, neither refusing nor accepting positively; but shuffling as usual, in a wayward manner'. Spanish policy had been plunged even more than usual into chaos in the summer by Philip V's ill health and his attempt to abdicate once more. The situation in Spain was believed to be chaotic. Townshend wrote in June that 'affairs at Madrid are at present in the utmost confusion, so that no judgment can be made as yet what course things will take.'[64] Elisabeth Farnese had succeeded however in preventing the attempted abdication and had taken advantage of her husband's weakness to consolidate her control of Spanish policy. She disapproved of the projected treaty, because it failed to safeguard Carlos's Italian pretensions and brought a Habsburg marriage no nearer.[65] Negotiations continued at Paris in an effort to produce a more acceptable project, and a new article was agreed in which Britain and France confirmed their undertaking of 1721 to assist in the establishment of Don Carlos in Italy and accepted the need to introduce Spanish garrisons.[66] One of the Spanish Plenipotentiaries, Bournonville, left for Spain in October with the new project. It was hoped that Spanish agreement would permit the signing of the Provisional Treaty, a move which would allow the British government to assure Parliament that peace was secure.

The Hanoverian Dimension

The Congress had not developed, therefore, as the British had hoped. Though Fleury had not abandoned his allies, as had indeed been feared, his willingness to negotiate in secret had kept the British Plenipotentiaries in the dark for much of the time, and had enhanced Fleury's position as the arbiter of Europe. Slingelandt had predicted in April 1728 that Fleury would be the de facto mediator of the Congress, a development George II was opposed to. The *Craftsman* referred to 'the extraordinary deference paid to Cardinal Fleury.'[67] The Congress sessions at Soissons had soon ceased to be of any significance, with important matters being handled privately in Paris.[68] The opposition press in Britain criticised the Congress and claimed that it was devoted to pleasure. Eleven years later the *Craftsman* wrote of the Plenipotentiaries, 'They took their seats, complimented one another, spent several months in diversions, and at last broke up, without adjusting any one material point in dispute.'[69] The British had been unhappy about this development, but they were forced to accept it. Their wish to raise the marriage at the Congress had been thwarted, as had their attempt to turn the Congress into a platform for challenging Imperial authority. Initial hostility to the Provisional Treaty had been replaced by support for it. In September Townshend informed Chesterfield that,

> there is more of name and sound, than of substance and reality between a definite treaty, and a provisional and suspensive one, as now proposed; By the present project all our engagements are answered, our former treaties are renewed, and things brought back to the foot they were before the making the dangerous Treatys of Vienna . . . as Treatys commonly last, and are interpreted according to times and circumstances, nothing could be so decided, as to expect a longer duration than this intended treaty provides for.[70]

This sober reflection was doubtless true, but it represented a different attitude to the more blustering and self-confident tone that had characterised British diplomacy the previous winter and spring.[71] It was the deterioration in the German situation and the smaller range of British diplomatic manoeuvre which accounted for this change. The bold talk of reconciliation with Austria, Prussia, Saxony and Russia had been replaced by fears about the intentions of these powers, fears sharpened by the suspicion that Denmark was about to join them.[72] The schemes for an alliance of German princes had met less success than anticipated. Saxony had preferred to retain its links with Austria and Prussia. Chesterfield's approach to the Wittelsbach envoy Gansinot had been met with caution. The Bavarians did not wish to anger their powerful Austrian neighbours.[73] The Hessians were not too enthusiastic about angering Austria or fighting Prussia, however much they welcomed British subsidies. There were also doubts about the reliability of Brunswick-Wolfenbüttel[74] and fear of trouble in East Friesland. As George realised, the German princes needed to have their resolve stiffened by Anglo-French assistance, for it was these princes who would be the first to suffer Austrian attack.[75] Without France, Britain did not seem strong enough to tempt German support, and Fleury's talks with Sinzendorf, talks which were as well known as their contents were mysterious, suggested to many that Britain could not count on French support. In July 1728 Newcastle instructed the Plenipotentiaries to press Fleury to stand firm over the Mecklenburg, East Friesland and Holstein-Gottorp issues, 'especially since the Treaty which the Cardinal is informed has been lately concluded between the Emperor the Kings of Prussia and Poland and the Czar will make His Imperial Majesty so powerful particularly in the north, that no care ought to be wanting to guard against the ill consequences of it.'[76]

The representative of the Duke of Mecklenburg at The Hague, Sande, suggested to Chesterfield 'that he thought the king's Hanover dominions were so much concerned in the fate of Mecklenburg that they might almost give the law to his Majesty upon this occasion'. Although Chesterfield rejected this suggestion and Townshend corroborated his rejection,[77] it is indeed possible that the key to British policy should be sought in the myriad complexities of German politics and, in particular, in the need to protect Hanover. The Hanoverians in the German Chancery in London enjoyed little power and the few contemporaries who considered their role gave it little prominence. No Hanoverian in the late 1720s wielded the influence that Bernstorff and Bothmer had enjoyed in their heyday. Though Bothmer survived until 1732 he lacked influence with George II. Fabrice had returned to Hanover. The principal officials of the German Chancery in London, Jobst and Andreas von der Reiche and Johann Philipp von Hattorf, were credited with little power, and they represented less of a challenge to the British ministers than Schaub and St. Saphorin, though Hattorf was to play a major role in the unsuccessful attempt to bring Britain into the Polish Succesion War. When the Hanoverian diplomat Reck was sent to the Congress, Townshend ordered the British Plenipotentiaries to tell him nothing about the negotiations for a Wittelsbach alliance, and he wrote, 'he has no powers nor anything to do at the Congress, and was sent by the King with no other view but to inform and assist your Ex. cies in the affairs of the Empire'. Horatio Walpole also urged that the negotiations with the Wittelsbachs be kept a secret from the Hanoverians.[78] In 1729 D'Aix reported from Hanover that the Hanoverian ministers were denied information about negotiations. Chavigny noted opposition by some of the Hanoverian ministers to Townshend's negotiations with the Wittelsbachs, and George's support for Townshend. Count Watsdorf, appointed Saxon envoy in London in 1730, was ordered to attach himself to the British ministers, and informed that they had the direction in all matters , including even those involving Hanoverian interests, whilst the Electoral ministers were excluded from any role.[79]

Nevertheless, despite the weakness of the Hanoverian representatives in London, there is no doubt that George was very concerned about the defence of his Electorate. Under his father the Electorate had been greatly strengthened by territorial consolidation and expansion. In particular, the acquisitions of Lauenburg, Bremen and Verden had represented a considerable expansion towards the north and had given the Electorate a coastline. There is little evidence in the late 1720s that George II intended to continue his father's expansionism, although contemporaries were unsure about his intentions in Mecklenburg and the schemes he entertained in the 1740s suggest that he was not averse to the idea of territorial expansion. In 1737 it was reported that George was to purchase Wismar.[80] He was certainly determined that his father's acquisitions should not be lost. This accounted for his opposition to the restoration of the Duke of Holstein-Gottorp, because he feared this would endanger his hold upon Bremen and Verden, leading to Danish claims that they should serve as territorial compensation, or claims from the Duke of Holstein-Gottorp that he should enjoy the duchies as heir to their late possessor the crown of Sweden.

George's attempt to develop a party within the Empire was clearly linked to his interest in the defence of Hanover, but it is necessary to consider whether this represented a distortion of British policy, insofar as there could be one without the King. The defence of Hanover dictated a choice of alliance between Austria and France. Although the idea of a Protestant league of Prussia, Britain, Sweden, Denmark, the United Provinces and Hesse-Cassel was to be advanced in the mid 1730s, it was not feasible in the late 1720s, due to the ties between Prussia and Austria and the poor relations between George II and Frederick William. George considered both an Austrian and a French alliance in 1728. He would have agreed with the *London Journal*[81] in its claim that 'the balance of Europe has generally been agreed to be an equality of power in the hands of the Emperor and France' and that it was essential for the balance that the two powers did not become partners. Insofar as there were definable 'British' interests at stake in 1728 it is clear both France and Austria were willing to accept the British point of view on most of them. This was not surprising as most of the issues – Gibraltar, Minorca and depredations upon commerce – involved Spain. Both powers were unenthusiastic about British commercial pre-eminence, but were willing to surrender their own commercial schemes. Sinzendorf agreed at Soissons to suppress the Ostend Company, whilst in the summer of 1728 profuse French assurances quietened British fears about French intentions at Dunkirk. Neither France nor Austria cared deeply about the points at issue between Britain and Spain, though both found it useful to see the two powers divided, and neither wished to risk their own relations with Spain by supporting Britain fully.

It could be argued that Britain should have made more of an effort to satisfy Austria in 1728. Waldegrave could certainly have carried more conciliatory instructions, but there was more to the continuation of Anglo-Austrian differences than George's concern for Hanoverian interests and his anger over the Mecklenburg issue. In the months before the Congress, Austria was far from responsive to the idea of a British approach. Sinzendorf was more hopeful, correctly as it turned out, of an approach to Fleury, whilst Prince Eugene was more interested in the friendship of Russia, Prussia and Saxony. An enthusiastic response to Waldegrave would have angered Frederick William. The lack of Austrian interest was shown by their delay in sending an envoy to Britain. They insisted that Waldegrave should arrive in Vienna before they named their envoy, but their choice – Count Philip Kinsky – was a light-weight, only 24 when appointed, and he did not reach London until September 1728.[82] Eugene blamed George II for the bad relations between Britain and Austria, but the Austrians made little effort to remedy this situation at Soissons. Though the British Plenipotentiaries made several approaches to Sinzendorf, the response was poor, and Newcastle complained that Sinzendorf's statements to Stanhope were dark and unclear. The approach via the Saxons was discarded because, as Stanhope told Le Coq, George did not wish to upset his allies and the draft of the Provisional Treaty had caused George to change his mind about a personal approach to the Austrians.[83] Stanhope could have added distrust of the Saxons and anger with Austria, but the reasons he gave were sufficient. Britain's abandonment of her approach to Austria in 1728 was not simply due to Hanoverian interests but reflected the need, when faced with Austrian lack of interest, to rely on the French. Had Britain abandoned the latter also she would have been isolated, unable to hope for help in her disputes with Spain and lacking influence in the diplomatic deliberations at Paris.

The anger Broglie and D'Aix noted in George is understandable. By the autumn of 1728 his diplomatic strategy had been revealed as a failure. Fleury had ignored Britain's opinion on most matters. George had no illusions about the amount of support he could expect from France.[84] The Austrians had neither been intimidated by George's alliances nor responsive to his suggestion of a reconciliation. The King had been forced to accept the idea of a Provisional Treaty, not so much because of ministerial pressure but rather because of diplomatic developments. Despite hopes to the contrary the Austro-Spanish alliance had persisted, whilst Fleury and Sinzendorf had developed a good working relationship which threatened to develop into a broader arrangement. The opposition press warned that this was a possibility. It is unclear whether Fleury had any intention of creating an alliance with Austria. In 1734 the Austrians were to claim that Fleury had sought at Soissons to unite France, Spain and Austria.[85] It is possible Sinzendorf believed this to be Fleury's intention, but there is no evidence that he did intend to abandon Britain. Despite this the autumn of 1728 was to witness growing strains in the Anglo-French alliance.

Notes

1. Townshend to Horatio Walpole, 23 June (os) 1728, BL. Add. 9138.
2. Baudrillart, III, 430–1; Goslinga, pp. 252, 256.
3. Tilson to Waldegrave, 25 June (os) 1728, Chewton; Newcastle to the Plenipotentiaries, 13 June (os) 1728, PRO. 78/189.
4. *Wye's Letter* 24 Apr. (os), *Craftsman* 27 July (os) 1728.
5. Horatio Walpole to Newcastle, 20 Mar. 1728, BL. Add. 32754; Waldegrave to Townshend, 3 July 1728, PRO. 80/61.
6. Chesterfield to Townshend, 21 May 1728, PRO. 84/300.
7. Townshend to Chesterfield, 14 May (os) 1728, PRO. 84/300.
8. Marini, p. 111.
9. Chesterfield to Townshend, 3 Aug. 1728, PRO. 84/301; Marini, p. 105.
10. Chesterfield to Townshend, 20 July 1728, PRO. 84/301.
11. Horatio Walpole to Townshend, 24 July 1728, Bradfer Lawrence; Plenipotentiaries to Newcastle, 10 Aug. 1728, BL. Add. 32757.
12. Daniel to Tilson, 2, 24 Mar. 1728, PRO. 77/75.
13. Chauvelin to Chammorel, 29 July 1728, AE. CP. Ang. sup. 8; Le Coq to Augustus II, 11 Aug., 18 Sept. 1728, Dresden 2733.
14. Horatio Walpole and Stanhope to Newcastle, 20 July 1728, BL. Add. 32757; Chesterfield to Townshend, 3 Aug. 1728, PRO. 84/301; Chauvelin to Broglie, 24 June 1728, AE. CP. Ang. 362; Marini, p. 116; Goslinga, pp. 258–9, 261–2, 265–8.
15. Poyntz to Townshend, 9 June 1728, Coxe, II, 628–9.
16. Boyer, XXXIV, 39–40.
17. *Craftsman* 10 Feb. (os), 9, 16 Mar. (os), 4 May (os) 1728.
18. Townshend to Poyntz, 3 June (os) 1728, BL. Add. 48982; Townshend to Chesterfield, 9 July (os), Townshend to Slingelandt, 23 July (os) 1728, PRO. 84/301, 580; Chammorel to Chauvelin, 22 July 1728, AE. CP. Ang. 363; Goslinga, pp. 265–6.
19. Horatio Walpole to Townshend, 20 June 1728, Waldegrave to Newcastle, 24 Jan. 1732, BL. Add. 9138, 32766; Poyntz to Chesterfield, 13 July 1728, Robinson to Harrington, 28 Mar. 1731, PRO. 84/301, 80/73; Bussy, French Chargé d'affaires in Vienna, to Chauvelin, 6. Jan. 1730, AE. CP. Autriche 165; Poyntz to Townshend, 19 June 1728, Bradfer Lawrence.
20. Townshend to Chesterfield, 25 June (os), 2, 26 July (os), 2, 13 Aug. (os), Poyntz to Chesterfield, 13 July 1728, PRO. 84/300–1; Newcastle to the Plenipotentiaries, 26 July (os) 1728, BL. Add. 32757.
21. Stanhope to Newcastle, 14 July 1728, BL. Add. 32757; Townshend to Chesterfield, 9 July (os) 1728, PRO. 84/301.
22. Poyntz to Chesterfield, 13 July 1728, PRO. 84/301.
23. Ralph, *A Critical History of the Administration of Sir Robert Walpole* (1743) pp. 419–20; Huisman, p. 41; Goslinga, pp. 252–3.
24. Horatio Walpole to Newcastle, 9 July, Horatio Walpole and Stanhope to Newcastle, 13, 28 July 1728, BL. Add. 32756–7; Poyntz to Chesterfield, 13 July, Chesterfield to Townshend, 20 July 1728, PRO. 84/301; Goslinga, p. 253; Wilson, p. 202.
25. Cabinet Minutes, 26 June (os) 1728, PRO. 36/7.
26. Townshend to Horatio Walpole, 23 June (os) 1728, Bradfer Lawrence; Townshend to Chesterfield, 25 June (os), 2, 26 July (os), 2 Aug. (os) 1728, PRO. 84/300–1; Goslinga, pp. 257–8.
27. Newcastle to the Plenipotentiaries, 15 July (os), Chesterfield to Townshend, 27 July 1728, PRO. 80/326, 84/301.
28. Broglie to Chauvelin, 16 Aug. 1728, AE. CP. Ang. 363; George II to Townshend, no date, commenting on Townshend to Slingelandt, 12 July (os) 1728, BL. Add. 38507 f.244.

29. Chesterfield to Townshend, 27 July 1728, PRO. 84/301.
30. Stanhope to Newcastle, 30 July 1728, BL. Add. 32757.
31. Townshend to Horatio Walpole, 15 July (os) 1728, Bradfer Lawrence.
32. Tilson to Horatio Walpole, 26 July (os) 1728, Bradfer Lawrence.
33. D'Aix to Victor Amadeus II, 4, 11, 20 July 1728, AST. LM. Ing. 36.
34. D'Aix to Victor Amadeus II, 11 July 1728, AST. LM. Ing. 35.
35. 'J. D.' to Horatio Walpole, 18 July (os) 1728, Bradfer Lawrence.
36. D'Aix to Victor Amadeus II, 20 July 1728, AST. LM. Ing. 36; Chesterfield to Townshend, 1 June, Newcastle to the Plenipotentiaries, 3 June (os) 1728, PRO. 84/300, 78/189.
37. William Chetwynd junior, secretary to Sutton, to Sutton, 28 June, 8 July 1728, PRO 81/122; Newcastle to Horatio Walpole, 13 June (os) 1728, BL. Add. 32756; Chavigny to Chauvelin, 3 Aug. 1728, AE. CP. Allemagne 374.
38. Chesterfield to Townshend, 1 June, Newcastle to the Plenipotentiaries, 3 June (os) 1728, PRO. 84/300, 78/189.
39. Townshend to Glenorchy, envoy in Copenhagen, 2 July (os), Chesterfield to Townshend, 13 July 1728, PRO 75/51, 84/301.
40. Newcastle to Horatio Walpole, 16 Apr. (os), 13 June (os) 1728, BL. Add. 32755–6; Chetwynd to Sutton, 28 June, 8 July 1728, PRO. 81/122; Chavigny to Chauvelin, 3 Aug. 1728, AE. CP. Allemagne 374.
41. Townshend to Chesterfield, 2 July (os) 1728, PRO. 84/301; Newcastle to the Plenipotentiaries, 15 July (os) 1728, BL. Add. 32757.
42. Newcastle to Horatio Walpole, 29 Mar. (os), Townshend to Horatio Walpole, 15 Sept. 1728, BL. Add. 32755, 32758; Newcastle to Horatio Walpole, 21 May (os), Townshend to the Plenipotentiaries, 12 Sept., Townshend to Chesterfield, 6, 13 Aug. (os) 1728, PRO. 78/189, 84/301.
43. Zamboni to Manteuffel, 17 Aug. 1728, Bodl. Rawl. 120.
44. D'Aix to Victor Amadeus II, 23 Aug. 1728, AST. LM. Ing. 35; George II to Townshend, 3, – , July (os) 1728, BL. Add. 38507 f.242, 244.
45. Townshend to Chesterfield, 13, 20 Aug. (os) 1728, PRO. 84/301.
46. Townshend to Chesterfield, 2 Aug. (os) 1728, PRO. 84/301.
47. St. Saphorin to Townshend, 20 May (os) 1728, PRO. 80/61; D'Aix to Victor Amadeus II, 12 June 1728, AST. LM. Ing. 35; 'J. D.' to Horatio Walpole, 18 July (os) 1728, Bradfer Lawrence; Le Coq to Augustus II, 11 Aug. 1728, Dresden, 2733.
48. D'Aix to Victor Amadeus II, 19 July 1728, AST. LM. Ing. 35.
49. D'Aix to Victor Amadeus II, 17 May 1728, AST. LM. Ing. 35; Marini, p. 108.
50. Sutton to Townshend, 19 Aug. 1728, PRO. 81/122; Wye's Letter 7, 10 Sept.(os) 1728; Chammorel to Chauvelin, 27 Sept. 1728, AE. CP. Ang. 363.
51. Delafaye to Horatio Walpole, 14 May (os) 1728, Coxe, II, 623; Townshend to George II, no date, – July (os) 1728, [Tilson] to Horatio Walpole, 12 Oct. (os) 1727, BL. Add. 38507, 48982; Townshend to Horatio Walpole, 21 Aug. (os) 1727, 29 Oct. (os) 1728, BL. Add. 48982, Bradfer Lawrence.
52. Townshend to Horatio Walpole, 10 Oct. (os) 1728, BL. Add. 9138.
53. Newcastle to Stanhope, 14 May (os), 3 June (os) 1728, Coxe, II, 623–4, 629.
54. Stanhope to Newcastle, 8 June 1728, Coxe, II, 626–7; Poyntz to Townshend, 9 June, Townshend to Poyntz, 3 June (os) 1728, BL. Add. 48982.
55. Horatio Walpole to Townshend, 20 June 1728, BL. Add. 9138.
56. Poyntz to Delafaye, 19 May, 2 July 1728, PRO. 78/188; Stanhope and Horatio Walpole to Newcastle, 28 July 1728, BL. Add. 32757.
57. Newcastle to Stanhope, 3 June (os), Stanhope to Newcastle, 8 June 1728, Coxe, II, 629, 626–7.
58. Marini, pp. 112–13.
59. Townshend to Horatio Walpole, 18 July (os) 1728, Bradfer Lawrence; Chesterfield to Townshend, 17 Aug. 1728, PRO. 84/301.
60. Horatio Walpole to Townshend, 28 Aug., Townshend to Horatio Walpole, 22 Aug. (os) 1728, BL. Add. 32757; Horatio Walpole to Delafaye, 28 Aug., [Newcastle] to Horatio Walpole, 22 Aug. (os), Sutton to Townshend, 2, 13 Sept., 4 Oct. 1728, PRO. 78/188–9, 81/122.
61. Chesterfield to Townshend, 13 Aug., 19 Nov. 1728, PRO. 84/301–2; Kinsky to

Eugene, 11 Nov. 1728, HHStA., GK. 94(b); Goslinga, pp. 217–18; Chesterfield to Waldegrave, 10 Sept. 1728, Chewton.

62. Chesterfield to Waldegrave, 12 Oct. 1728, Chewton; Baudrillart, III, 442; Goslinga, pp. 279–82; Wilson, p. 202.

63. Keene to Horatio Walpole, 20 Dec. 1727, BL. Add. 32753; [Newcastle] to Horatio Walpole, 21 May (os) 1728, PRO. 78/189; De Buy to Manteuffel, 9, 16 Aug., 18 Oct. 1728, Dresden, 3105; Armstrong, pp. 223–4.

64. Tilson to Waldegrave, 6 Sept. (os) 1728, Chewton; Townshend to Diescau, 21 June, Waldegrave to Townshend, 3 July 1728, PRO. 95/50, 80/61; De Buy to Manteuffel, 21, 28 June, 19, 26 July, 2 Aug. 1728, Dresden 3105; D'Aubenton to Maurepas, 8, 28 June 1728, AN. AM. B7 292; Pentenriedter to Eugene, 5 July 1728, HHStA., GK. 102(a).

65. Baudrillart, III, 444–6; Goslinga, pp. 291–2.

66. Baudrillart, III, 449–53; Goslinga, pp. 294–5.

67. 'Heads of ye Pensionary's paper', 2 Apr., Newcastle to Horatio Walpole, - Apr.(os) 1728, PRO. 103/110, 78/189 f.132; *Craftsman* 22 June (os) 1728.

68. Le Coq to Manteuffel, 16 July, Le Coq to Augustus II, 23 July 1728, Dresden 2733; Poyntz to Delafaye, 30 July, 22 Oct. 1728, PRO. 78/188; Wilson, pp. 199–200; Goslinga, p. 248.

69. *Craftsman* 24 Mar. (os) 1739.

70. Townshend to Chesterfield, 6 Sept. (os) 1728, PRO. 84/301.

71. The idea of a truce was strongly criticised by the *Craftsman* 5 Oct. (os), 16 Nov. (os), 21 Dec. (os) 1728.

72. Horatio Walpole to Newcastle, 24 Apr., 5 Nov., Horatio Walpole and Stanhope to Newcastle, 20 July 1728, BL. Add. 32755, 32759, 32757; Townshend to Glenorchy, 6 Sept. (os), Glenorchy to Townshend, 21 Sept., Sutton to Townshend, 13 Sept., Newcastle to Horatio Walpole, 26 Sept. (os), Waldegrave to Townshend, 16 Oct. 1728, PRO. 75/51, 81/12, 78/189, 80/61; Townshend to Horatio Walpole, 26 July (os) 1728, Bradfer Lawrence.

73. Törring to Plettenberg, 26 Aug., 23 Sept. 1728, Münster NA 148; Chavigny to Chauvelin, 14 Sept. 1728, AE. CP. Allemagne 374; Marini, p. 114.

74. Chavigny to Chauvelin, 31 Aug. 1728, AE. CP. Allemagne 374.

75. Newcastle to Horatio Walpole, 13 June (os), 22 Aug. (os) 1728, BL. Add. 32756, PRO 78/189; Townshend to the Plenipotentiaries, 5 Aug. (os), 12 Sept. (os) 1728, BL. Add. 32757, PRO. 78/189.

76. Newcastle to the Plenipotentiaries, 15 July (os) 1728, PRO. 80/326.

77. Chesterfield to Townshend, 6 July 1728, PRO. 84/301.

78. Townshend to the Plenipotentiaries, 12 Sept. (os), Horatio Walpole to Delafaye, 12 Sept. 1728, PRO. 78/189, 188; Anon. memoir, 31 Dec. 1728, AE. CP. Ang. 364; Foord, *His Majesty's Opposition* p. 122; Horatio to Robert Walpole, 28 May 1727, BL. Add. 63749.

79. D'Aix to Victor Amadeus II, 23 June 1729, AST. LM. Ing. 35; Chavigny to Chauvelin, 19 Sept. 1729, AE. CP. Br. 47; Augustus II to Watsdorf, 12 Oct. 1730, Dresden 2676.

80. Chavigny to Chauvelin, 19 Sept. 1729, AE. CP. Br. 47; *Dublin Newsletter* 22 Jan (os) 1737; Dureng, p. 70; Nauman, *Österreich* p.152; Hughes, pp. 368–9, 376–7.

81. *London Journal* 24 Aug. (os) 1728.

82. Waldegrave to Townshend, 28 July, Townshend to Chesterfield, 3 Dec. (os) 1728, PRO 80/61, 84/302; D'Aix to Victor Amadeus II, 20 Sept. 1728, AST. LM. Ing. 35.

83. Eugene to Kinsky, 29 Aug. 1728, HHStA., GK. 94(b); Newcastle to the Plenipotentiaries, 15 July (os) 1728, PRO. 80/326; Le Coq to Augustus II, 18 Sept. 1728, Dresden 2733.

84. Broglie to Chauvelin, 19 Dec. 1728, AE. CP. Ang. 363; D'Aix to Victor Amadeus II, 23 Aug. 1728, AST. LM. Ing. 35, Townshend to Chesterfield, 6 Sept. (os), PRO. 84/301; Newcastle to Horatio Walpole and Stanhope, 6 Nov. (os); Stanhope to Newcastle, 9 Dec. 1728, BL. Add. 32759; Tilson to Waldegrave, 8 Nov. (os) 1728, Chewton.

85. Instructions to Bishop Strickland of Namur, sent by Charles VI to London on a special mission, sent to Philip Kinsky, 14 Sept. 1734, HHStA., EK. 73.

CHAPTER SIX

Autumn 1728
Growing Strain in the Anglo-French Alliance

'You will inform him that it is the unanimous voice of our people whose interests as they are dearer to us than all the other considerations we must consult in the first place, that we have been long amused with fruitless negociations, and that after all ye moderation that has been shewn on our part, and the endless chicanes and delays on that of ye courts of Vienna and Madrid it would be entirely giving up the dignity of our Crown and ye Honour of ye Nation to suffer things to continue any longer in ye same situation'.[1]

In the autumn of 1728 three developments undermined further the British diplomatic situation and caused fresh doubts about the policies then being followed. Louis XV's smallpox attack threatened the Anglo-French alliance with the possibilities of civil war in France or the accession of Philip V as King of France. Spain rejected the Provisional Treaty and Bournonville's mission failed to justify the hopes which had been raised that he would succeed in persuading Elisabeth Farnese to accept the treaty. The Austrian ministry decided to disavow Sinzendorf's diplomatic approaches to the Hanover allies, to reject the Provisional Treaty and to reaffirm their Spanish alliance. The combination of these developments led many within Britain to question the wisdom of British policy, and these doubts, voiced by members of the government as well as the opposition, created a dangerous political situation as the parliamentary session approached. Tilson observed in November, 'our negotiations have had a pretty issue, and all our work is to begin again; if people can bear patiently such usage.'[2]

The ministers assembled at Soissons had hoped Spain would be persuaded, by the loss of Austrian support, to accept the project of a Provisional Treaty. The British ministry had hoped Bournonville would succeed in persuading Elisabeth Farnese to accept the treaty, though sceptical voices had been raised.[3] The Dutch had suggested that Bournonville had lost all credit at Madrid. However, it was from Vienna that the blow which destroyed the Provisional Treaty came. On 10 October the Austrian conference of ministers rejected the project, and made it clear that they would not act against Spain.[4] All hope of coercing Spain was therefore lost. This sudden and unexpected[5] decision was widely attributed to the result of a struggle for power within the Austrian ministry between Eugene and Sinzendorf. It was believed, correctly, that Sinzendorf's French approach had been rejected in favour of Eugene's policy of alliance within the Empire and with Spain and Russia.[6] This decision was a surprise, although there had been considerable disquiet over the possibility of collusion between Austria and Spain. George II, according to Townshend, believed the two powers were in a league to spin out the Congress and delay matters. It was feared that both Spain and Austria wished to postpone developments until after the arrival of the treasure fleet due from the Indies. Austria hoped Spain would use her treasure to pay the subsidies due to Austria, which would in turn enable Austria to satisfy her obligations to her German allies.[7]

The reaffirmation of the Austro-Spanish alliance, a development that bore testimony to Elisabeth Farnese's continued hope that the Austrian alliance would produce advantages for Don Carlos,[8] was rendered more serious by Louis XV's smallpox attack in late October. This caused Philip V to prepare for the seizure of power in France, and produced suggestions of a civil war between his supporters and those of the Duke of Orléans, the son of the former Regent. All Europe followed the news and rumours of the illness with great attention. St. Saphorin wrote to Townshend from his Swiss estate, 'je suis saisi des agitations les plus vives'.

The news that Louis definitely had smallpox reached London on 30 October. It caused a fall in the stocks, and widespread speculation as to the likely consequences of his death.[9] *Farley's Bristol Newspaper* suggested that if he died, the French government would rely on British aid to keep Philip V out.[10] British policy was paralysed, as the government awaited news of Louis' fate. He recovered swiftly and resumed his attendance at councils on 14 November. To a certain extent the crisis was simply an exacerbation of fears which had been expressed for a long while that French policy would change with the death or replacement of Fleury. Such an opinion had been widely voiced in Britain, France and Europe.[11] Late in October 1728 Rialp, probing Waldegrave on the possibility of an Anglo-Austrian reconciliation, informed him that the Anglo-French alliance depended on the life of Fleury, 'and that he was of opinion that were the cardinal to dye, those who would succeed him in the administration would not be so zealous for England as he was'. Waldegrave's reply was rather lame. He assured Rialp that Louis XV had been so persuaded of the importance of the British alliance that a change of ministry could not lead to an alteration in French policy.[12]

Such assurances convinced few, and within Britain there was not only opposition to the French alliance but also doubts, among its supporters, as to how long it could last. Combined with the apparent failure of the Congress of Soissons to settle international problems, this produced a major debate in the press about British foreign policy. The government was attacked for its failure to protect British commerce from Spanish depredations, for the threats posed by the developing strength of the French nation, and for signs of French commercial and maritime activity, ranging from repairs to the harbour at Dunkirk, to French colonial activities in North America and the West Indies.[13] The difficulties affecting trade and industry were blamed on the international situation. The uncertainty in European affairs was blamed on the government, which was accused of being subservient to the French and unduly tolerant of Spanish activities.[14] Anxiety also affected the price of stocks. This was noted by the press, and by foreign diplomats such as Chammorel. Other diplomats noted the increase in opposition to the government.[15] The increase they were reporting was that of London. Diplomats were often unduly influenced by the opinions held by colleagues, by their links with members of the opposition, and by the, to them, unusual freedom of the press in Britain. However, the strong attacks mounted in such provincial newspapers as *Farley's Bristol Newspaper* suggest that not only London was influenced by criticisms of the government's foreign policy. The degree of concern felt throughout Britain is impossible to measure.

It was widely held in diplomatic circles that the government would encounter major difficulties with Parliament. Chesterfield was told by an Austrian supporter at The Hague, 'that if nothing were concluded before the meeting of the Parliament, the nation, that was already uneasy at the expense, would be extremely exasperated at the continuance of it'. Kinsky informed Eugene that the government was worried about what it would be able to tell Parliament and feared the continued uncertainty of affairs would produce unpopularity. Chesterfield wrote to Townshend that it was believed at The Hague that there would be trouble in Parliament, and that Slingelandt had asked him whether the government majorities were secure in both Houses of Parliament. Poyntz reported: 'The Court of Madrid have recd. letters from England wch. give them great hopes from divisions in the insuing session, with an acct. of a strong Imperial party in England, and the approaching ruin of Los Walpole . . .' St. Saphorin had noted that 'la Cour Impériale se flattoit, à chaque ouverture du Parlement, que les choses y prendroient un tour désagréable à feu sa Majeste'. Wych wrote to Townshend, 'I do not doubt, but that it has been generally observed by all those who have had the honour to serve His Majesty abroad, that our enemies have more depended upon a prospect of seeing difficulties arise at home and creating discontents and divisions among us, than upon their own force'. The Jacobites spread reports that there would be trouble in Parliament. The Prussians hoped that 'the business of Ostfrise and Mecklenburg might make a noise amongst us'. In the coming session Sir Robert Walpole was to attack those who sought 'to encourage His Majesty's enemies with the hopes that the Parliament would not approve of the late measures taken by him and to put it out of the King's power to give the support and assistance to his allies, which his own honour and the most solemn engagements oblige him to perform'. A draft government pamphlet produced after the Treaty of Seville claimed that the opposition had provided 'Spain with arguments to justify their seizing and detaining the South Sea Company's effects and their depredations.'[16]

Given these expectations it was obvious that the ministry had to ensure a successful session in order to maintain their credibility in Europe. Chesterfield wrote 'to suggest the necessity of the strongest addresses imaginable from both houses at the meeting of the Parliament, in order to undeceive people abroad'.[17] Walpole's political position seemed secure so long as the diplomatic situation did not deteriorate.[18] There are few hints of any serious challenges to him from within the ministry in the second half of 1728. Despite press reports that Carteret would replace Newcastle,[19] he remained in Ireland. There are a few scraps of evidence suggesting that tension still existed between Walpole and the ministers allied to Wilmington. Walpole claimed Wilmington was responsible for George's inconvenient demand that Parliament make good the deficiency in the Civil List Funds, and his threat to turn to other ministers. Scarborough appears to have got into trouble for a poem he wrote reflecting on the Queen and the political situation. Chammorel reported that it had been believed that Dorset, Scarborough and Wilmington would be removed. An anonymous French 'Mémoire sur l'État présent de la Grande Bretagne' written on 31 December noted that George still had a lot of confidence in Wilmington.[20]

However, these suggestions do not amount to much, and most contemporaries felt that Walpole was in secure control of the government. Relations with George had improved following the departure of Carteret, Chesterfield and St. Saphorin. George's early enthusiasm for intervening in all the departments of government had waned, and Walpole's control of financial affairs was unchallenged by the autumn of 1728. D'Aix reported that the ministry had gained George.[21]

George was not so easily satisfied in the sphere of foreign policy. He advocated the seizure of the Ostend ships as a way to intimidate Austria.[22] His response to the Spanish and Austrian disavowals of the Provisional Treaty was to argue that they must be coerced into accepting it. George hoped that the return of Sinzendorf to Vienna might lead the Austrians to reverse their disavowal of his actions, but he had no intention of relying on persuasion alone. On 16 November, when it was already clear that Louis XV had fully recovered from his smallpox attack, Townshend informed Chesterfield that 'a right spirit shew'd on the part of the Hanover Allys will be a justification of Sinzendorf's conduct'. He added:

H.M. is of opinion that the Allys of Hanover should fix a time to the Emperor and to his Catholic Majesty for accepting the said Provisional Treaty, declaring . . . that if the Emperor and the King of Spain shall not accept . . . the Allys of Hanover . . . will endeavour jointly to do themselves and their subjects justice.[23]

This approach failed due to an absence of support from Britain's allies. The Dutch opposed the scheme and Fleury argued that an ultimatum would serve only to exacerbate matters.[24] Both Fleury and the British plenipotentiaries claimed the acceptance of the Provisional Treaty was delayed by 'misunderstandings' between Spain and Austria, and not by disputes involving Britain.[25] Fleury felt that before the Hanover allies made any moves they should wait for a clarification of the relations between Spain and Austria. He hoped the alliance between the two powers would collapse and that it would then be easier to negotiate with them from a position of strength.

As D'Aix pointed out, the British alone could not fight. The ministry therefore abandoned their scheme, Fleury having 'given hopes to Mr Walpole that our common interests shall not suffer by this forbearance, and that he will bring matters to a greater certainty before the meeting of the Parliament'.[26]

The abandonment was made with a bad grace. The British were dissatisfied with the Dutch and the French, and suspicious of French attitudes. Horatio Walpole confessed that he was 'quite sick with these useless cautions and fears' of the French. Newcastle ordered the British envoys in Paris to persuade France to act vigorously,[27] but the British government realised France was disinclined to do so. Despite Horatio Walpole's assurances about Fleury's firmness, the government was displeased with the French, largely on account of what Horatio called 'the darling point of Mecklenburg'. George argued that the French were failing to support him over Mecklenburg. He believed Fleury should have insisted in his talks with Sinzendorf that a settlement of the question was a major priority, and he adopted the somewhat surprising argument that his difficulties over Mecklenburg were due to his French alliance. Townshend, who in his correspondence with the Plenipotentiaries paid much attention to German matters and Hanoverian pretensions, argued that 'the King can never submit to see his Prussian Majesty brought into Mecklenburg by the influence of the court of Vienna, and placed there as an instrument of their wrath and vengeance agt. H.M. for continuing to cultivate that strict union with France . . . ' He also claimed that should any power seek to drive the Hanoverian troops out of Mecklenburg, George would have the same right to assistance of his allies, by the defensive clauses in the Hanover treaty, as if they should attack his troops in any part of his own dominions.[28]

Tension was not restricted to the Empire, where George also felt the French were neglecting to keep him informed about their negotiations with the Wittelsbachs and failing to support the Dutch over the East Friesland question.[29] The French and the Dutch were very anxious about suggestions that the British would undertake naval action against the Spaniards, and, in particular, seize the Spanish treasure fleet. Zamboni reported that an attack on the galleons had only been prevented by pressure from Britain's allies. Hop, the Dutch envoy, pressed Townshend against such an attack. The French, who had a very large interest in the cargo of the treasure fleet, also made their opposition clear.[30]

The Hanover alliance was therefore in bad shape at the end of 1728, and Zamboni predicted its speedy demise. The British had distrusted Fleury's secret diplomacy, but had been willing to accept the situation, albeit grudgingly, whilst this diplomacy had appeared successful. The failure of the Provisional Treaty and the apparent collapse of the Soissons negotiations made it clear that Fleury's diplomatic control was not going to produce the necessary solutions. Fleury's response, a hope that Sinzendorf would regain control in Vienna and a reliance upon the incompatibilities of Austria and Spain as partners, was too passive not only for George, but also for the British ministry. Many of the British diplomats were heartily fed up with the French alliance.[31]

Fleury believed that in order to encourage the breakdown of the Austro-Spanish alliance, it was necessary to avoid antagonising either power, as he feared that would serve to unite them more strongly. Therefore, he resisted George's demands for forceful French intervention in German politics, and opposed any idea of an attack upon the Spanish treasure fleet. Nevertheless, French policy was not totally passive. Within the Empire, France was actively wooing the Wittelsbach Electors. In so doing she was looking not only to the immediate but also to the more distant future. By gaining the Wittelsbachs France would succeed in matching Britain's alliance system within the Empire and in weakening Austrian influence. In addition, there are signs that several French ministers, such as their envoy at the Imperial Diet, Chavigny, and Belle-Isle, were giving serious thought to the possibility of undermining Austrian power by supporting a Bavarian candidature for the Imperial throne on the death of Charles VI. There are few hints about British views on this matter. The absence of a British series in the State Papers comparable to the French 'Mémoires et Documents' makes it difficult to piece together British views on long-term diplomatic strategy. In 1725 Townshend had written that

> if His Impl. Majesty will drive us to a necessity of doing our utmost against him, there are Princes enough to be found, who having France and England at their head, would under their influence and with their assistance, undertake to tear the greatest part of his dominions from him.[32]

Such an attitude persisted in the early years of George II's reign, but alongside it was the view that Austria should be chastened in order to persuade her to follow sound policies. The idea of policies 'natural' to each particular state was very common in the period. Each state was believed to possess naturally only one policy, and any alteration from it was a distortion, a perversion of sound policy wrought by corruption or incompetence, the product of misguided monarchs and evil ministers. For the British in this period there was no doubt that a British alliance was the 'natural' policy for Austria, a policy made inevitable by immutable Austrian interests.[33] Such a mechanistic interpretation was in accord with and essential to the concept of the balance of power. A few brave spirits dismissed the balance of power as a childish and erroneous concept, but most saw it as essential to any correct operation of the international system.[34]

By allying with Spain and antagonising Britain, Austria was being not only foolish but perverse, but opinions were divided as to what Britain should do about it. The problems posed by the French alliance, and the uneasy awareness that the marriages of the Austrian archduchesses could wreck the precarious stability of the European system, lent added weight to talk of an Anglo-Austrian reconciliation. From the end of 1728 till the following summer a reconciliation was to be seriously considered as a means to escape from the position of diplomatic nullity and failure which the French alliance had produced.

Notes

1. Deleted section of draft instructions to the Plenipotentiaries, early spring 1729, PRO. 103/110.
2. Tilson to Waldegrave, 8 Nov. (os) 1728, Chewton; 'Some loose thoughts upon the present state of the negotiation', anonymous memorandum possibly by Stanhope, autumn 1728, PRO. 103/110.
3. Waldegrave to Townshend, 23 Oct. 1728, PRO. 80/61.
4. Baudrillart, III, 479; King, pp. 68–9; Sinzendorf to Chauvelin, 5 Jan. 1729, HHStA., Frankreich, Varia 12.
5. Horatio Walpole to Tilson, 12 Nov. 1728, Bradfer Lawrence.
6. Townshend to Stanhope and Horatio Walpole, 14 Nov. (os) 1728, PRO. 78/189; Kinsky to Eugene, 1 Dec. 1728, HHStA., GK. 94(b); McKay, *Eugene*, pp. 218–19.
7. Townshend to Chesterfield, 24 Sept. (os) 1728, PRO. 84/304; Horatio Walpole and Stanhope to Newcastle, 8 Nov., Stanhope to Newcastle, 9 Nov., Waldegrave to Horatio, 8 Dec. 1728, BL. Add. 32759, 9138; Delafaye to Poyntz, 20 Jan. (os) 1729, BL. Althorp, E3.
8. Newcastle to Stanhope and Horatio Walpole, 6 Nov. (os), Keene to Newcastle, 20 Dec. 1728. BL. Add. 32759; De Buy to Manteuffel, 29 Nov. 1728, Dresden 3105, 2; Eugene to La Paz, – Dec. 1728, HHStA., GK. 102a: A. Beer, 'Zur Geschichte der Politik Karl VI', *Historische Zeitschrift*, 19 (1886), p. 44.
9. St. Saphorin to Townshend, 16 Nov. 1728, Horatio Walpole to Delafaye, 27 Oct.1728, PRO. 80/61, 78/188; Horatio and Stanhope to Newcastle, 27 Oct., Keene to Newcastle, 8 Nov. 1728, BL. Add. 32758–9; De Buy to Manteuffel, 8 Nov. 1728, Dresden 3105, 2; D'Aubenton to Maurepas, 15, 22 Nov. 1728, AN. AM. B7 293; *Wye's Letter* 22, 24, Oct. (os), *Farley's Bristol Newspaper* 26 Oct. (os), *Ipswich Journal* 2 Nov. (os) 1728; Baudrillart, III, 415, 455–78.
10. *Farley's Bristol Newspaper* 2 Nov. (os) 1728.
11. [Delafaye or Newcastle] to Horatio Walpole, 16 Nov. (os) 1727, Newcastle to Horatio, 14 May (os), Townshend to Chesterfield, 25 June (os) 1728, PRO. 78/187, 189, 84/300; Horatio to Newcastle, 4 Dec. 1727, Townshend to Chesterfield, 25 June (os) 1728, BL. Add. 32752, 9138; Sinzendorf to Fonseca, 29 Nov. 1727, HHStA., Fonseca 11; *Wye's Letter* 19 Oct. (os), *Fog's Weekly Journal* 4 Oct. (os), *Stanley's Letter* 19 Oct. (os) 1727; [J. Morgan], *Whartoniana* (1727) p. 10; Horatio Walpole, 'Considerations', 19 July 1728, Bradfer-Lawrence; *Newcastle Courant* 7 Feb. (os) 1730.
12. Waldegrave to Townshend, 30 Oct. 1728, PRO. 80/63.
13. *Wye's Letter* 24 Oct. (os), 10, 24 Dec. (os), *Leeds Mercury* 26 Nov. (os), *Craftsman* 24 Aug. (os), 9 Nov. (os) 1728, 18, 25 Jan. (os), 1 Feb. (os) 1729; Broglie to Chauvelin, 15 June, Chammorel to Chauvelin, 22 July, 25 Oct., 6 Dec. 1728, AE. CP. Ang. 363; Newcastle to Horatio Walpole, 26 July (os) 1728, BL. Add. 32757.
14. *Craftsman* 21, 28 Dec. (os) 1728, 15 Feb. (os) 1729; Broglie to Chauvelin, 7 Mar. 1729, AE. CP. Ang. 365; Marini, pp. 121–2; Earl of March, *A Duke and his Friends* (2 vols., 1911) I, 165; Villars, pp. 156–7; *Farley's Bristol Newspaper* 9, 16, 30 Nov. (os) 1728.
15. Chammorel to Chauvelin, 14 Oct. 1728, Chauvelin to Chammorel, 23 Jan 1729, AE. CP. Ang. 363, sup. 8; D'Aix to Victor Amadeus II, 15 Nov., 13, 27 Dec. 1728, 24 Jan. 1729, AST. LM. Ing. 35; *Ipswich Journal* 14 Dec. (os) 1728; HMC. *Carlisle*, p. 57.
16. Chesterfield to Townshend, 1 Oct., 28 Dec., Poyntz to Delafaye, 25 Dec. 1728, 29 Jan. 1729, St. Saphorin to Townshend, – Aug. 1727, Wych to Townshend, 15 Feb., Sutton to Tilson, 11 Mar., Du Bourgay to Tilson, 22 Jan. 1729, PRO. 84/302, 78/188, 190, 80/61, 82/46, 81/123, 90/24; Kinsky to Eugene, 25 Sept., Fonseca to Eugene, 14 Nov. 1728, HHStA., GK. 94 (b), 85 (a); Anon. French mémoire, 8 Nov. 1728, AE. CP. Ang. 364; Waldegrave to Horatio Walpole, 8 Jan., Tilson to Waldegrave, 31 Jan. (os) 1729, Chewton; Solaro di Breglio to Victor Amadeus II, 5 Jan. 1729, AST. LM. Aut. 59; De Buy to Manteuffel, 29 Feb. 1729, Dresden 3105, 2; Knatchbull, p. 82; Thomas Pelham MP to Poyntz, 3 Feb. (os) 1729, misfiled in 1730 papers, BL. Althorp, E4; Draft pamphlet, Weston-Underwood papers, f.3; Poyntz to Horatio Walpole, 16 Jan. 1729, BL. Add. 63850.

17. Chesterfield to Townshend, 28 Dec. 1728, PRO. 84/302; Delafaye to Poyntz, 30 Jan. (os) 1729, BL. Althorp, E3.
18. Duncan to John Forbes, 6 Jan. (os) 1728, Warrand (ed.), *More Culloden Papers*, p. 27.
19. *Wye's Letter* 29 Oct. (os) 1728.
20. Hervey I, 100–1; *Wye's Letter* 22 Oct. (os) 1728; Chammorel to Chauvelin, 15 Nov., Broglie to Chauvelin, 15 June, mémoire, AE. CP. Ang. 363–4; Vignola to Venetian government, 26 Nov. 1728, ASV. LM. Ing. 98; Poyntz to Horatio Walpole, 16 Jan. 1729. BL. Add. 63750.
21. D'Aix to Victor Amadeus II, 5 Feb., 1729, AST. LM. Ing. 35; Kinsky to Eugene, 25 Sept. 1728, HHStA., GK. 94 (b).
22. George's undated comment on letter from Newcastle of 31 Oct. (os) 1728, PRO. 36/8.
23. Townshend to Chesterfield, 5 Nov. (os), 17 Dec. (os) 1728, memorial 'Some loose thoughts', PRO. 84/302, 103/110; Waldegrave to Horatio Walpole, 8 Dec. 1728, BL. Add. 9138; King, p. 70.
24. Horatio Walpole to -, 28 Nov., Chesterfield to Townshend, 23 Nov., 14 Dec. 1728, PRO. 78/188, 84/302.
25. Townshend to Chesterfield, 26 Nov. (os), Chesterfield to Townshend, 14 Dec., Horatio Walpole to [Delafaye], 30 Nov. 1728, PRO. 84/302, 78/188; Stanhope and Horatio Walpole to Keene, 29 Nov., 7 Dec. 1728, BL. Add. 32759.
26. D'Aix to Victor Amadeus II, 3, 17 Jan. 1729, AST. LM. Ing. 35; Townshend to Chesterfield, 26 Nov. (os) 1728, PRO. 84/302.
27. Horatio Walpole to [Delafaye], 28 Nov., 'Some loose thoughts', PRO. 78/188,103/110; Newcastle to Horatio and Stanhope, 3 Dec. (os) 1728, BL. Add. 32759; Wackerbarth to Augustus, 15 Jan. 1729, Dresden 3331; King, p. 69.
28. Horatio Walpole to Newcastle, 8 Dec., Townshend to Plenipotentiaries, 3 Dec. (os), Townshend to Horatio Walpole, 10 Oct. (os) 1728, BL. Add. 32759, 9138; Newcastle to Horatio, 11 Oct. (os), Townshend to Chesterfield, 29 Nov.(os) 1728, PRO. 78/189, 84/302; Kinsky to Eugene, 11 Jan, 1729, HHStA., GK. 94 (b).
29. Townshend to Chesterfield, 3 Dec. (os) 1728, PRO. 84/302; Newcastle to Stanhope and Horatio Walpole, 3 Dec. (os) 1728, BL. Add. 32759.
30. Zamboni to Le Coq, 2 Aug., Zamboni to Landgrave of Hesse-Darmstadt, 24 Dec. 1728, Bodl. Rawl. 120, Darmstadt, D. EI. M10/6; Townshend to Chesterfield, 6 Dec. (os) 1729, PRO. 84/302; D'Aix to Victor Amadeus II, 27 Dec. 1728, AST. LM. Ing. 35; *Craftsman* 5, 12 Oct. (os), 21 Dec. (os) 1728; *Wye's Letter* 17, 19 Oct. (os) 1728.
31. Zamboni to Manteuffel, 10 Dec. 1728, Bodl. Rawl. 120; Villars, p. 159; Stanhope to Newcastle, 9 Dec., Poyntz to Delafaye, 25 Dec. 1728, BL. Add. 32759, PRO. 78/188; Waldegrave to William Finch, 5 Jan. 1729, Chewton.
32. Townshend to Du Bourgay, 29 Oct. 1725, PRO. 90/19.
33. St. Saphorin to Tarouca, Aug. 1727, PRO. 80/61.
34. Black, 'The Theory of the Balance of Power in the First Half of the Eighteenth Century; A Note on Sources', *Review of International Studies* 9 (1983).

CHAPTER SEVEN

Early 1729
Parliamentary Disquiet: Approach to Austria

'Il y aura des débats et des harangues violent du parti contraire, mais
la cour s'en mocquera comme des cris en l'air, sans force et sans effet'
Anonymous French memoir of December 1728.[1]

The opening of the parliamentary session on 1 February 1729 saw a
sustained attack upon the government's foreign policy. The opposition
Whigs launched a furious assault. Vernon attacked the French as a threat
to British commerce and a false ally; John Norris proposed that the King
should be addressed to break the alliance with France; Sir Wilfred Lawson
argued that it was dangerous to trust to French mediation, adding that if
war broke out, France would never support Britain against Spain, a view
held by many diplomats. Pulteney 'questioned the steadiness of France.'
Stanhope and Horatio Walpole rebutted these views and 'they both gave
assurances of the readiness of His Most Christian Majesty to concur . . . in
any measures that should be judged requisite for obtaining a general
peace.' Sir Robert Walpole confessed there was uneasiness over the
diplomatic position. He stated that 'when the negotiations at Soissons
came to be laid before the House, they would be better understood than at
present.' There was no division in the Lords, and in the Commons the
ministry obtained a majority of over 160, but its size owed something to
divisions among the opposition. The Tories and the opposition Whigs had
not cooperated in their parliamentary tactics, which led William Shippen,
the Jacobite, to abuse Pulteney in the House. Delafaye wrote to Poyntz
'never troops were worse disciplined than our adversarys, no concert, no
scheme, between an unwillingness to fly in the King's face and a desire to
slap his administration, they made the most awkward figure in the world;
only Sir William Wyndham was *sibi constans*, saying he liked none of the
measures, and was willing to declare it now lest he should not stay long
enough in town to have another opportunity, which is no ill symptom'.[2]
Ten days later, in the debate on the size of the army, a debate which did
not produce a division, the government was again helped by the divided
state of the opposition. There were rumours, for which there is no
evidence, that the government was attempting to profit from the splits.
Broglie reported that George and Caroline were wooing the Tory leader Sir
William Wyndham, and that the ministry hoped to detach Pulteney from
Bolingbroke. On 14 February Delafaye noted 'no Parliament ever
approved and supported measures better', though he expressed the hope
that the ministry would have something different to say next session.[3]
   However, attacks upon the government persisted and became more

serious. Sir Thomas Saunderson, a brother of Scarborough's, who had been refused a peerage by George, went over to the opposition and launched a strong attack upon the French alliance.[4] The alliance was unpopular but the government was better able to defend it than their position over Spanish depredations. A petition had been prepared by merchants trading to America and the West Indies, complaining of the depredations. Poyntz noted that major efforts had 'been taken to animate the City against us by false suggestions that the Government *wilfully* declined granting Letters of Reprisal against the Spaniards.' On 24 March, during the debate on the petitioners' evidence, the government carried a procedural point by a majority of only 180 against 145. Zamboni reported it to be generally believed in Britain that whenever the opposition vote in Parliament exceeded 150 the government would fall. Delafaye wrote of the debate as 'a hot day'. John Selwyn, a ministerial MP, was concerned about the response in the City, and on 28 March Delafaye informed Poyntz that Horatio Walpole and Stanhope were still in London:

Your Excellency will easily judge that during the ferment we have had, and which you will find by the calling for more papers etc is not quite over, they could not be spared from the service in Parliament. Great industry has been used to spirit up the merchants, in order to blacken the administration as if it was regardless of the protection of trade and navigation; but the edge of the general resentment turns another way, against the Spaniards, whose depredations and ill usage of us are so very enormous, that were you to hear how people talk in all manner of places and conversations you would conclude there is scarce a man in England but would sell the coat off his back to venture his life to be revenged of the Spaniards: Had our allies, who I believe had not much reason to brag of their justice and kindness towards them, the same keen sense of the injuries they have received, and were the Court of Madrid thoroughly apprised of it, surely they would hearken to reason . . . the present temper of people here, is full as warm as can be described.[5]

The government majority fell during the session. In the early debates they had enjoyed substantial majorities, though smaller than those of the previous session. The government won on the motion to refer the mercantile petition to a committee of the whole House, by 240 against 129; Lord Morpeth's motion asking for an address to enquire about the help France had given Britain for the preservation of Gibraltar was defeated on 16 February by 235 against 80; the subsidy for the Hessians was renewed by 298 against 91 on 18 February, and a financial debate a week later produced a majority of 257 against 90.[6] Thereafter the majorities fell. On 1 April, in the debate over the Lords' resolution relating to Gibraltar and Minorca, the opposition proposal to insist 'that all pretensions on the part of the crown of Spain to the said possessions be specifically delivered up' was defeated by 267 against 111. Lady Irwin informed her father Walpole had been so pressed that he had asked George for permission to retire to the Lords. On 6 April, in the debates over the contested elections for Newton and Great Bedwyn, the majorities were 166 against 147 and 150 against 119. After the Easter recess the majorities in the debate on 27 April on the deficiency in the Civil List were 181 against 106, and 154 against 101, although in the debates on the same subject on 4 May the majorities rose to 296 against 122 and 241 against 115.[7]

The reason for these falling majorities is unclear. Division lists survive for only one debate in the session, that on 4 May. Thus an analysis such as that undertaken by Langford for the 1733 session, from which three division lists have survived, is impossible for the 1729 session. Judging from the votes it is clear that the decreasing majorities were due not to the small increase in the opposition vote but to the major drop in the ministerial vote. Possibly the abstentions reflected a feeling among governmental MPs that the ministerial majority was too strong to be shaken, and that they were therefore free to absent themselves after the major debates at the beginning of the session. Selwyn wrote of opposition pressure over Spanish depredations 'this will end in nothing that will give trouble, but we are frequently diverted with such sorts of attacks'. Colley suggested that the voting discipline of the Tories was stronger than that of the ministerial Whigs, which may account for the situation. Zamboni claimed that George's avarice limited the financial inducements at Walpole's disposal.[8] It was widely argued by the opposition, in Jacobite circles, and in Europe that the government was able to dominate Parliament thanks to corruption, to the tempting prizes it could offer.[9] This was an argument rejected by the government. The ministry claimed that it enjoyed its majorities thanks to an ability to persuade Parliament of the wisdom of its policies. Townshend informed Poyntz in February that Fleury was

mistaken, if he thinks that the Parliament is influenced by money, to be thus unanimous in the supporting HM in all he has done. This zeal proceeds from the chief men in both houses being convinced, that the measures HM has hitherto taken are right; but these persons, tho' they have heartily concurred in what has been done hitherto, are under the greatest anxiety, at the uncertain state of our affairs; and will not be kept much longer in suspence.

Townshend was writing in order to persuade Fleury to act 'a friendly part towards the king'. Later in the year Townshend replied with similar arguments to the French suggestion of a secret British declaration promising peacetime subsidies to the Elector of Cologne, and he made the same point in 1730 over Swedish subsidies. Newcastle informed Poyntz on 12 April 1729 that the ministry had been criticised in Parliament for being 'too pacifick and too restrictive. Long days and long enquiries are frequent in the House of Commons, and we are to have some with us after the holidays but I think notwithstanding the inveteracy of some people, our friends, who are as great a majority as ever was known, are as hearty and well satisfied as possible . . . since our moderation is a crime here, I hope our friends abroad will no more complain of the vivacité Angloise, but think it high time to assist us out of our present uncertain situation . . . good news from abroad will be the best help we can have here.'[10] Foreign diplomats often argued that the British ministry exaggerated its difficulties with Parliament in order to persuade its allies not to force it to undertake policies it disliked, such as the restitution of Gibraltar. There was probably some truth in this view, particularly when it came to the British government explaining why they were forced to take commercial steps, such as import prohibitions, unfavourable to their allies. However, in general Townshend's claim was better founded. There is little material surviving as to how the 'Robinocracy' operated in practice; evidence for Walpole's management of the parliamentary sessions of the late 1720s is scant. The seductive lures of place and pension doubtless existed for many but their operation in practice is difficult to confirm for MPs. It is too easy to resort to the glib view that Walpole's control over the resources of the Treasury ensured his control over Parliament. In practice the ministerial MPs, and their counterparts in the Lords, were capable of considerable independence. Many were extremely well-informed about European events, and foreign travel, personal contacts and correspondence, and the press, helped to spread knowledge about Europe. The quality of parliamentary debates upon foreign affairs has recently been savagely attacked by J. R. Jones:

> Wilful misrepresentation of facts, sensationalism and pandering to popular prejudices, partisanship and appeals to xenophobia characterised most parliamentary debates . . . the issues could be dramatised and presented in black and white terms of national honour or disgrace, of commercial prosperity or ruin, bravery or cowardice.[11]

An examination of the debates in the late 1720s would suggest that this is an unfair conclusion. The House of Commons contained several diplomats or former diplomats and some of these contributed their knowledge to debates. Though envoys such as Edward Finch and William Finch rarely attended Parliament and are never recorded as having spoken, this was not the case with such former envoys as Sir Robert Sutton, Methuen, Hedges and Dodington. The debates recorded for the session of 1729 reveal a high standard of argument. Much information was presented to the Commons, Horatio Walpole beginning his speech on 11 February in defence of the continuation of the same number of land forces as in the preceding year, with 'an account of the proceedings of several courts of Europe and the Ministers employed at them'.[12] The speeches which have been recorded reveal a knowledge of European developments and of the major points at issue in British foreign policy.

In the debates in 1729 the Walpoles found themselves forced to defend the Anglo-French alliance against strong attacks. They did so by claiming that France was a good ally to Britain as a result of structural factors in the international situation. Horatio Walpole 'affirmed France to be the most faithful to us through the whole course of these late differences, and for a good reason, she being the irreconcilable enemy to Austria'. Sir Robert Walpole declared 'that where some had compared Galica fides with Punica fides, we were to consider that states govern themselves by their interest and that the close alliance of Austria, the ancient enemy, with Spain made them as entirely sure to our alliance as heretofore they were enemies when they aimed at universal monarchy'.[13]

These arguments were, however, being made increasingly redundant for two reasons. First, public distrust of France, which had continued throughout the Anglo-French alliance, was perceived as an increasingly potent political weapon for the opposition. Timothy Shallow, a government supporter who appeared in a fictional before-dinner dialogue in the *Craftsman*, confessed that 'the French Alliance is a very tender point; and that it is unpopular to argue in its defence'. Edward Harrison, a placeman and former MP close to Townshend, observed on 14 March 'we go on swimmingly in Parliament for the present, but the uneasiness daily increases, and spreads far and near. We that are sanguine hope now the galleons are arrived, we shall see an end of our trouble and expence, but the malicious say when France has got their money home, they will leave us to shift for ourselves'.[14] Secondly, the ministry was increasingly ready to consider the possibility of an Austrian alliance. Linking these two developments, Chammorel reported in early April that in the face of opposition arguments for an Austrian alliance the ministry might adopt such an alliance rather than fall from power.[15]

Foreign diplomats were very impressed by the ministerial control displayed in the early debates in the session, but by March their attitude had changed. Increasingly they suggested that the ministry was losing control of the situation and they identified foreign policy as the area where the government was most under strain. On 7 March Broglie reported that the different parties in the nation had united to demand that as soon as the galleons had arrived in Spain, Austria and Spain should be presented with an ultimatum requiring that they accept or refuse the Provisional Treaty. He added that the government, not being strong enough to resist public opinion, would be obliged to act.[16] Other diplomats attributed British suggestions of naval action against the galleons to popular pressure. The desire to act, rather than pressure for any specific action, was indeed strong within Britain.[17] Due to the availability of naval power and the strong anti-Spanish nature of public opinion, pressure for action was directed against Spain. Over the preceding three years there had been a marked development of anti-Spanish feeling within Britain. Spanish depredations upon British commerce were viewed with considerable anger, as was the Spanish attempt to regain Gibraltar. The Spanish siege of Gibraltar in 1727 had been followed with great attention by all sections of the British press. In comparison, expressions of anti-Austrian feeling were more muted, a fact noted by the Austrians. Sinzendorf told the Dutch envoy in Vienna, Bruyninx, that the Austrian ministry 'thought the Parliament of England might advise H.M. to rupture with Spain but was in no apprehension that the Parliament would meddle with the Emperor'.[18]

The ministry could not ignore the pressure for action. Townshend informed Waldegrave that it was 'the universal sense of this nation, that a speedy decision, should one way or other be obtained . . . how necessary it is thought here to get out of the present uncertain situation of affairs'.[19] The need 'for bringing matters to a decision' was stressed. It was no longer satisfactory to argue that Britain should trust to the path of negotiation and the aid of France. The Walpoles adopted this attitude in Parliament, but it is not clear how far they held it privately. Horatio Walpole informed Fleury that Parliament was satisfied with governmental assurances of French fidelity, but he pressed the need for an end to diplomatic uncertainties and argued that the Hanover allies should come to a joint resolution to present an ultimatum and take action as in the spring of 1727.[20] This method was still being rejected by the French in early 1729 as it had been late in the previous year. Nevertheless, the French assured Britain of their continued support for the alliance, providing George with conspicuous diplomatic support over Mecklenburg in the winter of 1728–9. Chambrier, the Prussian envoy in Paris, was informed that France would oppose any Prussian attempt to occupy Mecklenburg and would give military support to Britain if Hanover were attacked.[21] The British ministry was pleased by the French stance over Mecklenburg, whilst the French also brought pressure to bear on the Austrians.[22]

French opposition also blocked any idea of an attack upon the Spanish treasure fleet. Faced with this situation and with the failure of the Austro-Spanish alliance to disintegrate, as had been hoped for by the French, the British ministry was in a difficult diplomatic situation. Hopes that Sinzendorf and Bournonville would persuade Austria and Spain to accept the Provisional Treaty had proved abortive. Suspicion increased that both powers were only trying to delay matters until the return of the galleons. Delafaye exclaimed

> would to God, our good friend the Cardinal would speak out! the question to be asked him seems to be a short, plain one: You have hopes from what Sinzendorf writes, that the Emperor will come, and from the matters depending between him and Spain that the latter will fall out with him for not executing his engagements about the marriages; But if you are disappointed of those hopes, what is it you will then do? That is to say after the Galleons are arrived. To this, His Eminence and the Garde de Sceaux [Chauvelin] seem to make no direct answer, but beat about the bush, cavil at the plan of operations, which was a child of their own begetting, talk of waiting to see etc and so we may wait on till Doom's Day, and not see a step of the way before us.

Frederick William doubted that the Anglo-French alliance could survive its failure to satisfy the views of the British nation. D'Aix, noting the threat to the government's position in Parliament and the pressure for war, reported that the ministry were opposed to following the French lead and continuing the negotiations to persuade Spain and Austria to accept the Provisional Treaty. Tilson expressed the hope that he would soon be able to 'answer directly those impertinent questions so often asked – peace or war.'[23] It was against this background that Britain considered a reconciliation with Prussia and Austria.

Prussian Interlude

In the autumn of 1728 George II received a letter from his sister Sophia Dorothea the Queen of Prussia, proposing, in the King of Prussia's name, the marriage of Frederick, Prince of Wales, and Wilhelmina, the Prussian Princess Royal. Queen Caroline sent a very vague reply, which produced an enthusiastic Prussian response. George then told Caroline to inform Sophia Dorothea that he wanted not only the marriage of Frederick and Wilhelmina, but also that of the Prussian Crown Prince, Frederick, and a British princess, though not the Princess Royal, who was intended for William IV of Orange.[24]

George's response was cautious and reflected his suspicion of Frederick William and his views upon his reliability.[25] Chesterfield however was sufficiently optimistic to seek appointment as the Ambassador to be sent to Prussia to arrange the marriages and Townshend was willing to help him in this. There was extensive press and diplomatic speculation concerning the issue, and it was widely assumed that the marriages would take place. Chesterfield pointed out to the Dutch minister Fagel 'that as the Royal family in England was confined to Protestant alliances, it was not so difficult to guess them'.[26] The Dutch ministers expressed pleasure at the prospect of the marriages. For them Anglo-Prussian diplomacy was safer than the scheme for a British marriage for William IV of Orange, a scheme which was to embitter Anglo-Dutch relations in 1729. Townshend sent a dispatch to Stanhope and Horatio Walpole which reflected an optimistic view of Prussian intentions, 'tho' his Prussian Majesty has a great mind to get some hold of Mecklenburg at this juncture, by the means of this new commission, yet he is desirous of doing it with our Master's good liking, and in concert with him; which by the help of this match, and of one of our Princesses with the Prince Royal of Prussia he hopes may be compassed'. Townshend ordered Edward Finch to inform the Swedish government of the negotiations, 'at the same time assuring them that whatever may be the fate of this negociation, there will be no alteration in the public measures, and that His Majesty will enter into no engagements with the King of Prussia without their participation and concurrence'. Fleury, when approached, said that France approved of the scheme for a double match with Prussia so long as Jülich and Berg were clearly assigned to the Sulzbach claimants. The British replied by stating that it was not in Hanover's interests for Prussia to acquire Jülich-Berg, and that Britain would only support Prussian schemes if France failed to help Hanover.[27] However, the Jülich-Berg issue proved to be a major stumbling block to the attempt to combine the British and French strategies for German diplomacy. The French, keen to acquire the support of the Wittelsbachs, demanded that George should guarantee the Sulzbach claim to Jülich-Berg as a precondition for any French action under the guarantee she was already engaged to with respect to Mecklenburg.

Prussia was believed to favour a reconciliation due to a deterioration in her relations with Austria, but the urgency of the Jülich-Berg issue produced by the ill-health of the Elector Palatine, and the need to retain French support for the session, helped to block the development of good relations. Frederick William was more hopeful of gaining his way by a deterioration in Anglo-French relations, and the British were unwilling to guarantee the Prussian claim to Jülich-Berg. The approach therefore came to nothing. Chesterfield attributed the breaking off of the marriage negotiations to difficulties created by Frederick William regarding them as a condescension.[28] It is difficult to establish how seriously George and Frederick William were willing to make an effort to establish good relations. Sophia Dorothea was always keener on British marriages than her husband, and Frederick William never displayed much enthusiasm for the double marriage project. He was keener on a single marriage, that of Wilhelmina and the Prince of Wales. Neither side displayed much willingness to yield over Mecklenburg, and both were unwilling to risk alienating their principal ally for the uncertainty of marital negotiations. By 1730 the situation was to have changed, but by then Austria appeared less able to support Prussia, and the British ministry was divided over the French idea of an alliance with the Wittelsbachs.

Approach to Austria

In October 1728 Rialp, sounding Waldegrave on the possibility of an Anglo-Austrian rapprochement, observed that 'it was the natural interest of both powers to be well together; that we could never be jealous of each other's greatness'. The arrival of Kinsky, the only Envoy of any of the powers in the Vienna alliance in London, led to speculation in the autumn of 1728 that Austria desired a reconciliation with Britain.[29] Soundings were taken by both sides during the late autumn and winter, and in the early spring of 1729 the British ministry took a major initiative in an attempt to produce an Anglo-Austrian alliance. The British approach was to fail, largely because of a poor Austrian response, but it was of great importance because it revealed the lack of support within the British ministry for the French alliance. Anglo-Austrian negotiations in this period have received little scholarly attention, and it is necessary to examine them in some detail in order to piece together the train of events.

The disavowal of Sinzendorf, suspected by the British of being overly keen on a French alliance, led to hopes in Britain that the Austrian ministry would be more sympathetic to British interests. Eugene was believed, correctly, to be more interested in approaching Britain than France. The Austrian envoy at The Hague 'made the strongest and most publick declaration imaginable of the Emperor's good dispositions towards England and this Republick'.[30] Kinsky was ordered to attempt to improve relations. His initial moves failed. Kinsky reported in early December that there was no prospect of his approach succeeding and the British displayed little confidence in him. Chesterfield argued that neither Kinsky, nor the Austrian envoy at The Hague, Sinzendorf, the son-in-law of the Chancellor, had any real knowledge of Austrian intentions.[31]

In late January 1729 the situation changed. Queen Caroline and Stanhope pressed Kinsky with the idea of an alliance, and Kinsky reported the revival of discussions with Townshend.[32] Kinsky himself knew little of the intentions of his court,[33] and the British, who had a low opinion of him, made it clear that they preferred negotiations to be handled at Vienna. In the summer of 1729 Stanhope informed Kinsky's brother,

Count Stephen Kinsky, one of the Austrian plenipotentiaries at the Congress of Soissons, that he had been instructed to approach Philip Kinsky by George II and Queen Caroline. From the evidence which survives it seems that the negotiations in London were undertaken, under royal instructions, by Townshend and Stanhope. The choice of Townshend, knowledgeable in German affairs, was an obvious one, as Vienna was in his department. It is however interesting that Stanhope, then, like Horatio Walpole, in England for the parliamentary session, should have been chosen to talk to Kinsky. It seems that Horatio Walpole knew nothing of the approach. According to Zamboni, when George questioned them as to whether France would, in case of necessity, act vigorously and sincerely to support Britain, Horatio Walpole said yes, but Stanhope refused to commit himself. Horatio Walpole was distrusted by the Austrians as pro-French.[34]

Kinsky told Stanhope 'that his master was most earnestly desirous to be reconciled to the King', and he bitterly attacked both the Spanish alliance and the projected marriages between the Austrian archduchesses and the sons of Elisabeth Farnese. He sounded Stanhope on George's views on a marriage between Maria Theresa and Francis, the heir to the Duchy of Lorraine. Stanhope replied that George was very much in favour of the match. The Lorraine match had been canvassed for some time, but France was opposed to it, due to the traditional antagonism between the Dukes of Lorraine and the Crown of France, and to the fear that, whatever renunciations might be made, a Duke of Lorraine who was in control of the Imperial title and Austrian resources might seek to reverse the seventeenth-century settlement of France's eastern border. By indicating his support for the match George was revealing that on the important issue of the future of the Empire his views were opposed to those of France.[35]

Townshend told Kinsky that Austria must agree to sign the Provisional Treaty. Kinsky replied that Austria did not want to lose her Spanish subsidies, and feared that in order to win Spanish support Britain might lend Spain unfair aid in her attempt to secure Carlos in Italy. Kinsky had indeed predicted that Austro-Spanish relations would inhibit an Anglo-Austrian reconciliation. The terms of the Treaty of Seville were to prove Kinsky correct, but Townshend told him that Britain would be bound by the terms of the Quadruple Alliance in her Italian policy. This alliance, signed in 1718, provided that Carlos's right to the Farnese and Medici successions be recognized, but stipulated that the duchies be treated as Imperial fiefs and that Carlos's right should be protected by neutral rather than Spanish garrisons. By declaring his continued support for these terms Townshend made it clear that Britain was willing, as part of the price for any Anglo-Austrian rapprochement, to support Austrian interests in Italy. In support of his demand that Austria should sign the Provisional Treaty Townshend argued that

by his Imperial Majesty's signing the said treaty, the system of Europe would be put precisely upon the same foundation it stood upon before these late disturbances began; which would naturally, and without any violence offered to any engagements, throw their court and ours into the old Friendship and good correspondence that had so long subsisted between them.

Kinsky accepted Townshend's argument and promised to do his best to persuade the Austrian government to approve the idea. He told the British he lacked the necessary instructions to open negotiations and would seek orders from Vienna.[36] The British thought little of Kinsky and distrusted his links with 'those whose views naturally lead them to keep up the misunderstanding between his majesty and the Emperour'. Townshend complained that Kinsky

> who seems not to be much versed in business and therefore may be more susceptible of jealousies and misapprehensions, is very apt to give ear to the dreams of little and underlying agents. If he follows such advisers . . . he will give things a wrong turn, and exasperate matters.

Tilson complained that 'our Dear Count is often hot and cold; sometimes easy, and sometimes out of humour, as fancys are inspired by him'.[37] One of these 'agents', the Modenese envoy Riva, persuaded Kinsky that Britain was secretly negotiating with Spain against Austria, a rumour which was reported by several, but which it is difficult to substantiate.[38] The British ministry was very suspicious of Riva, and of the Prussian and Saxon agents in London, Reichenbach and Zamboni. They were all close to Kinsky and were believed to possess strong links with members of the opposition.[39] Townshend therefore decided to transfer the negotiations to Vienna where the envoy, Waldegrave, was a friend who owed his position to Townshend's support.

On 27 February Townshend sent Waldegrave secret instructions via Brigadier Richard Sutton, then at Cassel. Sutton was instructed to choose a servant 'whose diligence and secrecy' could be relied upon and send him secretly to Vienna. Carrington, the courier taking Townshend's instructions, was delayed at sea by contrary winds. He arrived at Cassel on 5 March but further delay was caused by the fact that Sutton had travelled to Wolfenbüttel, and the instructions were not forwarded until 10 March. Caillaud, Sutton's domestic secretary, reached Vienna with them six days later.[40]

Townshend's instructions demanded satisfaction for Hanoverian claims:

> If the court of Vienna is sincerely desirous to renew the perfect friendship and harmony, which so long subsisted between them and us, they will of themselves see the necessity of doing His Majesty as Elector justice upon several points, upon which the King, and his father, have so long, and with so much reason, complained. These are matters of so little importance to the Emperor, and his Imperial Majesty has them so entirely in his own power, that it will be impossible for him ever to convince us that he sincerely desires our friendship, unless he does explain himself clearly and explicitly to the King's satisfaction upon these several articles.

Zamboni observed fairly that George demanded a lot from Charles VI.[41] The secrecy of the British approach was soon lost. Zamboni had reported it as serious on 25 February and the Saxon envoy in Vienna, Count Wackerbarth, was soon investigating the matter. He had already reported in January his suspicion that Britain would seek a reconciliation with Austria. On 19 March he suggested that talks were being conducted through Kinsky and on 20 April he noted the rumour that Waldegrave had received a secret courier. On 14 April Chauvelin sent Chammorel the copy of a report he had received from London. The report claimed that Britain had determined on an alliance with Austria and had sent Riva to Vienna to negotiate the matter. Chauvelin ordered Chammorel to investigate the report. Seckendorf claimed there would soon be an Anglo-Austrian alliance. Fleury questioned the British Plenipotentiaries 'upon the report of His Majesty's being concerned in a private negotiation with the Emperor by the canal of Monsr. Riva'. Prince Eugene noted that reports of Kinsky's discussions were widely disseminated.[42]

Riva set out for Vienna carrying a letter from Townshend instructing Waldegrave to support his negotiations in the dispute over the Italian Duchy of Massa between the Duke of Modena and the Emperor. Townshend sent a separate letter to Waldegrave informing him that George had no interest in the lawsuits the Duke of Modena had sought his support for, and that Riva was 'a dangerous and ill intentioned person'. Many were however convinced that he had been commissioned to undertake the Anglo-Austrian reconciliation. Waldegrave declared that Riva had nothing to negotiate on behalf of Great Britain, but Wackerbarth doubted this and noted that it was not usual for the representatives of small courts to dine with Sinzendorf, as Riva did on his arrival. The Austrian response to Waldegrave's approach was a negative one. Waldegrave had warned Townshend at the beginning of January that Austria was unlikely to abandon its Spanish alliance, and that she was likely to delay all diplomatic moves until after the arrival of the galleons, so as not to jeopardise her claim to share in the treasure. He had also warned that Sinzendorf had not lost influence, as had been believed, and that Sinzendorf, who had opposed the choice of Kinsky as envoy to Britain, intended that Kinsky's mission should fail. Waldegrave informed Townshend that when Visconti told the Emperor that George and the British nation supported a reconciliation with Austria, Charles gave the curt reply, 'leurs actions ne le montrent guère'.[43]

Replying to Townshend's instructions, Waldegrave reported that the Austrian ministers did not keep him informed and that they were opposed to the Provisional Treaty. The Austrian government was also firm over the Mecklenburg issue. Townshend meanwhile had had second thoughts, and on 5 April ordered Waldegrave not to open himself to the Austrians unless they did so to him.[44] The Austrians' 'response froide' did not end all moves towards a reconciliation, although it led the naturally brusque George II to show his displeasure to Kinsky. The Austrians distrusted George. Eugene informed Kinsky that the British were negotiating with Spain and Prussia and seeking to begin talks with the Russians. He therefore urged Kinsky to be very cautious in his conversations with the British ministers, although he was still very keen to discover whether the

British were sincerely in favour of a reconciliation.[45] Tension within the Empire increased difficulties. Both the Mecklenburg and East Friesland disputes gave rise to serious concern in the spring of 1729. George was very angry about the Austrian attitude to both disputes, and he was determined to protect the Hanoverian position in the Mecklenburg dispute. Eugene argued that the Hanoverian position did not suggest any interest in a reconciliation, and stressed George's interest in Hanoverian aggrandizement. Sutton reported that the Hessians were hopeful the Austrian actions in the Mecklenburg dispute would sustain the tension their subsidy depended upon.[46]

Anglo-Austrian contacts persisted during the late spring of 1729, but the negative Austrian response to the initial approaches and George's determination not to be snubbed too frequently reduced the pace of the British approach. The British were also dissatisfied with the Austrian position at the Congress. The Austrian Plenipotentiary Baron Fonseca made it clear that the Austrians did not intend to depart from the position they had taken after the disavowal of Sinzendorf. He stated that they were determined to maintain the Ostend Company, to demand an equivalent for the claims of the Duke of Holstein-Gottorp, and 'to hang all matters upon the concurrence of Spain'. In London Kinsky stressed that the Austrians were determined not to abandon their allies. Though he told the British that the Emperor was 'not averse to the Provisional Treaty', he was in fact ordered to withdraw from active negotiations.[47]

The reasons for the Austrian response were clear. As Waldegrave had stated, Austria, in grave fiscal problems and threatened with a serious weakening of its position within the Empire unless it could honour its subsidy treaties, was too dependent upon the prospect of Spanish gold to risk endangering its Spanish alliance by negotiating new treaties. Eugene had assured the Spanish government that Austria was firmly determined to maintain its Spanish alliance and would not sign the Provisional Treaty without Spanish consent.[48] To agree to George's proposals would also have endangered Austria's Prussian and possibly its Russian alliance. In Russia, although Peter II's government was less sympathetic to the claims of the Duke of Holstein-Gottorp than Catherine I had been, there was still a powerful Holstein interest. The Austrian government was opposed to abandoning the interests of the Duke of Holstein-Gottorp. Austro-Prussian links had been strengthened by the secret Treaty of Berlin signed on 23 December 1728. By this Charles VI had promised assistance in the Jülich-Berg dispute and Frederick William recognised the Pragmatic Sanction. The Austrians were greatly concerned about Prussian views, particularly over Mecklenburg, where Imperial jurisdiction was also at stake.[49] 'The affairs of Mecklenburg are at present the only object of the King's [Frederick William] and Prussian ministers' attention', Du Bourgay had reported in April. In March favourable sentiments expressed by the Prussian minister Borcke about the possibility of an agreement over Mecklenburg had led Townshend to write to him 'desiring to have a plan formed upon the principles he had laid down'. However, the British rejected Borcke's plan as unsatisfactory, and relations deteriorated sharply.[50] The Austrians were therefore correct in concluding that satisfying George over his Hanoverian demands would endanger their Prussian alliance.

There was to be a revival in Anglo-Austrian contacts in June, but by then the collapse of the Austro-Spanish alliance had greatly changed the diplomatic situation. In the two preceding months the British had lost hope of a reconciliation with Austria and had turned back to the French alliance. The government reassured the French about their talks with Prussia and Austria. George's fears about Prussian intentions in Mecklenburg led him to reverse his attitude towards the Wittelsbachs. He declared his willingness to authorise Fleury 'to answer for him, to the Electors as to the guaranty relating to Juliers and Bergues in the manner His Eminence desired'.[51] As George came into line behind French policy in the Empire, abandoning his approach to Prussia and showing increasing favour to Wittelsbach views, he also began to cooperate with French schemes to win Spain from Austria. By May 1729 the Anglo-French alliance had been reaffirmed, and the passivity and disunion of the previous winter had been replaced by an active cooperation.

The relationship between differences of opinion among the British ministers and developments in British policy in the first five months of 1729 is unclear. Although there are suggestions of serious differences of opinion, it is difficult to paint even a partial picture of the situation. Evidence does not accumulate to any real extent until the summer of 1729, when Townshend accompanied George to Hanover. The correspondence between Townshend and Newcastle preserved in the series *State Papers, Regencies* is a useful source for the clashes in policy that summer, but there is nothing comparable for the preceding months. This is a serious omission because it is likely the clashes of the latter half of 1729, clashes that were to conclude finally with Townshend's resignation on 26 May 1730, did not owe their origin to the issues and events of the summer, but rather to already existing suspicions and differences of opinion. In February 1729 Townshend wrote, with reference to the Anglo-French alliance, of 'the reproaches I have with patience born upon the account of the share I had in forming this alliance'.[52]

In the autumn of 1729 these personal and policy differences produced two groups, one led by the Walpoles, Stanhope and Newcastle and the other by Townshend, Poyntz and Chesterfield. This division was to a certain extent the accidental product of the fusion of several unrelated disputes. One of the major disputes was that between the two Secretaries of State. Such clashes were not new, because the policy of dividing responsibility for British foreign policy and British diplomats between two roughly equal ministers was one that was naturally inconvenient and productive of disputes. In the mid 1720s Newcastle, without experience in diplomacy, tended to follow Townshend's advice. He announced 'I shall in everything act in concert with My Lord Townshend and according to the advice and instructions I shall have the pleasure of receiving from him'. Newcastle's biographer has suggested this situation had altered by 1727, and that by the spring of that year Newcastle had defined a different policy to Townshend, one that was anti-Spanish rather than anti-Austrian. Browning saw Newcastle as gradually gaining experience, confidence and authority, and argued that by late 1728 'it was customarily Newcastle, not Townshend, who transmitted notes to the King about foreign affairs, even if the problems discussed fell solely within the sphere of the northern secretary'. No evidence is produced to support this assertion, and Browning's account of the struggle between Newcastle and Townshend is both largely based upon Coxe and overtly hostile to Townshend.[53] There is no evidence to support the claim that Newcastle had 'assumed command of foreign affairs' by late 1728. There is no sign of Newcastle playing any role in the talks with Kinsky early in 1729. It is clear that the secret correspondence between Townshend and Poyntz met with royal approval; and Townshend stated that his orders to Poyntz to press Fleury to action originated with the King. Rather than Townshend vainly resisting the growing strength and profounder ideas of Newcastle, as Browning suggests, it seems to be the case that Newcastle was angered by his own weak position.[54] Townshend corresponded with the British Plenipotentiaries at Soissons without consulting Newcastle, and there are no signs that Newcastle was consulted over the activities of Townshend's department, such as the instructions sent to Waldegrave. Townshend was determined to retain control of British foreign policy, or rather of those areas of policy which he regarded as being most important. Attention has been drawn to the fact that in the summer of 1729 control of Anglo-Spanish negotiations was transferred from Townshend and the King at Hanover to the British Plenipotentiaries in France operating under the orders of the Queen and the ministers in London.[55] In fact George and Townshend did intervene in the Anglo-Spanish negotiations.[56] Furthermore this issue has distracted attention from the fact that no such transfer occurred in the case of Anglo-Austrian negotiations. These were securely vested in the hands of George and Townshend. When Kinsky approached Newcastle and Robert Walpole, after George and Townshend had already left London for Hanover, they referred him to Hanover. The British Plenipotentiaries received no instructions about negotiations with Austria despite the fact that the Austrian representatives in Paris, Stephen Kinsky and Fonseca, were senior to Philip Kinsky and, in the late summer of 1729, ready to negotiate with the British. When Fonseca and Stephen Kinsky approached the British Plenipotentiaries they were referred to Hanover.[57]

Determined to retain control of the important areas of British foreign policy Townshend clashed not only with Newcastle, but also with Sir Robert Walpole. The latter was increasingly concerned about the domestic repercussions of British foreign policy, and he differed with Townshend over the best policy to follow. Newcastle and Sir Robert Walpole favoured making up with Austria, but Townshend 'differs toto coelo'. In the summer of 1728 Horatio Walpole had made clear his total opposition to any Anglo-Austrian reconciliation. The Austrian government regarded Townshend as particularly anti-Austrian.[58] Linked to these clashes were the conflicting ambitions of several major politicians. Methuen sought to become Secretary of State, as did Chesterfield. Stanhope wanted a peerage and an end to diplomatic postings. When Methuen resigned as Treasurer of the Household, Stanhope attempted unsuccessfully to gain the post. Chammorel noted tension involving Carteret. Horatio Walpole denied any interest in becoming Secretary of State, but his protestations were doubted by many. The British representatives in France, Poyntz, Stanhope and Horatio Walpole, operated in an atmosphere of mutual distrust receiving contradictory instructions from London. Poyntz was in close touch with Townshend, Stanhope with Newcastle.[59]

These varied ambitions and disputes were already of considerable importance before George and Townshend left for Hanover, though it is very difficult to distinguish their relation to developments in British policy. In particular, their influence upon the abortive Anglo-Austrian talks held in London is obscure. It is not clear whether Stanhope, who had returned to London for the session, or Kinsky made the first advances. After the talks had collapsed, both sides claimed the other had made the first approach. The Austrians sought to embarrass Britain with her allies, whilst the British were determined to defeat any such attempt and to show that they had rejected Austrian approaches and been faithful to their allies. Whether Kinsky or the British made the first approach, it is interesting that Stanhope had a more prominent role than Townshend. In November 1729 the Austrian Plenipotentiaries in Paris informed Charles VI that in the previous summer Stanhope, then in Paris, had told Stephen Kinsky that his role reflected the Queen's awareness of tension between Townshend and Philip Kinsky. The Austrian Plenipotentiaries saw Stanhope as well-intentioned.[60] Whether the Queen also attempted to keep Townshend in the dark is unclear, but if so, she failed. It could be suggested that the moves Townshend made in February 1729 were designed to hinder the Anglo-Austrian negotiations or at least to bring them under his personal role and restrict the participation of the Queen and Stanhope. Kinsky complained to Chesterfield 'of the unkind reception he had met with in England, and that notwithstanding his master's good disposition, and his own earnest endeavours to accommodate matters, he had found no willingness in England to contribute to so desirable an end'. By moving the negotiations from London to Vienna Townshend brought them under his own control. This was further secured by the fact that they would be conducted by his own protégé Waldegrave, and that the security of his communications with Waldegrave would be controlled by his friend Sutton. Having brought the negotiations under control, he remoulded them to conform to his own views. Waldegrave's instructions were firm, if not harsh, making it clear that Austria would have to discard Prussian interests and submit to the indignity of having a prince of the Empire dictate to the Emperor the settlement of several Imperial disputes. Townshend also denied the Austrian claim that the Queen had sent for Kinsky, and going further than Stanhope, had made advances for a reconciliation. It is interesting to note that in 1732, at the time of the Anglo-Austrian alliance, Townshend wrote of Caroline,

I am persuaded she never in her heart approved of my notions in foreign affairs.

She is now got into the Plan which she always wished to see formed, and I heartily pray to God that it may succeed, but am still under the apprehensions which I formerly explained to you and am more confirmed in them by the present behaviour of the courts of Spain and France.[61]

How far Townshend's actions in early 1729 reflected George's orders is unclear. The King's role in the abortive Anglo-Austrian negotiations is obscure. Given the insistence upon Hanoverian demands in the instructions to Waldegrave, it could be suggested that George had intervened in order to block any reconciliation ignoring Hanoverian interests, but equally it could be argued that Townshend used the Hanoverian issue in order to persuade George to support his own more sceptical approach to the reconciliation. The interest expressed in the marriage of Maria Theresa points towards the active participation of George II, who had caused such a fuss over the issue in the spring of 1728 and who was largely responsible for demands that the Austrians should commit themselves over the choice of partner. It also reveals that much more was at stake than a simple settlement of Austro-Hanoverian disputes.

Despite the prominence given to Hanoverian demands in the instructions sent to Waldegrave, it would be a mistake to conclude that the negotiations failed due to this issue or that they revealed George and Townshend to be selfishly concerned with Electoral points to the detriment of wider interests. Whichever party is held to have taken the initiative, it would have been easy for Austria to respond favourably to the British position, talk about 'natural allies' and then, once the British had committed themselves to a formal alliance, betray it to France, Spain or the British opposition. Fears were expressed that they would follow such a policy. Sinzendorf denied that the Austrians had any intention of settling without France.[62] The Austrians were suspected of seeking to destroy the Hanover alliance, and the British would have been quite correct to suspect Austrian statements advanced through a relatively low-grade diplomat, even were he not as volatile as Kinsky. Kinsky lacked the rank of Sinzendorf or the contacts of Seckendorf. Delafaye observed of the negotiation 'it is well notice was sent of it in time to the Cardinal, for the Count can keep no secrets.'[63] In addition, the disavowal of Sinzendorf's approval of the Provisional Treaty must have warned the British to be cautious about committing themselves to the Austrians, and to be suspicious of the ability of Austrian diplomats to influence their country's policies. The stress in Townshend's instructions upon Hanoverian demands was therefore at one level a sensible diplomatic move, for the settlement of them would prove Austrian sincerity. Whatever the talk about shared interests, natural allies and the balance of power, it was only possible, in the first instance, for Austria to indicate its good intentions by a settlement of Hanoverian demands. Chesterfield complained to Kinsky of the Austrian 'professions, which consisted only in words, at the same time that no one action of that court corresponded with them; but on the contrary seemed rather calculated to exasperate than to quiet affairs'.[64] The settlement of Hanoverian demands could be done speedily and would not fatally compromise Britain in the eyes of her allies.

Whether the decision to tie progress in any Anglo-Austrian reconciliation to the settlement of Hanoverian demands was approved of within the
British ministry, or even debated, is unclear. It is possible that the great
care taken to keep Waldegrave's instructions secret from Britain's allies
was matched by a determination to keep many of the British ministers in
the dark. Newcastle and Horatio Walpole do not appear to have had any
role in the matter, and it is possible that Newcastle's complaints about not
being kept informed refer to this episode. In the Commons debate on the
Address there was an interesting hint that Sir Robert Walpole was aware of
the prospect of a reconciliation. Knatchbull noted in his diary, 'Sir Robert
urged that, for argument sake suppose the Emperor was any way inclined
to a coolness with Spain and was any ways looking towards us, would it be
prudent to anger him at this time'. The *Craftsman* commented in August
1729 that during the session 'it was confidentially asserted, that we were in
a fair way of settling all kinds of differences with the Emperor'.[65]

Prior to the summer of 1729 the views of ministers on foreign policy
issues are largely unclear. It is possible to use the views advanced in the
summer as an indicator of attitudes held in the spring but this is a rather
dangerous procedure. The fact that Townshend in the summer was
opposed to naval action against Spain does not prove he held the view in
the early spring, because the commencement of Anglo-Spanish negotiations in the late spring could have altered his opinions. The arguments
advanced by various ministers during the summer represent as much their
response to recent events or predicted developments as they do their
long-term views on the European situation, and it is necessary, though
difficult, to attempt to disentangle these different threads, whilst accepting
that for some ministers they may have been inextricably confused. During
the summer of 1729 attitudes were to be affected by three major
developments. From May onwards the prospect of an alliance between
Spain and the Hanover alliance became more apparent. In 1730 Poyntz
was to claim that 'the conduct of the Imperial court in relation to the
Provisional Treaty forced us into the arms of Spain'.[66] The discussions
about an alliance between Britain and the Wittelsbach Electors, hitherto
desultory, became of growing importance, and the projected alliance
became a major and divisive issue. In August a threatened Prussian attack
upon Hanover led to a reinterpretation of George II's relations with his
allies. These three related developments increased the urgency of foreign
policy decisions but the unpredictability of developments made the
decisions harder to take. Whereas in the previous summer negotiations
had centred round the rather cosy world of Soissons and Paris, in 1729
there was an altogether more upsetting atmosphere of volatility and
violence.

Notes

1. 'Memoire sur l'Etat present de la Grande Bretagne', 31 Dec. 1728, Broglie to

Chauvelin, 3 Jan. 1729, AE. CP. Ang. 364–5; D'Aix to Victor Amadeus II, 15 Nov. 1728, AST. LM. Ing. 35.

2. *Wye's Letter* 23, 25 Jan. (os) 1729; Egmont, III, 330–2; Knatchbull, pp. 80–1; Townshend to Sutton, 21 Jan. (os) 1729, PRO. 81/123; Broglie to Chauvelin, 3 Feb., Chammorel to Chauvelin, 3 Feb. 1729, AE. CP. Ang. 365; Colley, *Defiance* p. 209; Thomas Winnington, MP for Droitwich, to Stephen Fox, 24 Mar. (os) 1729, Dorset CRO. D124/box 240.

3. Knatchbull, p. 82; Broglie to Chauvelin, 7 Feb., Chammorel to Chauvelin, 14 Feb. 1729, AE. CP. Ang. 365; Duff, *Culloden Papers* p. 104; Delafaye to Poyntz, 21 Jan. (os), 3 Feb. 1729, BL. Althorp, E3.

4. Broglie to Chauvelin, 21 Feb. 1729, AE. CP. Ang. 365; Sedgwick, II, 230.

5. Zamboni to Manteuffel, 29 Mar. 1729, Bodl. Rawl. 120; Knatchbull, pp. 86–7, 89–94; Carlisle, p. 58; Hervey, pp. 94–5; Sedgwick, I, 38; Thomas, *House of Commons*, p. 275; Winnington to Hervey, 9 Apr. (os) 1729, Dorset, D124/box 240; G.C. Gibbs, 'Parliament and Foreign Policy in the Age of Stanhope and Walpole', *EHR* (1962), pp. 31–2; *Wye's Letter* 5 June (os) 1729; Poyntz to Thomas Townshend, 19 Feb., Delafaye to Poyntz, 13, 17 Mar. (os), Selwyn to Poyntz, 17 Mar. (os) 1729, BL. Althorp, E5, E3.

6. Knatchbull, pp. 83–6; *Wye's Letter* 5, 8 Feb. (os) 1729; Horatio Walpole to Fleury, 6 Feb. (os) 1729, PRO. 78/193; Tilson to Waldegrave, 24 Jan. (os), Horatio Walpole to Waldegrave, 15 Feb. (os) 1729, Chewton; Villars, p. 161; Carlisle, p. 57; Sedgwick, I, 37.

7. Knatchbull, pp. 92–6; Carlisle, p. 59; Marini, p. 127; Hervey, pp. 100–1.

8. P. Langford, *Excise Crisis* (Oxford, 1975), pp. 77–83, 173; Colley, *Defiance*, p. 81; Hill, *Parliamentary Parties*, p. 199; Zamboni to Manteuffel, 24 May, 1729, Bodl. Rawl. 120; Duke to Duchess of Newcastle, 10 Dec. (os) 1741, BL. Add. 33073, Selwyn to Poyntz, 31 Mar. (os) 1729, BL. Althorp, E3.

9. Egmont, III, 341; Pentenriedter to Fonseca, 22 Mar. 1727, HHStA., Fonseca, 21; D'Aix to Victor Amadeus II, 15 Nov. 1728, AST. LM. Ing. 35; Dickinson, *Walpole*, pp. 81–2; 'Situation de l'Angleterre', 27 June 1739, AE. MD. Ang. 8.

10. Townshend to Poyntz, 12, 21 Feb. (os) 1729, Coxe, II, 639, BL. Add. 48982; Townshend to Broglie, 3 Nov. (os), Newcastle to Poyntz, 20 Feb. (os) 1729, Townshend to Edward Finch, 3 Feb. (os) 1730, PRO. 100/9, 78/193, 95/54; Fleury to Horatio Walpole, 6 Feb. 1729, AE. CP. Ang. 368; Newcastle to Poyntz, 1 Apr. (os) 1729, BL. Althorp, E3.

11. J. R. Jones, *Britain and the World 1649–1815* (1980), pp. 13, 185.

12. Egmont, III, 338; Duff, *Culloden Papers*, p. 104.

13. Egmont, III, 338, 347.

14. *True Briton* 7 June (os) 1723; Horatio Walpole to Newcastle, 4 May 1728, BL. Add. 32755; Chammorel to Chauvelin, 15 Jan. 1731, AE. CP. Ang. 373; *Craftsman* 30 Aug. (os) 1729; Ossorio to Victor Amadeus II, 20 Mar. 1730, AST. LM. Ing. 37; Harrison to Poyntz, 3 Mar. (os) 1729, BL. Althorp, E3.

15. Chammorel to Chauvelin, 6 Apr. 1729, AE. CP. Ang. 366; Villars, p. 171.

16. Robinson to Waldegrave, 10 Feb. 1729, Chewton; Kinsky to Eugene, 8 Feb. 1729, HHStA., GK. 94(b); Broglie to Chauvelin, 28 Feb., 7 Mar. 1729, AE. CP. Ang. 365; Villars, pp. 167–8.

17. Townshend to Waldegrave, 4 Feb. (os), Horatio Walpole to Fleury, 6 Feb. (os), Newcastle to Plenipotentiaries, 24 Apr. (os) 1729, PRO. 80/64, 78/193; Poyntz to Keene, 12 Apr. 1729, BL. Add. 32760; *Craftsman* 15 Feb. (os), 1, 8, 22, 29 Mar. (os) 1729.

18. Waldegrave to Townshend, 15 Jan. 1729, Chewton.

19. Townshend to Waldegrave, 4 Feb. (os) 1729, Chewton; Le Coq to Augustus, 4 Apr. 1729, Dresden, 2735, 1; *Craftsman* 7, 21 Dec. (os) 1728.

20. Poyntz to Newcastle, 27 Feb., 11 Mar., Horatio Walpole to Poyntz, 6 Feb. (os), Newcastle to Poyntz, 20 Feb. (os) 1729, PRO. 78/190, 193; Townshend to Poyntz, 12, 21 Feb. (os) 1729, Coxe II, 638, BL. Add. 48982; King, p. 85; Marini, p. 126; Delafaye to Poyntz, 10 Mar. (os), 1 Apr. (os) 1729, BL. Althorp, E3.

21. Chambrier to Frederick William, 10 Dec. 1728, 10 Jan. 1729, PRO. 78/190, AE. CP. Prusse 88; Poyntz to Newcastle, 14 Jan., 6, 27 Feb., 11 Mar. 1729, PRO. 78/190;

Delafaye to Poyntz, 3 Feb. (os) 1729, BL. Althorp, E3; Poyntz to Horatio Walpole, 16 Jan. 1727, BL. Add. 63750; Wych to Townshend, 8 Feb. 1729, PRO. 82/46.

22. Newcastle to Poyntz, 25 Dec. (os) 1728, PRO. 78/189; Fonseca to Eugene, 12 Dec. 1728, HHStA., GK. 85a; Hughes, pp. 382–3.

23. Frederick William to Chambrier, 1 Jan. 1729, AE. CP. Prusse 88; D'Aix to Victor Amadeus II, 27 Dec. 1728, 18 Apr. 1729, AST. LM. Ing. 35; Zamboni to Manteuffel, 1 Mar. 1729, Bodl. Rawl. 120; Delafaye to Poyntz, 21 Feb. (os), Tilson to Poyntz, 1 Apr. 1729, BL. Althorp, E3.

24. Townshend to Chesterfield, 12, 29 Nov. (os), Chesterfield to Townshend, 25 Dec. 1728, PRO. 84/302; Horatio Walpole to Tilson, 12 Nov., Townshend to Plenipotentiaries, 3 Dec. (os) 1728, BL. Add. 9138.

25. Newcastle to Horatio Walpole, 11 Oct. (os), Townshend to Chesterfield, 12 Nov. (os) 1728, PRO. 78/189, 84/302; Horatio Walpole to Tilson, 18 Dec. 1728, Bradfer Lawrence.

26. Chesterfield to Townshend, 30 Nov., 25 Dec., Townshend to Chesterfield, 29 Nov. (os) 1728, PRO. 84/302; *Wye's Letter* 29 Oct. (os), 17 Dec. (os) 1728, 16 Jan. (os), 13 Feb. (os) 1729; *Original Mercury* 10 Dec. (os) 1728; *Craftsman* 7 Dec. (os) 1728, 11 Jan. (os) 1729; *Political State of Great Britain* 37 (1729) p. 110; Zamboni to Manteuffel, 24 Dec. 1728, Bodl. Rawl. 120; D'Aix to Victor Amadeus II, 10 Jan. 1729, AST. LM. Ing. 35.

27. Townshend to Plenipotentiaries, 3 Dec. (os) 1728, BL. Add. 9138; Townshend to Edward Finch, 27 Dec. (os) 1728, PRO. 95/51.

28. Chesterfield to Townshend, 17 May 1729, PRO. 84/304.

29. Waldegrave to Townshend, 30 Oct. 1728, PRO. 80/63; Riva to Duke of Modena, 5 Nov. 1728, HHStA., Interiora, Intercepte I; O'Rourke to James III, 11, 17 Dec. 1728, HHStA., England, Varia 8; Zamboni to Manteuffel, 29 Oct. 1728, Bodl. Rawl. 120.

30. Chesterfield to Townshend, 26 Oct., 12 Nov. 1728, PRO. 84/302; Chesterfield to Waldegrave, 10 Dec. 1728, Chewton.

31. Kinsky to Eugene, 1 Dec. 1728, HHStA., GK. 94(b); Chesterfield to Townshend, 5, 12 Nov. 1728, PRO. 84/302.

32. Kinsky to Charles VI, 18, 25, 28 Jan., Kinsky to Eugene, 8, 25 Feb. 1729, HHStA., EK. 65, GK. 94(b); Tilson to Waldegrave, 21 Jan. (os) 1729, Chewton; Townshend to Waldegrave, 25 Mar. (os), 1729, PRO. 80/64; Braubach, *Eugen* IV, 338.

33. Kinsky to Eugene, 8 Feb. 1729, HHStA., GK. 94(b).

34. Höfler I, 26, 110, II, 108; Tilson to Waldegrave, 19 Sept. (os) 1729, Chewton; Zamboni to Manteuffel, 18 Jan. 1729, Bodl. Rawl. 120.

35. Townshend to Waldegrave, 16 Feb. (os) 1729, PRO. 80/64; Sinzendorf to Fonseca, 19 Apr. 1729, HHStA., Fonseca 13.

36. Townshend to Waldegrave, 16 Feb. (os) 1729, Chewton; Kinsky to Prince Eugene, 11 Jan. 1729, HHStA., GK. 94(G).

37. Horatio Walpole to Waldegrave, 11 Feb. (os), Tilson to Waldegrave, 18 Mar. (os) 1729, Chewton; Townshend to Waldegrave, 18 Mar. (os), Waldegrave to Tilson, 5 Feb. 1729, PRO. 80/64.

38. Zamboni to Manteuffel, 29 Oct. 1728, Bodl. Rawl. 120; Sinzendorf to Fonseca, 26 Nov., 14, 21 Dec. 1728, HHStA., Fonseca 13; D'Aix to Victor Amadeus II, 3 Jan. 1729, AST. LM. Ing. 37; Vignola, Venetian Resident, to Government of Venice, 25 Mar., 15 Apr. 1729, ASV. LM. Ing. 98; draft to Grimaldi, Genoese diplomat, 2 Apr. (os) 1729, PRO. 100/32; Baudrillart, III, 495, n.1.

39. Townshend to Waldegrave, 4 Feb. (os), 28 Mar. (os) 1729, Townshend to Newcastle, 24 May (os) 1726, PRO. 80/64, 35/62; Tilson to Waldegrave, 18 Mar. (os) 1729, Chewton; Wackerbarth to Augustus II, 22 June 1729, Dresden, 3331, 1; Townshend to Du Bourgay, 31 Jan. (os) 1729, PRO. 90/24.

40. Townshend to Sutton, 16 Feb. (os), Sutton to Townshend, 11 Mar., Waldegrave to Townshend, 19 Mar. 1729, PRO. 81/23, 80/64; Sutton to Waldegrave, 10 Mar. 1729, Chewton.

41. Townshend to Waldegrave, 16 Feb. (os) 1729, PRO. 80/64; Zamboni to Manteuffel, 25 Feb. 1729, Bodl. Rawl. 120.

42. Poyntz to Delafaye, 6 Feb. 1729, PRO. 78/190; Zamboni to Manteuffel, 25 Feb., 1 Mar. 1729, Bodl. Rawl. 120; Wackerbarth to Augustus II, 15 Jan., 5 Feb., 19 Mar., 13, 20 Apr., 4, 14 May 1729, Dresden, 3331, 1; Chauvelin to Chammorel, 14 Apr., Anon.

report, 4 Apr. 1729, AE. CP. Ang. sup. 8; Woodward to Tilson, 23 Apr., Plenipotentiaries to Newcastle, 25 Apr. 1729, PRO. 88/35, 78/190; Eugene to Kinsky, 2 May 1729, HHStA., GK. 94(b); Tilson to Horatio Walpole, 10 Apr. (os) 1729, BL. Add. 48982; Vignola to Doge of Venice, 1, 8 Apr. 1729, ASV. LM. Ing. 98.

43. Townshend to Waldegrave, 26, 28 Mar. (os), Waldegrave to Townshend, 1, 15 Jan., 23, 26 Feb., 18 Mar. 1729, PRO. 80/64; Wackerbarth to Augustus II, 28 May, 8 June 1728, Dresden, 3331, 1.

44. Waldegrave to Townshend, 18, 19, 26 Mar., Townshend to Waldegrave, 25 Mar. (os) 1729, PRO. 80/64; Sinzendorf to Fonseca, 14 May, Instructions for Fonseca, 14 May 1729, HHStA., Fonseca 13.

45. Charles VI to Stephen Kinsky, 26 June, Eugene to Philip Kinsky, 27 Apr., 11 May 1729, HHStA., Fonseca 13, GK. 94(b); Zamboni to Manteuffel, 26 Apr. 1729, Bodl. Rawl. 120; Beer, 'Geschichte der Politick Karl's VI', pp. 53–4.

46. Eugene to Kinsky, 2 May, Kinsky to Eugene, 8 Feb., Kinsky to Charles VI, 3, 8 Feb., 22 Mar. 1729, HHStA., GK. 94(b), EK. 65; Townshend to Diemar, 1 May, Sutton to Townshend, 24 Feb., Newcastle to Plenipotentiaries, 5 May (os), Charles VI to George II, 8 Apr., Wych to Townshend, 15 Mar. 1729, PRO. 100/15, 81/123, 78/193, 82/46; Villars, pp. 163, 166.

47. Townshend to Waldegrave, 25 Mar. (os), 15 Apr. (os) 1729, PRO. 80/64; Tilson to Waldegrave, 1, 4 Apr. (os) 1729, Chewton; Stephen Kinsky and Fonseca to Charles VI, 6 July 1729, Höfler, I, 26.

48. Waldegrave to Townshend, 19, 26 Mar. 1729, PRO. 80/64; Eugene to La Paz, – Dec. 1728, HHStA., GK. 102(a).

49. Instructions for Fonseca, 14 May 1729, HHStA., Fonseca 13; Du Bourgay to Townshend, 19 Feb., Instructions for Seckendorf, 30 June 1729, PRO. 90/24, 78/193; Eugene to Kinsky, 20 Aug. 1729, Vienna, Kinsky 2(b).

50. Du Bourgay to Townshend, 19 Mar., 5, 14 Apr., Townshend to Du Bourgay, 15 Apr. (os), Townshend to Newcastle, 13 Apr. (os), Townshend to Chesterfield, 29 Apr. (os), Chesterfield to Townshend, 17 May 1729, PRO. 90/24, 43/77, 84/304.

51. Newcastle to Stanhope, 12 June (os) 1729, Coxe, II, 644; Plenipotentiaries to Newcastle, 25 Apr., Horatio Walpole and Stanhope to Townshend, 4 July, Townshend to Newcastle, 13 Apr. (os), Chesterfield to Townshend, 17 May 1729, PRO. 78/190, 192, 43/77, 84/304; Villars, p. 172.

52. Townshend to Poyntz, 21 Feb. (os) 1729, BL. Add. 48982; Newcastle to Stanhope, 15 Apr. (os) 1729, Coxe, II, 643.

53. Browning, pp. 49–50, 54–5, 19; Newcastle to Stanhope, 22 May (os) 1729, Coxe, II, 641–2.

54. Townshend to Poyntz, 21 Feb. (os) 1729, Delafaye to Horatio Walpole, 14 May (os) 1728, Coxe, II, 640, 623.

55. Townshend to Newcastle, 29 July, 2 Sept. 1729, PRO. 43/79–80; King, p. 110; Chavigny to Chauvelin, 4 Sept. 1729, AE. CP. Br. 47.

56. Townshend to Keene, 18 June, Townshend to Plenipotentiaries, 11 Sept. 1729, PRO. 94/100, BL. Add. 32763.

57. Newcastle to Horatio Walpole and Poyntz, 22 Sept. (os), Horatio Walpole and Stanhope to Keene, 17 Sept. 1729, BL. Add. 32763, PRO. 78/192.

58. Newcastle to Stanhope, 2 June (os) 1729, Coxe, II, 641; Horatio Walpole to Townshend, 1 July 1728, Bradfer Lawrence; Charles VI to Kinsky, 26 June 1729, HHStA., Fonseca 13.

59. Chammorel to Chauvelin, 11 Aug. 1729, AE. CP. Ang. 366; Townshend to Poyntz, 21 Feb. (os), Newcastle to Stanhope, 22 May (os) 1729, Coxe II, 638, 640–2; *Wye's Letter* 17 May (os) 1729, Zamboni to Manteuffel, 31 May 1729; Bodl. Rawl. 129; Hervey, pp. 101–2; Poyntz to Townshend, 11 June 1729, BL. Althorp, E5.

60. Fonseca and Stephen Kinsky to Charles VI, 6 July, 28 Nov., Fleury to Charles VI, 19 Dec. 1729, Höfler, I, 26, 363, II, 56; Philip Kinsky to Eugene, 16 Apr., Instructions for Stephen Kinsky and Fonseca, 31 Aug. 1729, HHStA, GK. 94(b), Fonseca 13; Kinsky to Townshend, 11 Sept., Horatio Walpole and Stanhope to Keene, 17 Sept. 1729, PRO. 100/11, 78/192; Horatio Walpole and Poyntz to Stanhope, 27 Sept. 1729, BL. Add. 32763.

61. Chesterfield to Townshend, 11 June, Waldegrave to Townshend, 18 Mar., Townshend

to Waldegrave, 25 Mar. (os) 1729, PRO. 84/304, 80/64; Townshend to Poyntz, 26 June (os) 1732, BL. Althorp, E5.

62. Chesterfield to Townshend, 12 July 1729, PRO. 84/304; Sinzendorf to Fonseca, 19 Feb. 1729, HHStA., Fonseca 13.

63. Waldegrave to Townshend, 15 Jan. 1729, PRO. 80/64; Delafaye to Poyntz, 1 Apr. (os) 1729, BL. Althorp, E3.

64. Chesterfield to Townshend, 11 June 1729, PRO. 84/304.

65. Knatchbull, p. 83; *Craftsman*, 16 Aug. (os) 1729.

66. Poyntz to Waldegrave, 19 Jan. 1730, BL. Add. 32765.

CHAPTER EIGHT

The Summer of 1729
The Dissolution of the Alliance of Vienna:
Negotiations with the Wittelsbachs

'The Common people huzza'd his Excellency, and cry'd, God bless
our good King George, a lasting peace, and a flourishing trade'.
St. James's Evening Post, 16 April 1728.[1]

In the spring of 1729 many of the British ministers who had spent the
winter in London set off for the Continent. The trials of parliamentary
attendance over, they crossed the sea, determined that the success of their
negotiations would prevent a recurrence next session of the difficulties the
ministry had faced in defending their policies. Delafaye wrote to Poyntz 'I
hope we shall not have the same story to tell over again another session.'
The British Plenipotentiaries to the Congress of Soissons travelled to Paris
where the Congress was now in effect being held. Horatio Walpole arrived
there on 18 April, Stanhope two days later. In May George and
Townshend set off for Hanover, George leaving on 28 May. The Queen
was left in charge of the government at London with Newcastle and Sir
Robert Walpole as her principal advisers in the field of foreign policy.

By the time of this dispersal it was already clear that one of the basic
elements of the European political system since 1725, the alliance of Spain
and Austria, was, if not already destroyed, in serious danger of dissolution.
Spanish pressure for a firm Austrian commitment to a speedy marriage of
Maria Theresa and Don Carlos failed to elicit anything more than
prevaricating answers. The Austrians argued that the Archduchesses were
too tender for matrimony and that Don Carlos must wait.[2] It is possible
that Charles VI had no intention of making Carlos his son-in-law, and the
favour with which Francis of Lorraine was treated at Vienna suggests that
he was seen already as the likely husband of Maria Theresa. In the short
term it is probable that other factors also played a role in postponing the
Austrian decision. Waldegrave suggested that the Austrians had decided to
postpone all decisions until they saw whether Spain intended to honour
her promise to pay Austria the arrears of her subsidy out of the proceeds of
the treasure fleet. The acute fiscal crisis then affecting Austria lends
substance to Waldegrave's suggestion, for without her subsidy Austria was
unable to pay the subsidies she had promised to various Princes of the
Empire.[3] The Austrians were aware of the danger that Spain might
approach France.[4]

Enraged at the Austrian refusal, Elisabeth Farnese determined to
discover whether France and Britain were willing to support her interests.
At the end of March the Spanish minister La Paz wrote to Fleury offering
to reopen negotiations on the basis of the introduction of Spanish garrisons

into those Italian duchies whose succession Carlos claimed.[5] Neither the Austro-Spanish tension nor the Spanish approaches to France remained secret for long, but optimism within the camp of the Hanover alliance was tempered by several factors. First, as the British Plenipotentiaries commented, Spain seemed to expect support over the Spanish garrisons without being willing to promise anything more than a renewal of negotiations at the Congress.[6] The same situation had been noted the previous autumn.[7] The British were determined that their position in Gibraltar and Minorca should be secured and Spanish depredations halted, whilst the French were very concerned at the projected *indulto* upon the cargo of the treasure fleet.[8] Secondly, the Hanover allies were worried about Elisabeth Farnese's real intentions for Carlos. Fleury feared Elisabeth's vast projects[9] and wondered how it would be possible to get Austrian consent to the introduction of Spanish garrisons.[10] Thirdly, the unpredictability of the Queen of Spain in particular and of Spanish policy in general made Spain seem an undesirable ally.[11] Fears were expressed that Spain would dupe the Hanover allies and use her negotiations with them to scare Austria into accepting her demands.[12] These factors encouraged a cautious response to the initial Spanish approach.[13] This caution was particularly marked in the British case, for the early months of 1729 had seen rumours of Anglo-Spanish military conflict, rumours which had persisted into the late spring and had attracted much diplomatic attention. The British government was concerned at Spanish military moves, worried by her naval preparations and anxious about the possibility of a new Spanish attack on Gibraltar. Keene was ordered to report on Spanish military moves. Admiral Cavendish reported concern over Gibraltar, whilst Chesterfield informed Townshend of a rumour that a siege was intended. The arming of the Spanish navy was followed by foreign diplomats, and by the British press. In late April the *Daily Post Boy* noted that Spain had twenty-one men-of-war in its Spanish ports. On 5 May the representative of the French Ministry of the Marine in Spain, D'Aubenton, reported that eleven ships of the line were arming at Cadiz.[14]

The natural British response was naval armaments, and the British decided to send a squadron to protect Gibraltar. Zamboni noted that the British were concerned about the Spanish preparations and unsure where they were intended for.[15] Given the scope of possible Spanish action, major British preparations were clearly felt to be necessary. During the late spring a sizeable fleet was prepared. On 17 May Tilson informed Waldegrave that the fleet would be ready for 'any action that may be render'd necessary'.[16] These British preparations alarmed Spain[17] and worried Britain's allies. The Saxon representative in Spain, De Buy, informed Count Manteuffel that the Spanish decision to send more troops to the Indies was taken in response to fears that the British would attack their possessions there.[18] Britain's allies feared that the dispatch of a large British fleet to Spanish waters would increase tension and might lead to war.[19]

Fortunately for the negotiations between Spain and the Hanover allies, the representatives of Britain and France in Spain were not alarmists.

Keene, D'Aubenton, and William Cayley, the British Consul at Cadiz, took great care to report both the intended Spanish preparations and their limited success. On 15 May Cayley commented on the movement of the Spanish warships from the inner harbour at Cadiz into the Bay: 'It can hardly be with any other design than to make a noise and show of readiness, in which they are far from really being.'[20] Tyrawly at Lisbon was more concerned about the Spanish preparations.[21]

It is likely that these reports damped the pressure within Britain for naval action against Spain. The British fleet was still ordered to assemble off Spithead and to prepare for an expedition to Spanish waters, but alongside these preparations the British showed a willingness to negotiate with Spain. The failure to secure a rapprochement with Austria left Britain little choice but to follow the French lead in replying to the Spanish approach. On 9 May instructions drafted jointly by the British and French ministers were sent to the French Ambassador in Spain, Brancas, and to Keene, to assure the Spanish government that in return for an immediate Spanish acceptance of the Provisional Treaty, France and Britain would attempt to gain the agreement of Austria and of the Grand-Duke of Tuscany to the speedy introduction of the Spanish garrisons.[22] France yielded to British pressure and agreed to threaten Spain with war should she reject the Anglo-French approach.[23]

Fleury, however, had not only no intention of fighting Spain, but also did not wish to run the risk of Austria refusing to accept any settlement of the Italian problem devised by the Hanover allies and Spain. Poyntz complained that he seemed 'equally fearful of obliging or disobliging Spain.'[24] The introduction of Spanish garrisons had not been specified in the Quadruple Alliance, and Fleury feared Austria would reject the idea, seeing it as a threat to Austrian hegemony in Italy. He therefore suggested that neutral, rather than Spanish, garrisons should be specified; during the summer various expedients involving British, Papal, Sardinian and Swiss troops were advanced.[25] Elisabeth Farnese was totally opposed to any such arrangement[26] and in late May she threatened to return to the Austrian alliance.[27] The Austrian ambassador Count Königsegg declared that Austria would accept Spanish garrisons, and he worked hard to restore the Austro-Spanish alliance. In the negotiations at Seville in November 'the Spanish Ministers declared publickly that the articles of their project' for Spanish garrisons 'were copied almost word for word from some offers of Königseck.'[28] The British government feared that the Austrians would offer new and better proposals to Spain. Poyntz wrote to Townshend 'I only wish our offer through the Cardinal's dilatoriness don't come too late to work its effect. For I much suspect the Emperor will have been beforehand with us.'[29] By 23 June De Buy could report that the Hanover allies had lost the chance of a Spanish alliance due to Fleury's opposition to the Spanish garrisons.[30]

> By all the conversations I have had with Mor. Patino I am more and more persuaded that it will be impossible to content the Queen of Spain without the introduction of Spanish troops into Tuscany and Parma and

that upon this condition Spain will not barely resume the course of the negotiations at Soissons as laid down in the Marq. de la Paz's letter of the 29th March to the Cardinal but will finish and conclude all matters depending between the two courts by a formal and decisive treaty.

Benjamin Keene[31]

Whereas the French response to the prospect of a Spanish alliance was hesitant and affected by the animosity between Fleury and Elisabeth Farnese, the British were more positive in their response to the Spanish demands, though it was they, not the French, who were preparing for military action against Spain. A major reason for this was the willingness of the Spaniards to drop the issues of Gibraltar and Minorca, provided they secured their goal of the Spanish garrisons. The British seemed to be more favourable to the prospect of Spanish garrisons than the French, though they too would have preferred neutral troops. Newcastle regarded the issue as crucial, 'what I think must bring all things right, is the Emperor's aversion on any account to admit Spanish garrisons.' De Buy reported on 16 June that the British were now in favour in Spain.[32]

The issue of the Spanish garrisons might seem to be a rather petty one, but in fact it was of the greatest importance both at the time and subsequently. Brancas and Keene urged the Spaniards 'that at least in the publick treaty some regard should be had to cover our resolutions to introduce Spanish troops that it might not appear that we went directly contrary to the express words of the Quadruple Allyance'.[33] They were seen not so much as a minor infraction of the Quadruple Alliance, but as a possible means by which Spain might destroy the equilibrium in Italy and launch herself on a career of Italian conquest.[34] The Hanover allies were intensely suspicious of the intentions of Elisabeth Farnese. They were warned by their representatives in Spain that she intended to use the Spanish garrisons to further aims of her own totally incompatible with the Quadruple Alliance. Keene informed Newcastle that

> the Queen's great view is the securing D. Carlos's succession and next to that to have her revenge upon the Emp. for having so long amused her, both which points she thinks will be gained by the introduction of Spanish garrisons into Italy.[35]

However, a refusal to accept Spanish garrisons would have led to a failure of the negotiations with Spain.[36] Spain, already fooled by one ally (Austria), suspected neutral garrisons as an attempt to trick Don Carlos out of the succession to Tuscany and Parma. By insisting on the Spanish garrisons, Spain intended to serve two purposes: to secure Carlos's succession, and, by holding the Tuscan ports of Leghorn and Portoferrario, to retain the ability to move large numbers of troops into Italy. This tested the views of the Hanover allies on the major issues of the European balance of power. The talk of the previous four years of revising the territorial order in Italy and driving the Austrians out of all or part of the peninsula suddenly ceased to be speculation.[37] Though some argued that territorial changes in Italy were of no importance to the European balance of power, this was not a generally held view, and it was commonly believed that regional balances, whether in Italy, the Empire, or the Baltic, were an integral part of the general European balance of power. By aiding the introduction of Spanish troops into Italy the Hanover allies, however circumscribed their intentions were, could be accused of helping to destroy the regional balance of power, and indeed this accusation was to be made over the next few years. Bathurst claimed in the Lords' debate on the Treaty of Seville, that the change might cause 'a dangerous and expensive war' and 'destroy the balance of power in Europe'. Spanish garrisons were condemned in the debate as a contradiction not only of 'the letter, but the very sense, and intent of the Quadruple Alliance'.[38]

Negotiations with the Wittelsbachs

Challenging the Austrian hegemony in Italy by supporting Spanish interests was not the only policy possibly incompatible with long-term British aims being pursued by the British government in the summer of 1729. Just as the British risked committing themselves to a troublesome and unpredictable Italian policy, so their negotiations with the Wittelsbachs entailed the risk of a similar commitment in the Empire. Although these negotiations have received very little scholarly attention, they are of considerable importance and throw much light on British intentions toward Prussia and Austria in the second half of 1729. The only scholarly work devoted, at least in part, to the negotiations is a short but important work by Dureng. Dureng's book suffers from being based exclusively upon the French archives, and from adopting too credulous an attitude to his principal source, the dispatches of Anne Théodore Chevignard de Chavigny, the French envoy to the Imperial Diet.[39] Chavigny was sent to Hanover in the summer of 1729, in order to persuade George II to accept an alliance with the Wittelsbachs on the latters' terms. An attempt to supplement Chavigny's dispatches encounters several major problems. First, there is surprisingly little material extant which can throw light upon the attitudes of George and Townshend to the negotiations, or upon the talks held at Hanover that summer. As D'Aix pointed out, there were few foreign envoys in Hanover that year.[40] Only four men participated in the talks at Hanover: George, Townshend, Chavigny, and the Wittelsbach representative, Count Plettenberg, the principal minister of Clemens-August the Elector of Cologne.[41] Chavigny's dispatches are unreliable. George left no record of his role and Townshend's record is restricted to his correspondence with Newcastle and with the British Plenipotentiaries in Paris. In this correspondence he gave a less than full account of his meetings with Chavigny and Plettenberg.

Fortunately, Plettenberg's papers have survived and are accessible. The large deposit of his papers held in Münster contains his correspondence with most of the prominent Wittelsbach ministers, such as the Bavarian Count Törring, with the Elector of Bavaria, with the Bavarian representative at Paris, Count Albert, Prince of Grimbergen, with Chavigny and with Townshend. Unfortunately, he did not keep a diary, or rather none has survived, and he preferred to entrust confidential matters to verbal communication. Thus, he left very little material about his conferences with George and Townshend. The ease of movement between Hanover and the courts of the Electors of Cologne, Mainz and the Palatinate, at Bonn, Mainz and Mannheim respectively, meant that Plettenberg was able to report in person to the Electors on his conferences at Hanover. Aside from the problem of discovering what actually happened at Hanover, it is difficult to ascertain what Wittelsbach intentions were. The major source for them is the correspondence of Plettenberg, but it is a source which has to be handled with care as it tends to stress the interests of the Elector of Cologne rather than those of his relatives.

To coerce Austria into abandoning her provocative policies and to block her schemes for areas such as Mecklenburg and East Friesland at the Imperial Diet, it was necessary to secure the alliance of a number of German Princes. A long-term policy of weakening Austria and gravely restricting her authority and power required the assistance of the Wittelsbach Electors.[42] They wielded great potential power, controlling several votes in the Electoral College, the College which elected Emperors.[43] In addition, when the bishoprics held by members of the family were taken into account, they controlled most of the area of Catholic Germany that was not ruled by the Austrians. Fifteen per cent of Imperial territory was ruled by the Wittelsbachs. As such, they were an obvious ally for France, and, in particular, for those French ministers who wished to see a fundamental reordering of the European situation. For Chauvelin, Chavigny and Belle-Isle the best way to accomplish such an aim was to have a Wittelsbach elected as the next Emperor, and to woo the Wittelsbachs from their commitments to the Austrians.

In 1727–1728 the British had displayed less interest than the French in seeking the alliance of the Wittelsbachs. The ministry was aware of the potential importance of an alliance,[44] but Townshend distrusted them and was opposed to the idea of subsidies.[45] After St. Saphorin left Munich in December 1725 no British envoy visited the city until Onslow Burrish's mission in 1746, though Isaac Leheup and Sir Thomas Robinson received credentials as British representatives in 1726 and 1745 respectively. Leheup was also accredited to the courts of Cologne, Mainz and Mannheim, though he did not present his credentials. In the late 1720s there were no British representatives at any of the Wittelsbach courts and diplomatic relations between them and the Electorate of Hanover were similarly bad. George II, in 1727 and 1728, preferred to leave the negotiations with the Wittelsbachs to the French, and to concentrate on his attempt to create a Protestant German league.[46] It is possible that George's view of the Wittelsbachs was affected by their response to his father's approach in 1725, as a member of the Alliance of Hanover, for an alliance. The Elector of Bavaria, Max-Emmanuel, had demanded that he receive peacetime subsidies and a guarantee of the Bavarian claims to the Austrian succession. These demands, and the treaty signed on 1 September 1726 between Charles VI and Charles-Albert, the new Elector of Bavaria, ended Britain's interest in a Wittelsbach alliance.[47]

Interest was reawakened in late 1728 and the issue brought to the fore by French pressure. In 1727–1728 France had had considerable success in severing the ties between the Wittelsbachs and Austria. Agreements between France and Bavaria, and France and the Palatinate, were signed on 12 November 1727 and 15 February 1729 respectively,[48] but for a variety of reasons France wanted Britain to participate in her new agreements with the Wittelsbachs. The cost of subsidising the Wittelsbachs was a major reason and the French believed that George II both could and should bear his share of the subsidies.[49] However, important though they doubtless were, the core of the dispute was not the subsidies. By seeing the negotiations between George and the Wittelsbachs in 1729 as a matter of money, and by drawing attention to this issue in the quarrel between Townshend and Walpole, historians have misunderstood the essential issues at stake. The alliance between Britain and the Wittelsbachs was intended to last many years, and the latter sought a commitment for the long-term payment of subsidies. As such, the negotiations were of great significance for long-term British, and indeed Hanoverian, diplomatic strategy. An alliance with the Wittelsbachs would have committed Britain to a long-term anti-Austrian policy and would have made support for Wittelsbach pretensions a central feature of British policy. Because of the Wittelsbach demand that Britain should guarantee the Sulzbach claim to the Jülich-Berg inheritance,[50] it would also commit Britain to an anti-Prussian policy and serve to drive Prussia and Austria further together.[51] The consequences of these commitments were clear. The traditional Hanoverian interest in a league of Protestant German princes and in close dynastic ties between Hanover and Prussia would be replaced by a non-confessional league tied to Wittelsbach interests. As Elector of Hanover George was involved in disputes with the Electors of Cologne and the Palatinate. He had been unenthusiastic about the Elector of Cologne's election as Bishop of Osnabrück, and he was in dispute with this prelate over the municipal rights of Hildesheim.[52] The Palatine court argued that a Prussian acquisition of Jülich-Berg would threaten Hanover.[53] George II's policy of creating a position of strength, from which the Emperor could be coerced or cajoled into being a good ruler, would be replaced by a commitment to confront the Austrians and support those determined to destroy Austrian power. It would open the way to a territorial recasting of the Empire. Despite the noted anti-Austrian attitudes of Townshend and George, both angered by Austrian intransigence in European matters and obstinacy over Hanoverian interests, neither sought the destruction of Austrian power. The negotiations over the Wittelsbach alliance exposed an important ambivalence in the Anglo-French alliance, that towards Austria. George II and those British ministers who were hawks in Anglo-Austrian relations – Townshend and Chesterfield – were essentially short-term hawks.[54] Their French counterparts, particularly Chauvelin, were long-term hawks, and though the British knew that Fleury was not interested in war with Austria, and was on good diplomatic terms with the Austrians, they both suspected his real views and feared that his death would cause French policy to become more strident, if not violent.[55] The negotiations of the summer of 1729 with the Wittelsbachs were therefore of great importance. They brought into prominence a major difference of opinion between Britain and France over diplomatic policy. The British had had a poor view of the negotiations between France and the Wittelsbachs. In November 1728 Horatio Walpole and Stanhope informed Newcastle that the French government was neglecting to keep them informed of the negotiations. They also attacked the incompetence of Chauvelin 'who, instead of making a solid and good plan of union with the four Electors for the publick tranquility of Europe, has given the Guaranty of France to the Palatine family for the succession of Bergh and Juliers, for an exchange of a neutrality only on the Elector Palatine's side, and for some concessions for the benefit of France in Alsace . . . '[56]

In the winter of 1728–1729 the French altered their policy and decided to involve Britain more actively in the negotiations. The British Plenipotentiaries were told that French support for Britain's Prussian policy, whether it involved seeking Anglo-Prussian marriages or attempting to block Prussian moves in Mecklenburg, was dependent on British support for the French German strategy, and in particular on British support of the Sulzbach claim in Jülich-Berg. Newcastle proposed that British support for the Wittelsbachs over Jülich-Berg should be linked to Wittelsbach support over Mecklenburg.[57] French pressure, concern over Mecklenburg, the failure to improve Anglo-Prussian relations and, no doubt, the abortive Anglo-Austrian reconciliation, led Britain to adopt a more receptive attitude in the spring of 1729. George did not send any envoys to the Wittelsbach courts, possibly because he did not want to provoke Austria by such a step, but agreed to receive Plettenberg at Hanover. This contrasted with his refusal to see Count Seckendorf, the Austrian envoy at the Court of Berlin and the confidant of Frederick William I. George's decision to refer the negotiations to Hanover was interesting as talks between the French government, the British Plenipotentiaries and the Wittelsbach envoys were already in progress in Paris. In May 1729 a project for a treaty had been presented to the British and the French by the Bavarian envoy in Paris, Count Albert. The projected treaty called for subsidies and a guarantee of the Sulzbach claim to Jülich-Berg. The Elector of Cologne requested subsidies, assistance for Wittelsbach claims to episcopal vacancies and a satisfactory settlement of the Hildesheim issue. The treaty was projected for 14 years. Bavaria and Cologne expected compensation for the arrears in their subsidies from Austria. Bavaria sought 400,000 écus of German money annually and a British guarantee of the payment by Spain of one million piastres owed under treaties signed by Charles II of Spain. In George's view the projected treaty entailed excessive fiscal demands and inadequate support over Mecklenburg.[58] By referring the talks to Hanover, George indicated his great interest in the matter, and his determination to gain personal control of the negotiations. In late July Townshend informed the Plenipotentiaries that George had 'referred the further transaction of this matter to your Excys'. However, the next stage of the negotiations was handled by Townshend and Chavigny, and Albert claimed that they had been referred to Hanover because Horatio Walpole lacked the necessary instructions. Chauvelin complained that Walpole discussed the negotiations with the Wittelsbachs in a light and vague fashion.[59]

Plettenberg reached Hanover on 15 July. He had an audience with George the next day and several lengthy conferences with Townshend over the following week. The substance of their conversations is a matter for dispute, and in particular it is unclear exactly what Plettenberg demanded and how far George and Townshend indicated a willingness to meet his demands. Townshend wrote that he and Plettenberg had declared 'that nothing that has passed between us, should be looked upon as binding or conclusive on either side'.[60] The position is confused by the fact that in the autumn, when the negotiations had run into difficulties, Townshend accused Plettenberg of a lack of consistency in the demands he had presented on behalf of the Wittelsbach Electors.

Opinions differed as to the success of the talks in July. An optimistic note was struck by the Elector of Bavaria, Charles-Albert, and by Chavigny. Charles-Albert replied to a report from Plettenberg by stating that the negotiation was nearly complete and that Britain had only to change her policy a little in order to satisfy the Wittelsbachs. Boissieux, the French envoy in Cologne, reported that Plettenberg was very pleased with the manner in which he had been received at Hanover, and with George's willingness to settle various points at issue between the Elector of Cologne and the Electoral government of Hanover.[61] Chavigny, whose arrival in Hanover was delayed by the poor state of the roads that summer,[62] presented Townshend as being totally committed to the idea of an alliance with the Wittelsbachs. He informed Chauvelin that Townshend sought the alliance for his own glory, to justify his policy, and in order to please George by displaying concern for Hanoverian security.[63] Those who struck a less optimistic note seem to have been nearer to the truth. George had made it clear to Schleinitz on 26 June that he would not accept the Bavarian financial demands.[64] On 21 July Plettenberg sent Charles-Albert and Count Albert copies of Townshend's comments upon the Wittelsbach alliance project. He informed Count Albert that the British thought France should pay the entire subsidy demanded by Bavaria. Townshend also pressed for the inclusion of the Elector of Mainz, the Wittelsbach Franz Ludwig, Duke of Neuburg, in the alliance, and declared that Britain was not prepared to accept an alliance for fourteen years, but was determined to fix a limit of two years. Plettenberg was suspicious of the British views on the Jülich-Berg inheritance.[65] George was reported to be in favour of an alliance with the Electors, but dissatisfied with their proposals.[66] Fleury proposed a compromise by which George, as King and Elector, would undertake to make no engagements over Jülich-Berg incompatible with a Sulzbach succession. George and Townshend approved of this compromise,[67] but it was rejected by the Elector Palatine who demanded an explicit commitment to the Sulzbach succession.[68] Count Törring, the Bavarian foreign minister, argued that it was unlikely France would be willing to pay all the Bavarian subsidy, and that Britain should not only agree to pay half the subsidy, but should be keen to do so in order to have greater influence upon Bavarian conduct. He also stated that the British demand for Wittelsbach assistance over the Mecklenburg question was likely to meet with opposition, particularly from Mainz.[69] George was very concerned about Mecklenburg.[70] Albert pressed Chauvelin about Wittelsbach anxiety over the British attitude to the Jülich-Berg question. He was assured that France wanted Britain to give a guarantee for the succession similar to the French one, and that Chavigny would be ordered to lend the Wittelsbachs all possible assistance on the matter. Both Chauvelin and Albert were dissatisfied with the British position. Chauvelin argued that the British demand for an inclusion of Mecklenburg within the terms of the provisions for mutual defence, similar to the agreement being sought as part of the projected treaty with Spain,[71] was unacceptable, and that the only thing George could expect was an agreement to defend Hanover if it were attacked as part of a dispute involving Mecklenburg. The French and Albert agreed that the British demand for the inclusion of Gibraltar and Minorca was also inadmissible. Albert also informed the French that from the Wittelsbach point of view it was very insulting to be hired like a hackney cab.[72]

The difficulties Plettenberg encountered were soon to be faced by Chavigny. He took over the task of persuading George and Townshend to accept the Wittelsbach case, whilst Plettenberg set off on a tour of the Wittelsbach courts designed to counter Austrian intrigues at Mannheim and to discover how much of the British case would be accepted by the Electors.[73] On 12 August Chavigny reported that Townshend was firm on the subsidies and the Jülich-Berg guarantee. Chavigny argued that Britain should concede on the Jülich-Berg issue in return for help over Mecklenburg, but Townshend replied that the Dutch would never accept the Sulzbach succession, a somewhat misleading argument, for Chavigny realised the British were more concerned with the Prussian than the Dutch response. Chauvelin referred to the Jülich-Berg question as the most important difficulty.[74] Townshend argued that it was impossible to pay any new subsidies because Parliament would reject any such obligations, and, according to Chavigny, he claimed the proposal would lead to a domestic storm which would endanger the Anglo-French alliance.[75] Chavigny replied by stating that the domestic British response would depend upon the manner in which the issue was presented to Parliament.

The exchange between the two men is interesting, illustrating as it does that Chavigny, despite his trip to London in 1723, still, at least publicly, subscribed to the manipulative interpretation of Parliament so condemned by Townshend. Townshend however was, or at least claimed to be, very concerned about the British response. He and George were certainly ready to send the Wittelsbach project for a treaty, presented by Plettenberg, to London, in order to elicit the views of the 'Lords of the Council' on the matter.[76] These 'Lords' constituted a form of cabinet appointed by George II to advise the Regent, Queen Caroline, during his absence in Hanover. The only surviving records of their deliberations are to be found in Lord

King's *Notes*, and the reports of their proceedings sent to Hanover. Lord
King was a member of the group, but unfortunately he did not attend
many of the sessions. He made it clear that he was frequently ignored by
Sir Robert Walpole, and preferred the seclusion of his seat at Ockham to
the strains of Whitehall, strains which did not do his gout any good.[77]
Unfortunately neither the *Notes*, nor the reports preserved in *State Papers
Regencies*, specify the views of individual ministers. Care was taken to
prevent ministers not in the inner circle, probably Carteret and Wilm-
ington, from gaining information about government policy.[78] In 1738 the
French Ambassador was to refer to the difficulty of discovering British
Council decisions.[79]

On 22 August the 'Lords of the Council' met at Sir Robert Walpole's
house in Chelsea to discuss the Wittelsbach project. Present were Lord
King, Walpole, Newcastle, the Lord Privy Seal (Lord Trevor), the Lord
Chamberlain (the Duke of Grafton), and the first Lord of the Admiralty
(Viscount Torrington). They agreed that though an alliance would be
useful, as it would increase the number of troops within the Empire at the
disposal of the Hanover alliance, the terms proposed by the Wittelsbachs
were unacceptable. The Lords objected to the provisions concerning the
succession to Jülich-Berg as being too anti-Prussian. They were opposed to
the projected time-span of the treaty, and approved of Townshend's
suggestion that it should only last for two years. They argued that the
preamble of the projected treaty, confining it simply to 'the good of the
Empire', and the provisions specifying that the Wittelsbachs were under
no obligations if conflict arose over Gibraltar or the Ostend Company,
were unacceptable and might cause political difficulties in Britain. It was
however the seventh article of the projected treaty which was the most
disapproved of. By this article George undertook not to give any guarantee
to any power whatsoever not included in the projected alliance, without
the consent of all the contracting powers. As the Lords in London pointed
out, this referred principally to the guarantee of the Pragmatic Sanction.
The reasons advanced in the deliberations of the Lords sent to Townshend
on 23 August 1729 are of great interest as they indicate the long-term views
of the group of ministers left in London or at least of the most powerful of
them. They argued that such an undertaking

would be an unnecessary tying up H.M.'s hands from a thing, which perhaps
hereafter upon a change of circumstances, H.M. may think adviseable, if the
Emperor, should ever make such proposals as H.M. might think advantageous
for himself and his people, and safe and honourable for his allies. Their Lordps.
have the greatest dependence upon the present good disposition of the court of
France; But as considering the particular circumstances of that court, the same
confidence may not always be preserved, their Lordships have ever lookt upon it
as the wisdom of H.M.'s councils, that hitherto nothing has been done that
should make ye friendship of that Crown absolutely necessary, or a reconciliation with the Emperor impracticable.

This statement is probably the best summary of British policy in the
summer of 1729. It indicates the fears held about future developments in

French policy. Poyntz wrote that November: 'I have observed hitherto admirable effects from France's apprehension of our making up with the Emperor which would in some measure cease when we should have tied ourselves up from giving the guaranty or somewhat equivalent to it without her consent.' Persistent reports over the previous two years that Fleury would fall, or die, to be replaced by ministers less interested in pacific measures or the British alliance, had helped to sap confidence in the Anglo-French alliance. Instead of being seen as a stable feature in European diplomacy and an essential aspect of British foreign policy, a view which had been strongly advanced following the formation of the Alliance of Hanover, it was increasingly seen as a temporary measure, an expedient necessary for the pursuit of better Anglo-Austrian and Anglo-Spanish relations. Poyntz feared that France would try 'especially after the Cardinal's death, to press us into measures destructive to the Balance of Europe.'[80]

The difficulty was to determine how the Emperor was to be persuaded to offer advantageous proposals. Kinsky blamed the failure to negotiate Anglo-Austrian reconciliation on the rigidity of the Austrian position. Horatio Walpole and Stanhope referred to 'the usual haughtiness of the Imperial Court'.[81] Attempts over the previous two years to negotiate with the Austrians, whether alone or in conjunction with other powers, as at Soissons, had failed. The logical conclusion of this failure, that an attempt should be made to coerce the Austrians by diplomatic isolation and the threat of violence,[82] was in the summer of 1729 forcing the British ministry to crystallize their views and assumptions about foreign policy, and adopt specific policies by agreeing to treaties involving major commitments both in the short and long term.[83] In a sense, the summer of 1729 was the first major opportunity for fresh thinking since the Alliance of Hanover in the autumn of 1725, as it saw the need for the discussion of two treaties representing novel alignments. In the intervening years the treaties negotiated by Britain had largely been the consequence of the Alliance of Hanover and had mostly been with powers considerably weaker than Britain. The negotiations had usually been about the amount of money Britain was prepared to pay to secure the alliance of other powers. In the case of the negotiations of 1729 with Spain and with the French-supported Wittelsbachs, money was not the major issue. Horatio Walpole and Stanhope expressed their fear that Britain might 'be pushed and engaged by Spain . . . into new and extravagant projects for troubling the tranquility of Europe, contrary to former Treatys, or to carry things any further, than what is necessary to secure the succession of Don Carlos by the Introduction of Garrisons . . .'[84]

The report of the 'Lords of the Council' showed that the vague talk of the need for an Anglo-Austrian reconciliation which had been expressed in public by various government figures over the previous years represented not only a nostalgic feeling for the triumphs of the Grand Alliance in the 1700s,[85] but also a considered response to the long-term European situation. The relationship between the approach made to Austria in the early spring of 1729 and the views expressed by the Lords of the Council in

August is unclear, since it is not known how many of the Lords were aware of the approach and of its failure. What is clear is that the British ministry was seriously interested in a reconciliation. It will therefore be necessary to consider why Austrian approaches made in the summer of 1729 failed.

While Plettenberg, Chavigny, Townshend and George II were holding talks in Hanover, a dispute was in progress between the Lords of the Council and Townshend over Anglo-Spanish negotiations. Domestic criticism of the apparent impasse in relations with Spain was marked. Delafaye commented 'people of both sides never were in a worse humour than now . . . the spirit of grumbling prevails prodigiously, it is now become an epidemical distempter.' The Lords of the Council, worried that Spain intended to dupe Britain and concerned at the prospect of having nothing definite to present to the next session of Parliament, argued that Spain should be persuaded to settle by the presentation of an ultimatum supported by the threat of naval action from the fleet assembled at Spithead. A blockade of Spain and the Spanish West Indies was suggested, and an attack on Puerto Rico proposed.[86] Townshend believed that this course of action was hasty. He felt Spain would produce a satisfactory answer to the British approaches and argued that any British action would meet with French and Dutch disapproval. Townshend therefore blocked the plan by persuading the Dutch to add a squadron to the fleet assembling under Wager. As he had foreseen, the difficulties of ensuring cooperation between the British fleet and the Dutch naval command helped to delay plans for an expedition. Townshend also made it clear to the Lords of the Council that he regarded their policy as precipitate.[87] The Lords agreed to defer the plan until mid-July, and Newcastle informed Townshend that if by then no satisfactory Spanish answer had been received, naval squadrons would be sent to Gibraltar and the West Indies.[88]

These steps by Townshend did not mean that opinion at Hanover was opposed to the possibility of coercing Spain. On 1 June Townshend ordered the Plenipotentiaries to press Fleury to set a date, preferably in July, for initiating operations against Spain if she had not by then returned a suitable answer. Similar instructions were sent a month later.[89] Horatio Walpole and Stanhope told Fleury that George II had decided to delay sending the fleet until he received the Spanish answer. They reported being told by Fleury that it would be reasonable to send the fleet if the answer was unsatisfactory.[90] However, though Townshend was prepared to consider the possibility of action against Spain, he believed the time was not ripe, and that negotiations had to be attempted first. He therefore did his best to thwart the Lords of the Council. Accompanying his instructions to the Plenipotentiaries on 1 July was a private letter to Horatio Walpole:

You will see that the orders your colleagues received by this messenger take their rise from England. I am glad that orders fall into wise hands, who if they can do no good with them, will however not let them do harm. I am persuaded for my own part that we shall finish with Spain, and therefore cannot help fearing that our friends are too hasty.[91]

It is not clear whether this flagrant incitement to disobey orders was made with George's knowledge. Indeed, the extent to which Townshend's opposition to the plans for naval action stemmed from royal views is a mystery. However, it can be suggested that opinion in Hanover was affected by French pressure. The French were very concerned about the matter. They feared it would hinder negotiations and, indeed, Keene informed Townshend that the Spaniards were very angry about the naval preparations.[92] Chavigny was ordered to press George II against the dispatch of the fleet and to make him realise that it would probably lead to the revitalization of the Austro-Spanish alliance and an Austrian attack upon Hanover. Chauvelin attacked 'l'extrême vivacité du ministère Anglais' and believed pressure on George was the best method to thwart it.[93]

Whether George and Townshend opposed naval action because of fear of French reaction is unclear, although it should be noted that this factor had been important in preventing such action over the previous two years. It is likely Townshend's claim that the negotiations with Spain looked too promising to risk was an important factor. Equally important was the relation between the negotiations with Spain and those being conducted at Hanover. As the Wolfenbüttel minister Schleinitz, then at Hanover, pointed out, the progress of the negotiations in Spain was of great importance in determining the response at Hanover to the Wittelsbach propositions.[94] It was also of the greatest importance for Anglo-Prussian relations.[95] Should Spain reject the Anglo-French proposals and return to an Austrian alliance, then an alliance with the Wittelsbachs would be necessary to offset an increase in Austrian strength and to bind France clearly to a British alliance in opposition to Austrian interests. There would be little chance of Austria responding favourably to British approaches if she were sure of Spain. If the Spaniards accepted the Anglo-French proposals then there would be less need for the Wittelsbachs and their alliance could be secured on easier terms.[96]

The Spanish determination to hold their negotiations in Spain and not at Paris, and George's decision that his negotiations with the Wittelsbachs should be held at Hanover, not Paris, meant the British Plenipotentiaries enjoyed less influence than in the previous year. Virtually no important foreign envoys spent the summer in London, where anyway there was no accredited representative of Spain or of the Wittelsbachs. Horatio Walpole complained that he was not being informed, either speedily or fully, of the negotiations with the Wittelsbachs. Townshend told Chavigny that George was more concerned than his father 'de parôitre tout voir, et tout déterminer par luymême'.[97] It may seem a rather questionable exercise to assess the skill displayed by various ministers in relating the two sets of negotiations, particularly when there are no personal memoranda on which to base conclusions. However, it could be suggested that some of the clashes over policy within the British ministry stemmed not only from differences of opinion over policy but also from varying abilities in relating the diffuse negotiations. Walpole, Newcastle and the other 'Lords of the Council' appear to have viewed Anglo-Spanish relations in isolation and not to have related them to German matters. Chauvelin criticised the British Plenipotentiaries for the same fault.[98] They do not seem to have grasped as well as Townshend, George and Chesterfield that Spanish policy was not determined by fear of British naval action, that securing the active cooperation of France was essential if Spain were to be persuaded to adopt a favourable policy, and that French help over Anglo-Spanish disputes was linked to British support for French policy in the Empire. France viewed both sets of negotiations as parts of an anti-Austrian policy, but the Lords of the Council were both disinclined to adopt the French analysis and unable to produce a satisfactory alternative. Had Spain rejected an ultimatum then the policy of naval action would have been a failure, because it would have produced the risk of British isolation. Spain would probably have returned to her Austrian policy,[99] possibly with French connivance, and Austrian pressure upon Hanover would have forced the British to seek French help, and therefore to submit to French direction of Britain's Spanish policy. There are no signs that this was grasped fully in London, despite the knowledge that Austro-Spanish negotiations were continuing in Spain.

Notes

1. A description of Stanhope's passage through the City of London on 15 April, *St. James's Evening Post* 5 Apr. (os) 1729.
2. Delafaye to Poyntz, 27 Jan. (os) 1729, BL. Althorp, E3; Sinzendorf to Fonseca, 15 Mar. 1729, HHStA, Fonseca, 13; Waldegrave to Townshend, 23 Feb., Du Bourgay to Townshend, 5 Feb. 1729, PRO. 90/24, 80/64; Waldegrave to Poyntz, 26 Feb. 1729, Chewton; De Buy to Manteuffel, 29 Mar. 1729, Dresden 3105; King, pp. 72–4, 77–85.
3. Delafaye to Poyntz, 17 Feb. (os) 1729, BL. Althorp, E3; Waldegrave to Townshend, 15, 29 Jan., 23, 26 Feb., 1729, PRO. 80/64; Waldegrave to Poyntz, 26 Mar. 1729, Chewton.
4. Sinzendorf to Fonseca, 8 Jan. 1729, HHStA, Fonseca 13.
5. La Paz to Fleury, 29 Mar. 1729, PRO. 78/190; Baudrillart, III, 500–1; Goslinga, pp. 338–9; Wilson, p. 206.
6. Plenipotentiaries to Newcastle, 25 Apr. 1729, PRO. 78/190.
7. Stanhope and Horatio Walpole to Keene, 4 Oct. 1728, BL. Add. 32758.
8. Le Coq to Augustus II, 4 Apr. 1729, Dresden 2733; Goslinga, p. 347.
9. Fleury to Brancas, 14 Apr. 1729, Baudrillart, III, 505.
10. Fleury to Brancas, 20 Apr. 1729, Baudrillart, III, 506.
11. Newcastle to the Plenipotentiaries, 5 May (os) 1729, PRO. 78/193; Le Coq to Augustus II, 4 Apr. 1729, Dresden, 2733.
12. Newcastle to the Plenipotentiaries, 5 May (os) 1729, PRO. 78/193; De Buy to Manteuffel, 12 May 1729, Dresden, 3105.
13. Fleury to La Paz, 14 Apr., Vandermeer to Van Hoey, Dutch envoy in Paris, 28 Apr. Chesterfield to Townshend, 6 May 1729, PRO. 78/190, 84/304; Baudrillart, III, 498, 503–6; Goslinga, p. 339; Wilson, p. 206.
14. Delafaye to Poyntz, 19 Feb. (os) 1729, BL. Althorp, E3; Newcastle to Keene, 1 Apr. (os), Keene to Newcastle, 12 May, Poyntz to Delafaye, 6 Feb., Newcastle to the Plenipotentiaries, 29 May (os), Tyrawly to Newcastle, 5, 16 Jan., 25 Feb., 25 Mar., 8 May, Chesterfield to Townshend, 29 Apr., Cavendish to Burchett, Secretary of the Admiralty, 25 Apr. (os) 1729; PRO. 94/100, 78/190, 193, 88/35, 84/304, 42/19; D'Aubenton to Maurepas, 5 May 1729, AN. AM. B7 296.
15. Zamboni to the Marquis de Fleury, 24 May, 22 July 1729, Bodl. Rawl. 120; *Wye's Letter* 29 May (os) 1729.

16. Tilson to Waldegrave, 6 May (os) 1729, Chewton; Marini, p. 129.
17. D'Aubenton to Maurepas, 24 Mar. 1729, AN. AM. B7 296; Plenipotentiaries to Newcastle, 25 Apr., Cayley to Newcastle, 17 May, Keene to Townshend, 23 June 1729, PRO. 78/190, 94/219, 100.
18. De Buy to Manteuffel, 21 Apr. 1729, Dresden, 3105.
19. Chauvelin to Chammorel, 7 Apr. 1729, AE. CP. Ang. sup.8.
20. Cayley to Newcastle, 19 Apr., 17 May, 21 June, 9 Aug., Cayley to Keene, 15 May, Keene to Newcastle, 9 June 1729, PRO. 94/219, 215, 100; D'Aubenton to Maurepas, 26, 31 May 1729, AN. AM. B7 296.
21. Tyrawly to Newcastle, 25 Mar. 1729, PRO. 88/35.
22. Baudrillart, III, 512–4; Goslinga, p. 340.
23. Newcastle to the Plenipotentiaries, 5 May (os), Poyntz to Delafaye, 9 May 1729, PRO. 78/193, 191.
24. Poyntz to Townshend, 11 June 1729, BL. Althorp, E5; Goslinga, p. 340; Instructions for Fonseca, 14 May 1729, HHStA., Fonseca 13.
25. D'Arvillars to Victor Amadeus II, 26 May 1729, AST. LM. Spagna 61; De Buy to Manteuffel, 9 June 1729, Dresden 3105; Horatio Walpole to Delafaye, 5 July 1729, PRO. 78/192.
26. D'Aubenton to Maurepas, 5 June 1729, AN. AM. B7 297; Holzendorf to Delafaye, 10 June 1729, PRO. 84/304; Keene to Townshend, 2 Aug. 1729, PRO. 94/100; Villars, p. 175.
27. Keene to Townshend, 26 May 1729, PRO. 94/100.
28. Horatio Walpole to Tilson, 5 July, Keene to Townshend, 10 July 1729, PRO. 78/192, 94/100; Marini, p. 132; Poyntz to Waldegrave, 19 Jan. 1730, BL. Althorp, E1.
29. Newcastle to the Plenipotentiaries, 12 June (os), Horatio Walpole to Delafaye, 5 July 1729, PRO. 78/193, 192; Poyntz to Townshend, 15 June 1729, BL. Althorp, E5.
30. De Buy to Marquis de Fleury, 23 June, Wackerbarth to Augustus II, 30 July 1729, Dresden, 3105, 3331; D'Aix to Victor Amadeus II, 30 June, 7, 14 July 1729, AST. LM. Ing. 35.
31. Keene to Newcastle, 19 May, Keene to Townshend, 26 May, Newcastle to Queen Caroline, 3 June (os) 1729, PRO. 94/100, 36/12; D'Arvillars to Victor Amadeus II, 2 Apr. 1729, AST. LM. Spagna 61.
32. De Buy to Manteuffel, 16, 30 June 1729, Dresden, 3105; D'Aix to Victor Amadeus II, 30 June 1729, AST. LM. Ing. 35; Poyntz to Townshend, 15 June, Newcastle to Poyntz, 17 July (os) 1729, BL. Althorp, E5, 3.
33. Keene to Townshend, 2 Aug. 1729, PRO. 94/100.
34. Waldegrave to Poyntz, 12 Feb. 1729, Chewton; Instructions for Seckendorf, 30 June 1729, Thomas Robinson, Minister Plenipotentiary in Vienna, to Lord Harrington, Secretary of State for the Northern Department, 21 Oct. 1733, PRO. 78/193, 80/100.
35. Keene to Newcastle, 12 May 1729, PRO. 94/100; London Evening Post 19 Aug. (os) 1729; Baudrillart, III, 526.
36. Chauvelin to Chavigny, 21 Aug. 1729, AE. CP. Br. 47.
37. Chesterfield to Townshend, 28 June 1729, PRO. 84/304.
38. Cobbett, VIII, 773, 775–6; Robert Trevor to Poyntz, 5 Feb. (os) 1730, BL. Althorp, E4; I. G. Doolittle, 'A First-Hand Account of the Commons Debate on the Removal of Sir Robert Walpole', Bulletin of the Institute of Historical Research 53 (1980) p. 129; Eugene to Philip Kinsky, 17 June 1730, 2, 13 Mar. 1734, Vienna, Kinsky, 2; Robinson to Horatio Walpole, 29 May 1734, BL. Add. 23845; Cobbett, IX, 225, 822, 869, XI, 1000; Armstrong, p. 258.
39. Dureng, pp. 85–6.
40. D'Aix to Victor Amadeus II, 16 June 1729, AST. LM. Ing. 35.
41. M. Braubach, 'Ferdinand von Plettenberg' Westphalische Lebensbilder 9 (1962).
42. Chavigny to Chauvelin, 10 Jan. 1730, AE. CP. Allemagne 376; M. Sautai, Les Préliminaires de la Guerre de la Succession d'Autriche (Paris, 1907); P. C. Hartmann, Geld als Instrument europäischer Machtpolitik im Zeitalter des Merkantilismus. Studien zu den finanziellen und politischen Beziehungen der Wittelsbacher Territorien Kurbayern, Kurpfalz und Kurköln mit Frankreich und dem Kaiser von 1715 bis 1740 (Munich, 1978); Hartmann, Karl Albrecht-Karl VII (Regensburg, 1985). I would like to thank Professor Hartmann for discussing with me Wittelsbach policy in these years. Neither his books

nor Schmidt's *Karl Philipp* consider Anglo-Wittelsbach relations or use the Plettenberg papers.

43. On 16 April 1728 the Electors of Bavaria, Trier, Cologne and the Palatinate signed a treaty stipulating common action in support of their various pretensions, Dureng, pp. 77–8. There is a copy of the treaty in PRO. 103/100; Newcastle to Horatio Walpole, 13 June (os) 1728, BL. Add. 32756.

44. Newcastle to Horatio Walpole, 13 June (os) 1728, BL. Add. 32756; Townshend to Horatio Walpole, 3 June (os), Bradfer Lawrence; Newcastle to the Plenipotentiaries, 15 July (os) 1728, PRO. 80/326.

45. Townshend to Horatio Walpole, 22 Aug. (os), Horatio Walpole to Townshend, 26 Aug. 1728, BL. Add. 32757.

46. Delafaye to Horatio Walpole, 29 Aug. (os) 1727, PRO. 78/187.

47. A. Lebon (ed.) *Recueil . . . Bavière, Palatinat, Deux-Ponts* (Paris, 1889) p. 167; A. Rosenlehner, *München und Wien 1725–26* (Munich, 1906); Hartmann, *Geld*, pp. 112–20.

48. Newcastle to Horatio Walpole, 11 Oct. (os) 1728, PRO. 78/189; Naumann, *Österreich* pp. 136–7; Schmidt, *Karl Philipp*, pp. 184–7; Hartmann, *Geld*, pp. 127–40.

49. Horatio Walpole to Townshend, 26 Aug. 1728, BL. Add. 32757.

50. Horatio Walpole and Stanhope to Newcastle, 20 July, Poyntz to Newcastle, 30 Dec. 1728, BL. Add. 32757, 32759; Horatio Walpole and Stanhope to Townshend, 12 Sept. 1728, Townshend to Platen de Linn, Palatine Minister in London, 14 May (os) 1729, Papers relating to the succession of Berg and Julich, 1729–32, PRO. 78/188, 193, 103/112.

51. Townshend to Finch, 15 Aug. (os) 1727, Horatio Walpole and Stanhope to Townshend, 12 Sept. 1728, Townshend to Newcastle, 13 Apr. (os) 1729, PRO. 84/294, 78/188, 43/77.

52. Townshend to the Plenipotentiaries, 12 Sept. (os) 1728, PRO. 78/189.

53. 'Contre-Remarques Palatines avec Remarques faites par Mylord Townshend . . . sur le Traité d'amitié', 8 Aug. 1729, PRO. 103/110.

54. Townshend to Finch, 18 Mar. 1726, Townshend to Chesterfield, 14 June 1729, PRO. 84/289, 304. However, D. B. Horn referred to Townshend's 'bellicose anti-Hapsburg policy'. Horn, *Great Britain and Europe*, pp. 51, 121.

55. Stephen Kinsky and Fonseca to Charles VI, 6 July 1729, Höfler, I, 32; Chesterfield to Townshend, 28 June 1729, PRO. 84/304; Robinson to Harrington, 19 Aug. 1730, BL. Add. 9139.

56. Stanhope and Horatio Walpole to Newcastle, 30 Nov. 1728, BL. Add. 32759.

57. Newcastle to Horatio Walpole and Stanhope, 30 Sept. (os) 1728, PRO. 78/189.

58. Albert to Plettenberg, 11, 19, 26 May 1729, Münster, NB. 33 1; 'Draft of the Electoral Treaty', PRO. 103/110; 'Formulaire d'un art. touchant Bergh et Juliers', Plenipotentiaries to Townshend, 1 June 1729, PRO. 103/112; Townshend to Plenipotentiaries, 11 June 1729, PRO. 78/193.

59. Townshend to Plenipotentiaries, 22 July, Tilson to Horatio Walpole, 5 Aug. 1729, PRO. 78/193; Albert to Plettenberg, 9 Aug. 1729, Münster, NB. 33 1; Chauvelin to Schleinitz, 7 Aug. 1729, PRO. 103/110.

60. Townshend to Plenipotentiaries, 22 July 1729, PRO. 78/193.

61. Charles Albert to Plettenberg, 26 July 1729, Münster, NB. 164; Boissieux to Chauvelin, 25 July 1729, AE. CP. Cologne 70.

62. Chavigny to Chauvelin, 1 Aug. 1729, AE. CP. Br. 47. Chavigny was still in Regensburg in mid-June. D'Aix had commented on the absence of a French representative at Hanover, and Schleinitz had argued that Chavigny's presence was necessary. D'Aix to Victor Amadeus II, 30 June, 7 July 1729, AST. LM. Ing. 35; Schleinitz to Fleury, 1 July 1729, PRO. 103/110.

63. Chavigny to Chauvelin, 18, 22 Aug. 1729, AE. CP. Allemagne 375.

64. Schleinitz to Fleury, 1 July 1729, PRO. 103/110.

65. 'Projet d'un Traité' with comments by Townshend and Plettenberg, PRO. 103/110; Plettenberg to Albert, 21 July 1729, Münster, NB. 33 1.

66. Townshend to Plenipotentiaries, 11 June, Tilson to Horatio Walpole, 5 Aug. 1729, PRO. 43/19, 78/193.

67. Schleinitz to Fleury, 1 July, Chauvelin to Schleinitz, 3 Aug. 1729, PRO. 103/110.

68. Chauvelin to Schleinitz, 24 July, 'Contre Remarques Palatines . . .', 8 Aug. 1729, PRO. 103/110.

128   THE COLLAPSE OF THE ANGLO-FRENCH ALLIANCE

69. Törring to Plettenberg, 30 July 1729, Münster, NA. 148.
70. Townshend to Plenipotentiaries, 11, 23 June 1729, Townshend to Chesterfield, 21, 28 June 1729, PRO. 78/193, 84/304.
71. King, p. 107.
72. Chauvelin to Schleinitz, 24 July 1729, PRO. 103/110; 'Contre Remarques Palatines . . . ', 8 Aug. 1729, PRO. 103/110; Albert to Plettenberg, 9, 16 Aug. 1729, Münster, NB. 33 1 f.173–4, 176, 182–4; Schleinitz, memorandum about the negotiations, no date, PRO. 103/110; 'Réponse de S.A.S.E. de Bavière sur les Remarques faites à Hanover par Mylord Townshend, et Monsr. le Comte de Plettenberg, sur le projet du traité à faire avec les quatre Electeurs', PRO. 103/110.
73. Törring to Plettenberg, 27 July, 6 Aug. 1729, Münster, NA. 148.
74. Chauvelin to Schleinitz, 3 Aug. 1729, PRO. 103/110.
75. Chavigny to Chauvelin, 12 Aug. 1729, AE. CP. 47; Villars, p. 191.
76. Townshend to Newcastle, 22 July 1729, PRO. 43/78.
77. King, p. 107.
78. King, p. 86.
79. Cambis to Amelot, 3 July 1738, AE. CP. Ang. 399.
80. Account of council meeting, PRO. 43/80; King, pp. 101–6; Poyntz to Thomas Townshend, 5 Nov. 1729, BL. Althorp, E5.
81. Kinsky to Ferdinand Albrecht, 2 Sept. 1729, Wolfenbüttel, 1 Alt 22, Nr. 590; Horatio Walpole and Stanhope to Townshend, 4 July 1729, PRO. 78/192.
82. Townshend to Chesterfield, 14 June, Chesterfield to Townshend, 7 July 1729, PRO. 84/304.
83. Kinsky to Ferdinand Albrecht, 20 Sept. 1729, Wolfenbüttel, 1 Alt 22, Nr. 590.
84. Horatio Walpole and Stanhope to Townshend, 4 July 1729, PRO. 78/192.
85. S. Baxter, 'The Myth of the Grand Alliance in the Eighteenth Century', in S. Baxter and P. Sellin, *Anglo-Dutch Cross Currents in the Seventeenth and Eighteenth Centuries* (Los Angeles, 1976) pp. 42–59.
86. Delafaye to Poyntz, 17 July (os) 1729, BL. Althorp, E3; Newcastle to Townshend, 13 June (os), Delafaye to Tilson, 3 June (os) 1729, PRO. 43/77; *Wye's Letter* 17 May (os), 7 June (os) 1729; Anon., *The Pacifick Fleet: A New Ballad* (London, 1729).
87. Townshend to Chesterfield, 1 July 1729, BL. Add. 48982; King, pp. 90–1; Chesterfield to Townshend, 7 July 1729, Black, 'A Fresh Chesterfield Letter of 1729', *Notes and Queries*, new series, 32 (1985), p. 209.
88. Newcastle to Townshend, 13 June (os) 1729, BL. Add. 9161.
89. Townshend to Plenipotentiaries, 1 June, 1 July 1729, PRO. 43/9, BL. Add. 48982.
90. Horatio Walpole and Stanhope to Townshend, 4 July 1729, PRO. 78/192.
91. Townshend to Horatio Walpole, 1 July, Townshend to Chesterfield, 1 July 1729, BL. Add. 48982.
92. Keene to Townshend, 23 June, Cayley to Newcastle, 17 May 1729, PRO. 94/100, 219.
93. Chauvelin to Chammorel, 26 June, 7, 21 July 1729, AE. CP. Ang. sup. 8; Instructions to Chavigny, 26 June, Chauvelin to Chavigny, 3, 24 July, 21 Aug., Chavigny to Chauvelin, 18 Aug. 1729, AE. CP. Br. 47; Dureng, p. 83.
94. Schleinitz to Fleury, 19 July 1729, AE. CP. Br. 47.
95. Du Bourgay to Townshend, 18 June 1729, PRO. 90/24.
96. Townshend to George II, 1 Oct. (os) 1729, PRO. 103/110.
97. Newcastle to Townshend, 24 June (os), Horatio Walpole to Delafaye, 29 July, Plenipotentiaries to Townshend, 4 Aug., Chauvelin to Schleinitz, 7 Aug. 1729, PRO. 43/78, 78/192, 103/110; Chavigny to Chauvelin, 12 Aug. 1729, AE. CP. Br. 47.
98. Chauvelin to Chavigny, 21 Aug. 1729, AE. CP. Br. 47.
99. Chesterfield to Townshend, 7 July 1729, PRO. 84/304.

CHAPTER NINE

Summer–Autumn of 1729
Negotiations with Austria, War-Panic with
Prussia, Settlement with Spain

A further element in the diplomatic situation in the summer of 1729 was the continuing contact between Britain and Austria. Given the increasing commitments being envisaged that summer as part of the strategy to coerce Austria (support for Spain in Italy and for the Wittelsbachs in the Empire), the opposition of the British ministers to war with Austria, and the obvious difficulties facing the coercive strategy (dependence upon the quixotic Elisabeth Farnese, Hanoverian vulnerability to Austrian and Prussian pressure, and the likelihood of successful Austrian resistance in Italy), it was not surprising that talks with Austria were considered. After the abortive British initiative in the early spring neither Britain nor Austria made any approaches in the late spring. The British were more concerned to exploit Austro-Spanish differences and they may have been affected by French disquiet at the Anglo-Austrian contacts earlier in the year. Adopting a charitable interpretation, it could be suggested that the Austrians were waiting until they could discover Spanish intentions.[1] Uncertainty over the degree to which Spain, once it had broken with Austria, would take anti-Austrian steps, was possibly an important factor.[2] A less charitable view would suggest that in the late spring the Austrian government, and in particular its foreign policy, was affected by the lethargy which seems to have crept over it so often during the reign of Charles VI.[3] This indolent and prevaricating monarch preferred hunting to the difficulties of decision making. Prince Eugene was also disinclined to commit himself to unpredictable courses of action, whilst Sinzendorf had suffered for his forwardness at Soissons. The unwillingness to take decisions at Vienna complicated a foreign policy already handicapped by the disorganised nature of the Austrian diplomatic corps. Both Eugene and Sinzendorf maintained an extensive private correspondence with Austrian envoys. Sinzendorf had close links with Fonseca, one of the Austrian Plenipotentiaries at Paris, whilst Eugene had similar links with, among others, Seckendorf, Kinsky and Wratislaw the Austrian envoy in Russia. Braubach has drawn attention to the range of Eugene's system and to the way in which he used it to follow a private diplomacy of his own, often in opposition to that of the Chancery under Sinzendorf. The effect of this confusion was that most Austrian envoys received contradictory instructions, and were uncertain about what to do. The bad relations between Kinsky and Seckendorf, both protégés of Eugene, were notorious. Seckendorf's claim that most Austrian envoys, himself naturally excepted, were unaware of the true intentions of the Austrian government, was partially true, though it begged the question whether there were any concerted views at Vienna.[4]

In late May 1729 the Austrians approached the British asking for talks. Sinzendorf, 'quite out of patience with Kinsky', approached Waldegrave, and suggested that he meet George II at Hanover and convey Austrian proposals for talks.[5] Kinsky intimated to Newcastle that Austria was ready to come to terms with Britain. Newcastle stated that Austria would have to sign the Provisional Treaty as a condition of any peace. Kinsky was against such a condition and told Newcastle that the treaty was bad for both Britain and Austria. He claimed, correctly, that the treaty would not settle the dispute over Gibraltar, and 'hinted to me that perhaps the Emperor might be disposed to go further lengths with us against Spain, in support of our pretensions, than possibly France would do'. Newcastle replied that Britain was perfectly satisfied with French conduct. Since France was known to be opposed to Britain's proposals for action against Spain this untruthful reply hardly suggested a British willingness to reply to Austrian approaches.

On 30 May Kinsky had a long conference with Sir Robert Walpole. They met in secret, in the house of the Lord Chamberlain, the Duke of Grafton, who acted as an interpreter in order to prevent any misunderstandings. Kinsky was more detailed in his approach to Walpole than he had been with Newcastle. Kinsky argued that nothing was so desirable, nor so much in the interests of both Austria and Britain, as a 'return to the old system of politicks in Europe', and a renewal of the alliance between the two powers. He blamed the fate of the approaches earlier in the year upon the British, arguing that their stance had been both too general and too harsh, and stated that the Emperor would never sign the Provisional Treaty in its present form. Kinsky said that his efforts to persuade Vienna of the good dispositions of Britain for a reconciliation had been hindered by the conduct of certain British envoys, but that he had eventually received full powers for negotiations from the Emperor. Kinsky stated that the Emperor would never comply with the unreasonable demands of Spain over the Spanish garrisons and the marriage of the archduchess, and that these demands had freed the Emperor to do what he could not previously have done with honour. He argued that the Provisional Treaty was not only unsatisfactory for the Emperor but also insufficient to secure British interests in Gibraltar and Minorca.

Walpole asked Kinsky to reconcile his protestations of good Imperial dispositions with the behaviour of the Emperor over Hanoverian interests. Kinsky attempted to differentiate between British and Hanoverian interests, but he suggested that a general reconciliation would produce a settlement of the Mecklenburg question which would be agreeable to Hanoverian interests. Kinsky told Walpole, as indeed he told the Queen, that he had powers to sign the Provisional Treaty.

Walpole's response was apparently unfavourable. He avoided 'saying anything more than what was absolutely necessary'. He told Kinsky his request that Britain should make no diplomatic moves until Austria had made proposals to George II at Hanover was unreasonable. He urged Kinsky to travel to Hanover at once and there offer his proposals to George and Townshend, but he refused to adopt an encouraging note. Aside from the official report upon the conference it is unclear what Walpole's reactions were. Three days after the conference between Walpole and Kinsky, a conference of which Newcastle was fully informed, Newcastle wrote to Stanhope of his preference for an alliance with the Emperor to one with Spain. He did not advance as his reason a belief in Anglo-Austrian relations as of essential importance to the European system, but claimed that the consequences of a breach with Spain were less serious than of one with the Emperor, and that a peace could probably be achieved with the latter 'att a cheaper rate' than one with the former. Although he did not expand on his argument it is probable that he was referring to the dangers of committing Britain to Spain's Italian policy.[6]

Newcastle certainly and Walpole possibly were advocates of an Austrian alliance by the late spring. It may then be asked why they did not succeed in their views, given that it is generally held that the two ministers succeeded in defeating Townshend and his policies the following winter. Several reasons can be advanced to explain the situation, relating to the role of Newcastle and Walpole in the formation of foreign policy and to the prospects for Anglo-Austrian reconciliation. Both Plumb and Browning have attributed too much influence to the two men.[7] It would have been unthinkable for them to detain Kinsky in London and seek to negotiate with Vienna through him. The King, jealous of his prerogatives and vitally concerned about relations with Austria, would never have accepted the situation. Equally there were limits to the amount of pressure the ministers in London could bring to bear upon Hanover. They made clear their disinclination to commit Britain to long-term support for the Wittelsbachs, but this was a view also held in Hanover. The Austrians persisted in their argument that Hanoverian demands threatened the Imperial constitution and the judicial position of the Emperor.[8] Given George's anger at Austrian opposition to Hanoverian interests and his suspicion that Austria was stirring up Prussia, it would have been foolish to press persistently the Austrian cause, and there are no signs that it was pressed during the summer. Furthermore, such a course of action would have endangered Newcastle's Secretaryship and threatened Walpole's position. It was probably for these reasons that comments from London tended to refer to peripheral aspects of British foreign policy, such as the cost of subsidies. The few comments which were made upon the desirability of particular alliances tended to be in response to demands from Hanover for the opinion of the London ministers, as when Townshend communicated the Wittelsbach project for a treaty. George would never have accepted dictation over his foreign policy, but he did realise the need to seek consent and advice over its financial aspects. It was therefore through their opposition to extensive subsidy commitments that the ministers in London were able to attempt to influence general policy. Discussions of general diplomatic strategy are rare in *State Papers Regencies*.

Particular problems faced any attempt to improve Anglo-Austrian relations in the summer of 1729. As Newcastle pointed out, Kinsky 'seems to drive at a separate treaty with us'.[9] This raised the problem of the relationship between such an alliance and the already existing Anglo-

French alliance, with its prospect of expansion to include Spain. Newcastle may have preferred settling with Austria to settling with Spain but, like the members of the Opposition who advocated the same policy, he failed to make clear what was to be done with Anglo-French relations, or to face up to the fact that French help was likely to be needed in order to restrain Spain in the Mediterranean; for however willing Austria might be to approach Britain, she could not be supposed to be willing to satisfy those very Spanish demands which had recently caused her to break her Spanish ties. In addition, there was the danger that Austria might use any British response to discredit Britain with her allies.

Aside from the possibility of separate negotiations with Austria, there was also the option of linking the negotiations with Spain to talks with Austria. Fleury was reported as being 'determined not to agree with Spain separately from the Emperor'.[10] There were several problems with this solution. It would have reintroduced the questionable element of French arbitration. The course of negotiations at Paris over Anglo-Wittelsbach relations, with France pressing Britain to accept the Wittelsbach position, suggested that negotiations in Soissons or Paris would not serve British interests. They would also be unpopular in Britain. More dangerous was the probability that a fusion of the negotiations would delay matters and thus increase the possibility that Austria would regain the alliance of Spain or the Wittelsbachs. Stanhope and Horatio Walpole informed Townshend of their concern that Austria might seek to enter the negotiations, and to spin them out over the Parmesan and Tuscan successions. Austrian procrastination over Italian matters in the early 1720s was not a hopeful precedent. It was feared that Austria would delay matters by insisting on the consent of the Empire for the introduction of Spanish troops. Kinsky was instructed to argue that the way was open for an Austro-Spanish reconciliation.[11]

Thus, despite disquiet over the negotiations with Spain and the Wittelsbachs, there was little pressure from London for a settlement with Austria or for the inclusion of Austria in the negotiations. There was more interest among the British Plenipotentiaries, Stanhope in particular making favourable comments to the Austrian Plenipotentiaries, but the British received no instructions for negotiations with the Austrians. Poyntz did not share Stanhope's views and wrote to Townshend 'I see such good reasons for preserving the friendship of France and Spain, to that of the Emperor in the present conjuncture, that I shall be in no great pain about being able to justify elsewhere what we have done.'[12] The issue of talks with Austria was left to George and Townshend and their control of the matter was unchallenged during the summer.

The Austrians made further direct approaches for talks with George through Seckendorf and through Kinsky. Kinsky's reports had given the Austrians room to hope that George was willing for a reconciliation, and Seckendorf sought to handle the negotiations. However, his projected mission to Hanover was blocked by two developments: first, George refused to notify his arrival in the Empire to the Emperor, which Charles VI chose to regard as a slight; second, Seckendorf, who had asked the

Emperor to appoint him to carry the compliments which were the traditional response to this notification, found that George made it clear he did not wish to see him. According to the Saxon envoy in Vienna, Count Wackerbarth, usually a reliable source on Austrian policy, the Austrian diplomat and connection of Seckendorf, Gotter, informed the Hanoverian minister Münchhausen that Seckendorf wished to settle Anglo-Austrian differences, and that if George II notified Charles VI of his arrival at Hanover, Seckendorf would be sent with a compliment. Wackerbarth argued that George's response would show his attitude to a possible reconciliation and that Seckendorf would also probably negotiate on the Pragmatic Sanction if George wished to do so. Both Townshend and Hattorf denied Seckendorf's statement that letters had been sent to him inviting him to Hanover.[13] The British decision was taken by George and related, not to any disinclination to listen to Austrian proposals, but to a deep suspicion that Seckendorf, despite his professed interest in improving Anglo-Prussian relations, was actually seeking to keep the two powers apart.[14] Townshend was suspicious of the 'extraordinary intimacy . . . and very close and extensive engagements between the Emperor and the Kings of Prussia and Poland'. Chesterfield suggested that the Austrians hoped to use Seckendorf to sow discord among the allies.[15] It is very possible that George and the British exaggerated Seckendorf's influence in Berlin and minimised Frederick William's antipathy to George II. A major reason for this was their understandable wish to persuade themselves that if only Frederick William ceased hearing anti-British reports he would at once settle with George on George's terms. Such a view was foolish, but the reports from Berlin which stressed Seckendorf's malevolent role make it understandable. The refusal to permit a visit to Hanover did not end Seckendorf's hopes. He attempted to establish a correspondence with George through Diemar, an old friend and fellow correspondent of Prince Eugene, who accompanied George to Hanover. Seckendorf suggested, unsuccessfully, that Townshend and Diemar could meet him in Hamburg. He urged Diemar to tell George of his good intentions and to communicate his letters to George. Diemar, unwilling to take such a step without the authority of his court and probably indisposed to associate Seckendorf with Anglo-Hessian relations, declined to do so, and George persisted in his refusal to receive Seckendorf.[16]

Kinsky, rebuffed at London, set off for Hanover, but on the way he chose to spend several days at The Hague. This led Townshend and Chesterfield to surmise that his delay was in order to give the Austrians time to ascertain the success of their efforts to regain Spain and they concluded that the Austrians were not sincere when they talked of reconciliation. Kinsky did not leave The Hague until 13 June. In discussions with Chesterfield 'he insisted strongly upon the affairs of Ostend and Mecklenburg, and declared the Emperor could never give up those two points'.[17] Meanwhile Townshend had informed Newcastle that the King was very satisfied with the manner in which Newcastle and Walpole had spoken to Kinsky.[18] Kinsky, when he arrived at Hanover, received as negative a reply as he had got in London, though it does not seem that he made a particularly strong approach. On 21 June he had a long conversation with Townshend. Kinsky stated that the Austrian government doubted that Britain was at all interested in the resumption of good relations, and he drew attention to Townshend's personal commitment to anti-Austrian policies. The two men quarrelled over the fate of Tuscany and Parma, and Kinsky claimed the Emperor was not bound to stand by the terms of the Quadruple Alliance unless they were confirmed by the Treaty of Vienna, a statement Townshend contradicted. Townshend complained that Kinsky was very hesitant in explaining himself and far from forthcoming, but this was not surprising, given Townshend's refusal to consider any extension to the Anglo-Austrian talks earlier in the year, and his insistence that Britain would take no steps without the concurrence of France and the Netherlands and that she was entirely satisfied with French conduct. Kinsky suggested that the negotiation of Hanoverian demands, the so-called 'Electoral Points', should be handled after British demands had been discussed.[19] Given the British unwillingness to tie their hands by agreeing not to negotiate without the concurrence of the Wittelsbachs and given the conduct of Britain earlier in the year, Townshend's statement must have seemed rather harsh. It reflected the determination of George and Townshend not to endanger the negotiations with Spain by holding talks with Austria.[20] Thus, it naturally complemented their opposition to the dispatch of a fleet to Spanish waters.

The Austrians remained interested in negotiating with George II. On 26 June Charles VI sent Kinsky plenipotentiary powers for a negotiation, ordering him to press the British on a guarantee of the Pragmatic Sanction. Charles urged compliance with the system of the Quadruple Alliance, claimed that as Austria had guaranteed the Hanoverian succession, so Britain should guarantee the Pragmatic Sanction, and declared that Maria Theresa would not be married in such a way as to threaten the balance of power. Two months later Eugene informed Kinsky that the sole Austrian demand was the guarantee of the Pragmatic Sanction. He argued that it was essential for the balance of power, and suggested that Britain and the United Provinces were at least as concerned in the balance as often as other powers, if not more so.[21]

This change in the Austrian attitude, a change doubtless produced by the growing tension in Austro-Spanish relations, led to fresh approaches by the Austrian representatives in Hanover and Paris. In September Waldegrave, then in Hanover performing the duties of Secretary of State in the gap between the departure from Hanover of Townshend and of George, recorded a conversation with Kinsky. Kinsky outlined a settlement of Anglo-Austrian differences which included a suppression of the Ostend Company, an Austrian signature of the Provisional Treaty negotiated by Fleury and Sinzendorf, Austrian concessions over Mecklenburg, Bremen and Verden, British support for the terms of the Quadruple Alliance, and a British guarantee of the Pragmatic Sanction, 'but the guarantee not to extend to any P. of the house of Spain or to any other P. who by his other dominions might endanger the Libertys of Europe'.[22]

Anglo-Austrian discussions in Paris began slowly. On 2 July Horatio Walpole had complained that Stephen Kinsky

> has not opened his mouth since his arrival to any purpose but that of eating and drinking. We are feasting him plentifully each in turn, and when he seeks to take you aside, and affects to talk in confidence, it is a routine discourse that we have heard often; general professions; secrecy as to what he shall say; enquiry about our having made any new engagements, ancient friendship and ye old system; and at last ends; when he has received no more than generall answers, to his general questions; with insisting upon a limited commerce [for the Ostend Company]. Never any court acted so unaccountable a part . . . I flatter myself we shall end with Spain without ye Imperiall court and then I think we shall have nothing to fear from it.[23]

More concrete Austrian proposals were advanced in Paris in August. Stephen Kinsky informed the French ministry and the British Plenipotentiaries that Charles VI would never accept any alteration to the terms of the Quadruple Alliance, and would fight rather than accept Spanish garrisons. He told the British Plenipotentiaries that the issue of the Ostend Company would be settled to British satisfaction if George II, as King, would agree to guarantee the Pragmatic Sanction under the condition that the guarantee would only be binding if George II approved of Maria Theresa's spouse.

The Plenipotentiaries assured Stephen Kinsky of British good intentions towards Austria, but informed Townshend that they thought Stephen Kinsky's purpose was 'to interrupt or slacken our present transaction with Spain, and to create jealousies between His Majesty and France'. Keene reported that the Spanish ministry was keeping a close watch on Stephen Kinsky's negotiations. The British and the Dutch Plenipotentiaries made clear their support for the Pragmatic Sanction and their belief that it was vital for the balance of power, but they informed the Austrians that they had no instructions on the subject, and that the Austrians should address themselves directly to George II and the Dutch government. On 1 August Stanhope told Stephen Kinsky that his court held the same views which had been expressed the previous winter in discussions with Philip Kinsky, but that as he had no instructions he could not negotiate.[24]

The crisis over relations with Prussia intervened at the end of August, with the British accusing the Austrians of stirring up Prussia, accusations Austria denied. Poyntz claimed that Stephen Kinsky had spoken of 'letting the Russians, Prussians and Poles loose upon the Empire'.[25] By then, however, the negotiations with Spain were sufficiently advanced to lead Britain to rebuff Austria, a situation Eugene had foreseen. Whilst Britain needed French help to obtain a Spanish guarantee of British commercial and territorial claims, it was understandable that Townshend should rebuff Kinsky, and claim that Britain would do nothing without her allies.[26]

Negotiations with Spain had progressed more slowly than the British had hoped.[27] This led to renewed pressure in August for the presentation of an ultimatum to Spain, and Newcastle instructed the Plenipotentiaries to have the project of a treaty with Spain, agreed with France and the United Provinces, delivered to Spain as an ultimatum.[28] Such a method was unnecessary as Spain had already rejected the approaches made by the Austrian envoy in Spain. Königsegg had suggested that Austria would accept Spanish garrisons in Tuscany and Parma. However, he failed to receive sufficient support from Vienna, where Eugene and Sinzendorf disagreed over the extent to which Austria should make concessions to Spain, and the Spaniards rejected his promises as too vague.[29]

On 14 June new instructions had been sent to Keene and Brancas, ordering them to agree to the Spanish garrisons if Spain insisted on the issue.[30] This satisfied Elisabeth Farnese, but negotiations were delayed as a result of the idiosyncratic nature of the Spanish government. Writing to Townshend Keene commented, 'Your Lordship must be justly surprised and impatient of these delays . . . I cannot attribute to any other cause than to its [Spain's] natural and invincible slowness . . . to their Catholick Majesties unaccountable conduct with regard to their two ministers. . .'.[31]

Attempts to persuade Spain to accept neutral garrisons failed, and only served to increase Spanish suspicion of France and Britain. The British believed the Spaniards were deliberately delaying the negotiations in order to benefit from British difficulties with Austria and Prussia.[32] Once Britain was fully and openly committed against these powers, it was possible she would have to offer Spain better terms. The British, suspicious that Spain would reserve difficulties to the last moment in the negotiations, and hope to profit thereby from the government's need to settle matters before the beginning of the parliamentary session,[33] also feared that Spain would commit Britain to an aggressive warlike policy in Italy.[34] New Austrian offers were also feared.[35] It was therefore decided to send Stanhope to Spain. It was believed that his diplomatic skills, combined with the high regard the Spanish court held him in, would enable him to finish the negotiations and sign a treaty. Poyntz supported the choice, writing to Thomas Townshend, son and Under-Secretary of Viscount Townshend, 'if there be any man living who can bring this about it is Mr. Stanhope. The King of Spain loves him personally and says he is the only minister who never told him a falshood; besides which he has a most universal and deserved credit with the whole Spanish court and nation as well as our own.' It was also felt that the dispatch of such a high-ranking diplomat would convince Spain Britain was in earnest. Furthermore, the decision to supersede Keene, a decision resented by the latter, possibly owed something to a fear that Keene would yield to pressure, as he had done with Rottembourg in 1727.[36]

Setting out from Paris on 21 September, Stanhope moved at great speed despite the bad roads made worse by heavy rains, and the difficulty in securing enough mules for his baggage in north Spain. On 25 October he reached Seville. That evening he was received by Philip V and Elisabeth Farnese and treated 'extremely graciously'. D'Aubenton, who was both suspicious and jealous of Stanhope, had predicted major difficulties for him unless he brought new concessions. The Saxon agent De Buy shared these views, and in common with D'Aubenton reported that neither Philip nor his wife approved of Stanhope. Both were to be proved wrong. Stanhope succeeded in settling matters, and at 7 pm on 9 November the Treaty of Seville was signed. The treaty settled outstanding differences between Britain, France and Spain, and committed the two former powers to the support of Spanish pretensions in Italy. The treaty stipulated that Spanish garrisons should be introduced into Leghorn, Porto Ferrajo, Parma and Piacenza. Four months were to be devoted to securing the consent of the Emperor and the Grand Duke of Tuscany to this stipulation. If they refused consent, force was to be used, and the garrisons were to be introduced not later than 9 May, six months after the signature of the treaty.[37]

The British had been less successful than the Spaniards in achieving their goals. Despite efforts to obtain an explicit confirmation of their rights to Gibraltar and to trading privileges in the Spanish Empire, as the *Craftsman* had urged, the Spaniards proved unwilling to make any such declaration.[38] The British attempted to gain French support for their efforts, arguing that if they failed, Parliament would reject the settlement. The French proved unwilling to support the British demand, and disagreement over this point played a part in increasing Anglo-French tension in the autumn of 1729.[39] Major differences of opinion over negotiations both with Spain and with the Wittelsbachs helped to exacerbate mutual suspicions, and to ensure that discussions over the response to the Austrian demand for the guarantee of the Pragmatic Sanction, and over the best method to ensure Austrian compliance over the Spanish garrisons, took place within an alliance made unstable by distrust.

The Treaty of Seville, a copy of which reached London on 29 November, stipulated that any articles of the Treaty of Vienna which conflicted with articles in treaties signed prior to 1725 were to be revoked. British and French commercial privileges were to be restored to the pre-1727 situation. Although the *Prince Frederick* was to be immediately restored, outstanding claims relating to the activities of illicit British merchants and to the depredations of Spanish *guarda-costas* were to be referred to a specially created commission. This was also ordered to consider the Spanish claim for the restitution of the Spanish ships taken by Byng after the battle of Cape Passaro. These terms, combined with the failure to mention Gibraltar specifically, were to lead to press and parliamentary criticism in Britain.[40] There was a widespread suspicion that the government was failing to protect British interests and it was thanks to this suspicion that credence was given to reports which suggested that, by a secret clause in the treaty, the ministry was engaged to restore Gibraltar and Minorca within six years and to bring this restoration before Parliament within three years.[41] Stephen Kinsky believed that a secret article stipulated the return of Naples and Sicily to Spain.[42] It was probably partly because of this already strong disquiet over ministerial intentions that the opposition was able to make so much headway in February 1730 with claims that the government had failed to prevent the improvement of the harbour and fortifications of Dunkirk.

This atmosphere of distrust obliged the ministry to move sharply over the issue.

Clash with Prussia

'We are on the verge of war in the middle of our negotiations for peace, and upon a matter that has no connection with the differences we are trying to settle'.[43]

George Lyttelton[43]

The diplomatic situation was made more urgent in the late summer of 1729 by the threat of a Prussian invasion of Hanover. When George II arrived in Hanover Anglo-Prussian relations were far from cordial, but there had been no talk of war. The Anglo-Prussian marriage talks had failed because of what the British saw as a negative Prussian attitude,[44] but the British still hoped for an improvement in relations. Their refusal to guarantee the Sulzbach succession to Jülich-Berg was seen in this light, and there were rumours of a projected meeting between George and Frederick William I. Sauveterre, the French agent in Berlin, suspected that Seckendorf's object was to reopen Anglo-Prussian marriage talks.[45] No such meeting took place, and George seems to have made no attempt to arrange one. George appears to have thought that any approach to Prussia was pointless until Prussia could be persuaded she was not powerful enough to defy Britain. This would happen when successful negotiations with Spain and the Wittelsbachs had weakened Austria and Prussia, and until then it was best to wait for Prussia to make approaches, as it was necessary to convince Britain's allies that George did not intend to neglect their interests, threatened by Frederick William. The Dutch and French were opposed to Prussian schemes for Jülich-Berg, the Swedes suspicious of Prussian views on Swedish Pomerania. For these reasons George did not use the opportunities for personal diplomacy presented by his first trip to Hanover as King to launch any initiatives for a Protestant German league, as was to be suggested on his 1735 and 1736 trips.

The responsibility for the Anglo-Prussian crisis of 1729 rests with both monarchs.[46] Frederick William's determination to increase the size of his army had produced vigorous recruiting policies which infringed the rights of his neighbours most of whom he had upset by the summer of 1729. George retaliated in July by arresting various Prussian soldiers then in Hanover. According to Charles VI this was unreasonable, as the soldiers had valid passports and were on the public way, and because George refused to see the Prussian minister Kannengieser sent by Frederick William to discuss the matter. Charles argued that for Hanover to arrest Prussian soldiers as a reprisal for Prussian recruiting methods was against the constitution of the Empire, which forbade reprisals.[47] George argued that the Prussian methods were a breach of the peace of the Lower Saxon Circle. The somewhat petty dispute, no different in character from several had occurred between Prussia and other powers over the preceding decade, was made more serious by a Prussian military mobilization in mid-July. George appears to have neglected to consider the possibility that

Prussia would react violently. On 12 July Sühm, the Saxon envoy in Berlin, reported that Frederick William had ordered the encampment on the Elbe near the frontier of Hanover of fifty-two battalions by mid-August. Sühm commented that Prussia had made warlike preparations before, but that hitherto they had been done openly. He believed the secret nature of the current preparations indicated that Frederick William intended to attack, though he stated his conviction that Seckendorf would prevent this. However, when Seckendorf told Frederick William he could expect no Austrian help if he was the aggressor, the latter replied that he only wanted an absence of Austrian opposition, and that Prussia was ready to attack alone. Despite Prussian suggestions of a joint commission to settle the troubles, George continued to arrest Prussian soldiers, and Frederick William to assemble his troops, though George made no similar moves. The Prince of Anhalt, one of the leading Prussian generals, was sent to reconnoitre the valley of the Elbe down which the Prussians hoped to advance, cutting off Mecklenburg from Hanover. On 19 July Guy Dickens, Du Bourgay's secretary, reported from Berlin that Frederick William was eager for action: 'the King of Prussia waits with impatience for an opportunity to do some action, which, to use his own expressions, may make some affronting stroke on the side of Hanover'.[48]

The Hanoverian response to the Prussian suggestion of a mediating commission was too general to please the Prussians, but opinions differed as to Prussian intentions. Prussian war preparations continued. On 6 August Du Bourgay informed Townshend that the constant tergiversations of Frederick William made it difficult to form any firm conclusions but that 'the general opinion is that he will not undertake anything'. Du Bourgay dismissed the suggestions, made to him by the Prussian minister Knyphausen, that Prussia was really in earnest, and that Seckendorf was secretly encouraging this policy. Three days later Sühm argued that the fact that both powers were still negotiating their dispute suggested there would be no conflict. Sutton, then at Brunswick, noted Prussian preparations at Magdeburg and Halberstadt, but stated that no Prussian troops had yet left their quarters.[49]

The response at Hanover had been muted in July and early August, but by mid-August the continued Prussian preparations led to a change in tone. The British pressed their allies to urge Prussia to desist from violent measures, and to prepare to support their representations by force. The French were asked to press the Prussians and to encourage other powers to do likewise. The French ministry gave the Plenipotentiaries assurances to this effect, and urged Denmark to assure Britain of her support. Sauveterre declared to the Prussian government that France would support George II if he was attacked. On 23 August the situation suddenly became more serious. Townshend received reports from Du Bourgay stating that Prussia had decided to attack. Requests for assistance were dispatched the same day to Britain's allies. Copies of these reports were sent by express to Cassel with a call for military assistance. Sutton was ordered to travel to Copenhagen and persuade Denmark to hold ten or twelve thousand troops ready to march to assist George in repelling either a

Prussian invasion of Hanover, or the movement of Prussian troops into Mecklenburg. Townshend also ordered Chesterfield and the Plenipotentiaries to secure Dutch and French support.[50]

On the 25th Townshend sent Newcastle copies of the recent dispatches from Du Bourgay and commented on the envoy's statement that Frederick William intended to attack:

> . . . these advices are confirmed from all hands, so that there is not the least room to doubt of these being his Prussian Mty.'s present intentions . . . the King of Prussia's temper and character is such that we shall not be justified either before God or man if we do not take all necessary precautions.

Townshend informed Newcastle that if war broke out George would order a sizeable section of the British army to Hanover, and he conveyed George's orders that 'the Lords of the Council' should send an account of the state of the regiments in England, and an estimate of how long it would take for these regiments to be prepared for shipping to Germany.[51]

Frederick William hoped that George's allies would desert him. He sounded his own allies, Russia, Austria and Saxony, about the possibilities of assistance. Prussia pressed France not to intervene, arguing that the conflict was an internal affair of the Empire.[52] Frederick William was swiftly disabused. None of his allies was willing to send troops, whilst George's allies produced a generally good response. Hesse-Cassel received the British request on 25 August and at once ordered all her regiments to be ready to march at the first warning. The Dutch readily promised assistance, and the States General voted 8,000 troops to go to the aid of Hanover. The French, Danes and Swedes promised aid. The Elector of Cologne refused to give the Prussians permission to move troops across his Westphalian possessions.[53]

The British were delighted by the response of their allies and attributed to it the Prussian decision not to invade Hanover. The following February, when a Prussian attack again appeared imminent, Poyntz was certain that with the assistance of his allies George would win: 'he will certainly find France most steady and active against him in all parts, where by themselves or their allies they can possibly infest him.'[54] George was particularly grateful for the Hessian assistance. On 6 September 1729 Townshend informed Newcastle:

> I am by the King's express command to acquaint your Grace that H.M. thinks himself in a very particular manner obliged to the Landgrave of Hesse Cassel upon this occasion, who by his great fidelity and readiness in executing his engagements, has extreamly contributed to the happy turn which this affair seems now to have taken; his Prussian Majesty's present peacable desposition being, in the King's opinion in great measure owing to the early motion of the Hessian troops, and to the apprehensions of a strong diversion on that side in favour of H.M.

The reiterated reference to George's personal view would not have been lost on Newcastle whose conclusion, advanced on 9 September, was a good deal less specific:

The king's Allies have, with so much justice, vigour and resolution, exerted in the support of His Maty., which must have undeceived those, who vainly imagined that H.M. would not have had their assistance upon this occasion.[55]

It is probable that the swift response of George's allies was the decisive factor in persuading Frederick William not to attack. As Townshend pointed out, the Prussian dominions were far-flung and many of them were vulnerable to attack. In particular, Frederick William's Rhenish territories of Cleves and Mark, and his Westphalian lands of Minden, Lingen and Tecklenburg, as well as the Prussian possession of Upper Guelderland, were all vulnerable to French and Dutch attack. George II pressed for the French and Dutch to threaten Cleves.[56]

Whatever the reason, Prussia changed her tone in the last week of August. Though she continued her military preparations, and Du Bourgay indeed urged George to maintain his, Prussia indicated a willingness to negotiate. Frederick William suggested an arbitration by Brunswick-Wolfenbüttel and Saxe-Gotha, the powers chosen by Britain and Prussia respectively. They agreed that the arbitrators should hold a Congress at Brunswick and that until a settlement had been reached the men seized by both sides were to be detained by the arbitrating powers. The convention arrived at Hanover on the 8th and was immediately ratified by George.[57]

The consequences of the Anglo-Prussian war scare are difficult to elicit, and its relationship to British diplomatic thinking and foreign policy in 1729 has therefore received little study. Quazza, suggesting that Austria was responsible for the crisis, claimed that it failed to delay the negotiations in Spain. Dunthorne argued that the crisis made the defence of Hanover an important priority, and therefore persuaded Britain to adopt a more conciliatory attitude towards Spain. Dunthorne is certainly correct in suggesting that the crisis highlighted the vulnerability of the Electorate of Hanover. Writing to Sutton on 2 September Townshend stated:

You are very well acquainted with the exposed situation and extent of his Majesty's frontiers, and that, as he has no fortifications to defend it, if he be not supported by a considerable body of his allies, there will be great danger from the first impression.[58]

This may well have been realised by Townshend, by George II and by Sutton with their military training, and by visitors to the Electorate, but it is questionable how far they were aware of the acute nature of the situation prior to the 1729 war-scare. Prussian boasts that she could conquer the Electorate in less than four weeks were far from foolish.[59] Whatever the views held by George and Townshend there seems to have been little awareness in Britain of the vulnerable nature of the Electorate, and the war-scare must have come as a nasty surprise. Though preparations had been made in early 1727 for the movement of British troops to the United Provinces, the prospect of British troops fighting for the defence of Hanover as a result of local disputes was very different from the situation in 1727, when an attack on Hanover could have been presented as part of an attack upon the Hanover alliance, an alliance formed to protect British interests.

The Prussians argued that the British people would be unwilling to support a war fought for the benefit of Hanover. Sasstroff, the Prussian Resident in Cassel, stated that Parliament would never support George II in any war he might undertake for the defence of Hanover, and he claimed 'that the Hessian troops being voted for by Parliament, were not to act in any cause that did not regard Great Britain in particular'; a point also made by the opposition press. George Woodward, the British Resident at the Court of Augustus II, reported that the Saxon minister Count Manteuffel had told him he doubted whether George would enjoy the support of the English ministers. In attempting to persuade George to accept arbitration Chavigny argued that, should he refuse, the Opposition would claim that Britain had no obligation to defend Hanover. There was no doubt there was little enthusiasm within Britain for a war with Prussia. John Selwyn, a placeman and ministerial MP, noted opposition criticism of Hessian assistance for Hanover. Townshend seems to have been concerned about the amount of backing he could expect from London.[60] What is unclear is how far the crisis affected the views of the 'Lords of the Council'. In their correspondence with Hanover they made clear their willingness to support George, and there is no reason to doubt that had Prussia attacked, British troops would have been sent to the defence of the Electorate. Such a move however would have been costly and unpopular.[61] It could be suggested that the prospect of an unpopular war made the ministers in London, and in particular Walpole and Newcastle, less happy with the direction of British foreign policy. The anti-Austrian policy, represented by the negotiations with Spain and with the Wittelsbachs, did not make a conflict over Hanover less likely, and it was possible that next time Prussia would be supported by her allies. The vulnerability of Hanover in a cause having no obvious bearing upon British interests had not been an issue for many years. When it became one in the summer of 1729 it posed major problems for British foreign policy and for the position of the government in Parliament.[62] For these reasons it is not surprising that the relations between Hanover and Austria, Prussia and the Wittelsbachs became of greater concern to the British ministers in the autumn of 1729, and that they were increasingly less happy about leaving British policy in the Empire under the control of George and Townshend.

Notes

1. Horatio Walpole to Townshend, 4 July 1729, PRO. 78/192.
2. Instructions for Fonseca, 14 May 1729, HHStA., Fonseca 13.
3. St. Saphorin to Townshend, 23 Jan. 1722, Waldegrave to Townshend, 1 Jan., Stanhope to Townshend, 4 July 1729, Robinson to Essex, envoy in Turin, 14 Oct. 1733, Robinson to Harrington (ennobled Stanhope), 24 Aug. 1736, PRO. 80/46, 64, 78/192, 80/100, 118; Visconti to Zamboni, 3 July 1729, Bodl. Rawl. 129; Poyntz to Waldegrave, 19 Jan. 1730, BL. Add. 32765.
4. Colman to Newcastle, 10 July 1725, Robinson to Harrington, 5 July, Harrington to Robinson, 31 July 1735, PRO. 98/25, 80/116; Sinzendorf to Fonseca, 31 May 1729, Diemar to Eugene, 15 Jan. 1734, HHStA., Fonseca 13, GK. 85a; D'Aix to Victor Amadeus II, 7 July 1729, AST. LM. Ing. 35; Kinsky to Eugene, [late Aug. 1729], Vienna, Kinsky, 3a.

5. Waldegrave to Tilson, 18 June 1729, Chewton.
6. Newcastle to Townshend, 20 May (os) 1729, PRO. 43/77; Newcastle to Stanhope, 22 May (os), 12 June (os) 1729, Coxe, II, 641–2, 644; Tilson to Waldegrave, 19 June 1729, Chewton.
7. Browning, p. 56; Plumb, p. 198.
8. Instructions for Seckendorf, 30 June 1729, PRO. 78/193.
9. Newcastle to Townshend, 20 May (os) 1729, PRO. 43/77.
10. Chesterfield to Townshend, 6 May 1729, PRO. 84/304.
11. Stanhope and Horatio Walpole to Townshend, 4 July 1729, BL. Add. 32761; Horatio to Tilson, 4 July, Plenipotentiaries to Townshend, 4 Aug., Delafaye to Horatio, 2 Dec. (os) 1729, PRO. 78/192; Charles VI to Kinsky, 26 June 1729, HHStA., Fonseca 13; Chavigny to Chauvelin, 19 Sept. 1729, AE. CP. Br. 47.
12. Stephen Kinsky and Fonseca to Charles VI, 22 Aug. 1729, Höfler, I, 105; Poyntz to Townshend, 15 June 1729, BL. Althorp, E5.
13. Wackerbarth to Augustus, 9 July, Sühm, Saxon envoy in Berlin, to Augustus, 5, 12 July 1729, Dresden, 3331, 3378; Schleinitz to -, 12 July 1729, AE. CP. Br. 47; Townshend to Plenipotentiaries, 15 July 1729, PRO. 78/193; Eugene to Kinsky, 16 July 1729, HHStA., GK. 94(b); D'Aix to Victor Amadeus II, 21 July 1729, AST. LM. Ing. 35.
14. Kinsky to Eugene, 27 July 1729, HHStA., GK. 94(b); Du Bourgay to Townshend, 11 Sept. 1729, PRO. 90/25.
15. Townshend to Plenipotentiaries, 15 July, Chesterfield to Townshend, 12 July 1729, PRO. 78/193, 84/304.
16. Seckendorf to Diemar, 30 July, 9 Aug., Diemar to Seckendorf, 6 Aug., Diemar to Landgrave Karl, 8, 13 Aug. 1729, Marburg, England 195, 197.
17. Townshend to Newcastle, 14 June, Chesterfield to Townshend, 14, 28 June 1729, PRO. 43/9, 84/304.
18. Townshend to Newcastle, 10 June 1729, PRO. 43/77.
19. Townshend to Newcastle, 21 June, Townshend to Plenipotentiaries, 23 June, Townshend to Kinsky, 9, 10 Aug., 20 Sept., Horatio Walpole and Stanhope to Keene, 17 Sept. 1729, PRO. 43/77, 78/193, 100/11, 78/192; Kinsky to Eugene, 5 Sept. 1729, HHStA., GK. 94(b); Chavigny to Chauvelin, 12 Aug., 4 Sept. 1729, AE. CP. Br. 47.
20. Plenipotentiaries to Keene, 19 Aug. 1729, BL. Add. 32762.
21. Charles VI to Kinsky, 26 June, Eugene to Kinsky, 25 Sept. 1729, HHStA., Fonseca 13, GK. 94(b).
22. Undated note in Waldegrave's 'Journal of his Embassy in France', Chewton; Waldegrave to Horatio Walpole, 26 Apr. 1730, Coxe, II, 690.
23. Horatio Walpole to Delafaye, 2 July 1729, PRO. 78/192.
24. Plenipotentiaries to Townshend, 4 Aug. 1729, PRO. 78/192; Stephen Kinsky and Fonseca to Charles VI, 3, 22, 24 Aug., 26 Sept. 1729, Höfler, I, 88–90, 105, 110, 227; Keene to Plenipotentiaries, 25 Aug. 1729, BL. Add. 32762.
25. Poyntz to Delafaye, 7, 12 Aug., Horatio Walpole and Stanhope to Keene, 17 Sept., Townshend to Chesterfield, 2 Sept. 1729, PRO. 78/192, 84/305; Sinzendorf to Fonseca, 5 Aug. 1729, HHStA., Fonseca 13; Stephen Kinsky and Fonseca to Charles VI, 22 Aug., 1, 26 Sept., Charles VI to Stephen Kinsky and Fonseca, 8 Oct. 1729, Höfler, I, 102, 200, 247, 250–2.
26. Eugene to Kinsky, 24 Aug. 1729, Vienna, GK. 94(b).
27. *Wye's Letter* 5 Aug. (os), *Newcastle Courant* 16 Aug. (os), *Craftsman* 23 Aug. (os) 1728.
28. Newcastle to Plenipotentiaries, 29 Aug.(os) 1729, PRO. 43/80; King, pp. 88–9; Goslinga, pp. 344, 348.
29. Keene to Townshend, 10 July, Plenipotentiaries to Townshend, 4 Aug. 1729, PRO. 94/100, 78/192; Plenipotentiaries to Newcastle, 21 Aug., Keene to Townshend, 1 Sept. 1729, BL. Add. 32762; Bussy to Chauvelin, 27 July, 17 Aug. 1729, AE. CP. Aut. 163; Newcastle to Stanhope, 17 July (os) 1729, Coxe, II, 651; De Buy to Marquis de Fleury, Saxon minister, 30 June, 14 July 1729, Dresden, 3105, 2.
30. Townshend to Plenipotentiaries, 11 June 1729, PRO. 43/9; Instruction enclosed in Plenipotentiaries to Keene, 14 June 1729, BL. Add. 32761; King, p. 89; Baudrillart III, 520–1; Goslinga, p. 347; Conn, pp. 16–7.
31. Keene to Townshend, 28 July 1729, PRO. 94/100; Tilson to Waldegrave, 23 June 1729,

Chewton; D'Aubenton to Maurepas, 27 Oct. 1729, AN. AM. B7 299.
32. Keene to Townshend, 22 Sept., Keene to Plenipotentiaries, 5 Oct., Horatio Walpole and Poyntz to Newcastle, 12 Oct. 1729, BL. Add. 32763.
33. Horatio Walpole to Delafaye, 17 Sept. 1729, PRO. 78/192; Horatio and Poyntz to Keene, 3 Oct., Keene to Townshend, 5 Oct., Horatio to Newcastle, 18 Oct., Keene to Newcastle, 20 Oct. 1729, BL. Add. 32763.
34. Keene to Townshend, 5 Oct., Keene to Newcastle, 13 Oct. 1729, BL. Add. 32763.
35. Horatio Walpole to Delafaye, 8, 11 Aug. 1729, PRO. 78/192; Fonseca and Stephen Kinsky to Philip Kinsky, 22 Aug. 1729, Vienna, Kinsky, 2(b).
36. Poyntz to Townshend, 4 Aug. 1729, BL. Althorp, E5; Horatio Walpole to Keene, 18 Oct. 1729, BL. Add. 32763; D'Aubenton to Maurepas, 20 Oct. 1729, AN. AM. B7 299.
37. Doctor Lidderdale to Horatio Walpole, 26 Sept., Stanhope to Horatio Walpole and Poyntz, 30 Sept., Stanhope to Keene, 12 Oct., Stanhope to Newcastle, 5, 14 Oct., Stanhope and Keene to Newcastle, 27 Oct. 1729, BL. Add. 32763; D'Aubenton to Maurepas, 20 Oct. 1729, AN. AM. B7 299; De Buy to Manteuffel, 6 Oct., 10 Nov. 1729, Dresden, 3105, 2; Chauvelin to Chammorel, 3 Nov. 1729, AE. CP. Ang. sup.8; Königsegg to Stephen Kinsky and Fonseca, 8 Nov. 1729, HHStA., Frankreich, Varia 12; Treaty, PRO. 108/490; Baudrillart, III, 540–2.
38. *Craftsman* 16 Aug. (os) 1729; Horatio Walpole and Poyntz to Newcastle, 13 Aug. 1729, PRO. 78/192; Stephen Kinsky and Fonseca to Charles VI, 4 Sept. 1729, Höfler, I, 206.
39. Chauvelin to Chavigny, 21 Aug., 4, 19 Sept., Chauvelin to Chammorel, 3 Nov., Chauvelin to Brancas, French envoy in Spain, 24 Aug., 1729, AE. CP. Br. 47, Ang. sup. 8, Mém. et Doc. France 449; Keene to Townshend, 1 Sept., Horatio Walpole and Poyntz to Stanhope, 27 Sept. 1729, BL. Add. 32762; Chesterfield to Townshend, 6 Sept. 1729, PRO. 804/304; King, p. 109.
40. *Craftsman* 13 Dec. (os) 1729; HMC. *Carlisle* p. 67.
41. Delafaye to Poyntz, 25 May (os) 1730, BL. Althorp, E4; Broglie to Chauvelin, 16 Jan., Chammorel to Chauvelin, 19 Jan. 1730, AE. CP. Ang. 369; Dowager Countess of Portland to Count Bentinck, 24 Feb. (os) 1730, Broglie to Chauvelin, 9 Apr. 1731, BL. Eg. Mss. 1715, Add. 32772; Tilson to Waldegrave, 17 Feb. (os) 1730, Chewton; Edward Finch to Townshend, 25 Feb. 1730, PRO. 95/54; Kinsky to Ferdinand Albrecht, 25 Feb., Seckendorf to Ferdinand Albrecht, 4 Mar., Ferdinand Albrecht to Kinsky, 13 Mar. 1730, Wolfenbüttel, 1 Alt 22, Nr. 590, 585d; Ossorio, Sardinian envoy in London, to Victor Amadeus II, 23 Jan., 27 Feb. 1730, AST. LM. Ing. 37; Zamboni to Manteuffel, 28 Apr. 1730, Bodl. Rawl. 120; Anon, *A Letter to a Member of Parliament, relating to the Secret Article concluded and ratified by the Treaty of Seville, concerning Gibraltar and Minorca* [1730], French mss translation, AE. CP. Ang. 370 f.96–8.
42. Poyntz to Delafaye, 24 Nov. 1729, PRO. 78/192.
43. George Lyttelton to Sir Thomas Lyttelton, – Aug. 1729, M. Wyndham, *Chronicles of the Eighteenth Century* (2 vols, 1924) I, 18.
44. Chesterfield to Townshend, 17 May 1729, PRO. 84/304.
45. Sauveterre to Chauvelin, 21 June 1729, AE. CP. Prusse 89; Seckendorf to Ferdinand Albrecht, 24 May 1729, Wolfenbüttel, 1 Alt 22, Nr. 585(b); Wackerbarth to Augustus, 2 July 1729, Dresden, 3331, 2; *Wye's Letter* 26 Apr. (os), 13 May (os), *London Evening Post* 13 May (os) 1729.
46. Schleinitz to Fleury, 8 July 1729, AE. CP. Br. 47.
47. Sühm to Augustus, 5 July, Dresden 3378, VI; Schleinitz to Fleury, 12 July 1729, AE. CP. Br. 47; Charles VI to Fonseca and Stephen Kinsky, 31 Aug., 10 Sept. 1729, Höfler, I, 144–6, 211.
48. Sühm to Augustus, 12, 19, 23 July 1729, Dresden, 3378, VI; Dickens to Du Bourgay, 19 July 1729, PRO. 90/24.
49. Du Bourgay to Townshend, 6, 9 Aug., Sutton to Townshend, 12 Aug. 1729, PRO. 90/24, 81/123; Sühm to Augustus, 26 July, 2, 9 Aug. 1729, Dresden, 3378, VI; D'Aix to Victor Amadeus II, 28 Aug. 1729, AST. LM. Ing. 35; Villars, p. 183.
50. Du Bourgay to Townshend, 20, 21, 22, 23 Aug., Townshend to Du Bourgay, 25 Aug., Townshend to Sutton, 23 Aug., Townshend to Titley, 23 Aug. 1729, PRO. 90/24, 81/123, 75/53; Declaration by Sauveterre, 22 Aug. 1729, Höfler, I, 146; Chauvelin to

Chavigny, 21 Aug., Chavigny to Chauvelin, 23 Aug. 1729, AE. CP. Br. 47; Diemar to William of Hesse-Cassel, 23 Aug. 1729, Marburg, England 195; Frederick William to Ferdinand Albrecht, 22 Aug. 1729, Wolfenbüttel, 1 Alt 22, Nr. 532.
51. Townshend to Newcastle, 25 Aug. 1729, PRO. 43/80; King, p.108.
52. Frederick William to Chambrier, 20 Aug., 3 Sept. 1729, AE. CP. Prusse 88; Du Bourgay to Townshend, 20, 27 Aug., Woodward, British envoy to Augustus II, to Townshend, 8 Sept., Chetwynd to Tilson, 9 Sept., PRO. 90/124, 88/35, 81/123; Pretsch, *Manteuffel*, pp. 56–7; Charles VI to Stephen Kinsky and Fonseca, 31 Aug., Stephen Kinsky and Fonseca to Charles VI, 1, 4 Sept. 1729, Höfler, I, 145–6, 301, 206.
53. William of Hesse-Cassel to Diemar, 27 Aug. 1729, Marburg, England 195; Caillaud, Sutton's secretary, to Tilson, 29 Aug., Sutton to Townshend, 30 Aug., Chesterfield to Townshend, 2, 9 Sept., Horatio Walpole to Delafaye, 31 Aug., Horatio to Tilson, 9 Sept., Plenipotentiaries to Townshend 21 Aug., 2, 3, 12 Sept., Poyntz to Tilson, 12 Sept., Titley to Townshend, 13 Sept., Woodward to Townshend, 21 Sept. 1729, PRO. 81/123, 78/192, 75/53, 88/35; Chavigny to Chauvelin, 4 Sept., Chauvelin to Chammorel, 3 Oct., Boisseaux to Chauvelin, 2 Sept. 1729, AE. CP. Br. 47, Ang. sup. 8, Cologne 70; Stephen Kinsky and Fonseca to Charles VI, 1 Sept. 1729, Höfler, I, 201; *Sbornik* 66, p. 94; BL. Add. 33006 f.17–9.
54. Newcastle to Plenipotentiaries, 19 Aug. (os) 1729, BL. Add. 32762; Poyntz to Du Bourgay 9 Feb. 1730, BL. Althorp, E1.
55. Townshend to Newcastle, 6 Sept., Newcastle to Townshend, 29 Aug., Townshend to Sutton, 11 Sept., Horatio Walpole to Delafaye, 12 Sept., Newcastle to Chesterfield, 2 Sept. (os) 1729, PRO. 43/80, 81/123, 78/192, 84/580; Newcastle to Poyntz, 22 Jan. (os) 1730, BL. Add. 32765.
56. Townshend to Du Bourgay, 25 Aug. 1729, PRO. 90/25; Chavigny to Chauvelin, 23 Aug., 4 Sept. 1729, AE. CP. Br. 47.
57. Du Bourgay to Townshend, 30 Aug., Townshend to Sutton, 6, 9 Sept. 1729, PRO. 90/25, 81/123; Townshend to Horatio Walpole, 4 Sept. 1729, BL. Add. 9139: Robert Trevor, sent to Berlin to report on Prussian military moves, to Poyntz, 15 Sept. 1729, BL. Althorp, E3.
58. Quazza, p. 129; Dunthorne, p. 183; Townshend to Sutton, 2 Sept. 1729, PRO. 81/123; Chauvelin to Chavigny, 21 Aug. 1729, AE. CP. Br. 47.
59. Du Bourgay to Townshend, 27 Aug. 1729, Dickens to Harrington, 21 June 1738, PRO. 90/25, 44.
60. Caillaud to Tilson, 5 Sept., Woodward to Townshend, 29 Aug. 1729, PRO. 81/123, 88/35; *Fog's Weekly Journal* 30 Aug. (os), *Craftsman* 23 Aug. (os) 1729; Chavigny to Chauvelin, 4 Sept., Chammorel to Chauvelin, 15 Sept. 1729, AE. CP. Br. 47, Ang. 366; Townshend to Newcastle, 25 Aug. 1729, PRO. 43/80; Zamboni to Manteuffel, 2 Sept. 1729, Bodl. Rawl. 120; Selwyn to Poyntz, 8 Dec. (os) 1729, BL. Althorp, E3.
61. Delafaye to Tilson, 22 July (os) 1729, PRO. 43/79; Black, 'Foreign Inspiration of Eighteenth-Century British Political Material: An Example from 1730', *Trivium* 21 (1986).
62. Notes in Newcastle's hand, probably for parliamentary speech in 1730, PRO. 36/21 f.215.

CHAPTER TEN

Winter 1729–30: Ministerial Crisis

'At present things are at a stand, and in all likelyhood there will not be
much to doe untill we hear the success of Mr. Stanhope's journey'.
Horatio Walpole, October 1729.[1]

The lengthy negotiations with Spain led to most other issues being placed
in abeyance. Austrian approaches to the Plenipotentiaries at Paris, requesting negotiations over a guarantee of the Pragmatic Sanction, were met
with delaying tactics. It was agreed to defer the answer to Austria until the
success of Stanhope's mission was known.[2] This decision was taken
despite the wish of Slingelandt to combine the negotiations with Austria
with those with Spain. Philip Kinsky claimed Townshend wished to finish
both sets of negotiations at once, but he advanced no evidence for this
assertion. The British were against any such combination. They believed
the state of negotiations with Spain depended heavily on the state of
relations between Austria and the Hanover allies, and that Spanish pliancy
depended on Spanish fears of an improvement in Anglo-Austrian relations. It was necessary to strike a balance between angering the Spaniards
by continuing talks with the Austrians, and making them obdurate by
closing the door to any such talks. Newcastle suggested that, 'if the
Spaniards believed 'all sort of negociation between the allies and the
Emperor is at an end', they might think 'they may insist upon what terms
and conditions they please with us, and we must be obliged to submit to
them'. Horatio Walpole wrote to Delafaye 'It is plain to me that the
Imperialists are put to their last shifts; and I don't doubt, but if we would
have entered into their proposition to Guaranty the order of their
succession they would give up all other points; but we must keep off and
stand by our allies as long as they stand by us'.[3]

Negotiations with the Wittelsbachs continued to be of major importance
for the rest of the year and played their part in exacerbating Anglo-French
tensions. George II left Hanover on 16 September, reaching Britain on the
22nd after a rushed journey and a hasty embarkation at Helvoetsluys.
Townshend's rapid departure meant that negotiations, in the absence of
Wittelsbach diplomatic representatives in London, had to be handled by
post. On 28 September Chavigny sent Townshend the project for a treaty
with the Wittelsbachs. Townshend's response was hostile.[4] The Wittelsbachs judged Townshend's reply inadequate. The Elector of Bavaria wrote
a memorandum on the subject. He was willing to accept George's views on
Mecklenburg and, in view of the approaching peace with Spain, to include
Gibraltar in the provisions of the Treaty, but he made it clear that he

supported Palatine demands over the Jülich-Berg succession and that he expected Britain to pay subsidies to Bavaria, arguing that George would be able to obtain a parliamentary majority for this. The French were also certain that Parliament would provide the necessary funds.[5] Far from being a simple quarrel about money, the negotiations were closely related to the issue of British diplomatic strategy in the Empire. Suggestions had been made that Britain should use the talks at Brunswick as a springboard for an Anglo-Prussian alliance, an alliance that would isolate Austria, facilitate negotiations with Russia, reduce dependance upon France and the Wittelsbachs, lessen tension over Mecklenburg and solve some of the marital problems of George's children.[6] The need to avoid committing themselves over Jülich-Berg was therefore clear. Törring noted that it was over this issue that the British and Wittelsbach points of view were furthest apart. The Cologne minister Bellanger was aware of this. After his conferences with Chesterfield at The Hague he informed Plettenberg that George wished to do nothing over Jülich-Berg which would upset Prussia. Poyntz claimed that Townshend agreed with his view that the negotiations 'should be forwarded or dropped, as the Emperor's behaviour on our communicating the Treaty with Spain shall make it necessary'. Delafaye saw them as useful 'for keeping the Imperial Court in order.'[7]

Chavigny was informed there was a danger that an Anglo-Prussian settlement would be effected before the treaty with the Wittelsbachs could be signed. On 22 October Bellanger had received (from Chesterfield) Townshend's reply to Chavigny's project. He had been most surprised by Townshend's failure to propose any expedient for adjusting the points at dispute. The French put pressure on the British to accept the Wittelsbach claims. Broglie pressed the government in London, whilst the British envoys in Paris were repeatedly urged to yield.[8] Townshend rejected the French expedient of a secret guarantee of the Cologne claim to peacetime subsidies, refused to yield over subsidies to Bavaria and peacetime subsidies to Cologne, and continued to press for George's demands over Mecklenburg, Jülich-Berg and the inclusion of Gibraltar and the Ostend Company in the reciprocal provisions of the treaty. Robert Trevor blamed the Cologne subsidy demands for the halting of the negotiations.[9] Neither among the British ministry nor amongst the Wittelsbach Electors was there a whole-hearted commitment to the treaty which matched the French determination to secure its signature. Poyntz reported that Fleury and Chauvelin 'labour the conclusion of the Treaty with the Electors with all their might'. In the same month Newcastle wrote 'His Maty. thinks it by no means advisable that this Treaty should be concluded till we can see further what turn the publick affairs are like to take', and Tilson made the same point.[10]

'Public affairs' involved not only the European situation, but also the struggle for control within the British ministry. This struggle persisted until the resignation of Townshend in May 1730. It is a struggle which has received relatively little scholarly attention. The absence of a biography of Townshend is particularly serious for this period, as is the restricted access to the papers of Horatio Walpole held in Wolterton, and the large gaps in the surviving Townshend material. Given the restricted nature of the archival sources available it is not surprising that scholarly comment on Townshend's fall has been brief, and at times superficial. Browning argued it was Townshend's loss of control over foreign policy to Walpole and Newcastle which made his fall inevitable: 'If he could no longer command foreign policy, it seemed but a matter of time until he either left or was asked to leave the government'. Speck also saw foreign affairs as decisive. He stated that Walpole 'negotiated the Treaty of Seville . . . behind Townshend's back . . . this independent initiative in foreign policy brought to a head a growing antagonism between the two ministers . . . After some months waiting for events to justify him, Townshend resigned'. Langford's analysis was similar:

> Once Walpole began to formulate his own line in foreign policy, there could be only one conclusion, and that a direct clash . . . Townshend was committed to a strategy . . . based on the assumption that the Emperor was the greatest menace to the peace of Europe and to the interests of Britain. Walpole, under the pressure of his domestic difficulties, could only see that Spain . . . posed an equal threat . . . Walpole's chief concern was . . . peace and retrenchment. There could be no compromise . . . Townshend, in no position to challenge Walpole's predominance at court and in the Commons . . .

The general consensus, therefore, is to link Townshend's fall to a major difference of opinion over foreign policy, and to regard it as the inevitable consequence of his disagreement with Walpole. Walpole is not seen as having been in danger, and George's role is discounted.[11] Such an analysis underestimates the severity of the crisis and ignores its longevity. Government policy, particularly its foreign policy, was gravely affected by the clash between the two ministers, a clash made more serious by its coincidence with the commencement of the parliamentary session. Had Walpole been as strong as is believed, he would have removed Townshend before May 1730. Once the attempts of George and Caroline to reconcile the two men had failed at the end of 1729, there was no reason for Walpole to keep Townshend in the ministry, unless he either feared his opposition in the House of Lords, a possibility which casts doubt on Walpole's control of the peers; or was unable to persuade George to dismiss him, a possibility which casts doubt on Walpole's influence with his royal master.

The parliamentary session of 1730 witnessed a determined effort by the opposition to use foreign policy issues to ensure the removal of Walpole. This coincided with a continued lack of control by Walpole over the ministry. Wilmington, Dorset and Dodington were unreliable, and the government lost the support of Townshend, Carteret and Winchelsea. George's support for Walpole was unclear; it was widely believed in diplomatic circles in late 1729 that George preferred Townshend's policies to those of Walpole. If this is correct then the crisis of 1729–1730 is of greater importance than historians have perhaps recognised. 1730 could be seen as a foretaste of 1742 and 1744, when George was forced to part with Walpole and Carteret respectively, against his better judgement.

A lengthy examination of the available archives does not suggest any definite conclusions. It does, however, suggest that the situation was more complex than has been realised hitherto, and that differences of opinion over diplomatic issues were crucial to the quarrel between Walpole and Townshend.

The views of George II in the winter of 1729–30 are unclear. There are only a few hints as to his opinions, and most of them are not completely reliable. In particular George's views with regard to relations with Austria, France, Prussia and the Wittelsbachs are unclear. In addition, there is little evidence about his relations with Walpole, Townshend, and the principal, actual or potential competitors for the Secretaryships of State, Chesterfield, Methuen, Stanhope and Horatio Walpole. The major source for George's views are the dispatches of foreign diplomats in London. The King's attitudes were only rarely alluded to in the correspondence of the leading British ministers.

The surviving evidence suggests that George was interested in an alliance with the Wittelsbachs, but only upon his own terms. He did not wish to pay large subsidies, had little interest in supporting the Wittelsbach claim to the Jülich-Berg succession, and demanded that the Wittelsbachs support him over Mecklenburg.[12] George's attitude towards Austria was not one of simple hostility. Rather, like Townshend and Poyntz, he was deeply suspicious of Austria, but hoped to persuade or force the Austrians into good relations. On 11 November, before the news of the Treaty of Seville had reached London but when it already seemed likely that Stanhope would succeed in his negotiations, Townshend informed Waldegrave of his views on Anglo-Austrian relations:

> however the Maritime Powers may be engaged in interest to prevent any division of the Austrian territories, this is by no means a proper time to propose a guarantee of the Pragmatic Sanction.

He argued that much would depend on Maria Theresa's marriage, and stated that it was best for Charles VI 'to put an end to the present disturbances as soon as possible, and by so doing put the Maritime Powers in a condition to renew their ancient friendship with him'.

This was hardly the language of the anti-Austrian hawk, seen by many historians. It seems that George shared Townshend's views, though there is no evidence supporting the claim advanced in the *Amsterdam Gazette* that George had written two letters to Charles VI promising never to execute the Treaty of Seville by force.[13] As soon as Austria was prepared to cooperate in the Empire with Hanover, and in Europe with Britain, then an alliance could be negotiated. There were two problems with this approach. First, it left the future of the French alliance in doubt. Broglie claimed George needed to retain the French alliance in order to protect Hanover, and in early 1730 the British ministry pressed the French to threaten Prussia with military action in the event of a Prussian attack upon Hanover. They were pleased with the response.[14] However, if Anglo-Prussian relations improved this situation would not pertain, and whatever the British ministry might need France for, George II would need her for nothing. It was only partly due to Hanoverian territorial interests in Bremen, Verden and Mecklenburg that George wanted an Austrian and/or Prussian alliance. The principal spur for him came from the more general need for Hanoverian security. Thus, far from George being defeated on 16 March 1731, when the Second Treaty of Vienna was signed and Hanoverian territorial demands shelved, albeit temporarily, the treaty was a triumph for George because it brought Hanover security. Broglie was sceptical about the degree of commitment against Austria shown by both Townshend and George. In December 1729 he reported that Townshend wanted to maintain an Austrian presence in Italy, and to diminish, not destroy, Austrian authority in the peninsula.[15]

Aside from French support, the second major problem with Townshend and George's Austrian policy was Walpole's impatience with the progress of British foreign policy. It was not that Walpole disagreed substantially with Townshend's Austrian policy. Browning's claim that 'Walpole and Newcastle, by repudiating Townshend's anti-Habsburg policy, were preparing for the day when the artificial situation that induced Britain and France to be allies had dissolved', is inaccurate.[15] Townshend's policy was not 'anti-Habsburg', and his insistence that a guarantee of the Pragmatic Sanction was dependant upon an Austrian commitment over Maria Theresa's husband was to be maintained, after his resignation, in the negotiations for the Second Treaty of Vienna. Walpole's concern was rather with the cost, in time and money, produced by Townshend's policy. He wanted a swift settlement of European problems, an end to heavy British military expenditure and extensive subsidy obligations, and a reduction in taxation. The political cost of the French alliance, in terms of providing ready issues for the parliamentary opposition, was also a factor, and in 1730 disputes with the French over Dunkirk and St. Lucia made this problem more serious. Whether Walpole, in the autumn of 1729, already sought to discard the French alliance, is unclear. Dureng argued that the Walpoles had already determined upon a reconciliation with Austria. It is more likely that the acute parliamentary crisis over Dunkirk in February 1730 and the return of the pro-Austrian William Stanhope to Britain in the summer of 1730, led Walpole to this conclusion, and that he had not already decided to abandon France at the time of his quarrel with Townshend. At that time it is probable Walpole had already determined to seek to lessen British dependence upon France. This was a wish shared by George and Townshend, Chesterfield and Stanhope.[16] Thus, both Walpole and Townshend had a similar long-term diplomatic strategy: reconciliation with Austria, the guarantee of the Pragmatic Sanction, upon terms, and a lessened dependence upon France. Such a situation would permit Walpole to retrench, and leave Townshend and George in a glorious diplomatic position. In diplomatic circles there was little doubt of George's support for Townshend, and hostility to Walpole's attempt to supplant him. The correspondence between Townshend and Chavigny was kept secret from the other ministers, with George's approval.[17] There was less agreement as to the cause of the dispute between the two ministers, though most blamed it on differences over the Wittelsbach negotiations, and in particular over the subsidies. It was generally held that Townshend was in favour of the latter and Walpole against. A particular problem appears to have arisen from the Palatine demand for the payment of a debt they claimed due to them, for the expenses of their troops who had fought in Catalonia during the War of the Spanish Succession, as a result of a subsidy treaty with Britain and the United Provinces. The Elector Palatine had long pressed for the payment of this debt and in 1729 Baron Beveren, the Palatine envoy in Hanover, told Townshend that its payment was a precondition of negotiations. It was presumably from this that a report of a secret promise by Townshend to pay the debt arose. On 4 August 1729 Horatio Walpole informed Townshend that Fleury had shown him a letter from Schleinitz claiming Townshend had offered to pay the debt and a subsidy to the Elector of Cologne, but insisted that it be kept a secret from the Plenipotentiaries. On the same day Poyntz wrote to Thomas Townshend:

My Lord will have a private letter from Mr. Walpole by this messenger on a very disagreeable incident. You will find that the Cardinal communicated to us a letter from Schleinitz which he had been desired to keep secret; I am entirely convinced that he either had not read the decyphering or had forgot that clause . . . I could have wished that Mr. Walpole would have written to my Lord on this subject, before he had written to England; but as he appears firmly convinced that the asking this additional expense in Parliament after the £115,000 will break the back of the administration, and that there was therefore a necessity of acquainting his brother with it, his communicating to my Lord what he has wrote was acting an honest and open part. In the other points of closing with Spain preferably to the Emperor and of not rendering the negotiations desperate by sending out our squadron precipitately, whatever diversity of sentiments there may have been in England, those of Mr. Walpole have been entirely conformable to my Lords, and I believe he has asserted them strenuously in private letters as well as in our dispatches, so that I verily believe his differing upon this point arises solely from the inconveniences he apprehends in Parliament. For my own part I cannot but hope that if our affairs with Spain should take such a turn, as to enable us to lay up the fleet, to disband the Hessians, and to reduce part of our land forces, Sir Robert Walpole might find it practicable from these savings to induce the Parliament to some share of the expence for the Electoral Treaty.

A variation of this episode was reported by Plettenberg, who blamed the ministerial rift on a project devised by Townshend and Schleinitz for the payment of the debt in return for an agreement that George should not have to guarantee the Jülich-Berg succession. According to this account, which was substantially corroborated by Chavigny and reported independently by D'Aix, Townshend stated that the money could be found by George, but that Walpole had to be kept in ignorance of the project; Fleury revealed it to Horatio Walpole, and though Townshend said that he knew nothing of any agreement and claimed that the project was Schleinitz's, a breach was caused. It is impossible to state how accurate this report was. Schleinitz was not the most reliable of men, Townshend had expressed distrust of him in 1728, and the scheme bore all the hallmarks of one of his over-ambitious projects. Tilson was scathing about his unsteadiness. It is possible that Townshend encouraged Schleinitz, who was known to be in touch with the French ministry, in order to convince the latter of his good intentions, without having any design of implementing his promise. In 1752, when the Elector Palatine sought again to have the debt paid, the Palatine envoy in Hanover delivered a memorandum claiming that Beveren had persuaded Townshend to seek further information on the case and to promise to settle it as soon as he returned to London.[18]

Coxe included in his biography of Sir Robert Walpole an explanation which also attributed the rift to actions and policies commenced by Townshend, a contrast to the view of Townshend as dispirited, enfeebled by illness, and largely passive in the face of Walpole's growth in authority and power. Coxe claimed that Townshend was resolved to form 'a new administration', and sought to replace Newcastle by Chesterfield. Coxe's account is not very sympathetic to Townshend: 'He became more obsequious to the King's German prejudices, paid his court with unceasing assiduity, and appeared to have gained so much influence that he thought himself capable of obtaining the appointment of Chesterfield'. According to Coxe the Queen, never a supporter of Chesterfield, whom she thought a client of Lady Suffolk's, helped Walpole to block Chesterfield's widely-anticipated appointment, and Townshend's second choice, Methuen, failed also, though Coxe does not explain the latter failure.

Horatio Walpole's account was different. He presented Townshend as vacillating over whether to resign and claimed he had promised George, if he did so, to wait till after the session; and had urged that Harrington, Poyntz and Horatio be considered as his replacement and not, to the surprise of others, Chesterfield 'with whom alone he acts in perfect confidence, and crys up beyond all persons.' Robert Trevor, in contrast, thought that Chesterfield would replace Townshend and Newcastle go to Ireland. Coxe's account attributes much to the influence of the Queen, and there was general agreement among the diplomats in London that Caroline actively backed Walpole against Townshend. In 1732 Townshend wrote of Caroline 'I am persuaded she never in her heart approved of my notions in foreign affairs'.[19] How important this support was, is less clear. However successful Walpole and Caroline might have been in preventing the appointment of Chesterfield, Walpole failed to remove Townshend at the end of 1729. It seems to be the case that Walpole attempted to transfer Townshend to the Lord Presidency of the Council, a post made vacant by the death of the Duke of Devonshire. Zamboni attributed the ministerial rivalry to this issue, and to Walpole seeking to appoint his brother Secretary of State. Robinson wrote to Horatio Walpole of the possibility of his 'coming to the chief direction of foreign affairs'. Peter Wentworth clearly had a different source, for he noted that Townshend was to have the Presidency added to his Secretaryship. The basis of this report was apparently the fact that Townshend acted as President during the vacancy in the post.[20]

It would be easy to multiply these various reports, but such a process is not very helpful. All the monocausal explanations of the rift are dubious, and it is probably more helpful to note that the divisions over policy seem to have been linked to differences over the composition of the Ministry and quarrels over place. The relationship between the disputes over policy and those over place is an obscure one. Comments such as Hervey's 'they say the conclusion of this Treaty has not secured Don Carlos's succession in Tuscany more effectually than it has defeated the hopes of Ld. Chesterfield in the Cockpit' are unclear. Whether ministers supporting the same policy naturally coalesced and sought posts for each other, or whether the quest for office took precedence, is difficult to ascertain. Given the fact that negotiations with the Wittelsbachs only became a divisive issue in the early autumn of 1729, whilst Townshend had been actively sponsoring Chesterfield, and Newcastle, Stanhope, from before this period, it is clear that however much these negotiations provided an occasion for conflict, they were not the original cause of division. It could be suggested that a conflict fuelled by ambition for office required an issue of policy in order to give credibility to the dispute, but it is hardly likely that Walpole would have chosen the Wittelsbach negotiations out of preference. The personal interest of the King, and Townshend's knowledge of, and willingness to support, Hanoverian interests, made it a dangerous issue. Townshend was heavily criticised by the other ministers for his pro-Hanoverian stance. In January 1730 Horatio Walpole informed Poyntz of Townshend's 'endeavours to make all measures electorall, preferrable to all other considerations, which is entirely agreeable to the King's sentiments'. Of all the ministers Townshend was the most sensitive to Hanoverian interests, and this shared concern of King and minister is more in evidence in the winter of 1729–30 than the few signs of personal disagreements between the two.[21]

Aside from the Wittelsbach negotiations, another diplomatic issue developed that winter which attracted George's personal interest and was directly related to Hanoverian interest: an alliance with Prussia. The progress of the Congress held at Brunswick to settle Anglo-Prussian differences was, despite hopes to the contrary, slow. Robert Trevor reported from London on Frederick William I's actions:

his animosity towards our King seems by his present behaviour to be grown more furious, and inveterate than ever; he detests his own children for their being related to him, and makes it his chief pleasure to torment them on that account. Within these few days he had forced his wife to write an insolent letter of his dictating to our queen, insisting upon her speedy performance of the hopes, she has given her of marrying Prince Frederick to her eldest daughter, and this before February next, and unconditionally, or else that she cannot hinder her husband from disposing of her to somebody else. I'll leave you to judge how this manner of treatment is relished at St. James's, especially after our King has opened himself so ingenuously, and kindly as he has very lately done upon a plan of reconciliation sent hither from Berlin; in his answer to which after having approved of the methods proposed for terminating the differences of the two Courts about Mecklenburg etc, he offers to exchange the two Princesses with, or without portions, and even to allow the Prince of Prussia, if he lives at London, wherewithall to support his rank, provided the King of Prussia returns him hither his present allowance. You certainly know, that our King's contempt for his brother in law is as great as one man can have for another, and I dread the probable consequences of a rancour so violent and so reciprocal.

British suspicions of Prussia increased, and at the beginning of 1730 the British pressed Sweden to increase their garrisons in Swedish Pomerania. Anglo-Swedish subsidy talks were seen, by the British ministry, as a basis for securing Swedish forces against Prussia in the event of war. The Electorate of Hanover remained on a war-footing, to the anger of Frederick William. The British were very concerned by the improvement of Prusso-Saxon relations over the winter, and feared that the journey which took Frederick William to Dresden in February had produced a secret treaty. On 31 January Townshend informed Edward Finch that he had been ordered by George to instruct him 'that he has received secret advices concerning the warlike preparations of the King of Prussia, and his dangerous designs of disturbing the peace of that part of Germany. These advices have been confirmed from several quarters, and we also learn from Holland, that the King of Prussia reinforces his garrisons on those frontiers and appears inclinable to do all the mischief he is able, as soon as he can have a proper occasion. His scheme seems to be, if the Emperor does not agree with the allys of the Treaty of Seville, to begin hostilitys by attacking the King's German Dominions.[22]

There was no doubt of Townshend's and George's fears of Prussia. Equally, Frederick William made no secret of his anger with George and his ministers, particularly his Hanoverian ministers, and he blamed George for the slow progress at Brunswick. Caroline and Walpole hoped to end these disputes and to secure a marital union between the houses of Hanover and Prussia. It was probably this which accounted for their marked opposition to Wittelsbach pretensions. The repeated entreaties of Sophia Dorothea, the Queen of Prussia, had finally borne fruit, even if they had had more effect upon her sister-in-law Caroline than her brother George. Caroline resumed her efforts to secure a marital alliance. Sir Richard Lodge, who referred to Caroline as 'an ardent patroness of the scheme', nevertheless saw Walpole as its prime exponent, although he produced no evidence for his view: 'His first expedient for the preservation of peace was a supreme effort to detach Prussia from the Austrian alliance'. Reichenbach, the Prussian agent, informed Grumbkow on 7 April that Walpole supported the marriage project and had urged George to yield in the Brunswick conferences in order to detach Prussia from Austria, and Chammorel presented Walpole as a keen supporter of the approach to Berlin.[23] There is no doubt of George's lack of enthusiasm for a new approach to Prussia. His correspondence with Townshend about the projected mission of a British diplomat to Berlin to propose a marital alliance reveals distrust of Prussia and dislike of the mission. George believed, correctly, that the mission would fail; he feared that it would irritate France and Spain, and was worried his honour would be insulted by Frederick William. George realised that the mission was incompatible with the negotiations with the Wittelsbachs, and he made it clear to

Townshend that he regarded the latter as 'of much more consequence'.[24]

Given this attitude it might be suggested that the eventual dispatch of Sir Charles Hotham to Berlin was as much proof of George's inability to control the situation as the failure of the Wittelsbach negotiations, the fall of Townshend, and the defeat of the aspirations of Chesterfield, a diplomat who had received much praise from both George and Townshend since he began his mission at The Hague. If such an interpretation is adopted then Walpole can be seen to have defeated both Townshend and George in 1730. However, this was not the case. The selection of Hotham for the mission seems an interesting indication of George's power. Hotham was a Gentleman of the Bedchamber to George II, and a serving army officer. Grumbkow referred to him as a 'créature' of George II. Reichenbach had a low opinion of him, and commented on his lack of experience. Whatever his merits as a diplomat the crucial factor about Hotham, who was also Chesterfield's brother-in-law, was that the King could rely upon him. Du Bourgay the British Envoy Extraordinary at Berlin had, in 1727, been severely reprimanded for exceeding orders, and it is clear that in 1730 George no longer trusted him. It is possible the reason for this distrust was Du Bourgay's close contacts with the Queen of Prussia and the ministers linked to her. Tilson, who usually reflected the views of Townshend, claimed that there was a need for an 'active and alert' envoy in Berlin 'able a little to cope with Seckendorf'. He said nothing about the marriages. George wanted his children married, but he had no intention of yielding to Prussian political demands. The element of personal hostility between the rulers of Britain and Prussia was already significant. A plan drawn up by Townshend, approved by George and transmitted to Poyntz for discussion with the French, proposed that if war broke out and Frederick William supported Austria, the allies 'ought then to begin by falling upon him' with all their forces 'in order to strip him of two or three places, which give him opportunitys of being a very uneasy neighbour to the Dutch; and to reduce him to the necessity of living upon better terms with all the princes of Lower Saxony, than he has hitherto done'.[25]

Hotham was ordered to insist on the double marriage of Frederick Prince of Wales and Wilhelmina, the Prussian Crown Princess, and of Crown Prince Frederick of Prussia and Princess Amelia. Anne, the Princess Royal of Britain, was designed for William IV of Orange. This was despite the fact that Frederick William was known to be keen on the former marriage, but opposed to the latter, as he believed that it would serve to increase the ties between the Crown Prince and his Hanoverian uncle. Seckendorf, who feared Hotham would propose the single marriage project, was correct in claiming that even it was full of difficulties, as Frederick William would not hear any talk of conditions. When Hotham reached Berlin he found Frederick William determined on the single marriage.[26] Despite Hotham's reports, and the knowledge that Frederick William had already declared the marriage of the Prince of Wales and Wilhelmina, George and Townshend remained firm. On 27 April Townshend sent Hotham fresh instructions:

The King continues firm in the resolution of having the double marriage, as most expedient, and most proper and desirable on both sides. And from this he will never depart, or be brought by any means to consent to make the one, either without, or at any distance of time from the other.

In reply to the Prussian suggestion that, if there was to be a marriage between Crown Prince Frederick of Prussia and Amelia, one of them should be created Stadtholder of Hanover, and the Electorate placed under their authority, Townshend noted that George was willing for Amelia to be Stadtholder on condition that she and Frederick should first come to England 'and make such stay there as His Majesty shall judge convenient'. Finally, George expected Frederick William to settle the Mecklenburg issue on George's terms.[27] These instructions were hardly calculated to produce good relations. Frederick William could not be expected to yield on Mecklenburg, nor on the departure of his heir for an unspecified term to England. Townshend's ability to send these instructions indicates that a month before his resignation he was still in control of at least the important negotiations with Prussia and that George still trusted him to draw up these crucial instructions. Further evidence of Townshend's activity can be found in a letter of Delafaye written on 27 March. Poyntz had complained about being sent an inaccurate secret article concerning Jülich-Berg from Newcastle's office. He was told

We copied what MyLord Duke gave to be copied and sent, and his Grace knows of no other secret article than that. I take the truth to be, that MyLord Townshend, who has had some conferences with M. Broglie at which his Grace was not present being then out of town, settled this new draught of a secret article with the ambr. and that My Lord Duke either was not told of it or did not attend to it.

Whatever the significance of his failure to enlist support for the Palatine arrears and the other Wittelsbach demands, Townshend had clearly not been crushed in the disputes with Walpole in late 1729.

Since at least October 1729 Townshend had been threatening to resign. On 3 March 1730 his son Thomas Townshend wrote to Poyntz informing him of his father's intention to do so. However, despite the talk of resignation, Townshend continued very active. Horatio Walpole doubted his intentions, and noted that despite Townshend's declaration that he would acquiesce in the views of others and 'barely give his opinion', he was in fact 'as active and eager in business as ever I knew him'. Six weeks later, Horatio still doubted Townshend's intention of resigning, and Newcastle shared his scepticism. Townshend's continued activity with foreign diplomats aroused disquiet, and it is clear that he criticised his rivals for failing to support Hanoverian interests:

His Lordship has represented us, as giving up Hanover quite, and has worked much upon the king upon that head; and also, that we had neglected pushing the plan of operations . . . I must begg you would do all you can about the German points, Mecklenburgh etc . . . Let us have some brisk resolution about the plan of operations, and some strong assurances about Hanover, and we shall be able to defy him, and all he can do . . . Hanover is Lord Townshend's great merit, and we have been all represented as wanting zeal . . . We have here great hopes of the king of Prussia . . . You may imagine somebody will not be sorry that things should miscarry hereafter.[28]

It is clear from the instructions sent to Hotham that Townshend was indeed very concerned with Hanoverian interests, and that he and George were able to control the mission, and in the event so direct Hotham that it failed. It is also clear that the ministerial dispute, far from being centred on the Wittelsbach issue and the late months of 1729, was still of great importance in the early spring of 1730. Coxe attributed Townshend's resignation to the success of Walpole and the Queen in overturning his strategy that before any proposals of accommodation were presented to the Emperor a plan of hostile operations should be concerted between the Seville allies. In a letter printed by Coxe whose original has been misfiled in the Public Record Office in the 1723 *State Papers Regencies* Series, Townshend argued that the news of such a plan would cause Prussia and Austria to submit, and George agreed. Townshend also argued that if it was decided to delay the formulation of the plan until after the negotiations with the Austrians commenced

I very much fear that considering the temper and disposition of the Cardinal, as well as of the Dutch, no plan of operations will be formed; and in that case any declaration to be made at Vienna, will rather be insulted than agreed to. And your Majesty will be next year at the meeting of the parliament under the same difficulties you at present labour, not only with regard to Prussia, but likewise in regard to the affairs in general, and one may easily foresee the evils that must attend such a situation.[29]

Townshend's schemes were opposed by Newcastle, Stanhope and the Walpoles. Thomas Townshend wrote to Poyntz at the beginning of March,

My Father approved extremely of your conversation with Monsieur Goslinga, and did, by the King's order . . . transmit the substance of that conference to the Pensionary as His Majesty's and your thoughts relating to the future conduct of our negotiations. However, he is afraid that Lord Harrington's instructions will not tally, so much as he could wish, with the plan which you and Mr. Goslinga laid down, being drawn up and settled by the Duke of Newcastle, Sir Robert Walpole and Lord Harrington, and my father not having been able to prevail upon them to alter them. He hopes therefore that, when you are acquainted with the situation he is in at present, you will not be surprised if you should hear of his resigning at the end of the session.[30]

Townshend was to be proved correct. The Seville allies, their disputes notorious, failed to persuade the Austrians to accept the Spanish garrisons, and the attempt to concert a plan of operations to coerce Austria collapsed in confusion and recrimination. Why George allowed himself to be persuaded into accepting the policy of delaying the formulation of the plan is unclear. Though Reichenbach claimed that Townshend was fed up with George's brutal manners, it was widely accepted that Townshend was still

George's favoured minister. Reichenbach reported that George did not want Townshend to go, but was obliged to maintain good relations with Walpole in order to obtain money.[31] Townshend resigned; George did not dismiss him. He appears to have finally decided to resign because of his frustration at the constant opposition of Walpole to his plans, rather than because of his anger over any particular issue. Selwyn claimed that Townshend's determination to stay had 'been giving way for some time'. Reichenbach reported that Walpole wanted everything to depend uniquely on his will and that Townshend did not wish to be treated like a small boy. Horatio Walpole suggested that Townshend's stance was due to his general feeling of frustration rather than to anger over a specific issue.[32] It is also probable that the ill-health Townshend told Chammorel about was indeed a factor. It had given cause for concern throughout the winter.[33]

As in 1733, when Walpole was unable to persuade George to dismiss Harrington and Scarborough, so in 1730, Walpole had to wait for Townshend to resign. He had clearly succeeded in making life difficult for Townshend, and by May 1730 Townshend was refusing to do anything involving cooperation with Walpole.Delafaye stated that a resignation was essential 'to make the service easy'.[34] The differences between the two men certainly involved foreign policy issues, but by the spring of 1730 these had become expressions of a struggle for power and control. Walpole succeeded in thwarting Townshend over the plan of operations and the negotiations with the Wittelsbachs, though Townshend and George had their way over Hotham's mission. Exasperated and unwell, Townshend resigned even though he still enjoyed the confidence of the king. The crisis was not a defeat for George, however. Though he did not make Chester-field Secretary of State, George's protégé William Stanhope, recently ennobled as Lord Harrington for his success at Seville, replaced Townshend. It was claimed that Walpole and the Queen had attempted to gain the post for Horatio Walpole, who denied any interest in it, but had been thwarted by George.[35] Newcastle, Harrington and the Walpoles were forced to consider Hanoverian interests and to press the French to support Hanover.[36] George could not have hoped that the ailing Townshend would continue as Secretary for many more years. He succeeded in gaining a pliant successor whose tenure of the northern Secretaryship was marked by very few disagreements with the king.[37] Indeed, Harrington was a more dependable Secretary than Townshend had been. It is unclear how far Horatio Walpole sought to become Secretary, but he was too independent for George, and it is possible that the king would have found Chesterfield a difficult subordinate for the same reason. If anything, the replacement of Townshend by Harrington, however difficult for George, helped to increase his control of the direction of British foreign policy.

Notes

1. Horatio Walpole to Waldegrave, 3 Oct. 1729, Chewton. Black, 'Fresh Light on the Fall of Townshend', *Historical Journal* 29 (1986) was written before the Poyntz papers were deposited in the British Library.

2. Horatio Walpole and Poyntz to Newcastle, 5 Oct., Horatio to Newcastle, 26 Oct., 9 Nov. 1729, BL. Add. 32763.
3. Kinsky to Ferdinand Albrecht, 8 Nov. 1729, Wolfenbüttel, 1 Alt 22, Nr. 590; Newcastle to Horatio Walpole and Poyntz, 6 Oct. (os), Horatio Walpole and Poyntz to Newcastle, 5, 12 Oct., Horatio to Chesterfield, 18 Oct., Keene to Horatio and Poyntz, 20 Oct., Horatio to Stanhope and Keene, 7 Nov. 1729, BL. Add. 32763; Horatio to Delafaye, 21 Sept. 1729, PRO. 78/192.
4. Chavigny to Townshend, 28 Sept. 1729, AE. CP. Ang. sup. 8; Townshend to George II, 1 Oct. (os) 1729, PRO. 103/110.
5. Elector's remarks, Münster, 5474 f.29–32; Chauvelin to Chammorel, 29 Jan. 1730, AE. CP. Ang. sup. 8.
6. Poyntz to Thomas Townshend, 26 Nov. 1729, BL. Althorp, E5; Horatio Walpole to Poyntz, 4 Nov. 1729, Coxe, II, 659–65; Seckendorf to Ferdinand Albrecht, 1, 8 Nov. 1729, Wolfenbüttel, 1 Alt. 22, Nr. 585.
7. Törring to Plettenberg, 11 Nov., Bellanger to Plettenberg, 28 Oct., Bellanger to Chavigny, 29 Oct. 1729, Münster, NA. 148, VE. 133; Townshend to George II, 17 Oct. (os) 1729, and George's undated reply, PRO. 103/110; Chavigny to Chauvelin, 10 Nov., Bellanger to Chavigny, 5 Dec. 1729, AE. Allemagne 47, Cologne 70; Poyntz to Thomas Townshend, 26 Nov. 1729, Delafaye to Poyntz, 6 Feb. (os) 1730, BL. Althorp, E5, 4.
8. Albert to Plettenberg, 23 Oct., 28 Dec., Townshend to Plettenberg, 12 Dec. (os) 1729, Münster, NB. 33, 5474; Townshend to Broglie, 3 Nov. (os) 1729, Minutes of conference with Broglie, 10 Feb. (os) 1730, PRO. 100/5, 36/17; Poyntz to Newcastle, 11 Jan. 1730, BL. Add. 32765; Chauvelin to Chammorel, 23 Jan., Chammorel to Chauvelin, 9 Feb., Broglie to Chauvelin, 9 Jan., 23 Feb. 1730, AE. CP. Ang. sup. 8, 369.
9. Townshend to Plettenberg, 11 Nov. (os), 12 Dec. (os), Townshend to Chavigny, 11 Nov. (os) 1729, Münster, 5474; 'Account of the Difference between the several projects of the Treaty with the Four Electors', PRO. 103/110; Chammorel to Chauvelin, 19 Jan. 1730, AE. CP. Ang. 369; Poyntz to Newcastle, 11 Jan., 10 Feb., Newcastle to Poyntz, 6 Feb. (os) 1730, BL. Add. 32765; Trevor to Poyntz, 21 Dec. (os) 1729, BL. Althorp, E3.
10. Newcastle to Poyntz, 12 Feb. (os) 1730, BL. Add. 32765; Horatio Walpole to Poyntz, 4 Nov. 1729, Coxe, II, 659–63; Poyntz to Keene, 9, 13 Feb., Tilson to Poyntz, 12 Feb. (os) 1730, BL. Althorp, E1, 4.
11. Browning, p. 57; Speck, p. 232. The claim that Walpole negotiated the treaty behind Townshend's back is unfounded; Langford, *The Eighteenth Century*, pp. 99–100; Jones, *Britain and the World*, pp. 191–2; Owen, *Eighteenth Century*, p. 43; Coxe, I, 332–9; Dickinson, *Walpole*, pp. 125, 166–7; Williams, p. 201.
12. Chavigny to Chauvelin, 20 Dec. 1729, AE. CP. Allemagne 375.
13. Chesterfield to Townshend, 7 July, Townshend to Chesterfield, 10 Oct. (os), Townshend to Waldegrave, 31 Oct. (os) 1729, Poyntz to Delafaye, 8 Apr. 1730, PRO. 84/304–5, 80/65, 78/194; Poyntz to Keene, 14 Feb. 1730, BL. Add. 32765.
14. Broglie to Chauvelin, 2 Jan. 1730, 1 Dec. 1729, AE. CP. Ang. 369, 367; Newcastle to Poyntz, 22 Jan. (os), Poyntz to Keene, 9 Feb. 1730, BL. Add. 32765; Delafaye to Poyntz, 6 Feb. (os) 1730, BL. Althorp, E4.
15. Browning, p. 56.
16. Dureng, p. 90; George II to Townshend, no date, Coxe, II, 536–7.
17. Tilson to Poyntz, 20 Jan. (os) 1730, BL. Add. 48982; Townshend to George II, 1 Oct. (os), PRO. 103/110.
18. Chavigny to Chauvelin, 19 Sept., Broglie to Chauvelin, 28 Nov., 15 Dec. 1729, AE. CP. Br. 47, Ang. 367; D'Aix to Victor Amadeus II, 5, 19, 26 Dec. 1729, AST. LM. Ing. 35; Memorandum on Palatine demands, enclosed with Schmidman, Palatine Resident in London, to -, 6 Feb., Townshend to Schmidman, 17 May 1728, Townshend to Beveren, 18 Aug., Horatio Walpole to Townshend, 4 Aug., Horatio to Robert Walpole, 4 Aug. 1729, PRO. 100/15, 103/110, 78/192; Poyntz to Thomas Townshend, 4 Aug. 1729, BL. Althorp, E5; Plettenberg to Chavigny, 5 Feb. 1730, AE. CP. Cologne 71; Chavigny to Plettenberg, 16 Feb. 1730, Münster, NB. 286; D'Aix to Victor Amadeus II, 17 Oct. 1729, AST. LM. Ing. 35; Townshend to Horatio Walpole, 28 Oct. (os) 1728, Tilson to Poyntz, 20 Oct. (os) 1729, 20 Jan. (os) 1730, Bradfer

Lawrence, BL. Althorp, E4; Palatine memoire, 11 June 1752, Munich, Kasten Blau 9/11, Black, 'Britain and the Wittelsbachs in the Early Eighteenth Century', *Mitteilungen des Österreichisches Staatsarchivs* 40 (1987); Earl of Holdernesse, envoy at The Hague, to Henry Pelham, 16, 20 Oct. 1750, Nottingham, University Library, Clumber papers, 1167–8.

19. Coxe, I, 335; Horatio Walpole to Poyntz, 30 Dec. (os) 1729, Trevor to Poyntz, 15 Jan. (os) 1730, BL. Althorp, E3, 4; Ossorio to Victor Amadeus II, 3 Apr. 1730, AST. LM. Ing. 37; *Wye's Letter* 21 Apr. (os) 1730; Kinsky to Ferdinand Albrecht, 8 Nov. 1729, Wolfenbüttel, 1 Alt. 22, Nr. 590; Broglie to Chauvelin, 7 May 1730, AE. CP. Ang. 370; Dowager Duchess of Portland to Count Bentinck, 13 Jan. (os), 10 Feb. (os) 1730, BL. Eg. 1715; Townshend to Poyntz, 26 June (os) 1732, BL. Althorp, E5.

20. Zamboni to Manteuffel, 4 Oct. 1729, Bodl. Rawl. 120; Robinson to Horatio Walpole, 7 Feb. 1730, Wentworth to Earl of Strafford, 25 Sept. (os) 1729, BL. Add. 9139, 22227; HMC. Carlisle, p. 64; D'Aix to Victor Amadeus II, 17 Oct. 1729, AST. LM. Ing. 35; Ferdinand Albrecht to Kinsky, 24 Oct., Kinsky to Ferdinand Albrecht, 8 Nov. 1729, Wolfenbüttel, 1 Alt 22, Nr. 590; Broglie to Chauvelin, 28 Nov. 1729, AE. CP. Ang. 367; Zamboni to the Duke of Modena, 13 Jan. 1730, AS. Modena, LM. Ing. 19.

21. Hervey to Stephen Fox, 18 Nov. (os) 1729, West Suffolk CRO. 941/474; Townshend to Chesterfield, 22, 25 Apr. (os) 1729, PRO. 84/304; Horatio Walpole to Poyntz, 21 Jan. (os) 1730, Coxe, II, 667.

22. Trevor to Poyntz, 21 Dec. (os) 1729, Poyntz to Waldegrave, 5 Feb. 1730, BL. Althorp, E3, 1; Townshend to Finch, 20 Jan. (os), 3 Feb. (os) 1730, Du Bourgay to Townshend, 20 Sept., Townshend to Baron Stain, 21 Nov. 1729, Du Bourgay to Townshend, 3, 17, 21 Jan., 21 Mar., Townshend to Diemar, 27 Jan. (os), Townshend to Dehn, 20 Feb. (os), Poyntz to Delafaye, 8 Feb., Titley to Townshend, 18, 21 Feb., Titley to Tilson, 25 Feb. 1730, PRO. 95/54, 90/25, 100/15, 90/26, 100/16, 78/194, 75/54; Seckendorf to Ferdinand Albrecht, 8 Dec., Kinsky to Ferdinand Albrecht, 23 Dec. 1729, Frederick William to Ferdinand Albrecht, 24 Feb., Seckendorf to Ferdinand Albrecht, 4 Mar. 1730, Wolfenbüttel, 1 Alt. 22, Nr. 585(c), 590, 532, 585(d); Ferdinand Albrecht to Kinsky, 16 Jan. 1730, Vienna, Kinsky, 2(b); Sauveterre to Chauvelin, 7 Feb., Broglie to Chauvelin, 12, 16 Jan. 1730, AE. CP. Prusse 90, Ang. 369.

23. Lodge, *Great Britain and Prussia in the Eighteenth Century* (Oxford, 1923), p. 21; Reichenbach to Grumbkow, 7 Apr. 1730, Hull, DDHO 3/3; Chammorel to Chauvelin, 15 June 1730, AE. CP. Ang. 370; Seckendorf to Ferdinand Albrecht, 8 Nov. 1729, 30 Jan. 1730, Wolfenbüttel, 1 Alt 22, Nr. 585(c), (d); copy of paper from Villa, Queen of Prussia's agent in London, no date, Hull, DDHO 3/10.

24. George to Townshend, no date, in reply to Townshend to George, 8 Feb. (os) 1730, Coxe, II, 534–5; Hotham to Townshend, 13 May, Frederick William to Reichenbach, 13 May 1730, PRO. 90/28.

25. Grumbkow to Reichenbach, 25 Mar., Reichenbach to Grumbkow, 4 Apr. 1730, Hull, DDHO 3/3; Coxe, II, 534; Portland to Bentinck, 24 Feb. (os) 1730, BL. Eg. 1715; A. W. Stirling, *The Story of the Hothams* (2 vols, 1918), I, 142–8; Tilson to Poyntz, 20 Jan. (os) 1730, BL. Althorp, E4; Du Bourgay to Tilson, 29 Jan. 1729, PRO. 90/24.

26. Horatio Walpole to Harrington and Poyntz, 23 Apr. (os) 1730, Coxe, II, 692; Seckendorf to Ferdinand Albrecht, 25, 28 Nov. 1729, 4, 8 Apr. 1730, 1 Alt 22, Nr. 585 (c-e); Hotham to Townshend, 4 Apr. 1730, PRO. 90/106; Hotham to Poyntz, no date, Hull, DDHO 3/2; Poyntz to Delafaye, 12 Apr., Holzendorf to Tilson, 14 Apr., Grumbkow to Reichenbach, 25 Apr. 1730, PRO. 78/194, 84/307, 90/28.

27. Townshend to Hotham, 16 Apr. (os) 1730, PRO. 90/27; Drafts of instructions in Weston-Underwood papers and BL. Add. 9147 f. 89–90.

28. Delafaye to Poyntz, 16 Mar. (os) 1730, BL. Althorp, E4; Poyntz to Townshend, 11 Oct. (os), Poyntz to Thomas Townshend, 26 Nov. (os), 1729, 26 Mar. (os), Horatio Walpole to Poyntz, 21 Jan. (os), Horatio Walpole to Waldegrave, 13 Mar. (os), Newcastle to Harrington, 24 Mar. (os), 23 Apr. (os) 1730, Coxe II, 659–89; Hervey, p. 118; Diemar to William of Hesse-Cassel, 5 May 1730, Marburg, England, 199; Reichenbach to Grumbkow, 24 Mar. 1730, PRO. 90/27.

29. Townshend to George, George to Townshend, undated, Newcastle to Harrington, 24 Mar. (os), Newcastle to Harrington and Poyntz, 24 Mar. (os) 1730, PRO. 43/5 f.335–6, Coxe II, 540–1, 678–84, I, 337; Harrington to Newcastle, 10 Apr., Tilson to Poyntz, 20

Jan. (os), Chauvelin to Broglie, 9 May 1730, BL. Add. 32766, 48982, Egerton Mss. 3134; Chammorel to Chauvelin, 18 May 1730, AE. CP. Ang. 370.
30. Thomas Townshend to Poyntz, 19 Feb. (os) 1730, BL. Althorp, E4.
31. Reichenbach to Grumbkow, 24, 28 Mar. 1730, Hull, DDHO 3/3; Diemar to William of Hesse-Cassel, 5 May 1730, Marburg, England, 199.
32. Reichenbach to Grumbkow, 19, 9 May, 24, 28 Mar. 1730, Hull, DDHO 3/3; Horatio Walpole to Poyntz, 21 Jan. (os) 1730, Coxe, II, 667; Chammorel to Chauvelin, 7 May 1730, AE. CP. Ang. 370; Hervey, p. 118; Selwyn to Poyntz, 12 Feb. (os) 1730, BL. Althorp, E4.
33. Chammorel to Chauvelin, 7 May 1730, AE. CP. Ang. 370; Dehn to Duke of Wolfenbüttel, 4 June 1729, Wolfenbüttel, 2 Alt 3631; Townshend to Du Bourgay, 21 Oct. (os) 1729, PRO. 90/25; Thomas Townshend to Poyntz, 16 Oct. (os), Delafaye to Poyntz, 20 Oct. (os) 1729, BL. Althorp, E3.
34. Delafaye to Poyntz, 13 Apr. (os) 1730, BL. Althorp, E4; Reichenbach to Grumbkow, 19 May 1730, Hull, DDHO 3/3; Hervey, p. 118.
35. Zamboni to Manteuffel, 7 Apr. 1730, Bodl. Rawl. 120; Kinsky to Ferdinand Albrecht, 8 Nov. 1729, Wolfenbüttel, 1 Alt. 22, Nr 590; Ossorio to Victor Amadeus II, 3 Apr. 1730, AST. LM. Ing. 37; Egmont I, 77; Poyntz to Thomas Townshend, 26 Nov. 1729, Coxe, II, 666.
36. Newcastle to Harrington, 24 Mar. (os) 1730, Coxe, II, 678.
37. Broglie to Chauvelin, 7 May 1730, AE. CP. Ang. 370.

CHAPTER ELEVEN

The Session of 1730

The prolonged crisis within the ministry in the winter of 1729–1730 and the following spring coincided with an unstable international situation and a troublesome parliamentary session. The three are usually treated separately, but their juxtaposition lends substance to the suggestion that British foreign policy cannot be treated separately from her political history. The Treaty of Seville had stipulated an approach to Austria, in order to obtain agreement to the admission of the Spanish garrisons. Opinion in London was divided over whether the Austrians would accept the proposal. The government argued that the choice of Spanish garrisons, instead of the Swiss ones stipulated in previous treaties, was a minor variation, and encouraged an optimistic attitude to the possibility of Austrian agreement. Delafaye suggested that the Austrians would cave in: 'my notion is that we shall have a good deal of bullying on that side; till the season for action comes on, and then possibly they will talk in a more moderate strain.' Waldegrave hoped that when the Austrians discovered 'that we are in earnest, and determine to stand to our point, they will consider better of it, and see that the difference is not worth contending for'.

Others were less sure, and noted reports of Austrian military moves, and in particular of the beginning of an Austrian build-up in Italy.[1] Partly as a result of Austrian diplomatic approaches in the autumn, the Dutch, particularly the Pensionary Slingelandt, were greatly in favour of associating the approach to Austria for an implementation of the Seville treaty with the offer of a guarantee of the Pragmatic Sanction.[2] The French were opposed to the idea. Both powers pressed Britain for her view, and it is interesting to note that the supposedly 'anti-Habsburg' Townshend was not unwilling to support the Pragmatic. He argued that it was not the time to offer the Austrians the guarantee, as it would upset Spain and Sardinia, but that the Emperor ought to be informed that a settlement of the points at issue would lead to a negotiation of the guarantee. Townshend did not wish to take agreeing with the Dutch to the point of offending Fleury or Spain. Poyntz warned of the danger of angering France and driving her to a unilateral peace with Austria. The Spaniards made clear their opposition to any guarantee. With regard to the Pragmatic, George was 'of opinion not to declare my intention about this matter, as long as it will be possible'. Townshend did not wish to anger the Dutch and delay their accession to the Treaty of Seville, but it is clear in December 1729 that he was being consistent with the Anglo-Austrian policy he had advocated over the previous three years, namely, that once Austria indicated its readiness to satisfy the demands of other powers, including Hanover, Britain should commit herself to the long-term stability of Austria. Tilson informed Poyntz, 'His Lordship thinks the Imperial Court has so strong a claim upon us, as to the guaranty, by the Quadruple Alliance itself, that they might let it stand upon that foot, without pushing it further at present; because we and the Dutch shall naturally lay hold of that engagement, whenever it is seasonable, it not being our interest to see the Austrian dominions pulled to pieces.' This policy was to be encapsulated in treaty form, by the Walpole ministry, in the Second Treaty of Vienna of 16 March 1731, and indicates the continuity of policy between Townshend and Walpole.[3]

The Austrians had no intention of complying with the introduction of the Spanish garrisons. On 28 December the Emperor informed his representatives in Paris that he would not accept them, and this decision was swiftly conveyed to the Seville allies. The allies continued until the summer to harbour the hope that the Austrians would change their minds, if the terms offered were slightly improved, or if they were frightened by the allies' preparations. Delafaye predicted that the Austrian ministers would act with characteristic slowness until they received 'a good banging'.[4] Negotiations with the Austrians continued but, largely under pressure from the British and the Spaniards, an attempt was made to devise a plan for operations against Austria. Conferences were held at Fontainebleau and several different schemes were proposed. The major issue discussed was whether operations in Italy should be matched by operations north of the Alps. The French were very interested in an invasion of the Austrian Netherlands; a scheme, as Sinzendorf had predicted, opposed by the British and the Dutch. Horatio Walpole noted with concern Bolingbroke's assurances to his close friends that France would only act in the Austrian Netherlands and would suddenly attack there. Britain and the United Provinces were concerned about the security of Hanover and the Netherlands, and wanted the deployment of a French army specifically designed for their protection. They were also unimpressed by a Spanish suggestion that the Austrian Netherlands be allocated to a Spanish prince. The Dutch wished to confine offensive operations to Italy. The British tended to concur with this view.[5]

There was less disagreement over operations in Italy. It was generally agreed that if the Tuscan ports were closed to the Spaniards, Sicily should be invaded, whilst the French would seek to gain Sardinian support and invade the Milanese. However, there was a dispute over the timing of the intended invasion of Sicily, and over the French demand that no offensive moves should be undertaken until agreement had been reached on war aims and on the extent and nature of the territorial changes which should be sought in the war. This was referred to as a treaty of equilibrium, and it had indeed been specified in the event of war, in the Treaty of Seville. This angered both the British government and the Spaniards, who saw it as an indication of French unwillingness to fight. Poyntz noted in February 'how hard it is on one side to keep the Cardinal up to the firmness necessary in the present situation of affairs, and how impossible on the other to bring him ever to think of giving an absolute unconditional guaranty to the Emperor's succession'. Furthermore the Spaniards, anxious to regain their former Italian possessions now held by Austria, did not wish to see their potential gains confined by treaty. Rather than wanting the simple introduction of their garrisons, the Spanish government, and in particular Elisabeth Farnese, wanted a war which would provide opportunities for Italian conquests. Delafaye commented, 'The Spaniards take large strides in their projects. Ripperdá's negotiations have brought them into the way of disposing of kingdoms and provinces, but I fancy they will find their allies a little more phlegmatic'.[6] The British ministry was worried by these delays and suspicious of its allies. Aware of Spanish impetuosity, they were particularly concerned with the delays caused by the French insistence on the need to concert a treaty of equilibrium. They feared it would cause Spain to doubt the commitment of her allies to the introduction of Spanish garrisons, and that this might lead Spain to renounce the Treaty of Seville and resume negotiations with Austria.[7] There was no doubt that such a course of action would be disastrous for the British government, both diplomatically and for internal political reasons. Diplomatically, it would increase Austrian power, thereby making Prussia less likely to settle with Britain and the Wittelsbachs less willing to offend Austria, and thus force Britain into greater dependence upon France. In Britain the ministry had proclaimed the commercial clauses of the Treaty of Seville as a great triumph. If Spain renounced them, and the ministry had nothing to show for the preceding years of diplomatic effort, military expenditure and higher taxation, then the opposition would be handed a brilliant basis for press attack and parliamentary criticism.

Thus, by the time of Townshend's resignation on 26 May, there was already disquiet about French intentions. On 12 April Harrington and Poyntz complained to Newcastle that the French were blaming the British for the delays in concerting plans, and were seeking to embitter Anglo-Spanish relations. On 4 May Newcastle confessed his concern about the possibility of an Austro-Spanish reconciliation. The embittered nature of the Paris conferences, suspicion that the French did not want the Anglo-Prussian initiative to succeed, anger at continued French sponsorship of the Wittelsbach claims and growing irritation with the conduct of Broglie, helped to create a situation of great strain in the Anglo-French alliance.[8]

The difficulties created for the Anglo-French alliance by diplomatic disagreements were matched by the strains placed upon it as a result of the parliamentary session of 1730. One of the factors encouraging the Austrians in their opposition to accepting the terms of the Seville allies was their conviction that the British ministry would be defeated in the session. Assurances to this effect were also given to the Prussians, both by the Austrians and by their Resident in London, Reichenbach, who was closely in touch with opposition politicians such as the Earl of Strafford. Poyntz suggested that Charles VI would not risk war 'except our divisions in England encourage him to it'. Waldegrave noted the Austrian conviction that the British ministry would fall, and the ministry was intensely suspicious of links between the British opposition and the envoys of

Austria and Prussia. Delafaye was sure that the opposition hoped to influence Austria by causing a storm over Dunkirk. The governmental tendency to castigate opposition as treasonable, and to blame the difficulties of their diplomatic position upon the activities of the parliamentary opposition, must be treated with caution. Nevertheless, the excellent resources of the government's interception system, by producing decyphered copies of the correspondence between Reichenbach and Grumbkow, gave the ministry's fears a basis of truth. Reichenbach sought information from Berlin about the Hotham mission, information which he claimed the opposition had asked him for, and he conveyed to Berlin supposed opposition advice to reject Hotham's terms, and thus gain concessions.[9] It was unnecessary to believe that the opposition was manipulated by foreign envoys, in order to realise that the relationship between foreign policy and parliamentary developments was a close one. Horatio Walpole referred to 'the relation which the affairs here in Parliament must have with those abroad'.[10] The course of the session revealed the truth of this assertion, and also produced disquieting evidence of the fragility of the ministerial position, particularly over foreign affairs.

A troublesome session had been anticipated by ministerial and opposition figures, and by foreign envoys. Delafaye had predicted there would be trouble over Dunkirk, St. Lucia and Gibraltar, points at issue between Britain and her allies, whilst Horatio Walpole and Lord Hervey expected the major conflict in parliament would be over the governmental wish to continue the subsidies for the Hessians. Selwyn was optimistic about the session: 'In my opinion it will not be very terrible though I hear the enemy flatter themselves with giving great trouble and I believe have mustered their troops in order to it. But 2 shilling per pound and no more will stop a great deal of clamour. That argument is felt more sensibly than the righteous reasoning of a Patriot. The charge of Hessian troops may serve for the purpose of clamour'. He maintained his optimism after the start of the session, confident of continued ministerial majorities. Horatio claimed that the opposition had planned to attack the ministry 'for their indolence and neglect in suffering so patiently the insults of the Spaniards' upon British trade, but that the Treaty of Seville had forced them to change their tactics. There is no evidence for this assertion, though it seems probable. The Venetian envoy Vignola noted that the treaty plunged the opposition into confusion.[11]

The session began on 24 January with a royal speech setting out the benefits of the Treaty of Seville and a debate in the Commons on the address. Thomas Wyndham failed 'to confine whatever assurances the Parliament should give His Majesty of making good his engagements, and of standing by him to attempts upon his Britannic dominions.' The ministry claimed to be well satisfied with the debates, and British envoys were instructed to convey an optimistic view. Britain's allies were certainly impressed by the ministerial success. However, though there had been no division in the Lords, the opposition motion in the Commons to amend the address attracted a substantial opposition vote. Horatio

Walpole saw this as a success for the opposition Whigs' plan to create a workable alliance with the Tories.

> . . . the Discontented Whigs had concerted a perfect coalition with the Torys of all degrees, and it had been agreed to act heartily and vigorously in the same opposition, and that for the purpose a summons should be made of all the Torys to be present without suffering any excuse, and this was pursued with so much zeal, that I believe there has been in town this year about 110 Torys, which is within a very few of the whole number elected.

This alliance was not a surprise. In December Edward Weston, who had replaced Thomas Townshend as an Under Secretary, had noted major opposition preparations for the session, and an alliance between the opposition Whigs and Tories 'to counterballance the Treaty of Seville'. He attributed the rise in the opposition vote to 'the great pains they have been at this winter to bring up their friends, the halt, the lame, and the blind'.[12]

On 6 February, in the Commons, Lord Morpeth moved that the King be addressed to communicate to the House any engagements he had entered into for the payment of subsidies to foreign troops, or for the hire of foreign troops, which he had not laid before the House. The motion made little impact and the government, on a division of 200–107, obtained a majority of 93.[13] Next day, Townshend spoke in favour of the ministry, when the Lords came to consider the Treaty of Seville. The opposition moved three motions, asserting that the Treaty of Seville violated the clauses of the Quadruple Alliance and threatened to involve the nation in a dangerous and expensive war, did not extinguish Spanish claims to Gibraltar, and provided for insufficient reparation for mercantile losses. The ministry defeated the motions with votes of 86–31, 85–31 and 79–30.[14] The following day, 8 February, the Commons debated the estimates for the land forces for 1730, and, thanks partly to indiscreet expressions by the Jacobite MP, Shippen, the debate was shorter than expected and the government majority rose, on a division of 243–121, to 122. Given this situation it is not surprising that ministerial optimism was maintained, and that both Newcastle and Chauvelin were confident of the government's ability to retain control of the Commons.[15]

This optimism also reflected the ministerial success in carrying the Hessian subsidies. On 9 February, on an opposition address to seek a further reduction of the army by the end of this, or before the beginning of the next session, the majority in the Commons fell to 68 on a division of 201–133 and on 15 February, the day of the debate over the Hessians, to 79. Trevor wrote to Poyntz, 'there were 169 No's. You see from hence that there is an ugly spirit gone out abroad, and I fear will give us a great deal of trouble.' Despite these figures, the ministry could feel satisfied that they had carried the issue they had most feared trouble over. On 17 February Delafaye observed 'The Danverians continue bickering in the House of Commons, but without any other effect but keeping our friends to close attendance there'.[16] The government was to be surprised by the storm which was to arise over the French restoration of Dunkirk. Since 1725 the facilities at the port of Dunkirk had been restored, despite specific prohibitions in the treaties of Utrecht of 1713, and of The Hague of 1717. The British government had been well aware of this restoration, and had complained to the French in 1727, 1728 and 1729. The issue had been exploited by the opposition press over the previous three years, and it was widely known that the harbour at Dunkirk was capable of receiving fairly large ships.[17] The existence of a regular trade between Dunkirk and London was no secret. The ministry were aware that Dunkirk might be used as an issue by the opposition in the session of 1730, though they appear to have taken no precautions to ensure that they could deflect criticism easily. On the evening of 18 January the Lords of the Admiralty met to consider the progress of the works at Dunkrik, and they noted that they were contrary to treaty. Given this governmental concern, and the knowledge that the opposition was keen to criticise the Anglo-French alliance, it is surprising that no real precautions were taken. Horatio Walpole offhandedly replied to criticism in the *Craftsman* when it was drawn to his attention. He reported that the French had obeyed the treaty and that the improvement of the port was due to tidal action and unauthorised work. He complained that the ministry was 'transported and frightened with the least good or bad thing, and without considering the real state of the matter we call for help from abroad upon trifles'. Townshend assured Newcastle in July 1729 'there is no fear that the harbour can be re-established by these small works'. It might be suggested that the poor French response to previous approaches and the wish to win French cooperation over the negotiations with the Prussians and the Wittelsbachs led to a decision not to press France over the issue.[18]

On 21 February, the House of Commons formed itself into a Committee of the Whole House to consider a motion of Sir William Wyndham's for an examination of the state of the nation, the first committee on the state of the nation since the Hanoverian succession. After a lengthy attack upon the policies and practices of the ministry, Wyndham advanced, as a proof of the government's failure to protect national interests, the restoration of the harbour of Dunkirk. The unsuspecting ministerial speakers lost control of the house and were unable to prevent the hearing of evidence about the restoration. On the following day it was resolved to address the King for the laying before the House of all correspondence about Dunkirk. In order to give time for this to be prepared, the debate on the state of the nation was adjourned for a fortnight.[19] The seriousness of the situation was clear. The opposition had found an issue which captured the concern of many MPs over the French alliance. The historical concern over the use of Dunkirk as a privateering base made the issue a concrete and readily grasped example of the more general opposition criticisms of the ministry. Broglie noted that 'La chambre en général a paru approuver les raisons du parti opposé . . .' Perceval referred to it as 'so popular and national a point', and Charles Howard noted that most MPs believed France to be restoring the harbour. Support for the ministry certainly diminished in late February. On 23 February the ministerial MP Anthony Duncomb complained that 'he saw the members fall every day from the Court, and . . . at last there would be a majority against it'. An air of anticipation hung over Westminster. Opposition leaders scented the prospect of office, and foreign envoys speculated on the fall of the ministry. Hervey noted 'People's expectations are mightily raised by the affair of Dunkirk'.[20]

On 27 February Samuel Sandys, an opposition Whig MP, proposed in the Commons that a bill be brought in to 'render the laws more effectual by disabling people that had pensions from the crown or offices in trust for them to be Members of the House of Commons'. The ministerial speakers 'were violently against it', but they lost the division by 134 to 144, an opposition majority of ten. Perceval attributed the defeat to Whig defections, noting that 'above sixty persons who were used to vote with the court deserted Sir Robert on this occasion, some by voting for the motion, others by leaving the House'. He claimed that Walpole 'it is probable may date his fall from this day'. Selwyn wrote that the opposition 'have gained ground upon us of late considerably insomuch that we lost a question by ten votes this week on the subject of Places and Pensions, which though I own it is a popular point in a House of Commons yet would not have been lost in the late King's time but the £115,000 of the last year had its effect in that and will be remembered for some time to come. Something may likewise be attributed to our misunderstandings amongst ourselves'. Kinsky was sufficiently impressed to send a courier to Vienna with the news of the defeat, and in Austria expectations were raised of the fall of the Walpole ministry. Holzendorf noted that the Imperialists at The Hague 'lay such a stress upon it as if the court had lost all their interest in the House'. Zamboni suggested that the government would be unable to win a majority in the Commons when the debate on the state of the nation was resumed.[21]

The ministry was therefore threatened not only with a loss of control in the Commons, but also with a collapse of European confidence in its ability to control Parliament. It was not surprising that the French were pressed hard over Dunkirk. Poyntz and Armstrong, the British military representative at Paris, who was an expert on the Dunkirk issue, were instructed to secure the demolition of the works. Armstrong was informed by Newcastle that, could he but execute these orders, nothing would 'more contribute to damage the efforts of those who oppose his Majesty's measures and have chiefly in view to discredit our alliance with France'. Horatio Walpole sought Fleury's personal intervention. The British diplomatic pressure succeeded. Fleury gave an official assurance that the works at Dunkirk had been performed without the authorisation of Louis XV. Louis XV ordered their demolition and copies of this order were sent to Britain. On 10 March the Commons resumed their deliberations on Dunkirk. Wyndham produced fresh evidence of the French works but, after a lengthy debate, the ministerial proposal for an address to thank the king for his care of the national interest over the Dunkirk issue and to 'declare satisfaction in the firm union and mutual fidelity, which so happily subsist, and are so strictly preserved, between the two crowns', was carried by 270 to 149, a majority of 121. The government was delighted, and proclaimed it as a proof that Parliament was really behind ministerial policy. Newcastle informed Harrington that 'many of our friends that had before left us came back upon this occasion' and wrote that 'justice has been done to the fidelity of France'. Delafaye predicted the French order would 'perfectly reconcile to our alliance some weak though well meaning men, who by false insinuations had been prejudiced against it'. Woodward hoped the issue would 'have a very good effect, by convincing the world of the steadiness of the Allies to one another'.[22] The French assurances were printed in the newspapers, and British envoys were instructed to cite the debate as a demonstration of parliamentary support for the Anglo-French alliance.[22] The period of the Dunkirk debates was the high-point of parliamentary tension in the session of 1730. On 17 March Tilson wrote 'since the Dunkirk affair has been quash'd, we have had calmer doings in the House, and I hope we shall have no more very troublesome struggles'. After the government's victory, the opposition lost much of their energy. On 21 February, when the examination of the state of the nation was continued, a desultory debate on the Anglo-French dispute over the possession of St. Lucia, over which Newcastle and Delafaye had predicted trouble, ended with a government majority of 112. The dispute was a long-standing one, which arose from conflicting claims to the island. The interest of the British government in it was not particularly strong, especially since the British rights had been granted to the Duke of Montagu. The Duke had angered the ministry by his conduct, and the government had made it clear to the French that they were not greatly concerned by this issue, a view shared by Parliament. St. Lucia lacked the historical importance of Dunkirk, and in no way approximated to the latter as an issue capable of arousing anger and concern. Furthermore, the position of St. Lucia in international agreements was obscure and contested.[23]

The opposition failure over St. Lucia led to the end of the Committee of the State of the Nation, and to the departure of many opposition MPs from London. Parliament became more quiescent. Tilson noted 'we are somewhat in a state of indolence, no furious attacks, nor any vigorous defence at present'. Horatio Walpole claimed that the 'skirmishes that have happened since the day of Dunkirk, have served only to expose the weakness of the opponents'. Delafaye informed Poyntz 'the Enemy gain no ground nor can carry any point'. On 27 March Weston noted 'people are pretty quiet at Westminster . . . we reckon the business of the session pretty well over', and three days later Delafaye wrote 'The House of Commons seem to have done with plaguing us'.[24] Many of these 'skirmishes' involved foreign affairs. On 28 March the Loan Bill, a measure designed to prevent loans to foreign powers without royal licence and, in particular, to block Austrian moves to borrow money in London, was passed by the Commons, after only a short debate, with the government receiving more than twice the opposition vote in a division of 176–76 on the opposition amendment.[25] Two days later the government enjoyed a majority of 86–31 in a Lords debate on the Pension Bill, a measure rejected on 1 April.[26] On 2 May Norris moved in the Commons for an address to the king to lay before the House the secret and separate articles of the Treaty of Seville, but the ministry defeated his motion by 197–78 votes.

Horatio Walpole concluded, 'it plainly appeared by the debate and by the complexion of the house that they will support His Majesty in fulfilling his engagements for the execution of the Treaty of Seville'. Though Parliament was not prorogued until 26 May Norris's motion was the last major conflict that session involving foreign affairs, and after the debate was over Horatio Walpole wrote 'This session of Parliament is in a manner come to a conclusion'.[27]

In the session of 1730 the ministry found itself forced to defend the Anglo-French alliance against strong attacks. The parliamentary opposition's assault upon the ministerial foreign policy was based upon a strong attack on this alliance, and a demand for the revival of the Anglo-Austrian alliance of the first decade of the century.[28] Similar arguments were advanced in the opposition press. On 18 March 1730 the *Daily Post Boy* carried the following advertisement 'This Day is published – Dedicated to his Grace the Duke of Bedford – 'Remarks on the Proceedings of the French Court, from Charles VIII, to the latter part of the reign of Lewis XIV". Shewing what little regard has been had to the Faith of Treaties; the Ties of Blood, Marriages, Friendship and Oaths etc . . . Proper to be compared with the present Times, and to be perused by all True Englishmen; by which they may judge how far the French are to be depended on by their Allies, either in Time of Peace or War'. In adopting this plan the opposition chose to discard the parliamentary strategy which had been largely followed the previous session, the attack upon the 'Hanoverian' bias of British foreign policy, and its consequences such as the Hessian subsidies. The French alliance had been attacked in previous sessions of the Parliament, but never with the ferocity that marked the attacks of 1730, whilst in this year the attacks upon Hanover were not pressed so hard. This was despite the fact that the war-panic of the previous summer had threatened to drag Britain into a war with Prussia as a result of Hanoverian quarrels, and that the decision to continue subsidies to the Hessians in 1730 clashed obviously with ministerial assurances of a forthcoming peace.

However, in concentrating on the French alliance, the opposition chose well. The attacks struck a popular chord, appealing to the persistent francophobia of large sections of the British political nation. Selwyn indicated the limited nature of the support for the alliance when he wrote 'an alliance with France is not so unpopular now, but it is admitted there may be cases in which it is expedient'. Furthermore, the opposition arguments that the balance of power in Europe and British interests would be endangered by a war with Austria, reflected disagreements within the ministry over the French alliance. Perceval recorded in his journal a story of Lord Lovel arriving in London at the start of the session, and telling Chesterfield that he did not know how to vote. When the Earl replied 'with the Court', Lovel retorted 'the Court is so divided that I don't know which way it leans.' On 31 March Zamboni claimed that if the ministry did not abandon its anti-Austrian policies it would lose its parliamentary majority, and reported his certainty that a large group had been formed, of political figures not in the opposition determined to prevent Britain declaring war on Austria. Two weeks earlier Chauvelin had argued that the Austrians were fomenting opposition in Britain. Reichenbach suggested that the Opposition wished to help Austria and Prussia by embroiling France and Britain. Chauvelin's view, that the Austrians were behind the Opposition, cannot be established, but Zamboni's suggestion of a powerful pro-Austrian lobby within the ministerial camp appears more convincing. It is very possible that this group was the same as that recorded by Perceval on 16 February. That day he dined at Dodington's and noted:

I found by Mr. Dodington's free way of talking that I have not been in the wrong in thinking a long time past that the speaker is forming a party in the House of reasonable Tories and discontented Whigs, to rise upon the ruins of Sir Robert Walpole.

By the 'speaker' Perceval meant not the current Speaker, Onslow, but his predecessor, Wilmington. On 28 April Perceval referred to Wilmington as 'the head of the party which opposes Sir Robert Walpole', and Dodington, that evening, informed Perceval that he was in favour of an Austrian alliance. Perceval was informed by his son 'As for war, our Politicians in the country don't talk much of it, they seem to expect a change of measures, I believe they hope it, because they think it can't happen without a change of Ministers'. Horatio Walpole wrote to Waldegrave 'There is one thing which certainly encouraged the opposition of the enemy, which was some misunderstanding among the great men here'. Broglie reported that Wilmington was the head of a very strong group including Chesterfield and Scarborough, committed to removing Walpole. The French ministry feared that if Walpole fell he might be replaced by a pro-Austrian government. The composition of Wilmington's party is a mystery, although it is probable that it included Dodington and Dorset, and may have comprised former members of the court of George II, as Prince of Wales, such as Scarborough.[29] Zamboni's reports were sometimes inaccurate, and he was no friend of the ministry, which had indeed sought his recall.[30] Perceval made mistakes, and Dodington was unreliable. The reports are of considerable importance, however, because in the government reshuffle at the end of the session Wilmington was given an important post, that of Lord Privy Seal. Horatio Walpole stated that this was 'done by a perfect union and concert with those already employed'. It was even suggested that Wilmington was considered as Townshend's replacement, though there is little evidence for this assertion. Delafaye commented 'Lord Wilmington's coming in, is a blow to our malcontents, among whom he was deeply engaged'.[31]

A major reconstitution of the ministry took place in May 1730. Important as the changes were it is difficult to establish much more than the eventual distribution of offices. The vacant Lord Presidency was conferred on Lord Trevor, Harrington succeeded Townshend, and Wilmington, created an Earl, succeeded Trevor as Lord Privy Seal, 'with some douceurs of larger salary and higher dignity in the House of Lords'.

Trevor's death on 30 June 1730, led to Wilmington being appointed Lord President, and Devonshire Lord Privy Seal. Newcastle's brother, Henry Pelham, replaced Wilmington as Paymaster-General of the Forces, and was in turn replaced by Sir William Strickland, as Secretary at War. Dorset succeeded Carteret as Lord Lieutenant of Ireland. Carteret, who had been mentioned as a possible Lord Privy Seal, refused Dorset's place of Lord Steward, which was given to Chesterfield. Horatio Walpole stated that Chesterfield receiving the Stewardship had 'been entirely done by the proposal and credit of Sir Robert Walpole and his Lordship looks upon this preferment in this light, and will I am persuaded as he has solemnly declared act upon that foot'. Carteret's political ally, Lord Finch, the new Earl of Winchelsea, declined Methuen's former place, the Treasurership of the Household. Reichenbach suggested that Walpole did not wish to give Carteret a place of importance, and Selwyn described the Stewardship as 'of less state and profit' than the Lieutenancy, but in fact household posts in the early Georgian period could be not only extremely remunerative but also very influential, and Horatio Walpole was made Cofferer of the Household in May 1730. Hervey suggested that Carteret declined the offered post as a result of Winchelsea's influence. Whatever the reason, his decision had the important effect of removing from the court a major rival of Walpole's.[32] These changes were matched by new diplomatic postings. Harrington, Horatio Walpole and Poyntz were recalled from France; the last, a potential Secretary of State, to become Governor of the Duke of Cumberland. Neither Walpole nor Poyntz returned to Britain until September 1730, and both of them were therefore absent during the period when the decision was taken to resume negotiations with Austria. Britain's new representative in Paris was James Waldegrave, created Earl Waldegrave the previous year, and not Chesterfield as had been discussed. Waldegrave's appointment was supported by both Townshend and Horatio Walpole, though Waldegrave suspected that Newcastle wanted his cousin Thomas Pelham, who had served as Secretary of the Embassy to the Congress of Soissons, to gain the post. Waldegrave arrived in Paris on 21 June, and received his instructions as Ambassador Extraordinary and Plenipotentiary the following month. He was replaced at Vienna by Thomas Robinson, who had been Secretary of the Embassy at Paris and was a protégé of the Walpole family, and in particular of Horatio Walpole and his brother-in-law, Isaac Leheup. Robinson, who arrived in Vienna on 17 June, symbolised the new role in the Northern Department of Walpole family influence.[33]

Whatever their effect on Sir Robert Walpole's political position, the governmental changes led to the promotion of less anti-Austrian opinions. The resignation of Townshend, the departure of his protégé Poyntz from Paris, and the decision not to create Chesterfield Secretary of State, represented major blows for those who wanted Britain actively to confront Austria. The French had been in no doubt of Townshend's willingness to use force in order to make Austria reasonable. Newcastle complained to Chammorel about his preference for Townshend, and Chauvelin wanted Townshend to continue in office.[34] Equally the changes represented a victory for those who advocated milder methods with Austria. Newcastle had not been sent to replace Carteret in Ireland, as many had anticipated. The Austrians regarded Harrington as one of the more pro-Austrian of the British ministers. Robinson was disillusioned with the French alliance, and was to be accused, throughout the 1730s, of being pro-Austrian. The exact importance of these governmental changes is difficult to ascertain. Townshend and Newcastle assured Chammorel, Horatio Walpole, and Waldegrave that they would lead to no change in policy, and Zamboni came to the same conclusion. However, Chauvelin feared that the fall of Townshend would lead to policy changes.[35] The influence of the ministerial changes upon the decision to resume negotiations with Austria is obscure. The timing of the approach, soon after the return of Harrington to England on the morning of 24 June 1730, could suggest that it was Harrington, a minister who had enjoyed close links with George II in recent years, who was instrumental in persuading George and the ministry to resume negotiations, a decision strongly opposed by Horatio Walpole. Harrington's role in the foreign policy of the 1730s is largely unknown, and too often the dismissive and witty phrases of Hervey are remembered.[36] Harrington was doubtless indolent, but he also possessed ability and diplomatic skill, and his role in the negotiation of the Second Treaty of Vienna was an important one.

The session of 1730 closed with a considerably rearranged ministerial team. The government had survived a serious onslaught in Parliament. French readiness to meet British demands over Dunkirk had played a major role in enabling the ministry to face the attack. However, the opposition claim that the nation would not accept an endlessly uncertain diplomatic situation, and a dangerous and expensive alliance system, had come close to fruition. Throughout the summer and autumn of 1730 ministers anxiously surveyed issues, such as Dunkirk or the recruitment in Ireland for the French army,[37] which might produce trouble in the forthcoming session. In the midst of his delight over the French order for the Dunkirk demolitions, Newcastle had remarked wisely 'all will depend upon the Court of France's executing what they have now undoubtedly ordered . . . if the works there be not forthwith destroyed, and everything put upon the foot of the Treaties of Utrecht and the Triple Alliance, it will have the worse consequence imaginable with regard to France, and greatly tend to set people here against them and their alliance'. Selwyn wrote in mid-March 'it behoves us to look a little forward and to prevent such an attack in another sessions, which will not turn out so favourable to us'. A month later Delafaye complained 'I am teased every day with questions about the progress that is made in the demolition', adding 'We cannot help insisting upon Dunkirk; our letters may be called for next winter'. In May Horatio Walpole attacked French conduct over Dunkirk as 'a perfect farce', and warned of 'the greatest confusion in England but also in all Europe next winter by the dissolution of the present system of affairs, for it is impossible to imagine that the nation will grow cooler on this head'.[38] It was normal, particularly in the early winter, to exercise such fears, but in 1730 the level of anxiety, though unmeasurable, was certainly higher than in preceding years. A strong conviction grew in ministerial circles, a conviction stemming from opposition arguments[39] and drawing sustenance from the events of the preceding session. It was a conviction, not of the correctness of an Anglo-Austrian alliance, but rather of the need to escape from the situation of diplomatic uncertainty Britain was in. In the circumstances of 1730 this conviction produced pressure, first, for an alliance with Prussia, and, after this had failed, for one with Austria. No tide of pro-Austrian sentiment swept ministerial circles in the summer of 1730. There was little sympathy for the Austrian case over the Spanish garrisons, and suspicion of Austrian chicanery and diplomatic dishonesty persisted.[40] Instead the pressure for a new departure in British foreign policy, pressure which came from a variety of sources, led to a decision to attempt a reconciliation with Austria. It was a decision taken with few illusions. Ministers were aware of the difficulties facing a reconciliation. However, as Chammorel noted, 'un point sur lequel tout le monde convient c'est un grand désir de la paix'.[41]

Notes

1.　Delafaye to Poyntz, 8 Jan. (os) 1730, BL. Althorp, E4; Townshend to Horatio Walpole and Poyntz, 2 Dec. (os) 1729, BL. Add. 48982; Tilson to Waldegrave, 23 Dec. (os) 1729, Chewton; Delafaye to Thomas Clutterbuck, Secretary to the Lord Lieutenant of Ireland, 27 Dec. (os) 1729, PRO. 63/391; Sinzendorf to Fonseca, 11 Jan., 26 Apr. 1730, HHStA, Fonseca 14; Villars, p. 199; Frederick William I to Chambrier, 11, 21 Mar. 1730, AE. CP. Prusse 91; Grumbkow to Reichenbach, 6 Mar. 1730, Hull, DDHO 3/3; Waldegrave to Robinson, 1 Feb. 1730, Leeds District Archives, Vyner Mss 6018, 13463.
2.　Tilson to Waldegrave, 12 Dec. (os) 1729; De Brais, Saxon envoy in Paris, to Augustus, 10 Oct. 1729, Dresden, 2735, 1; Goslinga, pp. 353, 365–6, 368–71, 379–85; Villars, p. 199; Huisman, pp. 451–2.
3.　George to Townshend, undated, in reply to Townshend to George, 15 Dec. (os), Townshend to Horatio Walpole and Poyntz, 2 Dec. (os) 1729, Poyntz to Newcastle, 26 Jan. 1730, BL. Add. 38507, 48982; Townshend to Broglie, 4 Dec. (os) 1729, PRO. 100/5; Poyntz to Thomas Townshend, 26 Nov. 1729, Poyntz to Waldegrave, 5 Feb. 1730, Weston to Poyntz, 20 Jan. (os), Tilson to Poyntz, 30 Dec. (os) 1729, BL. Althorp, E1, 5, 4, 3.
4.　Charles VI to Stephen Kinsky and Fonseca, 28 Dec. 1729, Höfler, I, 438; Eugene to Kinsky, 25 Jan. 1730, HHStA., GK. 94(b); Holzendorf to Tilson, 3 Jan., 'copy of Emperor's answer to the communication . . . of the Treaty of Seville', PRO. 84/307, 100/11; Wilson, p. 215; Delafaye to Poyntz, 30 Jan. (os), 5 Mar. (os), 2 Apr. (os) 1730, BL. Althorp, E4.
5.　Poyntz to Waldegrave, 19 Jan., Poyntz to Keene, 6 Mar., Horatio Walpole to Poyntz, 14 Apr. 1730, BL. Althorp, E1, 4; 'Draft to Mr. Poyntz relating to the Advices from Berlin as it was sent to Your Majesty yesterday morning', 21 Jan. (os), Poyntz to Keene, 6 Mar., Harrington and Poyntz to Newcastle, 25 Mar., 12 Apr. 1730, BL. Add. 32765–6; Sinzendorf to Fonseca, 4 Feb. 1727, HHStA., Fonseca, 14; Villars, pp. 226–9, 232–3, 237–41; Baudrillart, IV, 35–60.
6.　Keene to Poyntz and Harrington, 16, 24 Mar., Poyntz to Newcastle, 1 Feb., 10 Mar., Harrington and Poyntz to Keene, 1, 16 Apr., Harrington and Poyntz to Newcastle, 12, 27 Apr. 1730, BL. Add. 32765–6; Chesterfield to Harrington, 25 Aug., 'Short Abstract of what has past about ye Treaty of Equilibre', anon. memorandum, summer 1730, PRO. 84/307, 103/113; Delafaye to Poyntz, 20 Feb. (os), Poyntz to Holzendorf, 9 Feb. 1730, BL. Althorp, E4, 1.
7.　Poyntz to Keene, 19 Jan., Poyntz to Newcastle, 19 Feb. 1730, BL. Add. 32765.

8. Poyntz to Newcastle, 11 Jan., 10, 14, 19 Feb., Harrington and Poyntz to Newcastle, 12 Apr., Newcastle to Harrington and Poyntz, 23 Apr. (os), 7 May (os), Paper sent to Chesterfield, 10 Feb. (os), Newcastle to Poyntz, 12 Feb. (os), Newcastle to Waldegrave, Horatio Walpole and Poyntz, 24 Aug. (os) 1730, BL. Add. 32765–7, 9139, 32769; Harrington and Poyntz to Holzendorf, 1 Apr., Delafaye to Poyntz, 2 May 1730, BL. Althorp, E2, 4.

9. Chetwynd to Townshend, 9 Sept., Du Bourgay to Townshend, 25 Oct., Townshend to Du Bourgay, 31 Oct. (os) 1729, Holzendorf to Tilson, 20 Jan., Newcastle to Harrington and Poyntz, – Apr. (os), Waldegrave to Tilson, 22 Apr. 1730, PRO. 81/123, 90/25, 84/307, 78/195 f.126, 80/67; Sauveterre to Chauvelin, 7 Feb. 1730, AE. CP. Prusse 90; Grumbkow to Reichenbach, 3 Mar., Reichenbach to Grumbkow, 17 Mar., 14, 18 Apr. 1730, Hull, DDHO 3/3; Waldegrave to Tilson, 15 Mar., 12, 16, 26 Apr. 1730, Chewton; Delafaye to Poyntz, 20 Feb. (os), Poyntz to Thomas Townshend, 24 Feb. 1730, BL. Althorp, E 4, 5.

10. Horatio Walpole to Waldegrave, 13 Mar. (os) 1730, Chewton; Horatio Walpole to Harrington and Poyntz, 2 Mar. (os) 1730, Coxe, II, 668–9; Harrington and Poyntz to Keene, 1 Apr. 1730, BL. Althorp, E2.

11. Horatio Walpole to Waldegrave, 13 Mar. (os), Delafaye to Waldegrave, 7 Jan. (os) 1730, Tilson to Waldegrave, 23 Dec. (os) 1729, Chewton; Hervey to Henry Fox, 24, 29 Jan. (os) 1730, Ilchester, pp. 45–6; Selwyn to Poyntz, 8, 22 Jan. (os) 1730, BL. Althorp, E4; Vignola to Government of Venice, 9 Dec. 1729, ASV. LM. Ing. 98; Horatio Walpole to Poyntz, 21 Jan. (os) 1730, Coxe, II, 667; Kinsky to Ferdinand Albrecht, 8 Nov. 1729, Wolfenbüttel, 1 Alt 22, Nr. 590; Zamboni to Manteuffel, 20 Jan. 1730, Bodl. Rawl. 120; *Craftsman* 29 Nov. (os) 1729.

12. Trevor to Poyntz, 15 Jan. (os) 1730, BL. Althorp, E4; Horatio Walpole to Waldegrave, 13 Mar. (os) 1730, Chewton; Townshend to Du Bourgay, 13 Jan. (os), Townshend to Edward Finch, 13 Jan. (os), Holzendorf to Tilson, 31 Jan. 1730, PRO. 90/26, 95/54, 84/301; Kinsky to Charles VI, 27 Jan. 1730, HHStA., EK. 67; Newcastle to Poyntz, 13 Jan. (os) 1730, BL. Add. 32765; Zamboni to Manteuffel, 27 Jan. 1730, Dresden, 637, 2; D'Aubenton to Maurepas, 16 Feb. 1730, AN. AM. B7 301; Chammorel to Chauvelin, 26 Jan., Chauvelin to Broglie, 5 Feb. 1730, AE. CP. Ang. 369; Sedgwick, I, 68; Knatchbull, pp. 97–8; Hervey, pp. 112–4; Egmont, I, 3–6; H. McMains, *The Parliamentary Opposition to Sir Robert Walpole 1727–31* (unpublished Ph.D. thesis, Indiana State University, 1970) pp. 163–5; Weston to Poyntz, 29 Dec. (os) 1729, 30 Jan. (os) 1730, Delafaye to Poyntz, 13 Jan. (os) 1730, BL. Althorp, E3, 4.

13. Egmont, I, 10; Carlisle, p. 65; Knatchbull, pp. 100, 143–5; Delafaye to Poyntz, 26 Jan. (os) 1730, BL. Althorp, E4.

14. Newcastle to Poyntz, 30 Jan. (os) 1730, newsletters for Lord Perceval, 27, 29 Jan. (os) 1730, BL. Add. 32765, 27981; Kinsky to Charles VI, 18 Feb. 1730, HHStA., EK. 67; Egmont, I, 11; Cobbett, VIII, 773–4; Thomas Pelham to Poyntz, 30 Jan. (os), BL. Althorp, E4.

15. Egmont, I, 11–12; Knatchbull, pp. 101–2, 145–6; Newcastle to Poyntz, 30 Jan. (os) 1730, BL. Add. 32765; Chauvelin to Chammorel, 16 Feb. 1730, AE. CP. Ang. sup. 8; Villars, p. 212; Dayrolles to Tilson, 21 Feb. 1730, PRO. 84/310; Weston to Poyntz, 30 Jan. (os), 6 Feb. (os) 1730, BL. Althorp, E4.

16. Trevor to Poyntz, 5 Feb. (os), Delafaye to Poyntz, 6 Feb. (os), 1730, BL. Althorp, E 4, 3; Egmont, I, 12–13, 24–31; Hervey, pp. 114–5; Carlisle, p. 66; Knatchbull, pp. 102–3, 147–51; Portland to Bentinck, 10 Feb. (os) 1730, BL. Eg. 1715; Diemar to William of Hesse-Cassel, 17 Feb. 1730, Marburg, England, 199; Winnington to Henry Fox, 3 Feb. (os) 1730, Ilchester, p. 47; Plumb, p. 207; Hill, *Parliamentary Parties*, p. 200.

17. Townshend to William Finch, 15 Aug. (os), Townshend to d'Ittersum, 18 Aug. (os) 1727, Newcastle to Horatio Walpole, 14 May (os), – July (os) 1728, PRO. 84/294, 296, 78/189; C(H) Mss. papers 25; *Craftsman* 29 June (os), 20 July (os) 1728; *Fog's Weekly Journal* 2 Aug. (os), *London Evening Post* 22 Nov. (os), *Daily Post Boy* 21 Nov. (os) 1729; Chammorel to Chauvelin, 2 Aug. 1728, AE. CP. Ang. 363.

18. Wager to Delafaye, 8 Jan. (os) 1730, Horatio Walpole to Delafaye, 14 Dec. (os) 1729, PRO. 42/20, 78/192; Townshend to Newcastle, 12 July 1729, C(H) Mss. papers 25/41; Delafaye to Waldegrave, 7 Jan. (os) 1730, Chewton.

19. Portland to Bentinck, 13 Feb. 1730, BL. Eg. 1715; Chammorel to Chauvelin, 22 Feb., Broglie to Chauvelin, 27 Feb. 1730, AE. CP. Ang. 369; Hervey, pp. 116–17; Egmont, I, 34–8; Knatchbull, pp. 104–6; McMains, *Parliamentary Opposition*, pp. 192–213; Dickinson, *Bolingbroke* pp. 225–8; Hill, *Parliamentary Parties* pp. 200–1.

20. Broglie to Chauvelin, 22 Feb. 1730, P. Mantoux, *Notes sur les Comptes Rendus des Séances du Parlement Anglais* (Paris, 1906), p. 52; Egmont, I, 38–40; Carlisle, p. 67; Diemar to William of Hesse-Cassel, 24 Feb. 1730, Marburg, England, 199; Hervey to Henry Fox, 17 Feb. (os) 1730, Ilchester, p. 48; Chammorel to Chauvelin, 27 Feb., 2 Mar. 1730, AE. CP. Ang. 369; *Daily Post Boy*, 12 Feb. (os) 1730; Plumb, p. 212.

21. Egmont, I, 50; Selwyn to Poyntz, 21 Feb. (os) 1730, BL. Althorp, E4; Diemar to Frederick I, King of Sweden, 31 Mar. 1730, Marburg, England, 201; Knatchbull, p. 106; George II to Townshend, no date, in reply to Townshend to George II, 19 Feb. (os)1730; Coxe, II, 536; Waldegrave to Tilson, 15, 18 Mar., Woodward to Tilson, 19 Apr., Holzendorf to Tilson, 7 Mar. 1730, PRO. 80/67, 88/36, 84/307; Zamboni to Manteuffel, 3 Mar. 1730, Bodl. Rawl. 120; Tilson to Waldegrave, 24 Mar. (os), Horatio Walpole to Waldegrave, 24 Mar. (os) 1730, Chewton.

22. Chauvelin to Broglie, 2 Mar., Chammorel to Fleury, 9 Mar., Broglie to Chauvelin, 13 Mar., Chauvelin to Chammorel, 12 Mar. 1730, AE. CP. Ang. 369, sup. 8; Newcastle to Poyntz and Armstrong, 12 Feb. (os), Newcastle to Armstrong, 12 Feb. (os), Armstrong to Newcastle, 27 Feb., 'Order from the King of France', 27 Feb., Newcastle to Harrington, 2 Mar. (os), Newcastle to Harrington and Poyntz, 2 Mar. (os) 1730, BL. Add. 32765–6; Horatio Walpole to Fleury, 23 Feb. 1730, A. R. Saint-Leger, *La Flandre Maritime et Dunkerque sous la domination Française, 1659–1789* (Paris, 1900), p. 321; Newcastle to Poyntz, 20 Feb. (os), Thomas Townshend to Poyntz, 20 Feb. (os), Delafaye to Poyntz, 21 Feb. (os), 2 Mar. (os) 1730, BL. Althorp, E4; Woodward to Tilson, 29 Mar., Townshend to Du Bourgay, 3 Mar. (os), Townshend to Edward Finch, 3 Mar. (os), Newcastle to Keene, 5 Mar. (os) 1730, PRO. 88/36, 90/26, 95/54, 94/105; Villars, p. 224; Reichenbach to Grumbkow, 14 Mar. 1730, Hull, DDHO 3/3; Egmont, I, 71–5; Knatchbull, pp. 109–10; Carlisle, pp. 68–9; *St. James's Evening Post* 5, 7 Mar. (os), *Whitehall Evening Post* 5, 7 Mar. (os), *British Journal* 7 Mar. (os) 1730.

23. Tilson to Waldegrave, 6, 13 Mar. (os) 1730, Chewton; Chammorel to Chauvelin, 22 Feb., 16, 23 Mar. 1730, AE. CP. Ang. 369; Egmont, I, 78; Knatchbull, pp. 112–13; Diemar to William of Hesse-Cassel, 21 Mar. 1730, Marburg, England, 199; Reichenbach to Grumbkow, 24 Mar. 1730, Hull, DDHO 3/3; Townshend to Plettenberg, 6 Mar. (os) 1730, Münster, 5474; Portland to Bentinck, 13 Mar. (os) 1730, BL. Eg. 1715; Newcastle to Poyntz, 20 Feb. (os), Delafaye to Poyntz, 20 Feb. (os) 1730, BL. Althorp, E4.

24. Tilson to Waldegrave, 17, 20 Mar. (os), Horatio Walpole to Waldegrave, 21 Apr. (os), 1 May (os) 1730, Chewton; Tilson to Hotham, 13 Mar. (os) 1730, Hull, DDHO 3/3; Carlisle, p. 70; Egmont, I, 78; Delafaye to Poyntz, 9, 19 Mar. (os), Weston to Poyntz, 16 Mar. (os) 1730, BL. Althorp, E4.

25. Diemar to William, 4 Apr. 1730, Marburg, England, 199; Egmont, I, 81–2; Knatchbull, pp. 113–14.

26. Egmont, I, 82–4; Carlisle, p. 70; Tilson to Hotham, 24 Mar. (os) 1730, Hull, DDHO 3/1; newsletter, 21 Mar. (os) 1730, BL. Add. 27981.

27. Horatio Walpole to Waldegrave, 21 Apr. (os) 1730, Chewton; Egmont, I, 95–6; Carlisle, p. 71.

28. Egmont, I, 52; Reichenbach to Grumbkow, 14, 24 Mar. 1730, PRO. 90/27; Poyntz and Harrington to Newcastle, 16 Apr. 1730, BL. Add. 32766.

29. Selwyn to Poyntz, 22 Jan. (os) 1730, BL. Althorp, E4; Egmont, I, 10; Zamboni to Manteuffel, 24 Feb., 31 Mar. 1730, Bodl. Rawl. 120; Reichenbach to Grumbkow, 14 Mar. 1730, Hull DDHO 3/3; Chauvelin to Brancas, 14 Mar. 1730, AE. MD. Espagne 158; Egmont, I, 31, 93–4; Perceval to father, 22 May (os) 1730, BL. Add. 47032; Horatio Walpole to Waldegrave, 13 Mar. (os) 1730, Chewton; Broglie to Chauvelin, 7 May, Chauvelin to Broglie, 13 July 1730, AE. CP. Ang. 370.

30. Townshend to Woodward, 27 Feb. (os) 1730, PRO. 88/36.

31. Horatio Walpole to Harrington and Poyntz, 23 Apr. (os) 1730, Coxe, II, 693; Newcastle to Boulter, Primate of Ireland, 20 June (os) 1730, PRO. 63/392; Broglie to Chauvelin, 7 Mar 1730, AE. CP. Ang. 370; Delafaye to Poyntz, 13 Apr. (os) 1730, BL. Althorp, E4.

32. Selwyn to Poyntz, 13 Apr. (os) 1730, BL. Althorp, E4; Perceval newsletter, 20 June (os), Harrington to Keene, 30 Jan. (os) 1730, BL. Add. 27981, 32765; Reichenbach to Grumbkow, 19 May 1730, Hull, DDHO 3/3; Hervey, p. 120; Ossorio to Victor Amadeus II, 29 May 1730, AST. LM. Ing. 37; Williams, p. 80; Horatio Walpole to Poyntz, 21 May (os), Selwyn to Poyntz, 23 Apr. (os), 4 May (os) 1730, BL. Althorp, E4; 'Disposition of Employments', BL. Add. 63750.
33. Townshend to Waldegrave, 1 May (os) 1730, Robinson to Leheup, 4 Feb., Robinson to Horatio Walpole, 7 Feb. 1730, BL. Add. 48982, 9139; Horatio to Robert Walpole, 23 July 1730, BL. Add. 63749; Newcastle to Waldegrave, 22 June (os), Robinson to Waldegrave, 28 June 1730, Chewton; Selwyn to Poyntz, 12 Feb. (os) 1730, BL. Althorp, E4.
34. Chauvelin to Chammorel, 27 Apr., 9 May, 12 June 1730, AE. CP. Ang. sup. 8.
35. Chammorel to Chauvelin, 22, 29 May, Chauvelin to Broglie, 12 May 1730, AE. CP. Ang. 370; Horatio Walpole to Waldegrave, 13 Mar. (os) 1730, Chewton; Zamboni to Manteuffel, 2 June 1730, Bodl. Rawl. 120.
36. Horatio to Robert Walpole, 16 Aug. 1730, BL. Add. 63749; Hervey, pp. 174, 345–6.
37. Broglie to Chauvelin, 24 Aug. 1730, PRO. 107/2; Newcastle to Plenipotentiaries, 28 Aug. (os) 1730, BL. Add. 32769; King, pp. 115–18; Zamboni to Manteuffel, 2 June 1730, Bodl. Rawl. 120; Anon. ballad, *The Square and the Cardinal*, Bodl. Firth.
38. Newcastle to Poyntz, 20 Feb. (os), Selwyn to Poyntz, 5 Mar. (os), Delafaye to Poyntz, 2, 14, 30 Apr. (os), Horatio Walpole to Harrington and Poyntz, 16 Apr. (os), Horatio Walpole to Poyntz, 21 May (os) 1730, BL. Althorp, E4.
39. Chauvelin to Chammorel, 22 June 1739, AE. CP. Ang. sup. 8.
40. Horatio Walpole to Poyntz, 14 Apr. (os) 1730, BL. Althorp, E4; Waldegrave, Horatio Walpole and Poyntz to Robinson, 16 July, Newcastle to Horatio Walpole, 17 Aug. (os) 1730, BL. Add. 23780, 32769.
41. Chammorel to Chauvelin, 14 Aug. 1730, AE. CP. Ang. 370.

CHAPTER TWELVE

The Collapse of the Seville Alliance

'Mr. Keene should be explicit, not only in our readiness but even our desire not to pass this summer in inaction'.

Sir Robert Walpole.[1]

Whatever the importance of the alterations in the ministry, developments in the diplomatic situation made imperative a reconsideration of British foreign policy. Two developments were of particular importance. The first was the collapse of Britain's northern strategy, her hopes of profiting from developments in Prussia and Russia. The failure of Hotham's mission marked the effective end of this approach, and it was replaced by fears that Prussia and Russia would take advantage of the revival of difficulties in Mecklenburg to attack Hanover. This in turn led to a reconsideration of the degree to which Britain could rely on her allies for assistance. The second major development was the degeneration of the Alliance of Seville into a feuding and distrustful group of powers pursuing independent policies. Possibly this had been predictable, and was inevitable once the alliance had failed to intimidate Austria into compliance with its demands. Tension between Britain and her allies was not new, but the increased hostility of the summer of 1730 marked the effective end of the Anglo-French alliance, and placed major strains on relations between Britain and Spain.

'His Majesty has had intelligence that the Russians were making preparations to march a body of men to attack His Majesty's German Dominions and that they had sounded the King of Poland about granting them passage through his country, and that it was suspected that the King of Prussia was privy to this enterprize.'

Harrington, June 1730.[2]

In the spring of 1730 in Britain there had been considerable expectation of a major alteration in the diplomatic situation in northern Europe. Great hopes had been raised about the Hotham mission, and it had been widely anticipated that a new period in Anglo-Prussian relations would be ushered in, with marital links between the ruling houses, a visit by Frederick William I to England, and Anglo-Prussian cooperation in European diplomacy. It had been felt that such a realignment would affect Saxony and Austria.[3] At the same time developments in Russia suggested other major changes. The unexpected death from smallpox of the young Peter II, the grand-son of Peter I, led to the accession of Peter I's niece, Anne, the widowed Duchess of Courland. The greater aristocracy succeeded in making Anne's accession conditional upon her accepting a new constitution which drastically limited regal powers, and suggested to various foreign commentators the Swedish, Polish or British constitution. It was widely believed that Russia would revert to her pre-Petrine state, and that the circumscribed power of the new monarch would be too weak to prevent internal disorders and the reversion of Russia to what western-Europeans unfairly described as barbarism. In the specific field of foreign affairs it was believed that the developments in Russia would harm her ally, Austria. In particular, the Russian treaty obligation to send 30,000 men to the defence of Austria, if attacked, seemed in danger, and the role of the Austro-Russian treaty in keeping Prussia in alliance with Austria was threatened by the apparent collapse of Russian power. It was also believed that the change in Russia would open the way to an easing of relations between Russia and the powers of the Treaty of Seville, particularly Britain. Perceval noted in his diary 'it is not improbable but that the apprehension of civil disturbances will induce the court of Muscovy to cultivate the friendship of all the Princes of Europe capable of hurting the present election, and particularly of Great Britain, and if so the late Czar's death, who was nephew of the present Emperor of Germany, will have a great influence over him to accede to the Peace of Seville'. Dayrolle suggested that the pro-Austrian British opposition would be upset by the death of the Czar. Seckendorf viewed the death as a catastrophe and the British stocks rose on the news. It was believed that the changes in Russia would cause Prussia to be more cautious in making anti-Hanoverian moves.[4]

These hopes were to be shattered. There was far less disorder than had been anticipated. The Duke of Liria, the Spanish Ambassador in Russia, wrote to Prince Eugene of the extraordinary tranquillity following Peter's death. As a result of a military coup Anne was able to reject the new constitution. The new Russian ministry lost no time in promising Austria the 30,000 men, and Anne pledged herself to the Austrian alliance.[5] These developments upset British hopes, though the British ministry continued to claim the new Russian government was less stable than it seemed, and that it would therefore be unable and unwilling to send troops to the aid of Austria. However, British hopes of Russia had been far less than those of Prussia. Little attempt had been made to establish an alliance, and no high-ranking British diplomat had been either sent or selected for Russia. On 27 May the Consul-General, Thomas Ward, had been promoted to Minister Resident, and a new Consul-General, Claudius Rondeau, appointed. Both men had been in Russia for some time, and each had claimed that the possibility of an Anglo-Russian alliance existed. They had sought instructions from London. However, no instructions were sent from London in 1730 until early June. On 9 June Newcastle informed Ward that it was time to put aside the disputes dating from Peter I's reign, 'as many changes have happened since both in Muscovy and England and as those disputes were wholly personal it is to be hoped they are forgotten on all sides'. Ward was congratulated on his approach to Count Osterman, the Russian foreign minister, but Newcastle made it clear that Britain expected reciprocity to be the basis of any relationship.

> You did very right in shewing him the real instances His Majesty had given of the sincerity of his intentions to live in perfect amity with Russia, and it is very reasonable that His Majesty should find some proofs of a mutual good disposition on their side.[6]

The lack of instructions earlier in the year, and the guarded tones of those which eventually arrived made it clear that, whilst the ministry in London was actively interested in securing an alliance with Prussia, as indeed it was also, in 1730, with Saxony-Poland, there was considerable caution about Anglo-Russian negotiations. There were several reasons for this hesitation. The apparently unstable nature of Russian factional politics, and the desire not to offend Sweden and Denmark, allies whose interests were incompatible with Russia, were important. Responding to Swedish fears of Anglo-Russian negotiations, Newcastle had in June 1728 given the assurance that 'no negociation of this sort will be entered into by His Majesty without previously communicating it to the King of Sweden and Count Horn, and having their concurrence and approbation'. The confused nature of Russian politics following the death of Peter II led to a revival in Sweden of schemes for a reconquest of the Baltic provinces surrendered, only nine years earlier, at the Treaty of Nystad. Edward Finch was pressed on the subject by Frederick I of Sweden and his ministers.[7] The ministry of Peter II had displayed little interest in supporting the anti-Danish interests of the Duke of Holstein-Gottorp, and indeed, during the reign of Peter II, when the Russian capital returned to Moscow and 'German' influences were muted, Russian expansionism had not been a European problem, and relations with Russia were not a high priority in British foreign policy. The possibility that the new reign of Anne would see a revival in Russian expansionism could not but remind the British government of their treaty obligations to Denmark and Sweden. There were probably other reasons which helped to account for the lack of a British diplomatic approach to Russia. Newcastle's mention of the importance of a good Russian disposition is significant. George II believed that any moves toward good relations had to be the product of efforts by both powers. It is also possible the British ministry felt that, if they succeeded in winning Prussia, Austria would yield over the Spanish garrisons and Russia would be forced to avoid diplomatic isolation by settling her differences on the terms of Britain and her allies. Rather than compromising over the rights of the Dukes of Mecklenburg and Holstein-Gottorp, the British ministry could hope that, by holding out, the Russians would yield. In the absence of material which could cast light on thinking within the British ministry about relations with Russia, the role of Townshend, never noted for his sympathies with Russian interests, is open to speculation. The decision to promote Ward, appoint Rondeau and dispatch instructions, coincided with Townshend's resignation. Possibly Townshend, well-informed of Swedish views and seeking to persuade the Swedes to follow an anti-Prussian policy and increase their forces in Swedish Pomerania, simply preferred to avoid antagonising Sweden.

The reaffirmation of the Austro-Russian alliance after the consolidation of Anne's power would not have been a terribly serious blow to British foreign policy had it not been followed by the failure of Hotham's mission. The relationship between developments in Russia and in Prussia is obscure. Frederick William I certainly revealed, throughout his reign, a well-developed consciousness of Russian strength, and the idea of using Prussian fears of Russia to hold Frederick William in check was recognised in the diplomatic plans of the period. Russian developments were believed to influence decisions in Berlin.[8] However, in the spring and early summer of 1730, contemporaries did not ascribe the failure of Hotham's mission to events in Russia, and there is no reason to doubt their views. Arriving in Berlin at the beginning of April 1730 Hotham found Frederick William more interested in the single than the double-marriage scheme. This was a serious blow, though the possibility of a compromise involving two marriages and the establishment of Crown Prince Frederick in Hanover was investigated. It is not clear that George II envisaged the succession of Frederick of Prussia and his intended wife Amelia to both Prussia and Hanover and the eventual union of these two territories, but the possibility of such a development was certainly more tempting for Prussia than their more usual schemes of a Hohenzollern ruling Courland and of dynastic links with the house of Brunswick-Bevern. On 12 April Hotham reported to Townshend that his negotiations were complicated by Frederick William's inconstancy and 'excessive jealousy'. At the end of a drunken feast, an intoxicated King of Prussia had declared the marriage of his eldest daughter and the Prince of Wales, but eventual sobriety led the King to renege on this declaration. Hotham noted that a compromise, albeit a difficult one, was possible in the case of Crown Prince Frederick: 'It is very plain he will sell his son, but not give him'. Good progress was made in the Brunswick conferences, and there was optimism in Britain about the chances of a reconciliation. The press confidently predicted it. Slingelandt urged the British to demand only the single marriage, in order to avoid antagonizing Frederick William. On 8 April Frederick William wrote to his envoy in Paris, Chambrier, that as his differences with George II were settled, he assumed this would have a considerable influence in the military conferences at Paris.[9]

Hotham was less optimistic, and he cannot be accused of misleading the British ministry about the difficulties facing his mission. On 18 April he informed Townshend that he was finding it difficult to treat with Frederick William personally.[10] A major problem confronting Hotham was the division between the Prussian ministers. Throughout the late 1720s the Prussian ministry had been badly divided, and the situation had not eased by 1730. The ministry was split into two factions, one led by General Grumbkow, and the other by Knyphausen. Frederick-Ernst Knyphausen, a diplomat of some experience, was associated, albeit not always to the satisfaction of the British ministry, with the policy of a British alliance, and with the schemes for Anglo-Prussian marriages. He had lost influence following the death of his father-in-law, the Prussian minister Ilgen, in December 1728, and in 1730 he relied heavily upon the British marriages to restore his power. His principal rival Grumbkow was to be described in 1732 by Chauvelin as 'un homme vif, pour ne pas dire féroce, sans principes, assez opposé aux Anglois . . . '. He was closely associated with pro-Austrian policies, and with the very active Austrian envoy in Berlin, Seckendorf. Complicating Hotham's mission was the fact that he had been ordered to attempt to secure the disgrace of Grumbkow and the recall of Reichenbach, whose correspondence with Grumbkow had been intercepted by the British. It had been argued that Prussian policy would not alter until Frederick William changed his ministers. On 9 April Townshend sent Hotham the intercepted correspondence and ordered him to 'communicate them to Monsieur Knyphausen, and concert with him the use you are to make of them'.[11] However, by linking Hotham to Knyphausen, Townshend was complicating the mission to a fatal degree. Possibly the marriages and their desired consequence, a Prussian breach with Austria, could have only taken effect had Grumbkow been removed.[12] If so, the mission's chances of success were limited, as Frederick William did not wish to see his choice of ministers dictated by foreign powers. Hotham sought to stir up the King against Grumbkow, but he had to inform Townshend of a lack of success. On 12 April he wrote:

> I see no one instance of Cnyphausen's superiority or Grumkau's credit being lessen'd . . . He [Knyphausen] even told me himself that he stood alone, that the whole court was sold to the Empr. and I saw plainly, that he stands in that awe of the King, that he will never venture to lead his master into anything, which he does not see the King already disposed to: and it is most certain, that the few friends we have are timorous and indolent and our enemys enterprizing and active.

Hotham's pessimism about his mission did not diminish. On 6 May he informed Townshend that Borck, the Prussian minister then much in favour with Frederick William 'follows Seckendorf's direction'. A week later, he reported that Frederick William, opposed to the idea of the Crown Prince leaving the country, had rejected the suggestion that the Stadtholderate of Hanover be conferred on Princess Amelia, adding 'the proposal the King of Prussia has now rejected was sometime ago the thing in the world he was the most fond of'. However, Frederick William was also willing to order the recall of Reichenbach, much to the latter's distress, and to tell Hotham that he wished for nothing more than to live well with Britain. Hotham's conclusion was that the King was unreliable.[13]

Another factor complicating Hotham's mission was Frederick William's concern about its consequences for the Austrian cause in the Empire. Seckendorf was adept at exploiting the King's fears that a war would harm the Empire, and by defeating Austria overturn the balance of power. At dinner with Hotham in Potsdam on 21 April, Frederick William 'always returned to that; that suffering the French to attack Luxemburg or invade the Low Countries would in the end have very pernicious consequences, and that we ourselves should soon be sensible to it, and that he did not doubt but in a year or two, we should return to the old system, as he termed it, and join hands against France . . . ' Several days later he told Hotham that Luxemburg and the Austrian Netherlands were too near to his own possessions for him to permit an attack upon them. The relationship between Prussian fears, and British opposition at the conferences at Fontainebleau to war north of the Alps, has not been brought out by those historians who have considered the conferences. A major reason why the British devoted so much energy, in April and May 1730, to persuading their allies that operations against Austria should be confined to Italy, was their awareness of the danger of Prussian military assistance to Austria, either by virtue of treaty obligations, or because of Prussian obligations as a member of the Empire. Frederick William expressed particular concern about Luxemburg, whilst he allowed Hotham to form the opinion that the Prussians would not send help to the Austrians in the event of the war being confined to Italy. The British hoped that even if they could only make Prussian policy waver it would affect Austrian conduct.[14]

By early May Hotham's mission had clearly failed. Whether it could have succeeded had George pressed for only the single marriage, as Slingelandt and the Wolfenbüttel minister Stain urged, and as those who opposed the reconciliation feared, or if George had offered the Stadtholderate of Hanover to Crown Prince Frederick, as some of the British ministers had urged, is unclear. Frederick William sought the latter solution, and later in the year he blamed the failure of the marriage negotiations on the British refusal to accept the Prussian conditions.[15] However, it is probable that Frederick William's indecisiveness would have prevented him accepting any expedient until the European situation had been resolved by peace. On 13 May he wrote to Reichenbach restating his insistence on the single marriage, and stating that he would not support a British marriage for Crown Prince Frederick until the disputes over the Treaty of Seville were settled. The mission ended suddenly as a result of Hotham's attempt to discredit Grumbkow by a revelation of the contents of Reichenbach's intercepted correspondence. Frederick William regarded the opening of his minister's letters as a personal insult, and he reacted violently when Hotham pressed him on the matter on 10 July. Treating the King's violent anger as an affront to George II, in the person of his envoy, Hotham left Berlin without an audience of leave.[16]

The failure of Hotham's mission was a serious blow to British foreign policy. The deterioration of British relations with Prussia and Russia led to a revival of fears that the two latter powers would initiate military action against Hanover. Earlier in 1730, when there had been fears of Prussian action against Hanover, Britain had turned to her allies, particularly France, for assistance, and had been greeted with promises of help. In the summer of 1730 the situation was less promising, and the renewed perception of a threat to Hanover led to an awareness of the practical difficulties created by the distrust and disagreements affecting Anglo-French relations. On 3 May Townshend told Broglie that George II wanted France to hold a corps ready to assist Hanover in the event of an Austrian or Prussian attack.[17] Disagreement between Britain and France was particularly acute over the German policies of the two powers. The dispute over British subsidies to the Wittelsbachs had continued throughout the spring of 1730. Just as the British felt letdown over Dunkirk, so the French felt that British parsimony was destroying the possibility of creating an effective anti-Austrian coalition within the Empire. The revival of the disputes over Hildesheim angered the French.[18] Without Prussia or the Wittelsbachs the British position in the Empire was weak. In the spring they had sought to benefit from the prospect of improved relations with Prussia by opening talks with the Saxons for an alliance. Woodward was ordered to press for good relations, but on 16 June he had to report that the Saxon minister, Count Hoym, had informed him that the basis of any alliance would have to be British subsidies, and that it was the prospect of these which would be most likely to lead Augustus II to consider a treaty. Suspicious of Prusso-Saxon links, the British ministry was unwilling to offer a subsidy. They were also sceptical of the value of any Saxon promises. The well-known factionalism of the Saxon court made it appear particularly unstable.[19] The return of the exiled Duke, Charles Leopold, to Mecklenburg aroused British fears that Russia, Austria and Prussia were seeking to create difficulties for Hanover, his principal foreign opponent. There were still Hanoverian troops in Mecklenburg. Robinson wrote of the possibility 'of drawing on an universal war from the least disturbance in Lower Saxony', and informed Newcastle of the danger that Russian troops would be sent to Mecklenburg. Charles Leopold was the brother-in-law of the new Czarina, and it was widely feared that she had been responsible for his return to Mecklenburg and was seeking to enlist support for him.[20] Opinions were divided as to the extent of Austrian support for Charles Leopold. Chammorel reported that some British ministers believed Austria was determined to persuade Russia to intervene in Mecklenburg either to force George II to retire his troops from the duchy or to risk a parliamentary storm by seeking a continuation of his subsidies to German allies.

Developments in Mecklenburg certainly aroused the concern and anger of George II. Ossorio, D'Aix's replacement, noted George's anger. Broglie reported that the Queen and Walpole were cooperating to quieten George's anxiety.[21] The situation was made yet more serious by the continued deterioration of Anglo-Prussian relations. Frederick William had decided to replace Reichenbach by Count Degenfeld, and the British hoped the arrival of the latter in Britain would provide an opportunity for a resumption of good relations. Borck and Harrington exchanged messages calling for such a resumption, and when Degenfeld arrived in London, Newcastle told him that Hotham's folly was to blame for the failure of his mission, and that the marriage negotiations should be resumed by Degenfeld and the ministry in London. On 25 July Tilson informed Robinson 'the King of Prussia seems concerned at his sudden flirt of passion . . . we expect Count Degenfeld here in all haste to set matters right . . . ' Zamboni was assured that Frederick William had relented of his conduct to Hotham. Degenfeld reached London in early August. Newcastle approached Degenfeld and proposed new negotiations over the double marriage. According to Zamboni, who was well acquainted with Degenfeld, having known him before his mission to London, Hotham was sent to Degenfeld to ascertain whether he had been instructed to apologise for Frederick William's insult to George II, in the person of his minister. Degenfeld replied that he had not come to make excuses, and that it was rather the part of George to apologise for his minister's conduct. Zamboni nevertheless reported that all was likely to finish well as both courts, particularly Britain, wanted a reconciliation.[22] He was to be proved wrong. Anglo-Prussian relations were not helped by George's refusal to give Reichenbach an audience of leave, and other difficulties, created by George, delayed Degenfeld's initial audience. When it finally took place on 21 September he was treated badly by the royal family. However, it was to be developments in Prussia which proved Zamboni wrong. The attempted escape of the Crown Prince, and the disgracing of those who had opposed Grumbkow, destroyed the chances of a reconciliation. On 25 September Borck declared to Guy Dickens that Frederick William would not consider any marriage, single or double. British anger at the treatment of the Crown Prince, and Prussian suspicion that George II was responsible for Frederick's attempt at escape, which he had indeed known of, helped to embitter relations. Plans to send Sutton to Berlin were cancelled.[23] Serious moves towards an Anglo-Prussian rapprochement were not to be made again until 1732, and the legacy of personal bitterness between the two monarchs was to wreck that attempt and the others made in the latter half of the 1730s. The failure to ensure good relations was to be a major handicap to British foreign policy in the 1730s.

It is difficult to establish the nature or extent of the relationship between developments in Prussia, Russia and Mecklenburg on the one hand, and the British decision to pursue actively the option of an Austrian alliance on the other. The British approach to Prussia had been intended as part of a diplomatic strategy aimed at restoring relations with Austria by isolating her and compelling her to sue for terms. Its failure, and the replacement of a reasonably satisfactory situation in northern Europe by a threatening one, was paralleled by the failure of the conferences at Fountainebleau to produce much more than discord and distrust. Townshend had apparently been proved correct within a few months of his resignation. His belief that the only way to achieve the aims of the Treaty of Seville was its vigorous enforcement seemed vindicated by the discord at Fountainebleau. The failure of the Hotham mission and the resumption of tension in northern Germany suggested that, unless there were some major diplomatic changes before January, Walpole would be forced to ask for the continuation of the unpopular subsidies to foreign powers.

Parliamentary trouble could also be anticipated over Dunkirk. Louis XV's promise had been followed not by the demolition of the works there, but by prevarication on the part of the French, and anger on that of the

British. Maurepas, the Naval minister, was opposed to the destruction of the works, and took steps to ensure that whatever demolition took place was slow and partial. Within a month of the French promise to demolish the works, British complaints at the failure to honour the promise began. Horatio Walpole claimed

the behaviour of France towards England with regard to Dunkirk is a perfect farce, and exposes the honour, and credit of his Majesty, and his ministers, as well as the faith of France to the greatest ridicule. The most solemn promises, and orders pretended to be sent so long since for destroying what has been done contrary to treaty have been eluded, and remain unexecuted in the most shameful manner, and it is notorious that there are more officers, intendants, governors, and engineers under pretence of inspecting that work who delay and prevent the demolition, than there are workmen employed in what has been agreed on all hands to be demolished; and our enemys laugh, and flatter themselves with a full persuasion that France will deceive us in this affair, the consequence of which must inevitably be not only the greatest confusion, in England but also in all Europe next winter by the dissolution of the present system of affairs, for it is impossible to imagine that the nation will grow cooler on this head.

The French representatives in London were pressed by the British ministers and, in response to frequently reiterated orders, the British representatives in Paris urged the French to fulfil their promise. Fleury complained about the degree of British pressure over Dunkirk, which Horatio Walpole considered excessive. The British felt tricked by the French failure to honour repeated promises, and French questioning of their claims led to angry scenes. On 23 August Waldegrave recorded in his journal a meeting which had taken place that morning between Fleury and Horatio Walpole:

His Eminence seemed still to doubt whether the works that were now insisted should be demolished had been really so in 1713. Mr. Walpole took fire at this, and with a good deal of agitation told the Cardinal he was abused, and that he would go away, and not take his leave of the Court, for he could not say in his compliment which would be undoubtedly made public in England that he was pleased with the good harmony etc. which ought to subsist between the courts whilst France was so little complaisant in an affair which was so clear.

Sir Robert Walpole was clearly concerned about the danger of the issue being raised in Parliament, and this accounted for his instruction to his brother to present a Memorial on the subject. Parliament would have to be convinced that the ministry had not been remiss over the issue. Delafaye observed in August 'we must take comfort in having done all that was possible, and stand it as well as we can next session.' In the summer of 1730 the opposition press drew attention to continued activity at the port of Dunkirk, and to the French failure to begin the demolition of the illegal jetties. The importance of the Dunkirk issue in embittering Anglo-French relations cannot be over-estimated. Far from being a 'little local difficulty', of no consequence for more general diplomatic developments, Dunkirk served to produce frustration and anxiety among the British ministers. It represented the manner in which the Anglo-French alliance was no longer producing any tangible benefits, but was instead threatening the parliamentary position of the British ministry.[24]

At the same time as conferences were being held at Fountainebleau in order to produce an agreed allied strategy in the event of war with Austria, an attempt was made to settle by compromise the differences with Austria. The British and the French had rejected the Austrian attempt to link negotiations for the admission of the Spanish garrisons to a guarantee of the Pragmatic Sanction. However, in order to keep the negotiations going, the Seville allies had informed Austria that they were ready to listen to further Austrian proposals. In addition, they decided to offer Austria a guarantee of the undivided inheritance of the Emperor's Italian dominions in return for his consent to the admission of the Spanish garrisons. In late May Fleury proposed this solution to the Austrian representatives in the name of all the allies. Charles VI rejected the idea.[25] The continuation of negotiations with the Austrians created tension between the Seville allies. Spain was opposed to talks,[26] and Britain, Spain and Bavaria suspicious of links between France and Austria.[27] Furthermore, the disagreements at Fontainebleau became worse as the summer progressed. The British suspected both that the French did not want war, but were seeking to shift the blame for inaction upon them,[28] and that, if the French did decide to fight, they would insist upon doing so in areas, such as the Austrian Netherlands, where the British were opposed to French gains. The British ascribed the Austrian refusal to negotiate to their knowledge of the divisions amongst the Seville allies. These divisions were indeed no secret. The Austrians were sure that there would be no hostilities in 1730, and anticipated the collapse of the Seville alliance and the fall of the British government.[29] The latter was also feared by the French, who regarded the British ministry as very weak.[30]

The Austrians were correct in their belief that delay would cause some of the Seville allies to change their tone. On 2 August the British representatives in France reported that the Dutch government had ordered their representatives to propose 'a negotiation with the Emperor about granting him a general guaranty of his dominions'. The Dutch suggested the Spaniards should accept neutral garrisons. Fleury dismissed the idea: 'the Cardinal in a formal speech rejected what relates to the Guaranty of the Emperor's dominions on the foot of the Pragmatick Sanction, as what would bring a scandal upon the Alliance of Seville, disoblige the Princes of Italy and the Empire and subject them to a perpetual bondage to the Imperial Court'.[31] It was therefore clear that the French would oppose any guarantee of the Pragmatic Sanction.[32] Yet for the British this was increasingly looking like the only solution to their diplomatic difficulties. When Charles VI had rejected the suggestion of a guarantee of the succession to his Italian dominions, the British representatives in Paris had written to Robinson 'You will easily conclude that this negociation is at an end, and the allys must think of other means for bringing him to reason'.[33] However, the resort to violence hinted at in this letter had been blocked by disagreements among the allies. The Austrian rejection of the proposed expedient led the British to press their allies for an immediate attack upon Sicily. The British hastened their military preparations for such an expedition. French insistence on the prior settlement of a treaty of equilibrium thwarted the British plan.[34] The British had wanted to see hostilities begin in 1730, and feared that without this Spain would attempt a fresh alliance with Austria. Austro-Spanish talks were reported and the British ministry feared that the Spanish would not observe the commercial provisions of the Treaty of Seville. Horatio Walpole stressed the need 'that care be taken, that we do not disoblige Spain.'[35] The French argued that it was better to settle plans for a general war in 1731, and that, before hostilities were commenced, efforts should be made to win the alliance of the Wittelsbachs. Furthermore, the French argued that the major Austrian military build-up in Italy made any maritime invasion unwise, and that operations in Italy required Sardinian assistance. A. M. Wilson has suggested that the French were disinclined to force the issue, because their interests were not being harmed by the protraction of peace. This is probably correct, but it should also be noted that there were reasonable military considerations leading France to reject the British scheme. The military effort demanded of the French was large, for they were expected not only to invade Italy but also to protect Hanover and the United Provinces from attack.[36]

The French view of the desired equilibrium was an ambitious one. On 7 August at a conference of British, French and Dutch representatives held at Compiègne Chauvelin 'explained himself more clearly . . . upon the Equilibre than ever I had heard him, his discourse tended to divest the Emperor of all the dominions he had in Italy . . .'[37] The British were unwilling to accept such a plan and Chauvelin complained that they would only accept a scheme that did not harm the Emperor. On 2 August the British representatives in Paris informed Keene that 'it never was His Majesty's intention to new model the possessions of Europe, and to make a new distribution of dominions and territorys for pleasing the Queen of Spain.'[38]

The Anglo-French alliance had therefore become, by the summer of 1730, the basis of a possible recasting of the European system. British foreign policy was to be tied to the abasement of Austria, which was to become a matter of planning and action, rather than speculation. Such a situation had been advocated by various British ministers ever since the signature of the Treaty of Vienna, but its practical implementation had become, by the summer of 1730, an entirely different matter. Slingelandt told Chesterfield that 'the views of France all tended to the reduction of the House of Austria and the forming a new plan of Equilibre at their expence which he thought by all means ought to be prevented' by supporting the Pragmatic. The following January Harrington was to decry 'the extravagant schemes and plans of Spain and France, for involving the greatest part of Europe in a general and destructive war'. In the same month Rottembourg told Keene that it would be necessary to promise Bohemia and Silesia to rivals of the Habsburgs.[39] The Anglo-French alliance was no longer to be a defensive screen to protect Hanover, Gibraltar and British commercial privileges. It now entailed projected subsidies to Sardinia and the Wittelsbachs, the possibility of a British guarantee of the Saxon succession in Poland, and a war to drive the Austrians from Italy. Poyntz noted that Victor Amadeus would require, as the price of an alliance, a 'reward . . . out of the Emperor's Dominions in the Milanese . . . or Great subsidys'.[40] The Anglo-French alliance which the British ministry decided to abandon in the late summer of 1730 was being directed by the French toward goals very different from those which ministerial speakers had defended in Parliament for the previous five years. However difficult it had been to defend the alliance in those sessions, it would be even harder to confront the new session with demands for fresh subsidies. Horatio Walpole, aware 'of the clamour that may arise against our joyning with France to pull down the house of Austria', nevertheless urged that, in order to intimidate Austria, Parliament should be summoned to meet in November and asked to vote supplies sufficient to permit the raising of another ten thousand British troops. He argued that it was essential to be able to threaten the Emperor with 'the consequences of a dangerous war' in order to get him to be reasonable. Edward Harrison, an office-holder and former MP, feared political trouble if there was war.[41] It is not surprising that Sir Robert Walpole chose to ignore his brother's advice to maintain the Anglo-French alliance, when it was accompanied by suggestions of subsidies for Sardinia and settling with the Wittelsbachs which would have been politically disastrous had they been attempted. It was frequently claimed that Sir Robert Walpole's role in the direction of British foreign policy was minimal, and that he took his ideas and his information from his brother. In June 1730 Robert Trevor suggested that Horatio Walpole 'who without doubt thinks his councils much missed here' might try to return to London from Paris. On 13 July Chammorel reported that Sir Robert Walpole relied on his brother for foreign policy matters. This was an inaccurate view which paid insufficient attention to signs of his interest in and knowledge of foreign affairs. In the summer of 1730 Sir Robert Walpole read many of the diplomatic dispatches and took an active role in the drafting of instructions to British envoys. His letter of 5 July to Newcastle was very thoughtful on general diplomatic strategy and on Anglo-Spanish relations.[42] It seems reasonable to suggest that Sir Robert Walpole's awareness of the potentially fatal domestic repercussions of the continuance of the Anglo-French alliance played a large part in the decision to explore the possibilities of an Anglo-Austrian reconciliation. Equally, the views of Harrington must not be discounted. The Austrians and Chauvelin were convinced that Harrington was the most pro-Austrian of the British ministers. Harrington and Poyntz informed Fleury 'of the absolute necessity of putting an end to the present state of uncertainty one way or other immediately, without which both England and Holland must think of new measures'. Harrington's important role in the negotiation of the Second Treaty of Vienna suggests that he was also partly responsible for the decision to approach Austria. Though Browning claims that Newcastle played a significant role in the conduct of British foreign policy in the summer of 1730, the diplomatic papers of the period would seem to suggest that his role was largely confined to expressing increasing frustration with the French. He and Horatio Walpole played little part in the negotiations with Austria.[43]

Notes

1. Walpole to Newcastle, 24 June (os) 1730, PRO. 36/19.
2. Harrington to Woodward, 30 June (os) 1730, PRO. 88/37.
3. Paper sent to Chesterfield, 10 Feb. (os) 1730, BL. Add. 9139.
4. Egmont, I, 49; Dayrolle to Tilson, 21 Feb., Titley to Townshend, 21 Feb. 1730, PRO. 84/310, 75/54; Seckendorf to Ferdinand Albrecht, 4 Mar. 1730, Wolfenbüttel, 1 Alt 22, Nr. 585 (d); Ferdinand Albrecht to Kinsky, 13 Mar. 1730, Vienna, Kinsky, 2 (b); *Wye's Letter* 12 Feb. (os) 1730; Poyntz to T. Townshend, 24 Feb. 1730, BL. Althorp E5.
5. Liria to Eugene, 2 Feb. 1730, HHStA., GK. 97(b); Frederick William to Chambrier, 25 Mar. 1730, AE. CP. Prusse, 91; Grumbkow to Reichenbach, 7 May 1730, Hull, DDHO 3/3; Charles VI to Stephen Kinsky and Fonseca, 24 Mar. 1730, Höfler, II, 124; Robinson to Harrington, 2 Aug. 1730, BL. Add. 9139.
6. Newcastle to Ward, 29 May (os), Rondeau to Tilson, 15 June (os) 1730, PRO. 91/11; Rondeau to Townshend, 2 Feb. (os) 1730, *Sbornik*, 66, 133; Newcastle to Poyntz, Waldegrave and Horatio Walpole, 2 July (os) 1730, BL. Add. 32768.
7. Newcastle to Horatio Walpole, 20 June (os) 1728, PRO. 78/189; Finch to Townshend, 21 Jan., 4 Feb. 1730, PRO. 95/54.
8. Titley to Townshend, 21 Feb., Holzendorf to Tilson, 4 Apr. 1730, PRO. 75/54, 84/307.
9. Hotham to Townshend, 22 Mar., 4 Apr., Holzendorf to Tilson, 14 Apr. 1730, PRO. 90/106, 90/27, 84/307; Hotham to Poyntz, no date, Hotham to Townshend, 22 Mar., Alvensleben, Hanoverian minister, to Hotham, 30 Mar., Holzendorf to Hotham, 31 Mar., 11 Apr., Tilson to Hotham, 10 Mar. (os) 1730, Hull, DDHO 3/2, 10, 1; Seckendorf to Ferdinand Albrecht, 8 Apr., Ferdinand Albrecht to Ludwig Rudolf of Brunswick-Wolfenbüttel, 1 Alt. 22, Nr. 585 (e), 531; Frederick William I to Chambrier, 4 Apr. 1730, AE. CP. Prusse 91; Tilson to Waldegrave, 10 Apr. (os) 1730, Chewton; Diemar to William, 10, 18 Apr. 1730, Marburg, England, 199; *Stanley's Newsletter* 4, 7 Apr. (os), *Oedipus* 16 Apr. (os), *Wye's Letter* 14 May (os) 1730; Delafaye to Poyntz, 30 Mar. (os), Poyntz to T. Townshend, 19 Apr. 1730, BL. Althorp, E4.
10. Hotham to Townshend, 18 Apr. 1730, PRO. 90/28.
11. A. Waddington (ed.), *Recueil . . . Prusse* (Paris, 1901), p. 344; Newcastle to George II, 4 Apr. (os) 1730, Du Bourgay to Townshend, 30 Dec. 1727, Fagel to Hop, 22 Sept. 1730, PRO. 36/18, 90/22, 107/2; Townshend to Hotham, 8 Apr. (os) 1730, Hull, DDHO 3/1; Villa to Dickens, 3 Mar. (os) 1730, PRO. 90/27.
12. Hotham to Townshend, 13 May 1730, Hull, PRO. 90/28.
13. Hotham to Townshend, 12, 18 Apr., 6, 9, 13, 27 May, Frederick William to George 11, 13 May, Grumbkow to Reichenbach 28 Apr. 1730, PRO. 90/28; Robert Trevor to Poyntz, 8 May (os) 1730, BL. Althorp E4.
14. Hotham to Townshend, 22, 26 Apr. 1730, PRO. 90/28; Harrington and Poyntz to Keene, 1 Apr. 1730, BL. Add. 32766; Holzendorf to Hotham, 29 Apr., Reichenbach to Grumbkow, 31 Mar. 1730, Hull, DDHO 3/1, 3.
15. Ferdinand Albrecht to Ludwig Rudolf, 2 May 1730, Wolfenbüttel, 1 Alt 22, Nr. 531; Reichenbach to Grumbkow, 12 May, Frederick William to Reichenbach, 13 May 1730, PRO. 90/28; Horatio Walpole to Harrington and Poyntz, 23 Apr. (os) 1730, Coxe, II, 693; Frederick William to Chambrier, 30 Sept. 1730, AE. CP. Prusse 91.
16. Hotham to Harrington, 11 July 1730, 'Monsr. Borcke's account of what passed with Sir Charles Hotham', no date, PRO. 90/28, 106; Seckendorf to Ferdinand Albrecht, 14 July 1730, Wolfenbüttel, 1 Alt 22, Nr. 585(e).
17. Newcastle to Poyntz, 6 Feb. (os), Newcastle to Harrington and Poyntz, 30 Mar. (os), Harrington and Poyntz to Newcastle, 5, 12 Apr. 1730, BL. Add. 32765–6; Broglie to

Chauvelin, 4 May 1730, AE. CP. Ang. 370; Townshend to George II, 6 May (os) 1730, Coxe, II, 542; Törring to Meerman, Bavarian envoy in Vienna, 17 June 1730, Munich, Bayr. Ges. Wien 182.

18. Newcastle to Harrington and Poyntz, 28 May, (os), Harrington and Poyntz to Newcastle, 2 June, Newcastle to Horatio Walpole and Poyntz, 18 June (os) 1730, BL. Add. 32767–8; Albert to Plettenberg, 31 May, 3 July 1730, Münster. NB. 33 .

19. Woodward to Newcastle, 16 June, Newcastle to Horatio Walpole and Poyntz, 18 June (os) 1730, BL. Add. 32768; Townshend to Hotham, 24 Apr. (os) 1730, Hull, DDHO 3/3; Townshend to Woodward 11 May (os), Harrington to Woodward, 14 July (os) 1730, PRO. 88/37; Schleinitz to Ludwig Rudolf, 17 Apr., Seckendorf to Ferdinand Albrecht, 14 July 1730, Wolfenbüttel, 1 Alt 22 Nr. 470, 585(e); Diemar to William of Hesse-Cassel, 13 June 1730, Marburg, England, 199.

20. Robinson to Harrington, 22 July, Robinson to Newcastle, 5 July, Titley to Robinson, 18 July, Tilson to Robinson, 3 July (os), 2 July 1730, BL. Add. 9139, 23780; Schleinitz to -, 1730, AE. CP. Br. 48; Rondeau to Newcastle, 13 July (os), Harrington to Rondeau, 18 Aug. (os), Dickens to Harrington, 5 Aug. 1730, PRO. 91/11, 90/29.

21. Chammorel to Chauvelin, 3, 20 July, Broglie to Chauvelin, 2 July 1730, AE. CP. Aug. 370; Ossorio to Victor Amadeus II, 10 July 1730, AST. LM. Ing. 37; Newcastle to Waldegrave, 19 Nov. (os) enclosing 'Paper relating to the affair of Mecklenburg', BL. Add. 32770; Holzendorf to Tilson, 20, 27 June, Hotham to Harrington, 11 July, Harrington to Edward Finch, 20 Oct. (os) 1730, PRO. 84/307, 90/28, 95/56.

22. Tilson to Robinson, 14, 21 July (os) 1730, BL. Add. 23780; Borck to Harrington, 15 July, Harrington to Borck, 17 July (os), Degenfeld to Grumbkow, 15 Aug. (os), Delafaye to Newcastle, 12 Sept. (os) 1730, PRO 90/106, 107/2, 36/20; Zamboni to Manteuffel, 1, 18 Aug. 1730, Bodl. Rawl. 120; Villebois, French envoy at Frankfurt, to Chauvelin, 8 July, Chammorel to Chauvelin, 14 Aug. 1730, AE. CP. Allemagne 377, Ang. 370; Diemar to William, 8 Aug. 1730, Marburg, England, 199; Dickens to Hotham, 8 Aug. 1730, Hull, DDHO 3/1; Delafaye to Waldegrave, 17 Sept. 1730, Chewton.

23. Diemar to William, 11, 22 Aug., 29 Sept. 1730, Marburg, England, 199; Zamboni to Marquis of Fleury, 25 Aug., 22 Sept. 1730, Bodl. Rawl. 120; Hervey to Stephen Fox, 14 Sept. (os) 1730, Ilchester, p. 60; Tilson to Robinson, 14 Sept. (os), 16 Oct. (os) 1730, BL. Add. 23780; Hotham to Newcastle, 16 June, Harrington to Dickens, 20 June (os), Harrington to Hotham, 20 June (os), Harrington to Rondeau, 14 Sept. (os), Holzendorf to Chesterfield, 18 Aug. 1730, PRO. 90/28, 91/11, 84/307; Seckendorf to Ferdinand Albrecht, 23 Sept., 5, 14, 23 Oct., 4, 14 Nov., Frederick William to Ferdinand Albrecht, 14 Oct. 1730, Wolfenbüttel, 1 Alt 22, Nr. 585(e), 532.

24. Horatio Walpole to Poyntz, 21 May (os), Delafaye to Poyntz, 24 Aug. (os) 1730, BL. Althorp, E4, 5; Waldegrave journal, 12, 23, 28 Aug., 1, 2 Sept., Delafaye to Waldegrave, 27 July (os) 10, 20 Aug. (os), 11 Sept. (os), 5, 15 Oct. (os), 21 Dec. (os) 1730, Chewton; Robert Walpole to Newcastle, 3 July (os), Newcastle to Harrington and Poyntz, 28 May (os), Newcastle to Harrington, Poyntz and Horatio Walpole, 4 June (os), Newcastle to Poyntz, Horatio Walpole and Waldegrave, 29 June (os), 28 Aug. (os), Harrington and Poyntz to Newcastle, 3 June, Horatio Walpole to Newcastle, 10 Sept., Horatio to Robert Walpole, 28 Aug. 1730, BL. Add. 32687, 32767, 32769, 63749; Chammorel to Chauvelin, 5, 26 June, 31 July, Horatio Walpole to Fleury, 21 June 1730, AE. CP. Ang. 370, MD. France 459; *Craftsman* 24, 31 Oct. (os), 21, 28 Nov. (os), *London Evening Post* 6 June (os), *Fog's Weekly Journal* 13 June (os) 1730.

25. Harrington and Poyntz to Newcastle, 25 Mar., 12 June, Newcastle to Harrington and Poyntz, 7 Apr., Thomas Pelham to Robinson, 9 July, Horatio Walpole, Waldegrave and Poyntz to Robinson, 19 July 1730, BL. Add. 32766–7, 23780; paper delivered by Fleury to Count Königsegg, 28 May 1730, PRO. 103/113; Stephen Kinsky and Fonseca to Charles VI, 1 June 1730, Höfler, II, 188–93; Villars, p. 258; Wilson, p. 217; Vaucher, *Robert Walpole et la Politique de Fleury 1731–42* (Paris, 1924), p. 33; G. Steuer, *Englands österreichpolitik in den jahren 1730–35* (unpublished Ph.D. thesis, Bonn, 1957), pp. 25–6, 31–2.

26. Harrington and Poyntz to Newcastle, 2 June 1730, BL. Add. 32767.

27. Keene to Harrington, 5 Apr., Harrington to Newcastle, 12 Apr. 1730, BL. Add. 32766; D'Aubenton to Maurepas, 7 Apr., 26 May 1730, AN. AM. B7 302; Albert to

Plettenberg, no date, Münster, NB. 33I f.2.

28. Horatio Walpole to Poyntz, 21 May (os) 1730, BL. Althorp, E4; Newcastle to Waldegrave, Horatio Walpole and Poyntz, 27 July (os) 1730, BL. Add. 32769; Waldegrave Journal, 23 Aug. 1730, Chewton; Horatio to Robert Walpole, 28 Aug. 1730, BL. Add. 63749.

29. Newcastle to Waldegrave, Horatio Walpole and Poyntz, 10 July (os), Robinson to Newcastle, 5 June, 5 July, Harrington and Poyntz to Keene, 1 Apr. 1730, BL. Add. 32768, 9139, 32766; Waldegrave to Tilson, 10 Aug., Woodward to Townshend, 18 Mar., Robinson to Newcastle, 21 June 1730, PRO. 78/194, 88/36, 80/68.

30. Waldegrave journal, 21 Aug. 1730, Chewton; Horatio to Robert Walpole, 7 July 1730, BL. Add. 63749.

31. Horatio Walpole, Waldegrave and Poyntz to Newcastle, 2 Aug. 1730, BL. Add. 32768.

32. Waldegrave journal, 4 Sept. 1730, Chewton; Chesterfield to Harrington, 25 Aug. 1730, PRO. 84/307.

33. Horatio Walpole, Waldegrave and Poyntz to Robinson, 19 July 1730, BL. Add. 32780; Waldegrave journal, 9 Aug. 1730, Chewton; Sinzendorf to Fonseca, 31 Aug. 1730, HHStA., Fonseca 14.

34. Harrington and Poyntz to Keene, 23 May 1730, BL. Althorp, E2; Waldegrave journal, 31 July 1730, Chewton; Newcastle to Horatio Walpole and Poyntz, 22 June (os), Newcastle to Horatio Walpole, Waldegrave and Poyntz, 26 June (os), Horatio Walpole and Poyntz, to Newcastle, 7 July, Thomas Pelham to Robinson, 5 Aug. 1730, BL. Add. 32768, 23780.

35. Horatio Walpole to Poyntz, 25 May (os), Delafaye to Poyntz, 11 June (os) 1730, BL. Althorp, E4; Robert Walpole to Newcastle, 24 June (os), Holzendorf to Tilson, 8 Aug. 1730, PRO. 36/19, 84/307; Colman to Waldegrave, Poyntz and Horatio Walpole, 18 Aug. 1730, Chewton; Villars, pp. 253, 271, 295; Newcastle to Waldegrave, Horatio Walpole and Poyntz, 24 Aug. (os) 1730, BL. Add. 32769.

36. Waldegrave Journal, 20 Aug. 1730, Chewton; Thomas Pelham to Robinson, 24 Aug., Horatio Walpole and Poyntz to Newcastle, 25 June, Chauvelin to Broglie, 9 May 1730, BL. Add. 23780, 32767, Eg. 3124; Wilson, pp. 221–2.

37. Waldegrave journal, 7 Aug. 1730, Chewton.

38. Chauvelin to Chammorel, 20 Aug. 1730, AE. CP. Ang. sup. 8; Horatio Walpole, Waldegrave and Poyntz to Keene, 2 Aug. 1730, BL. Add. 32770.

39. Plenipotentiaries to Keene, 2 Aug. 1730, BL. Add. 32769; Chesterfield to Harrington, 29 Aug. 1730, Harrington to Robinson, 28 Jan. (os) 1731, Holzendorf to Chesterfield, 11 Aug., Chesterfield to Harrington, 22, 25 Aug., 1, 5 Sept., Harrington to Chesterfield, 20 Nov. (os) 1730, Keene to Newcastle, 18 Jan. 1731, PRO. 84/307-9, 80/71, 94/107; Fonseca to Sinzendorf, 27 Feb. 1730, Höfler, II, 104; Chavigny to Chauvelin, 17 Jan. 1730, 24 Apr. 1731, AE. CP. Allemagne 376, 379.

40. Poyntz to Holzendorf, 12 Feb., Horatio Walpole and Poyntz to Newcastle, 25 June, Newcastle to Waldegrave, Horatio Walpole and Poyntz, 24 Aug. (os) 1730, BL. Add. 32765, 32767, 32769.

41. Horatio to Robert Walpole, 16 Aug., 16 Sept. 1730, BL. Add. 63849; Horatio Walpole to Newcastle, 10 Sept. 1730, BL. Add. 32769; Harrison to Poyntz, 25 May (os) 1730, BL. Althorp, E4.

42. Chammorel to Chauvelin, 13 July 1730, AE. CP. Ang. 370; Delafaye to Newcastle, 31 July (os) 1729, Newcastle to George II, 23 Apr. (os), 25 June (os), Walpole to Newcastle, 24 June (os) 1730, PRO. 36/13, 18, 19; Ralph, *Critical History*, p. 404; D.B. Horn, 'The Machinery for the Conduct of British Foreign Policy in the Eighteenth Century', *Journal of the Society of Archivists* (1967), p. 234; Black, 'An "Ignoramus" in European affairs?' *British Journal for Eighteenth-Century Studies* 6 (1983); Trevor to Poyntz, 15 June (os) 1730, BL. Althorp E4.

43. Charles VI to Austrian Plenipotentiaries, 27 Aug. 1730, Höfler, II, 260; Chauvelin to Chammorel, 27 Nov. 1730, AE. CP. Ang. sup. 8; Harrington and Poyntz to Newcastle, 2 June, Thomas Pelham to Robinson, 20 Sept. 1730, BL. Add. 32767, 32780; Browning, pp. 59–60.

CHAPTER THIRTEEN

The Negotiation of the Second Treaty of Vienna

'I continue in the opinion I have had a long while that nothing but fear of an impending danger will bring the Imperial court to reason'.
                              Waldegrave to Newcastle, October 1730.[1]

On 1 August 1730 Kinsky reported to Charles VI that Harrington, who as Secretary of State for the Northern Department was responsible for relations with Austria, had hinted to him that the British were willing to sign a separate treaty with Austria. Harrington proposed an unconditional British guarantee of the Pragmatic Sanction. The Austrian response to Harrington's approach, and to Robinson's proposed expedient of British garrisons in Tuscany and Parma, was cautious. Charles VI was not disposed to yield over Mecklenburg, fearing that it would upset Austria's allies, and he was worried that if Austria replied favourably to the British approach, the British would use the reply to discredit Austria with her allies. In addition, wishing to avoid a repetition of the dispute between Kinsky and Townshend in 1729, Charles wanted it to be made clear that the approach for a reconciliation had been initiated by Britain. He therefore decided it was best for Austria to make no reply to Harrington's approach and to wait until better terms were offered. However, the Austrians made it clear they would welcome a British approach. Sinzendorf proposed a separate Anglo-Austrian peace to Robinson, and Stephen Kinsky made the same suggestion to Waldegrave after they dined together on 24 August.[2]

Possibly as a result of their experience the previous year the Austrians and British decided not to base the negotiations for a separate treaty on Philip Kinsky.[3] Having gained Dutch agreement to a joint guarantee of the Pragmatic Sanction, Harrington instructed Robinson to begin negotiations, on the basis of the offer of such a guarantee in return for Imperial acceptance of the Spanish garrisons, and an Imperial settlement of the Ostend, Mecklenburg, East Friesland and Bremen issues to the satisfaction of Britain and the United Provinces.[4] Negotiations were begun, both at Vienna, and between Chesterfield and the Austrian Ambassador, Count Sinzendorf (the son-in-law of the Imperial Chancellor), at The Hague, though the latter were of less importance.[5] The principal difficulty encountered was the Austrian refusal to entertain the idea of the Spanish garrisons, a refusal encouraged by the Dutch willingness to envisage the compromise of garrisons composed of Spanish and Swiss troops, in equal proportions. On the evening of 25 October Robinson pressed Chancellor Sinzendorf to admit the garrisons, and informed him that it was essential to settle matters before the opening of Parliament. He also stated that Britain, in regaining the Emperor's friendship, wished to do nothing to make Spain or France an enemy. Robinson claimed Fleury would support anything that would produce peace.[6] The British frequently repeated the theme that an Anglo-Austrian alliance would be useless to Britain unless Spain was satisfied over the garrisons, because, without this, Anglo-Spanish relations would collapse, and Britain would be forced to defend Gibraltar and her commercial concessions. Harrington informed Chesterfield that George II would 'insist upon the execution of the Treaty of Seville with respect to the introduction of the 6,000 Spaniards, as an absolute and indispensable condition of proceeding in this negociation'.[7]

The Austrian reply to the British proposals was judged unacceptable.[8] On 15 December Harrington informed Robinson that a prompt settlement was essential both for diplomatic and for domestic political reasons. George had to know what to tell Parliament. Harrington reiterated the link between the British guarantee of the Pragmatic Sanction and the admission of the Spanish garrisons:

> the King is absolutely resolved, in all events, to execute his engagements with Spain, in relation to the said garrisons, to which his own, and the nation's honour, as also the interest of his subjects indispensably oblige him. The being enabled to compass that end without a war, is what alone can induce the King to charge himself with the Guaranty of the Emperor's succession.

Another issue which caused difficulties was George's demand that the 'Electoral points' should be satisfied. Harrington wrote that it was the

> . . . highest injustice, that those vexations and injuries done to his majesty's electoral rights, and interests, purely on account of differences and animosities unhappily arisen betwixt the Empr. and the crown of Great Britain, should not, upon the renewal of the ancient good understanding and friendship betwixt those two powers, be at the same time removed and redrest.[9]

Charles VI's view was different. In August he had referred to George's wish to have the Mecklenburg issue settled in accordance with his fantasies. The Imperial answer to the British approach, conveyed by a paper given to Robinson on 17 September, was unyielding as far as the Electoral points were concerned. Though the demanded investiture of Bremen and Verden would not seriously anger any of Austria's allies, Prussia was concerned in both the Mecklenburg and the East Friesland disputes, and Russia interested in the former. The British ministry were prepared to compromise on the matter. On 15 December, when Robinson was sent the full powers to conclude a treaty, he was instructed to insist on the Electoral points. However, the following day, Harrington sent him a letter written in his own hand, 'coming from a private friend and not from a minister'. Robinson was ordered to obtain a declaration from Austria promising satisfaction of the Hanoverian demands, 'but if the Court of Vienna should obstenately refuse to give such a declaration, you will not absolutely break the treaty upon that head, but send an account of everything with all speed to England, and if you find you are not likely to agree upon these points, I believe you would not do amiss, to dispose that court to send at the same time full powers and instructions to their minister here to conclude them if possible without any loss of time'.[10]

Harrington's order reflected the realisation that the Austrians were not going to yield over both the Spanish garrisons and the Electoral points. It was essential to gain Austrian consent to the first, because otherwise Spain would be alienated, but none of Britain's allies would be offended if the Electoral points were not pressed. However, in December Harrington did not dare to mention this in Robinson's instructions. The situation had not changed by early February. When, on 8 February, Harrington sent Robinson a new project of a treaty, to be presented to the Emperor as an ultimatum, there was no mention in his official instructions of the shelving of the Electoral points. It was in a 'private and particular' letter that Harrington ordered Robinson to postpone the consideration of the Electoral points until after the treaty was signed.[11]

It is unclear how far George II was kept in ignorance of the decision to defer the negotiation of the Electoral points. It is possible that he was aware of Harrington's secret instructions to Robinson, but did not wish, for reasons of honour or prudence, to countenance them formally. Had George chosen to defy his ministers and insist upon the Electoral points, he would have found himself in a very weak position. As Chesterfield, no supporter of the Electoral points, noted, if the Austrians satisfied the British demands, 'then for reasons too obvious to mention, it will be impossible to break upon the Electoral points'. If the negotiations were to be broken off upon these points it would provide the opposition with a marvellous opportunity to attack the government for its subservience to Hanoverian interests. The *Craftsman*, in its issue of 13 January, 1731, had revealed the secret of the Anglo-Austrian negotiations, which had already been hinted at in late 1730, and the Austrians, had the talks collapsed, would have been able to provide the opposition with material which would harm the government. The opposition had already resumed its attacks on the Hessian issue.[12]

This was a serious consideration, though it could be suggested that it may not have been decisive with George II. More important probably was the knowledge that Spain and France were considering or had actually begun negotiations with the Emperor. British suspicions, already strong in the late autumn, had produced, by early 1731, a realisation that Britain was taking part in a race, with France and Spain, for an Austrian alliance.[13] Were Austria to settle with either or both of the other powers, then George would not obtain satisfaction for the Electoral points anyway. Furthermore, an Anglo-Austrian settlement which excluded these points would nevertheless assuage George's fear of an attack upon Hanover, and it can be suggested that, for George, this fear took precedence over the more specific Hanoverian demands.

The reasons which induced George to finally accept the postponement of the Electoral points are unclear, but the importance of this postponement is not. Watzdorf and Ossorio suggested that for domestic political reasons it was thought best to settle the Electoral points in a separate treaty. As Thomas Pelham noted 'the German affairs . . . have been the chief clog to this negociation'.[14] It is clear that the Austrians were concerned for more than Imperial authority. They had no wish to surrender their important Russian and Prussian alliances for the sake of Hanoverian interests. Whilst the British ministry, however hopeful they might be of persuading Fleury to concur in the new diplomatic arrangements, realised that they were seriously jeopardising the Anglo-French alliance and taking what was in effect 'a leap in the dark',[15] the Austrians were ready to take no such leap. They did not intend to abandon their allies and, their alliance sought by Britain, France and Spain, they were in a far stronger diplomatic position, at the beginning of 1731, than the British. The British government was aware of this, and it accounted for the somewhat frenetic and anxious tone of the Harrington-Chesterfield-Robinson correspondence in the first ten weeks of 1731. Weeks slipped by, the Austrians did not yield to the British demands, the Austrian diplomatic position became stronger as the Seville alliance publicly disintegrated, and the British ministers wondered whether they were following the correct policy. The opening of the parliamentary session caused further problems. The Prince of Wales observed 'all these unlucky accidents must be mended through eloquent peoples fine talking'.[16]

The negotiations were not confined to the Electoral points and 'the two great views of the Guaranty, and the Introduction'.[17] The Austrians suggested that George and the Czarina should reciprocally guarantee their dominions, and that George should undertake to obtain an equivalent for the Duke of Holstein-Gottorp for the lands he had lost to Denmark. George rejected both suggestions, and insisted that Anglo-Russian relations should be settled by the two powers in separate negotiations.[18] By rejecting the Austrian proposals George showed his determination to maintain his alliances with Sweden and Denmark. The failure to include Russia, Prussia and Holstein-Gottorp in the Treaty of Vienna was to cause major problems. Russia and Austria effectively abandoned the Holstein-Gottorp cause in the Treaty of Copenhagen of 1732. However, in 1731–33 a fatal ambivalence affected Austrian policy in the Empire and northern Europe. The conflicting diplomatic interests of, on the one hand Prussia and Russia, and on the other George II, proved very difficult to reconcile. Austria tended to support Prussia and Russia, and George II was angered and confused by actual or supposed Austrian support for the Prusso-Bevern marriages, the Prussian cause in Mecklenburg, the Prusso-Russian marriage project and the negotiations for the Treaty of Copenhagen, negotiations which were kept a mystery to the British. Disputes over these issues helped to embitter Anglo-Austrian relations, and in particular to anger George II, so that by early 1733 the Anglo-Austrian alliance was in a parlous condition.[19] It is doubtful whether these difficulties could have been avoided by widening the terms of the Treaty of Vienna to include Prussian and Russian interests. The postponing of the Electoral points meant that the negotiation of differences with Prussia was put off. The British refusal to undertake to guarantee Russian possessions and to support Holstein-Gottorp claims was understandable, given pressure from Denmark and Sweden and strong fears that France would attempt to gain their alliance.[20] In addition, there was simply not enough time to encompass these issues in the negotiations at Vienna. The initial requirements of secrecy demanded that as few powers as possible were informed of the negotiations, and the subsequent need for speed and, in particular, the wish of the British ministry to inform Parliament of the treaty, helped to ensure that the Vienna talks left many issues unsettled.

The British ministry was determined to attach one important condition to their guarantee of the Pragmatic Sanction. They wished to include in the treaty a stipulation that the guarantee would depend upon the husbands selected for the Archduchesses:

> His Majesty is willing still that none of the Arch-Dutchesses should be married to any Prince that might give any just grounds of jealousy as to the balance of power in Europe . . .'[21]

The Emperor, who had offered in May 1729 and May 1730 to guarantee that no marriage detrimental to the balance of power would be negotiated, felt it was dishonourable to have his daughter's marital choice restricted in a public treaty, and it was therefore decided that a secret article should be resorted to. This article released the Maritime Powers from their obligations to the Emperor in the event of a Bourbon or Prussian marriage for Maria Theresa. It is possible to suggest that George was responsible for this article. D'Aix had noted in 1728 that George had differed from Townshend in insisting upon such a stipulation, and the ban on a Prussian marriage reflected the fear that Crown Prince Frederick of Prussia would be forced to convert to Catholicism to enable him to marry Maria Theresa. The secret article served another important function. By linking the British guarantee to an exclusion of a Bourbon marriage it restricted the possibility of the Austrians reviving an Austro-Spanish alliance based on the 1725 agreements. This possibility was not a strong one in 1731, but it could not be discounted. In the event, Maria Theresa was married to Duke Francis III of Lorraine in 1736, and her sister married his brother Charles. These marriages had been strongly advocated by George II, who had been much impressed by Francis on his visit to England in the autumn of 1731. In the following years George urged the Austrians to declare that the marriage of Maria Theresa and Francis would take place. It is interesting to note, however, that at the time of the War of Polish Succession the Walpole ministry advocated an Austro-Spanish marriage as a way to settle differences between the two powers. They were less concerned than George about the possibility of a future union of Spain and Austria.[22]

Anglo-Austrian negotiations were complicated by the sudden death on 20 January, after a brief illness of two and half days, of Antonio, the last Farnese Duke of Parma. He left a will announcing that his wife, Henrietta, was pregnant, and declaring her Regent for the unborn child. In the will he called upon the Pope, and the rulers of Austria, France and Spain, to protect the Regency. The hopes of the Parmese government that the major powers would delay intervention until they saw the issue of the pregnancy were disappointed. The Austrians wished to prevent the movement of Papal troops into the Duchies and in the last week of January four thousand Austrian troops invaded and occupied, without resistance, the towns of Parma and Piacenza. The Duchess's complaints were ignored by the Austrian commander, General Stampa.[23] It was widely suspected that the Austrians would seek to block Don Carlos's right to succeed in Parma. The news of the death of the Duke and of Stampa's invasion reached Seville on 4 February, and Patiño promptly told Keene that he was sure the Austrians would never accept Carlos in Parma. Degenfeld reported from London that the news from Parma worried the ministry considerably. In order to remove the Austrians it was possible that Spain would turn to France. Rottembourg informed the Spaniards, who believed Henrietta's pregnancy was imaginary, that they could not rely upon the British to get Carlos put into possession of Parma. The French and the Spaniards formally complained about the Austrian invasion. The British dithered, regretting the invasion and seeking to persuade the Spaniards that the Austrians would withdraw, and the Austrians that they must avoid provocative actions.[24]

The invasion of Parma underlined the British need for a swift settlement with Austria. It was necessary to show the Spaniards that the Austrians were willing to accept the introduction of their troops, in order to prevent Spain heeding French suggestions of an anti-Austrian alliance. Furthermore, on 23 January the Duke of Liria, a high-placed Spanish diplomat (who was also Waldegrave's first cousin), reached Vienna, and on 28 January Patiño's brother, the Marquis of Castelar, the Spanish ambassador to France, solemnly announced Spain's repudiation of the Treaty of Seville. The unpredictability of Spanish diplomacy, and the danger of separate Spanish agreements with Austria or France, explained the British government's determination to push for Spanish garrisons rather than 'Electoral points' in the negotiations at Vienna. Castelar's declaration undermined the British ministry's claim to have secured British commerce, and, despite efforts to keep it a secret, it was exploited by the opposition in Britain. Horatio Walpole argued that it should be kept secret in order to prevent the opposition from using it as an argument 'to refuse the supplies necessary to enable His Majesty to make good his engagements with Spain'.[25] Fortunately for the British ministry the Austrians rejected the idea of a separate treaty with Spain. The Austrians were not interested in a Spanish marriage.[26] However, despite British pressure for speed, they moved slowly towards settling the terms of a treaty. Chesterfield feared Austrian chicanery, but Robinson was accurate when he reported on 9 March, 'I have more reason to impute those difficulties to a habit in this court of turning everything to its advantage and to the satisfaction of its innate pride, than to apprehend from such artifices any insincerity in the execution of what is now fixed'.[27]

A week later the treaty was signed. Britain, Austria and the United Provinces mutually guaranteed each others' territories, rights and immunities against attack. Britain and the United Provinces guaranteed the

Pragmatic Sanction with a secret proviso relating to a Bourbon or Prussian marriage for Maria Theresa. As security for Don Carlos's succession to Parma, Piacenza and Tuscany, 6,000 Spanish troops were to be immediately admitted. The Ostend Company was to be permanently suppressed, and the Emperor promised to satisfy the Dutch over East Friesland, as far as was consistent with Imperial justice.[28] Two widely reported secret clauses, which were not in fact in the treaty, were an agreement to compel France and Spain, by force if necessary, to guarantee the Pragmatic Sanction, and a British undertaking to pay Austria the equivalent of the subsidies owed her by Spain under the first Treaty of Vienna.[29] The treaty was ratified by George on 9 April and by Charles VI on 21 April. In the following month, George and the Emperor reached a compromise agreement on the 'Electoral points'. The Emperor refused to give way over Mecklenburg, but George was granted the investitures of Bremen and Verden.[30] The Mecklenburg issue continued to complicate relations with Austria over the next few years, but, given the Austrian wish to maintain the Prussian alliance, a desire fortified in late 1731 by suspicions of a French-backed alliance of Saxony and Bavaria, it was unrealistic to hope that Austria would satisfy George over Mecklenburg.

The treaty was proclaimed in Britain as a triumph for British diplomacy. Newcastle wrote of 'the honour and credit which our Royal Master has so justly acquired, by having singly given peace to all Europe'. The *Flying Post or Post Master* printed a poem by Joshua Nun praising the true patriot, Sir Robert Walpole

> . . . the Great Patriot whose propitious care,
> Averts the Horrors of all wasting War,
> And bids our Isle with peaceful Pleasure crown'd
> Command the Wonder of the World around.

More prosaic ministerial writers asserted that Walpole had brought peace to Europe and secured British national interests. 'Orator' Henley, the author of the ministerial newspaper the *Hyp-Doctor*, stated that 'the public interest is now in the most prosperous state, the most refined courts of Europe are manag'd with peculiar address in their turns; commerce and credit improve at home and abroad'. Opposition claims that the government was guilty of inconsistency in now proclaiming the virtues of an alliance with a power, Austria, which had been treated as a threat for the previous six years, were dismissed. The *Craftsman* claimed that the government's new alliance had been negotiated as a result of the newspaper's call for an Austrian alliance, but it also asserted that the only proper alliance with Austria was an 'equal' one, not one which sacrificed British interests to those of Hanover. The government press denied that such a sacrifice had taken place.[31]

Whatever the importance for the future of the press debate about the Austrian alliance, it in fact took second place in the spring of 1731 to the government's attempts to counter opposition charges that their foolish diplomacy had only served to unite France and Spain. The opposition thus chose, not to attack the new Austrian alliance, but rather to claim that incompetent diplomacy had served to create a Bourbon pact. The ministry claimed that Spain would accede to the new treaty, and France accept it. The opposition challenged both these assertions.[32] Castelar's declaration and the new Spanish fortifications near Gibraltar provided grounds for public scepticism from January 1731. The events of the following six months were to provide more material for the opposition press, for far from being a triumphant diplomatic success, the Second Treaty of Vienna threw Anglo-Spanish relations into total confusion, and produced in the summer of 1731 an Anglo-French war-scare which has been overlooked by most historians. The Second Treaty of Vienna was to be a failure in the end, and in the short-term it produced a very difficult diplomatic situation for the British government. However, in the circumstances of 1730–1, there had been no sensible alternative.

The British ministry failed to appreciate how their new alliance would be received in Europe. They were inaccurate in their supposition that French anger would be but superficial and that the French would accommodate themselves to the new settlement.[33] British attempts to excuse their action to Fleury met with rebukes. Fleury had little time for the efforts of Horatio Walpole and Waldegrave to argue that the new treaty simply ensured the provisions of that of Seville. Suspecting secret anti-French articles in the new treaty, the French attacked British duplicity. Chauvelin wrote to Chammorel that 'les coups d'infidelité ne sont pas un crime aux yeux de la nation, dans laquelle vous vivez'.[34] The French ministry had no intention of subscribing to any scheme which entailed the guaranteeing of the Pragmatic Sanction, and it made a determined effort to prevent Spain acceding to the new treaty, and to build up a party in the Empire and the Baltic pledged to resist the Pragmatic Sanction and Austrian power. Within a few months British diplomats were complaining of French activities in Spain, the United Provinces, the Empire and Scandinavia. The British ministry responded to these complaints, and urged the Austrians to take all possible steps to defeat French projects. By the summer of 1731 the British realised it would be totally impossible to reconcile the French to their new scheme. Suppositions based on Fleury's supposedly pacific dispositions were replaced by anxiety about French policy.

Plumb wrote of the Spanish response 'Elisabeth Farnese and her husband greeted this treaty with delight and joined it with surprising alacrity'. This statement is inaccurate, and historians have done less than justice to the difficulties affecting Anglo-Spanish relations in the first half of 1731. The British ministry were to be proved wrong in their view that Spain would accept the new treaty without hesitation. Sir Robert Walpole informed Parliament in February that 'there was nothing negotiated with the Emperor but with a comprehension of Spain's interest and to effectuate the admission of Don Carlos into Italy, according to the plan of the Seville Treaty'. Newcastle wrote to Keene 'it will not be difficult for you to make that Court sensible, that they owe everything to His Majesty, and can depend upon the execution of no part of it, unless they will comply with

His Majesty's just demands . . .'[35] However, as Chauvelin commented sardonically the following month, 'Les Walpoles vont beaucoup s'applaudir, même avant qu'on sache quel parti prendra l'Espagne'.[36] British attempts to gain a speedy Spanish accession to the new treaty were defeated by the quixotic character of the Spanish government. The personal views of Philip V were a major difficulty as, in the spring of 1731 at any rate, he had no wish to harm the interests of his native country, France. Furthermore, the perpetually imminent succession crisis which so confused Spanish court politics in the 1720s and 1730s was of great importance in this period. The eccentric lifestyle of Philip V and, in particular, his irregular hours and disinclination to sleep, led to fears for his life. Some envoys, such as the Sardinian Marquis D'Arvillars, took to cultivating his eldest son the Prince of Asturias (the future Ferdinand VI), who was believed to have little interest in his stepmother's Italian aspirations and whose accession, it was thought, would undo all the British efforts. In this situation the diplomatic approaches of the British and French envoys, Keene and Rottembourg, were met with delay and prevarication.[37] This refusal to accept their propositions was accompanied by two moves which disturbed the British: the continuation of negotiations by the Duke of Liria, and the exacerbation of Anglo-Spanish relations by acts of hostility. Liria pressed the Austrians to sign an Austro-Spanish alliance which would exclude Britain, and demanded an archduchess for Don Carlos. The Austrians rejected Liria's proposals but, as the British ministry realised, the success of their attempts to have the commercial clauses of the Treaty of Seville renewed depended on the success of Liria's negotiations. On 11 May Keene informed Delafaye: 'if they could come at Parma by the Emperor's means, without us, there is no doubt but they would refuse to renew our Treatys of commerce and particularly that of Assiento, which Patiño looks upon as the ruin of the Indies'.[38]

Threatening Spanish moves near Gibraltar, which had preceded the Second Treaty of Vienna, did not cease with its signature. In December 1730 new Spanish emplacements near Gibraltar were constructed, and the Spaniards threatened to dominate part of the Bày of Gibraltar with their artillery. This development attracted much press comment in Britain. Fears were expressed that Gibraltar would be closely blockaded or attacked. Pulteney contrasted the British wooing of Spain and the Spanish threat to Gibraltar. On 2 May Keene wrote to Waldegrave 'Mr. Rottembourg tells me he hears from France that the affair of Gibraltar makes great noise in England, and that I am to have very strong orders to execute upon it which they imagine will finish our negotiations with Spain'.[39] General Sabine, the commander of the Gibraltar garrison, was told to prepare against a possible Spanish attack; the British factory in Cadiz was warned that war was a possibility. Maritime insurance on ships trading with Spain rose considerably. The British merchantmen in the Bay of Cadiz and Alicante left in May in order to avoid possible seizure. A report circulated that the Spanish ministry had ordered their governors in the West Indies to prevent all further trade with Britain.[40] The *Daily Post Boy* announced the success of Rottembourg, and reports circulated of the disgrace of Elisabeth Farnese and the rise to power of the Prince of the Asturias. Spain was reported as being opposed to the guarantee of the Pragmatic Sanction, and as demanding the return of Gibraltar. Some commentators reported that the major British naval preparations of this period were intended to cajole Spain into acceding to the new treaty or to protect British trade in the West Indies from Spanish attack.[41] Waldegrave reported on 12 June that it was believed in Paris that the British had ordered the immediate return of the 'annual ship' of the South Sea Company, and had sent instructions to Admiral Stewart in the West Indies to prepare for action. The Sicilian priests, Waldegrave's informants on Spanish affairs, informed him that Castelar had reported that the British fleet was being prepared in order to intercept the galleons. The British ministry were very anxious about Spanish intentions. Newcastle referred to the behaviour of the Spanish court as 'very extraordinary', and Robinson thought it 'very unaccountable'. Harrington noted, 'there is no forming any sure judgement upon the future conduct of so capricious a court as that of Spain . . .', and he was to reiterate this theme on several occasions. This view was shared by British diplomats. The prospect of a Bourbon alliance worried the ministry. Such a development would be harmful domestically, and dangerous diplomatically. On 25 May Harrington referred to 'France, who by such a union will be enabled to keep the affairs of Europe in a continual state of agitation and uncertainty, and perhaps bring on a general war . . .'[42]

The tense situation in international affairs was made appreciably worse by the simultaneous arming of the British, French and Spanish fleets, and by a burst of reports about possible Jacobite action. The British ministry noted an upsurge of Jacobite activity, and received reports that James III had travelled secretly to France and met Louis XV and Fleury. Fears were expressed that France would support the Jacobites. Newcastle complained of Broglie 'having more than once said, talking of his own court, upon what has lately happened, *qu'on n'avoit qu'à jouer le Pretendant'*. British envoys were ordered to keep a close watch on Jacobite activities. On 12 April Newcastle wrote to Waldegrave 'It is certain the Jacobites begin to conceive hopes of France, and thereupon the greatest attention imaginable should be given to that'. Waldegrave was sceptical about the possibility of French aid, but his scepticism had little effect upon Newcastle. In fact, though James III did leave Rome, it was in order to visit Naples, and on 2 June Waldegrave was able to assure Newcastle that Fleury had refused a Jacobite request for James to be given permission to visit France. Concern about possible Bourbon support for the Jacobites helped to increase ministerial anxiety about European developments and, in particular, about Bourbon naval preparations.[43]

Spanish preparations against Gibraltar and naval armaments were less of a military threat than French preparations. The Spaniards were greatly hindered by a lack of sailors and, despite Patiño's attempts to improve the Spanish navy, it was still far from being a formidable force. Concern about French preparations had been expressed since April. On 5 May Newcastle ordered Waldegrave to send spies to the French naval bases at Toulon, Brest, Port Louis and Rochefort to report on the condition of the French ships and arsenals and to ascertain whether the French were making any naval preparations. Waldegrave's reply was far from alarmist. He reported the armament of a squadron of six or seven ships of the line at Toulon, and noted 'this expedition is said to be chiefly intended for the instruction of the young seamen, and . . . to awe the petty princes on the coast of Barbary'. Five weeks later Waldegrave, in denying the validity of reports of a French naval threat and of the capacity of the Toulon Squadron to support the Jacobites, informed Newcastle that the squadron consisted of only five ships of the line and one frigate, and he noted of the reports, 'I am almost ashamed to write such idle stuff'.[44]

Waldegrave was one of the very few diplomats not to be affected by the war hysteria of the summer of 1731, and his assurances were not believed. The British ministry was convinced that the French were arming a large fleet, and was aware that their own armaments, intended to produce a squadron to escort the 6,000 Spanish troops to Leghorn, were viewed with concern in Spain and France. On 24 May Newcastle instructed Waldegrave to assure the French that the British squadron was only intended to aid the peaceful introduction of the Spanish garrisons. These assurances failed to quell French anxiety. The French were suspicious of the size and intended destination of the British fleet and, as Waldegrave noted, believed 'the augmentation much greater than it is'. Speculation over the destination of the British fleet varied greatly. It was to intercept the Spanish galleons, seize a base in Cuba, challenge the French possession of St. Lucia, attack Spanish America or Martinique, destroy the Spanish emplacements near Gibraltar, seize the Isle d'Origny (an island 3 leagues off Cape La Hogue from where it was feared Britain would be able to interfere with French coastal commerce), prevent the junction of the French and Spanish navies, or destroy the harbour at Dunkirk.[45] On 18 June, fearing a British attack upon Dunkirk, the French Secretary of State for War, Dangervilliers, instructed the Marquis D'Asfeld to ascertain British intentions and take defensive precautions. A substantial force of French troops was ordered to march towards Dunkirk, Gravelines and Furnes. These moves alarmed the British ministry. On 10 July Harrington ordered Robinson and Chesterfield to secure promises of Austrian and Dutch assistance in the event of need. On the following day the Privy Council met in Whitehall. Grafton, Devonshire, Godolphin, Wilmington, Scarborough, Bolton, Newcastle, Harrington, Sir Robert Walpole and Sir William Strickland, the Secretary at War, discussed 'a design intended by France to make some attempt here'. They decided that an invasion was a possibility and ordered that a squadron should be assembled in the Downs. Orders were sent to the Lord Lieutenant of Ireland to make preparations for sending troops to Britain. Troops were moved from London to the Kent and Sussex coasts, and by the end of July most of the army then in England had been deployed along or near those coasts.[46] The British preparations in turn upset the French and contributed to the exacerbation of the situation. Reports circulated that the British had landed troops near Dunkirk and bombarded the town.[47]

British assurances, and the news that no troops had been embarked on the British fleet, led the French to accept that no attack upon Dunkirk was envisaged. The march of many of the troops ordered to Dunkirk was countermanded, and the French assured the British that the reason for the concentration of troops near the coast was the need to find new areas of pasture for the cavalry. On 20 July Townshend wrote to Poyntz, 'I am heartily glad our warlike bustle is over, and in my opinion the less that is said of it the better, for it is not much for the honour of either court. The Cardinal must dote if he could have taken any alarm from our squadron'. The British did not withdraw their troops from the coast for some time, the Guards not being recalled from Rochester till the end of August, but the countermanding of the march of most of the French regiments reassured the government. On 17 August the *Ferrett* sloop was sent to inspect the French ports from Dunkirk to Le Havre; Captain Smith reported that he had found only ordinary merchantmen in the ports and no signs of naval or military movements.[48]

The war panic did not prevent the desired Spanish accession to the new treaty. On 22 July the representatives of Britain, Spain and the Emperor signed an agreement at Vienna recognising Spain's acceptance of the provisions of the Second Treaty of Vienna. Three days later, at Florence, the Spanish and Tuscan representatives signed a treaty which recognised Don Carlos as the heir to Tuscany.[49] The new diplomatic alignment was symbolised by two journeys in the autumn. Francis of Lorraine arrived in England in October and, in a tour that took him to London, Newmarket, Euston and Houghton, made an excellent impression upon the British court and ministry.[50] Admiral Wager sailed from Spithead on 25 July, disproving Rottembourg's claims that British fears of France would prevent the dispatch of a fleet to the Mediterranean, and was very well received by Philip V and Elisabeth Farnese,[51] before convoying the Spanish troops to Leghorn, where Carlos arrived separately on 27 December. The Parma pregnancy having proved a sham, Carlos established his court in Parma. France appeared humiliated, isolated diplomatically and harmed internally by constitutional and religious disputes.

The war-panic of the summer of 1731 may not, therefore, appear particularly important. Indeed historians, concerned to summarise the overwhelming mass of diplomatic developments in this period, can be forgiven for ignoring what might appear to have been an inconsequential event. Such a conclusion is inaccurate, as the impact of the war-panic was probably of considerable importance for Anglo-French relations. It can be suggested that it played a role in worsening relations between the two powers, and helped to prevent the possibility of a successful British approach aimed at ascertaining the terms upon which France would agree to guarantee the Pragmatic Sanction.

On 30 July Poyntz wrote to Waldegrave:

The late alarm between us and France has astonished me above all the strange things I ever saw happen. I was in Norfolk when it first took rise, and had asserted to Lord Townshend (who seemed to apprehend something of this kind) that during the Cardinal's life, and our own inoffensive disposition at home, nothing of this kind could ever befall us; but upon coming back I found we have had secret intelligencers who – if I don't mistake, had been infusing jealousys of us into the Cardinal, and afterwards had been playing the same game here with regard to us.

The identity or indeed existence of these 'secret intelligencers' is unclear. Equally unclear are the views of the individual British ministers about the crisis. Chammorel reported that the British troop movements were due to George II, whilst Zamboni attributed them to Kinsky who, according to him, attended most ministerial meetings.[52] It is impossible to ascertain the truth of these remarks. If George II and/or Kinsky were responsible for the British moves it is necessary to consider whether it was as a result of fears that France would invade, or because they wished to see a deterioration in Anglo-French relations. Possibly George wished to convince Austria that Britain was a powerful ally capable of a strong military response to provocation.

In July 1731 Delafaye expressed the hope that the war-panic would prove to be only 'the falling out of lovers', and he urged a policy of 'forget and forgive'. Holzendorf, Chesterfield's secretary, suggested that 'if the Cardinal's pulse was felt now, he would perhaps be the first for promoting a general negotiation'. In Paris the Prussian and Russian envoys, Chambrier and Golofkin, told Thomas Pelham that

no general pacification can be made whilst France remains in the present situation with regard to the other powers, that she is too considerable to be left alone and if left alone will always be able to embroil matters so far as to endanger the tranquility that is now established among the contracting parties of the last Treaty of Vienna . . . it was necessary to make immediate use of the Cardinal's pacific temper, and not wait till by his death and demise any change of ministry should happen here . . . I agreed that . . . there was no harm in marking out a way for France to enter, with honour for all parties, into the same engagements with the Allies of Vienna.

Newcastle argued that it was essential to reassure Fleury about British intentions and the secret clauses of the new treaty. The Austrians were opposed to such a policy, possibly because they feared that a French entry into the new system would weaken Anglo-Austrian and strengthen Franco-Spanish ties. The attempts to ensure the cooperation of all four powers in the late 1710s and early 1720s hardly provided an encouraging precedent for Austria. In October 1731 Stephen Kinsky told Waldegrave that it was unnecessary for Austria to have an Ambassador in Paris. In 1731 the possibility of Britain using the Vienna Treaty as a stepping stone for a European peace, of Britain persuading France to assent to the new arrangements, was lost. Possibly such an attempt would have failed, defeated by Chauvelin and by French unwillingness to accept a dictated settlement. However, without French consent, no European peace settlement could be secure or long-lasting. Whilst France was isolated her diplomatic efforts, such as the attempts to gain the alliance of Sweden,

Bavaria, Denmark and Saxony and to prevent the Imperial Diet accepting the Pragmatic Sanction, were a threat to European tranquillity. As soon as France could gain allies, as in late 1733 when she negotiated alliances with Spain and Sardinia, she was to prove a major threat.[53]

The basis for any French accession to the Anglo-Austrian agreement was assumed to be a guarantee of the Pragmatic Sanction. France was unwilling to provide such a guarantee, but the eventual solution which was to be produced by the Third Treaty of Vienna, the acquisition of Lorraine in return for the guarantee, had already been considered in the late 1720s and early 1730s. Should Maria Theresa marry Francis of Lorraine, the dynastic union of Lorraine and Austria would become a strong possibility. France could not be expected to accept this. Indeed, in June 1731, Count Törring argued that an agreement over Lorraine was essential for the peace of Europe.[54] Possibly because of the legacy of Anglo-French bitterness dating from the spring and summer of 1731 the British ministry, which had pressed Austria to satisfy Spain and accept the introduction of the Spanish garrisons, was unwilling to press Austria to satisfy France by the cession of Lorraine. Possibly the effort would have met with Austrian refusal, but the failure to make it was to have serious consequences. When the British ministry attempted to use its good offices to end the Polish Succession War, the absence of any substance underlying the assurances of regard exchanged by Horatio Walpole and Fleury was to defeat the attempt. France and Austria were to settle their differences, including the Lorraine question and the French guarantee of the Pragmatic Sanction, without Britain, and the British were to be consigned to diplomatic isolation in the second half of the 1730s.

Notes

1. Waldegrave to Newcastle, 17 Oct. 1730, BL. Add. 9139; Richelieu to Morville, 19 July 1725, AN.K.K. 1394, p.26.
2. Kinsky to Eugene, 22 July 1730, HHStA., GK. 94(b); Charles VI to Austrian Plenipotentiaries, 27 Aug. 1730, Höfler, II, 258–67; Newcastle to Horatio Walpole, 17 Aug., Robinson to Harrington, 15 July 1730, BL. Add. 32769, 23781; Waldegrave journal, 24 August 1730, Chewton; Eugene to Kinsky, 17 June 1730, Vienna, Kinsky, 2(b); Charles VI to Kinsky, 27 Aug. 1730, HHStA., EK. 68.
3. Chesterfield to Tilson, 19 Sept., Robinson to Harrington, 18 Nov. 1730, PRO. 84/308, 80/69; undated note by Robert Walpole, C(H) Mss. papers 26/39a; Watzdorf to Augustus II, 30 Jan., 2 Feb. 1731, Dresden, 2676, 1. This is reflected in the scarcity of instructions to Kinsky in HHStA., EK. 68 and GK. 94(b).
4. Harrington to Chesterfield, 4 Aug. (os), Chesterfield to Harrington, 29 Aug., Harrington to Robinson, 14 Sept. (os) 1730, PRO. 84/307, Coxe, III, 33–9.
5. Chesterfield to Robinson, 27 Oct. 1730, BL. Add. 23780; Chesterfield to Tilson, 10 Oct. 1730, PRO. 84/308.
6. Robinson to Harrington, 28 Oct., 14, 18 Nov., Robinson to Tilson, 18 Nov., Newcastle to Henry Pelham, 24 Oct. (os), Chesterfield to Harrington, 22 Dec. 1730, PRO. 80/69, 63/393, 84/309; draft account by Sinzendorf of meeting on 25 Oct. 1730, HHStA., England, Noten, 2.
7. Harrington to Chesterfield, 10 Nov. (os), Robinson to Harrington, 18 Nov. 1730, PRO. 84/309, 80/69.
8. Newcastle to Waldegrave, 30 Nov. (os), Chesterfield to Robinson, 17 Nov., 12 Dec.

1730, BL. Add. 32770, 23780; Harrington to Chesterfield, 20 Nov. (os), 4 Dec. (os) 1730, PRO. 84/309.

9. Harrington to Robinson, 4 Dec. (os) 1730, PRO. 80/69; Delafaye to [Newcastle?], 5 Dec. (os) 1730, BL. Add. 32770.

10. Charles VI to Stephen Kinsky, Fonseca and Königsegg, 27 Aug. 1730, Höfler, II, 261; Harrington to Robinson, 5 Dec. (os), Delafaye to [Newcastle?], 5 Dec. (os) 1730, BL. Add. 23780, 32770; note by Robert Walpole on progress of negotiations, C(H) Mss., papers 26/39a.

11. Harrington to Robinson, 28 Jan. (os), Tilson to Robinson, 28 Jan. (os) 1731, Coxe, III, 83–8.

12. Chesterfield to Robinson, 2 Feb. 1731, Coxe, III, 88; *Whitehall Evening Post*, 6 Oct. (os), *Wye's Letter* 31 Dec. (os), *Craftsman* 28 Nov. (os) 1730.

13. Holzendorf to Tilson, 8 Aug., 24 Sept., 24 Nov. 1730, Daniel to Tilson, 2 Jan., Titley to Harrington, 20, 27 Feb. 1731, PRO. 84/307, 309, 77/78, 75/56; Chesterfield to Robinson, 24 Nov., Tilson to Robinson, 20 Nov. (os) 1730, Newcastle to Waldegrave, 25 Feb. (os), 26 Mar. (os) 1731, BL. Add. 23780, 32771; Villars, pp. 292, 299–300, 308; Baudrillart, IV, 62–3, 70–1; Vaucher, *Walpole*, pp. 39–40; Wilson, pp. 227–8.

14. Watzdorf to Augustus II, 24 Apr. 1731, Dresden, 2676, 1; Ossorio to Charles Emmanuel III, 12 Feb. 1731, AST. LM. Ing. 38; Thomas Pelham to Waldegrave, 23 Mar. (os) 1731, Chewton; Harrington to Newcastle, 11 Dec. (os) 1730, BL. Add. 32770; Robinson to Harrington, 16 Jan. 1731, PRO. 80/70.

15. Instructions for Chesterfield, 4 Aug. (os) 1730, PRO. 80/307.

16. Prince of Wales to Hervey, no date, West Suffolk CRO. 941/47/1.

17. 'Observations relating to the Counter Project sent from Vienna', sent to Chesterfield and Robinson, 28 Jan. (os) 1731, (hereafter Observations), PRO. 84/311 f.108, 114.

18. Observations, f.118–20; Robinson to Harrington, 16 Jan. 1731, PRO. 80/70; Diemar to William of Hesse-Cassel, 3 Apr. 1731, Marburg, England, 204.

19. Black, '1733 – Failure of British Diplomacy?', *Durham University Journal*, 74 (1982), pp. 203–4; Black, 'When "Natural Allies" Fall Out: Anglo-Austrian Relations, 1725–1740', *Mitteilungen des Österreichischen Staatsarchivs*, 36 (1983), pp. 145–6; Black, 'British Neutrality in the War of the Polish Succession', *International History Review* 8 (1986).

20. Watzdorf to Augustus, 15 June 1731, Dresden, 2676, 2; Eugene to Kinsky, 13 Dec. 1730, HHStA., GK. 94(b); Titley to Tilson, 21 July 1731, Harrington to Titley, 11 Feb. (os) 1732, Robinson to Tilson, 24 Mar. 1731, PRO. 75/57, 59, 80/73; Harrington to Edward Finch, 5 Mar. (os) 1731, J. Chance (ed.), *British Diplomatic Instructions, Sweden, 1727–89* (Camden Third Series, 39, 1928), p. 19.

21. Observations, f.109; Harrington to Robinson, 14 Sept. (os) 1730, Robinson to Harrington, 16 Jan. 1731, Coxe, III, 35, 58–9.

22. Instructions for Fonseca, 14 May 1729, HHStA., Fonseca 13; Harrington and Poyntz to Newcastle, 2 June 1730, BL. Add. 32767; D'Aix to Victor Amadeus II, 9 May 1728, AST. LM. Ing. 35.

23. Robinson to Harrington, 26, 27 Jan., 1 Feb. 1731, PRO. 80/71; Robinson to Waldegrave, 27 Jan. 1731, Chewton; Waldegrave to Newcastle, 31 Jan., 15, 21 Feb., Charles VI to Philip Kinsky, 31 Jan., Newcastle to Keene, 23 Feb. (os) 1731, BL. Add. 32771; Quazza, pp. 159–60.

24. Keene to Newcastle, 5, 9, 23 Feb., Degenfeld to Frederick William, 9 Feb., Chesterfield to Tilson, 16 Feb. 1731, PRO. 94/107, 107/3, 84/311; Robinson to Waldegrave, 10 Feb., Newcastle to Waldegrave, 11, 23 Feb. (os), 4 Mar. (os), Keene to Waldegrave, 23 Feb., Waldegrave to Newcastle, 15 Feb. (os), Chesterfield to Robinson, 16 Feb. 1731, BL. Add. 32771–2, 23781.

25. Castellar's declaration, Robinson to Harrington, 26 Jan. 1731, PRO. 103/113, 80/171; Horatio Walpole to Waldegrave, 25 Jan. (os), Thomas Pelham to Waldegrave, 19 Feb. (os) 1731, Chewton; *Craftsman*, 27 Jan. (os), 13 Feb. (os), *Daily Post Boy* 13 Feb. (os) 1731; Keene to Waldegrave, 18 Feb., Waldegrave to Keene, 27 Feb. 1731, BL. Add. 32771.

26. Robinson to Harrington, 28 Mar. 1731, PRO. 80/73; Robinson to Waldegrave, 25 June 1731, Chewton.

27. Robinson to Harrington, 9 Mar. 1731, PRO. 80/72.

28. Copy of treaty, 'Stipulations about the Garrisons in Tuscany and Parma in the Quadruple Alliance, Treaty of Seville, Treaty of Vienna', PRO. 103/113.
29. Newcastle to Waldegrave, 11 Feb. (os), Waldegrave to Newcastle, 24 Feb., Waldegrave to Keene, 28 Feb., Broglie to Chauvelin, 19 Feb., 9 Apr., Chammorel to Chauvelin, 19 Feb. 1731, Waldegrave to Newcastle, 16 Oct. 1734, BL. Add. 32771-2, 32786; Chavigny to Chauvelin, 24 Apr. 1731, AE. CP. Allemagne 379.
30. Hughes, pp. 387-90; Naumann, Österreich, England und das Reich, pp. 171-3.
31. Newcastle to Waldegrave, 26 Mar. (os), Chammorel to Chauvelin, 19 Feb. 1731, BL. Add. 32771-2; Flying Post, 22 Apr. (os), Hyp-Doctor 1 June (os), Craftsman 24 Apr. (os) 1731.
32. Newcastle to Waldegrave, 15 Mar. (os), Broglie to Chauvelin, 9 Apr. 1731, BL. Add. 32772.
33. Waldegrave to Newcastle, 20 Jan., 15, 28 Feb., Waldegrave to Keene, 1 May 1731, BL. Add. 32771-2; Delafaye to Waldegrave, 30 Nov. (os) 1730, Robinson to Waldegrave, 31 Mar. 1731, Chewton; Villars, pp. 313-14.
34. Chauvelin to Chammorel, 10 Apr. 1731, AE. CP. Ang. sup. 8; Newcastle to Waldegrave, 23 Feb. (os), Waldegrave to Newcastle, 15 Mar. 1731, BL. Add. 32771-2; Keene to Newcastle, 20 May 1731, PRO. 94/107; Stainville, Lorraine envoy in Paris, to Francis of Lorraine, 4 Feb. 1731, Nancy 86.
35. Plumb, p. 229; Egmont, I, 146; Newcastle to Keene, 1 Apr. (os) 1731, BL. Add. 32772.
36. Chauvelin to Chammorel, 26 Mar. 1731, AE. CP. Ang. sup. 8; Craftsman 27 Feb. (os) 1731.
37. Keene to Newcastle, 11 May 1731, PRO. 94/107; D'Aubenton to Maurepas, 6, 13, 20 Apr., 11, 25 May, 1 June 1731, AN. AM. B7 307; D'Arvillars to Charles Emmanuel, 1 May, 15 June, 6, 20 July 1731, AST. LM. Spagna, 63.
38. Keene to Delafaye, 11 May, Keene to Newcastle, 14 Aug., Robinson to Harrington, 22 Aug. 1731, PRO. 94/107-8, 80/78; Robinson to Harrington, 30 May 1731, BL. Add. 32773; 'Account of what passed at Vienna relative to the Introduction of Spanish Garrisons into Tuscany, and the Admission of Don Carlos to the fiefs of Parma and Piacenza . . . ' papers of Edward Weston in possession of Mr. John Weston-Underwood.
39. General Sabine to Newcastle, 21, 28, 29 Nov. 1730, Waldegrave to Newcastle, 2 Jan., Newcastle to Keene, 14 Jan. (os), Keene to Waldegrave, 2 May 1731, BL.' Add. 32771-2; Cayley to Newcastle, 12 Dec. 1730, Keene to Delafaye, 20 May 1731, PRO. 94/219, 107; Pulteney to Colman, 12 June (os) 1731, G. Colman the younger (ed.), Posthumous letters from various celebrated men addressed to Francis Colman and George Colman the elder (1820), pp. 32-3; Fog's Weekly Journal 17 Apr. (os), Daily Courant 8 May (os), Daily Post Boy 24 May (os), London Evening Post 29 June (os) 1731.
40. Keene to Newcastle, 2 May, Cayley to Newcastle, 8 May 1731, PRO. 94/107, 219; D'Aubenton to Maurepas, 11, 18, 25 May 1731, AN. AM. B7 307; Wye's Letter 22 May (os), Evening Post 27 May (os) 1731.
41. Daily Post Boy 26, 28, 31 May (os), 1 June (os) 1731; Newcastle to Keene, 31 May (os) 1731, BL. Add. 32773.
42. Newcastle to Waldegrave, 7 May (os), Robinson to Harrington, 4 Apr., Waldegrave to Newcastle, 12 June 1731, BL. Add. 32772-3; Harrington to Robinson, 14 May (os), 18 June (os), Chesterfield to Tilson, 27 Mar., Thomas Pelham to Delafaye, 23 May, Keene to Delafaye, 7 June 1731, PRO. 80/74-5, 84/312, 78/198, 94/107.
43. Colman to Waldegrave, 26 May 1731, Chewton; Newcastle to Waldegrave, 1, 15 Apr. (os), Broglie to Chauvelin, 9 Apr., Waldegrave to Newcastle, 10, 19 Apr., 2, 12 June 1731, BL. Add. 32772-3; Chesterfield to Harrington, 10 Apr., Allen, Consul in Naples, to Newcastle, 25 May, Dayrolle to Tilson, 29 May, Thomas Pelham to Delafaye, 18, 27 Aug. 1731, PRO. 84/312, 93/5, 84/317, 78/198.
44. Newcastle to Waldegrave, 24 Apr. (os), Waldegrave to Newcastle, 16 May, 16, 25 June 1731, BL. Add. 32772.
45. Newcastle to Waldegrave, 13 May (os), Waldegrave to Newcastle, 12, 16 June 1731, BL. Add. 32772-3; Chammorel to Chauvelin, 4 June, Chevalier de Caligny to –, 11 June, Chauvelin to Chammorel, 17 June 1731, AE. CP. Ang. 374, sup. 8; Wye's Letter 18 May (os) 1731; D'Aubenton to Maurepas, 1 June 1731, AN. AM. B7 307; Bustanzo,

Genoese Secretary at Seville, to government of Genoa, 4 July 1731, R. Ciasca (ed.), *Relazioni degli Ambasciatori Genovesi* VI, 146–7; Marquis D'Asfeld, French general, to Dangervilliers, Secretary of State for War, 6, 8, 11 July, Le Beau, French spy in London, to Segent, French military commissioner in Dunkirk, 12 July, anon., undated memorandum, AG. A1. 2676, Nos. 182, 185, 190, 193, 217.

46. Harrington to Robinson, 29 June (os), Harrington to Chesterfield, 29 June (os), minutes of the Privy Council, 30 June (os), Waldegrave to Delafaye, 16 July 1731, PRO. 80/75, 84/313, 36/23, 78/199; Kinsky to Charles VI, 7, 11 July 1731, HHStA., EK. 67; Le Beau to Segent, 12 July 1731, AG. A1 2676 No.193; Duke to Duchess of Newcastle, 2 July (os) 1731, BL. Add. 33073.

47. Lascelles, agent in Dunkirk, to Waldegrave, 4 July 1731, BL. Add. 32773; *Daily Post Boy* 9 July (os) 1731.

48. Waldegrave to Delafaye, 6, 16 July, Delafaye to Waldegrave, 9 July (os), Thomas Pelham to Delafaye, 16, 21 July, Smith to Burchett, Secretary of the Admiralty, 12 Aug. (os), Holzendorf to Tilson, 27 July 1731, PRO. 78/198–9, 42/20, 84/314; Townshend to Poyntz, 9 July (os) 1731, BL. Althorp, E5; Newcastle to Waldegrave, 9 July (os), Waldegrave to Newcastle, 16, 30 July 1731, BL. Add. 32773; J.M. Black and A. Reese 'Die Panik von 1731', in J. Kunische (ed.), *Expansion und Gleichgewicht. Studien zur europäischen Mächtepolitik des ancien régime* (Berlin, 1986), pp. 69–95.

49. Copy of agreement, 'An account of what passed at Vienna relative to the Introduction of the Spanish Garrisons', PRO. 103/113; Baudrillart, IV, 103–4.

50. Duke to Duchess of Newcastle, 7 Nov. (os) 1731, BL. Add. 33073; Watzdorf to Augustus II, 30 Oct. 1731, Dresden, 2676, 2; Countess of Strafford to Countess of Huntingdon, 25 Dec. (os) 1731, HMC. *Hastings Rawdon* III, 8.

51. Keene to Newcastle, 3 Aug., Keene to Delafaye, 23 Aug. 1731, PRO. 94/108; Delafaye to Waldegrave, 23 Aug. (os) 1731, Chewton.

52. Poyntz to Waldegrave, 19 July (os) 1731, Chewton; Chammorel to Chauvelin, 19 July 1731, AE. CP. Ang. 374; Zamboni to Marquis de Fleury, 13 July 1731, Bodl. Rawl. 120.

53. Delafaye to Waldegrave, 9 July (os), Waldegrave to Delafaye, 13 Oct., Holzendorf to Tilson, 24, 27 July, Pelham to Delafaye, 17 Aug. 1731, PRO. 78/199, 84/314, 78/198; 'Minutes of the King's orders for my discourse with Count Kinsky', 31 Aug. (os), Newcastle to Waldegrave, 26 July (os) 1731, BL. Add. 33006, 32774; Villars, p. 320.

54. Törring to Plettenberg, 21 June 1731, Munster, NA. 148; Perouse, Bavarian envoy in Dresden, to Törring, 18 May 1731, München, Bayr. Ges. 820; *Daily Post Boy* 14 July (os) 1731; Chavigny, memorandum, 10 Apr. 1733, AE. CP. Ang. 380; John, Danish envoy in London, to King of Denmark, 9 Dec. 1735, C(H) Mss. corresp. 2518; Robinson to Harrington, 4 Apr. 1731, PRO. 80/73; P. Boyé, *Un roi de Pologne* (Paris, 1898), p. 334.

Conclusion

In British politics the most important developments in the period 1727–1731 were the accession of George II, his decision to retain most of his father's ministers, the development of a working relationship between king and ministers, and the fall of Townshend. Compared to these events the activities of the Pulteney-Bolingbroke opposition, in both Parliament and the press, appear of less moment. Foreign policy was of great importance in these political developments. Issues of foreign policy provided much of the currency of political debate in the Council, in Parliament and in the press. An examination of these issues can serve to elucidate some of the divisions within the ministry, but much still remains obscure. In particular, the exact impact of differences over foreign policy upon the dispute between Sir Robert Walpole and Townshend is unclear. This study has cast light upon the relationship between foreign policy and domestic politics, but much is left in darkness. The destruction of archival material and the attitude of several manuscript owners are partly responsible for this, but the nature of politics in this period is a more significant factor. Much material survives about party disputes and it is relatively easy to undertake a study of parliamentary or press conflict. In these conflicts issues were publicly debated. This was not the case with divisions within the court or ministry, or between the king and his ministers. These disputes were conducted within a small group where everybody knew everybody else and where opportunities for meeting were frequent. Issues were debated face to face, and conversations took the place of memoranda. There was no institution which recorded the audiences ministers had with the king, and there is no equivalent for the British council of the records of the Austrian Privy Conference. In the latter case the views of the individual ministers were recorded separately. Distinguishing the views of George II is not easy and it is no accident that historians have hitherto neglected George as the subject of a full-length biography. Little of his private correspondence has survived. In the official instructions to British diplomats, George's own ideas are invariably hopelessly intertwined with those of his ministers.

This study has indicated some areas in which the king's views can be reasonably asserted, but it has not proved possible to state definitively what George's attitudes and achievements were for more than a few issues. It has proved possible to cast light on some of the aspects of British foreign policy in this period which were previously neglected. The discussions about the possibility of an Anglo-Austrian reconciliation have been rescued from an undeserved obscurity. An attempt has been made to indicate the importance of Hanoverian vulnerability in Anglo-French and Anglo-Austrian relations. The fragility of the Anglo-French alliance in the late 1720s has been stressed. It is clear that the usual view of British foreign policy in this period, of Britain firmly behind the Anglo-French alliance until the summer of 1730, is inaccurate. The customary view, that of Townshend's anti-Austrian policy being replaced by Walpole's pro-Austrian schemes, is not supported by the evidence. Rather, this study suggests that policy was far more complex and confused, that ministers were less fixed in their opinions than has been appreciated, and that the distinct administrative machinery for the formulation and execution of foreign policy was of less significance than the views and actions of individuals: George II and his ministers.

Epilogue

The diplomatic development of the period up to the fall of Walpole in 1742 casts some light upon British foreign policy in the period 1727–1731. Despite much diplomatic effort Britain's attempt to use her good offices to end the War of the Polish Succession of 1733–35 failed.[1] The terms of the treaty ending the war, the Treaty of Vienna, were not communicated to Britain. The new diplomatic configuration produced by this treaty, the Austro-French alliance, which lasted until 1741, ignored British and Hanoverian interests. Austria and France attempted to settle many of the outstanding European problems, such as the Jülich-Berg dispute, without heeding British views. The British ministry retorted by considering alliances with Prussia and Russia. Discussions about the possibility of an Anglo-Prussian alliance having failed in 1735 and 1736, George II and the British ministry pinned their hopes upon Crown Prince Frederick of Prussia. They were to be swiftly disabused when he came to the throne but it is important to note that a conviction that his accession would produce an alliance led the British ministry to assume in the late 1730s that their diplomatic isolation would only be temporary. In late 1738 the British government launched a diplomatic initiative intended to produce an Anglo-Russian treaty. Though such a treaty was not signed until April 1741, this was due to Russian, rather than British, obstinacy.

It is thus clear that far from welcoming diplomatic isolation and seeking to cut itself off from the problems of Europe, the Walpole ministry sought to replace the French alliance which had failed in 1730 by an Austrian alliance and, after this had run into major difficulties in 1732 and finally collapsed in 1733–4, by an attempt to win the support of Prussia and/or Russia. This suggests it would be inaccurate to argue that British foreign policy became isolationist after Townshend fell.[2] Whatever the views of the principal ministers, British foreign policy was committed to involvement in continental developments by royal interests, by concern for the security of Hanover, and by treaty obligations. Hanoverian security was to remain a major problem throughout the period of the Walpole ministry. It complicated Anglo-Prussian relations in the mid-1730s and early 1740s, just as it had embittered them in the late 1720s. The possibility of Prussia attacking Hanover affected George II's stance in the War of the Polish Succession. The threats by Prussia and France to attack Hanover in 1741 produced the Hanoverian neutrality which so harmed the Walpole ministry, both domestically and diplomatically, in its last months.[3] Thus, the Hanoverian issue continued to remain a problem. However successful Walpole might have been in persuading George II, in the spring of 1731, to shelve temporarily the 'Electoral points', he did not succeed in preventing similar points from complicating British foreign policy in the subsequent decade. This continuity puts into perspective the supposed changes produced in 1730 by the fall of Townshend and the collapse of the Anglo-French alliance. The failure of the Hotham mission, combined with the continued importance of Hanoverian interests, condemned Anglo-Prussian relations to hostility throughout the 1730s, and this drastically limited the freedom of manoeuvre enjoyed by the British ministry in its foreign policy. Whilst the fall of Townshend was followed by an attempt at a reconciliation with Austria, no such attempt was made in the case of Prussia. George II's views dominated Anglo-Prussian relations, to their detriment.

Walpole's ministry ended in war, the Anglo-Spanish conflict which began in 1739, and the War of the Austrian Succession which began with Frederick the Great's invasion of Silesia at the end of 1740. The Anglo-Spanish war was in no way inevitable. The issues at stake were not new, and Anglo-Spanish negotiations succeeded in resolving most of them by the Convention of the Pardo signed in January 1739. The war which commenced that autumn was not 'necessary' in diplomatic terms. Room for negotiation remained. War was brought about by the political weakness of the Walpole ministry. Had the ministry been united there would probably have been no war, but the ambivalent attitude of many leading ministers, such as Newcastle, weakened the ministry to a fatal degree. It is interesting to contrast the events of 1739 with those of 1729. In 1729 the ministry had also been split over war with Spain, but the timing of the crisis had been different. Whereas in 1729 the issue was most serious in the summer, in 1739 it coincided with the parliamentary session. In 1729 the opposition had planned to use the issue of Anglo-Spanish relations as the basis for their attack upon the ministry in the 1730 session. They had been pre-empted by the Treaty of Seville, whilst the ministers who had sought naval action against Spain were prevented from this by Townshend's skilful tactics. In both 1729–30 and 1738–39 British foreign policy was greatly affected by domestic political pressure. In the former case the ministry responded to it by linking the satisfaction of British mercantile complaints to the introduction of the Spanish garrisons, and by breaking with a French ministry whose policies were creating parliamentary difficulties in London. In the latter case the room for manoeuvre was smaller. Spanish acquiescence in British commercial demands could not be purchased by British support for Spanish claims in Italy. Such claims still existed in the late 1730s. Elisabeth Farnese wished to reverse the territorial settlement of the Third Treaty of Vienna and to establish her second son, Don Philip, in Parma. However, the Austro-French alliance made such aspirations hopeless, and they could not be pursued until the alliance disintegrated in the opening stages of the War of the Austrian Succession. It was this alliance, supported so ardently by Fleury and the Austrian minister Bartenstein, which circumscribed Britain's diplomatic position in the period 1735–41, and prevented a solution to Anglo-Spanish disputes by the methods utilised in 1729.

Whether it would have been wise to win Spanish support by promising aid in Italy is a different question. The Austrians feared in 1741 that the British would accept Spanish gains in Italy. Francis of Lorraine indicated to Robinson his unease 'at the reports which are spread over all Europe as if the Court of England might not be able to resist the real advantages the Queen of Spain may be capable to offer in the West Indies to have her hands free against Italy.'[4] At the end of 1735 the Spanish government had sought unsuccessfully to enlist British support against the third Treaty of Vienna. However the British ministry was not interested in schemes designed to limit the size of the Austrian Empire. This might seem to be a change from the policies associated with Townshend, but this change should not be exaggerated. In 1741–3 the British government helped to negotiate agreements by which Austria lost most of Silesia and much of the Milanese. Under the plans put forward by Horatio Walpole during the War of the Polish Succession, Austria would have lost Naples and Sicily. These agreements and plans were of course produced under the stimulus of Austrian defeat, but many of the attitudes which had informed British foreign policy in 1727–31 can be seen in the later years of the Walpole ministry. The notion that Sardinia, rather than Austria, must be built up to resist Bourbon plans in Italy was not new. The interest in acquiring a Prussian alliance, whilst preventing Prussian expansion in Mecklenburg and Jülich-Berg, was hardly novel. The British commitment to the Austrian cause during the War of the Austrian Succession also followed on from the policies enunciated by George II and Townshend in the late 1720s. Then, whilst opposing the policies of Austria, they had nevertheless made clear their determination to preserve the Habsburg inheritance as an essential counterweight to France. The negotiations with the Wittelsbachs in 1729–30 revealed a British ministry unwilling to contemplate major changes in the Empire, and Charles Albert was to find this attitude both in 1729–30 as Elector of Bavaria and in 1743 as the Emperor Charles VII.

There was therefore no decisive break in British foreign policy when Townshend fell. To assume such a break would be to neglect the role of the King and to misunderstand the position and attitudes of Townshend. The exact role of George II in many of the issues facing British foreign policy in the first decade and half of his reign is obscure. However, an examination of British foreign policy both before and after the changes associated with the fall of Townshend would suggest that his influence has been underestimated. A consideration of the King's actions would suggest that Owen's re-evaluation of the King, based upon his research on the 1740s, can be corroborated by work in the early period of his reign. Linked to the recent work of Gregg on Queen Anne and Hatton on George I this would suggest that the case for a reinterpretation of the role of the monarchy in early eighteenth-century Britain is a strong one.[5] By concentrating their researches on Parliament and party, historians have neglected, to some extent, the focus of political life in aristocratic Britain – the court – and have overlooked the activities of the arbitrator of court and ministerial conflicts, the King. It is interesting to note that whilst several scholars have written biographies of Walpole, there is no scholarly biography of George II. Whilst such a situation pertains it will be impossible to arrive at a well-based understanding of British politics in the second quarter of the eighteenth century.

Notes

1. Black, 'British Neutrality in the War of the Polish Succession, 1733–35', *International History Review* 8 (1986).
2. As suggested by Lodge, review of Vaucher 'Robert Walpole', *EHR* 40 (1925), p. 440; Dunthorne, p. 237.
3. Black (ed.), *Britain in the Age of Walpole* (1984), p. 155; Black, *Natural and Necessary Enemies* (1986), p. 41.
4. Robinson to Harrington, 25 Jan., 22 Feb. 1741, PRO. 80/144.
5. J. B. Owen, 'George II Reconsidered', in A. Whiteman, J. S. Bromley and P.G.M. Dickson, *Statesmen, Scholars and Merchants* (Oxford, 1973), pp. 113–34; E. Gregg, *Queen Anne* (1980).

Manuscript Sources

Bedford	*Bedfordshire Record Office* Lucas Papers
Bury St.Edmunds	*West Suffolk Record Office* Hervey Papers
Cambridge	*University Library* Cholmondeley Houghton Papers
Chelmsford	*Essex Record Office* Mildmay Papers
Chewton Mendip	*Chewton Hall* Waldegrave Papers
Chichester	*West Sussex Record Office* Richmond Papers
Darmstadt	*Staatsarchiv* El M. Austria, Britain, France, Hanover, United Provinces
Dorchester	*Dorset Record Office* Fox–Strangways Papers
Dresden	*Sachsisches Hauptstaatsarchiv* Geheimes Kabinett, Gesandtschaften. All revelant diplomatic series were consulted. The following were of particular importance: Le Coq, Watzdorf, De Löss and Zamboni, reports from London Le Coq's correspondence with Marquis de Fleury. Reports from De Brais (United Provinces), De Buy (Spain), Le Coq (France), Sühm (Prussia), Wackerbarth (Austria)
Edinburgh	*Scottish Record Office* Stair Papers
Florence	*Archivio di Stato* Lettere Ministri: Britain
Genoa	*Archivio di Stato* Lettere Ministri· Britain, France
Hanover	*Nieder Sachsisches Hauptstaatsarchiv* All relevant diplomatic material in Calenberg Brief Archiv and Hanover Des. 91 was consulted. In addition to the material cited by Hatton, Calenberg Brief Archiv. 11. El. 342, and St. Saphorin material in Hann. 91 were found of value.

Hertford	*Hertfordshire Record Office* Panshanger Papers
Hull	*University Library* Hotham Papers
Iden Green	*Home of John Weston-Underwood* Edward Weston Papers
Ipswich	*East Suffolk Record Office* Leathes Papers
Leeds	*City Archives Office* Vyner Papers
Leicester	*Leicestershire Record Office* Finch Papers
London	*Bank of England* Stock Ledger Books

British Library
Egerton Mss: Bentinck Papers.
Stowe Mss: Jacobite correspondence.
Loans: Portland and Bathurst Papers. Additional Mss: Blakeney, Blenheim, Bolingbroke, Caesar, Carewe, Carteret, Coxe, Dayrolles, Egmont, Essex, Gualterio, Hardwicke, Hatton-Finch, Holland House, Keene, Newcastle, Norris, Pulteney, Robinson, Skinner, Strafford, Townshend, Tyrawly, Wager, Walpole, Wilmington, transcripts from Dutch archives.
Microfilm 687: Stair–Sarah Malborough correspondence.
Althorp Mss: Poyntz Papers

House of Lords Record Office
Proxy Books

Post Office Archives
General Accounts

Public Record Office
State Papers: Domestic, Naval, Regencies, Scotland, Ireland, Miscellaneous, Austria, Denmark, Dunkirk, Flanders, France, German States, Hamburg, Holland, Malta, Poland, Portugal, Prussia, Russia, Sardinia, Spain, Turkey, Tuscany, Venice, Drafts, Royal Letters, Treaties, Confidential, Foreign Entry Books, Foreign Ministers in London, Foreign News Letters, Treaty papers

Lucca	*Archivio di Stato* Documents 'al tempo della liberta' – relevant instructions and reports
Maidstone	*Kent Record Office* Sackville, Stanhope, Sydney papers
Marburg	*Staatsarchiv* Series 4f. Britain, France, Hanover, Prussia, Sweden, United Provinces; Series 4g. newsletters

Modena	*Archivio di Stato* Lettere Ministri: Britain
Munich	*Bayerisches Hauptstaatsarchiv* Kasten Blau: Britain, France, Hanover. Kasten Schwarz: Austria, Britain, France, Prussia, Saxony, United Provinces
Münster	*Staatsarchiv* Dep. Nordkirchen, Papers of Count Plettenberg
Nancy	*Archives de Meurthe-et-Moselle* Fonds de Vienne, series 3F. diplomatic reports. Of particular use were reports from Schmidman (Britain), Jacquemin (Austria) and Stainville (France)
Newcastle	*Northumberland Record Office* Delaval papers
Northampton	*Northamptonshire Record Office* Isham, Finch-Hatton papers
Norwich	*Norfolk Record Office* Bradfer Lawrence, Ketton-Cremer, Townshend papers
Osnabrück	*Staatsarchiv* Rep. 100 Newsletters to the Prince-Bishop
Oxford	*Bodleian Library* Zamboni papers
	Christ Church Wake papers

Paris	*Archives Nationales*
	a) Archives de la Marine
	    1) B3 Service Général. Correspondance
	    2) B7 Pays´Etrangères
	    3) AE. BI. Correspondance Consulaire
	b) Archives Privée: entrée Fleury

	Bibliothèque de L'Arsenal *Gazette d'Utrecht* Archives de la Bastille: Gazetins secrets de la Police

	Bibliothèque Nationale
	a) Nouvelles Acquisitions Françaises
	    349 Blondel Remarques
	    9399 Mémoire sur la marine de Louis XV
	    9511 D'Aube, Réflexions sur le Gouvernment de France
	    10125 correspondence of Hoym
	b) Manuscrits Français
	    7149 Cambis correspondence
	    7177–98 Villeneuve papers

Quai d'Orsay, Archives du Ministère des Affaires Étrangères
a) Correspondance Politique
    Germany, Britain, Austria, Bavaria, Brunswick, Hanover, Cologne, Spain, Hesse-Cassel, United Provinces, Prussia, Turkey
b) Mémoires et Documents
    Austria, Germany, Britain, Spain, France, United Provinces

Vincennes. Archives de la Guerre
A1 Diplomatie

Parma

Archivio di Stato
Carteggio Farnesiano
Lettere Ministri: Austria, Britain, France

Stüttgart

Staatsarchiv
Gravanitz's mission to London 1727

Trowbridge

Wiltshire Record Office
Savernake papers

Turin

Archivio di Stato
Lettere Ministri: Austria, Britain, France, Spain, United Provinces

Venice

Archivio di Stato
Lettere Ministri: Britain, France

Vienna

Haus-, Hof-, und Staatsarchiv
a) State Chancellery
    Britain: korrespondenz, noten, varia. France: varia
    Interiora: intercepte
b) Grosse Korrespondenz
    Of particular interest was Eugene's correspondence with Ferdinand Albrecht, Kinsky, and Pentenriedter
c) Nachlass Fonseca

Palais Kinsky
Correspondence and papers of Count Philip Kinsky

Windsor

Windsor Castle
Royal Archives: Stuart papers

Wolfenbüttel

Staatsarchiv
All relevant diplomatic correspondence. Of particular interest were the reports of Thom (London) and the correspondence of Ferdinand Albrecht with Frederick I and Seckendorf.

Index of Proper Names